Microservices

Antonio Bucchiarone • Nicola Dragoni •
Schahram Dustdar • Patricia Lago •
Manuel Mazzara • Victor Rivera •
Andrey Sadovykh
Editors

Microservices

Science and Engineering

Editors
Antonio Bucchiarone
Distributed Adaptive Systems (DAS)
Research Unit
Fondazione Bruno Kessler
Trento, Italy

Nicola Dragoni
Department of Applied Mathematics
and Computer Science
Technical University of Denmark
Kongens Lyngby, Denmark

Schahram Dustdar
Distributed Systems Group
Vienna University of Technology
Vienna, Austria

Patricia Lago
Dept of Computer Science
Vrije Universiteit Amsterdam
Amsterdam, The Netherlands

Manuel Mazzara
Institute of Technologies and Software
Development
Innopolis University
Innopolis, Russia

Victor Rivera
Institute of Technologies and Software
Development
Innopolis University
Innopolis, Russia

Andrey Sadovykh
Innopolis University
Innopolis, Russia

ISBN 978-3-030-31648-8 ISBN 978-3-030-31646-4 (eBook)
https://doi.org/10.1007/978-3-030-31646-4

This Springer imprint is published by the registered company Springer Nature Switzerland AG.
The registered company address is: Gewerbestrasse 11, 6330 Cham, Switzerland

Preface

If the reader had ever looked in detail at the mainstream languages for development of server-side applications, he will have noticed that they provide abstractions to break down the complexity of programs into modules, but they are designed for the creation of a single executable artifact. This artifact in literature is often called a *monolith*. The modularization abstractions of these languages rely on sharing resources such as memory, databases, and files within the same machine. The modules of a monolith depend on these very shared resources and cannot be therefore independently executed.

The consequence is that monoliths are difficult to use in distributed systems without the addition of specific frameworks or ad hoc solutions. The reader will remember the popularity of, for example, RMI or CORBA. However, even these solutions suffer from the general issues affecting monoliths, such as difficult maintainability, problem dependencies, and, in particular, issues with scalability. Monoliths also represent a technology lock-in for developers, which are bound to use the same language and frameworks of the original application.

The *microservices architectural style* has been proposed exactly to cope with such problems. In its simplest definition "a microservice is a cohesive, independent process interacting via messages." The word "cohesive" here indicates that the service implements only functionalities strongly related to the concern that it is meant to model. This is the very idea of *micro*-services, which is not particularly about the size, but the cohesiveness. Microservices are meant to be independent components deployed in isolation and equipped with dedicated memory persistence tools (e.g., databases). In a microservice architecture, all the components are microservices. Here, the distinguishing behavior derives from the composition and coordination of its components via messages.

Despite the broad and extensive research in the field, especially conducted in recent years, many questions are still open, and this book tries to address some of them. We consider microservice an *evolutionary* rather than *revolutionary* architectural style, and we would like to assist the reader in sharing with us this perspective while reading this book. In this way we organized and structured the content. Our objective is to present the state of the art in the field and open the discussion towards the next evolutionary step. The volume is organized in six parts, each dedicated to a specific aspect of the topic.

Part I: Opening

The first chapter opens the dance by asking *"Microservices: The Evolution and Extinction of Web Services?"* This is a particularly important question for the service community, and for all the researchers and practitioners who worked in the field for the last 15–20 years. The first chapter analyzes the new (and old) challenges, including service design and specification, data integrity, and consistency management and presents an evolutionary perspective that captures the fundamental understanding of microservice architectures, encompassing their whole life cycle. This will help the readers to have effective exploration, understanding, assessing, comparison, and selection of microservice-based models, languages, techniques, platforms, and tools. Chapter 2, *"Size Matters: Microservices Research and Applications,"* is a summary of research performed in the field by some of the editors of this book. It consists of an overview that provides the introductory information that one should know before continuing reading.

Part II: Migration

Part II discusses the issue of migration from monoliths to microservices. Chapters 3 and 4 are indeed specifically on migration to a loosely coupled architecture. Microservices have received and are still receiving increasing attention, both from academia and industry. Migration to microservices is a sensitive matter for a number of companies involved in a major refactoring of their back-end systems. The chapters *"Migrating to Microservices"* and *"Assessing Your Microservice Migration Readiness"* are exactly covering this aspect.

Part III: Modeling

Aspects of modelization are covered in Part III. Chapter 5 introduces a catalog and a taxonomy of the most common microservices anti-patterns and identifies common problems. Chapter 6 introduces the concept of RESTful conversation and Chap. 7 presents insights from studying and developing two approaches for employing *"Graphical and Textual Model-Driven Microservice Development."*

Part IV: Development and Deployment

Part IV is dedicated to aspects of development and deployment. Chapter 8 is the perfect glue between Parts III and IV, presenting a formal model tailored for reasoning on the deployment of microservice architectures. Chapter 9 addresses the problem of autonomic and decentralized microservices management by using *GRU*, a tool that adds an autonomic adaptation layer for microservice applications focusing on Docker. Chapter 10 proposes a novel hybrid approach to microservices load balancing.

Part V: Applications

Part IV covers applications of microservices. Chapter 11, *"Towards the Digital Factory: A Microservice-Based Middleware for Real-to-Digital Synchronization"*, shows the relevance of the topic in the increasingly important Industry 4.0.

Chapter 12, *"Using Microservices to Customize Multi-tenant SaaS"* presents a novel approach to support customizing SaaS in a microservices architecture style. Here each customization is encapsulated as a microservice, which is on-boarded to the main service at runtime and replaces the standard functionality of the service. Chapter 13, *"You Are Not Netflix"*, explains why the success of Netflix cannot just be exported in any context with the same results.

Part VI: Education
The last Chap. 14 is dedicated to education, and opens to our new project: a series of yearly workshops focusing on education and another book on the very same topic as a result of this collaborative brainstorming.

Trento, Italy — Antonio Bucchiarone
Kongens Lyngby, Denmark — Nicola Dragoni
Vienna, Austria — Schahram Dustdar
Amsterdam, The Netherlands — Patricia Lago
Innopolis, Russia — Manuel Mazzara
Innopolis, Russia — Victor Rivera
Innopolis, Russia — Andrey Sadovykh
June 11, 2019

Contents

List of Reviewers

Marco Autili	Università dell'Aquila
Luciano Baresi	Politecnico di Milano
Mario Bravetti	University of Bologna
Antonio Bucchiarone	Distributed Adaptive Systems (DAS) Research Unit, Fondazione Bruno Kessler
Franck Chauvel	SINTEF ICT
Martina De Sanctis	Gran Sasso Science Institute (GSSI)
Elisabetta Di Nitto	Politecnico di Milano
Nicola Dragoni	Technical University of Denmark
Schahram Dustdar	Vienna University of Technology
Martin Garriga	Universidad Nacional del Comahue
Alexis Henry	Netfective technology
Patricia Lago	Vrije Universiteit Amsterdam
Valentina Lenarduzzi	Tampere University of Technology
Ivano Malavolta	Vrije Universiteit Amsterdam
Jacopo Mauro	University of Oslo
Manuel Mazzara	Innopolis University
Phu H. Nguyen	SINTEF
Cesare Pautasso	University of Lugano
Florian Rademacher	University of Applied Sciences and Arts Dortmund, Institute for Digital Transformation of Application and Living Domains
Victor Rivera	Australian National University
Sabine Sachweh	University of Applied Sciences and Arts Dortmund, Institute for Digital Transformation of Application and Living Domains

Andrey Sadovykh	Softeam
Jonas Sorgalla	University of Applied Sciences and Arts Dortmund, Institute for Digital Transformation of Application and Living Domains
Davide Taibi	Tampere University of Technology
Damian Andrew Tamburri	Technical University of Eindhoven—Jeronimus Academy of Data Science
Philip Wizenty	University of Applied Sciences and Arts Dortmund, Institute for Digital Transformation of Application and Living Domains

Part I
Opening

Microservices: The Evolution and Extinction of Web Services?

Luciano Baresi and Martin Garriga

Abstract In the early 2000s, service-oriented architectures (SOA) emerged as a paradigm for distributed computing, e-business processing, and enterprise integration. Rapidly, SOA and web services became the subject of hype, and virtually every organization tried to adopt them, no matter their actual suitability. Even worse, there were nearly as many definitions of SOA as people adopting it. This led to a big fail on many of those attempts, as they tried to change the problem to fit the solution. Nowadays, microservices are the new weapon of choice to achieve the same (and even more) goals posed to SOA years ago. Microservices ("SOA done right") describe a particular way of designing software applications as suites of independently deployable services, bringing dynamism, modularity, distributed development, and integration of heterogeneous systems. However, nothing comes for free: new (and old) challenges appeared, including service design and specification, data integrity, and consistency management. In this chapter, we identify such challenges through an evolutionary view from the early years of SOA to microservices, and beyond. Our findings are backed by a literature review, comprising both academic and gray literature. Afterwards, we analyze how such challenges are addressed in practice, and which challenges remain open, by inspecting microservice-related projects on GitHub, the largest open-source repository to date.

L. Baresi
Dipartimento di Elettronica, Informazione e Bioingegneria, Politecnico di Milano, Milan, Italy
e-mail: luciano.baresi@polimi.it

M. Garriga (✉)
Faculty of Informatics, National University of Comahue, Neuquén, Argentina

CONICET, National Scientific and Technical Research Council, Buenos Aires, Argentina
e-mail: martin.garriga@fi.uncoma.edu.ar

A. Bucchiarone et al. (eds.), *Microservices*,
https://doi.org/10.1007/978-3-030-31646-4_1

1 Introduction

Some 20 years ago, service-oriented architecture (SOA), web services, and service-oriented computing (SOC) were the buzzwords of the day for many in the business world [11]. Virtually every company adopted, or claimed to adopt, SOA and web services as key enablers for the success of their projects. However, there were nearly as many definitions of SOA as organizations adopting it. Furthermore, such panorama obscured the value added from adopting the SOA paradigm. The many proposed standards (e.g., WSDL and BPEL) were supposed to break the barriers among proprietary systems and serve as common languages and technologies to ease the integration of heterogeneous, distributed components, fostering the cooperation among independent parties. However, these approaches often failed when applied in practice, mainly because ever-changing business requirements, to which they were not able to (nor designed to) react timely [25]. In other words, many organizations applied SOA because of the hype and not given their actual needs.

Nowadays, we are witnessing the same hype for a new set of buzzwords: microservices and microservice architectures [26]. Microservices describe a particular way of designing software applications as suites of independently deployable services. One may also say that it is nothing but "SOA done right," as they preach for the same advantages, such as dynamism, modularity, distributed development, and integration of heterogeneous systems. However, now the focus is not on reuse and composition, as it is on independence, replaceability, and autonomy [28]. Services then become micro in terms of their contribution to the application, not because of their lines of code. They must be entities that can be conceived, implemented, and deployed independently. Different versions can even coexist and the actual topology of the system can be changed at runtime as needed. Each single component (microservice) must be changeable without impacting the operation and performance of the others.

However, as happened with SOA, microservices are not a silver bullet. With them, new challenges have appeared, as old ones regained attention. Just like any incarnation of SOA, microservice architectures are confronted with a number of nontrivial design challenges that are intrinsic to any distributed system—including data integrity and consistency management, service interface specification and version compatibility, and application and infrastructure security. Such design issues transcend both style and technology debates [49].

This chapter attempts to provide an evolutionary view of what services have been, are, and will be from the early times of SOA—with WSDL/SOAP-based services—through RESTful services, and finally to the advent of microservices and their possible evolution into functions-as-a-service (FaaS) [35]. By doing this, we shed some light on what is novel about microservices, and which concepts and principles of SOA still apply. Then, we complement this evolutionary view with a literature review (including both academic and gray literature) to identify the new (and the old) challenges still to be faced when adopting microservices. Finally, we analyze how practitioners are addressing such challenges by diving into the current microservices landscape in the biggest open-source repository to date: GitHub.[1] Our preliminary study on mining microservices on GitHub helps us understand the trending topics, challenges being addressed, as well as popular languages and tools.

To conclude, and summarize, the contributions of this chapter are threefold:

- An evolutionary view of SOA, from WSDL/SOAP to microservices and beyond
- A discussion regarding current challenges on microservices, based on a review of academic and gray literature
- A panorama of the current landscape of microservices on GitHub, and how those challenges are being addressed

The rest of this chapter is organized as follows. Section 2 presents the evolutionary view from first-generation SOA through REST to microservices and serverless. Section 3 revisits old and new challenges of SOA in the era of microservices. Section 4 discusses the microservices ecosystem on GitHub. Finally, Sect. 5 concludes the chapter.

2 Web Services Then and Now

This section provides an evolutionary view from the early days of WSDL/SOAP-based services (Sect. 2.1), to RESTful services (Sect. 2.2), then to microservices (Sect. 2.3), and the possible evolution into the novel functions-as-a-service (FaaS) [35] (Sect. 2.4).

2.1 SOA(P) Services

Service-oriented architectures (SOA) emerged as a paradigm for distributed computing, e-business processing and enterprise integration. A service, and particularly a web service, is a program with a well-defined interface (contract) and an id (URI), which can be located, published, and invoked through standard Web protocols [29]. The web service contract (mostly specified in WSDL) exposes public capabilities as operations without any ties to proprietary communication frameworks. Services decouple their interfaces (i.e., how other services access their functionality) from their implementation.

The benefits of SOA are multifaceted [10]. It provides dynamism, as new instances of the same service can be launched to split the load on the system. Modularity and reuse, as complex services are composed of simpler ones and the same services can be (re)used by different systems. Distributed development, since distinct teams can develop conversational services in parallel by agreeing on their

[1] https://github.com/.

interfaces. Finally, integration of heterogeneous and legacy systems, given that services merely have to implement standard protocols (typically SOAP—Simple Object Access Protocol [7]) to communicate over existing logic.

On top of that, specific workflow languages are then defined to orchestrate several services into complex compositions (e.g., WS-BPEL, BPEL4WS) [16]. As these languages share ideas with concurrency theory, this aspect fostered the development of formal models for better understanding and verifying service interactions (i.e., *compositions*), ranging from foundational process models of SOA to theories for the correct composition of services [10]. In the early years of SOAP-based service composition, according to different surveys [32, 40] the literature mainly focused on two aspects: Definition of clear/standard steps (modeling, binding, executing, and verifying) of Web Service composition, and classification of compositions into workflow-based industry solutions (extending existing languages, e.g., WS-BPEL and BPEL4WS) and semantics-based academic solutions, using planning/AI upon semantic languages such as OWL-S.

2.2 RESTful Services

Years after SOA irruption, stakeholders still disagreed about its materialization, and mostly failed to implement it [25]. First, the absence of widely accepted usage standards led organizations to develop and/or describe web services and compositions using divergent specification practices and concept models [16, 17]. Besides, daunting requirements regarding service discovery (e.g., UDDI registries [36]) or service contracts agreements (WSLA) hindered the adoption of early SOA models. Second, the claimed benefits and hype of SOA tempted organizations to adopt it even when their particular context said the contrary [25]. Pursuing flexibility too early, before creating stable and standardized business processes, plus the problems of interoperability and data/process integration (through too smart communication mechanisms such as the enterprise service bus), led traditional SOA to fail often.

In such a context, REST (REpresentational State Transfer) [13] appeared as a simpler, lightweight, and cost-effective alternative to SOAP-based services. Although the term was coined in 2000 by Roy Fielding, RESTful services gained traction around one decade after [30]. RESTful services use the basic built-in HTTP remote interaction methods (PUT, POST, GET, and DELETE) and apply their intended semantics to access any URI-referenceable resource. HTTP methods then became a standardized API for services, easier to publish and consume.

As the years passed, REST and HTTP (and JSON as data exchange format) became ubiquitous in the industry, in detriment of WSDL/SOAP-based solutions [36]. This dominance fits well with the characteristic of microservices being built on top of lightweight communication mechanisms, as we will see in the next section.

Still, reuse and composition issues were under discussion in the RESTful era. Humans being considered as the principal consumer/composer of

RESTful services explains the lack of machine-readable descriptions, and the massification of user-driven composition approaches (mashups) [17]. We can keep the aforementioned distinction between workflow- and semantic-based solutions; process-oriented mashups and extended business composition languages (such as BPEL4REST) belong to the first group, while semantic annotations, planning-based solutions, and formalization efforts define the second class [17].

2.3 Microservices

Nowadays, most of the issues related to defining, classifying, and characterizing services and composition solutions mentioned in the previous sections are overcome. However, yet new challenges appeared, posed by the internet of services/things, pervasive computing, and mobile applications.

The environment in which services are developed and executed has become more open, dynamic, and ever changing. This raises several malleability issues, including the ability of self-configuring, self-optimizing, self-healing, and self-adapting services. This may involve devices with limited resources and computational capabilities [6], and calls for novel algorithms for dynamically managing such lightweight and simple services. Also, to manage services in current pervasive environments, one must address context awareness, heterogeneity, contingencies of devices, and personalization. A pervasive environment claims for appropriate semantic technologies, shared standards, and mediation to assure interoperability of heterogeneous entities, such as mobile devices, sensors, and networks. Finally, as users are now becoming "prosumers" [22] (i.e., both producers and consumers), it is still unclear how to combine the need for aggregating several services, maintaining their QoS, and keeping the coupling level as low as possible.

In this context, microservices came to the scene as the weapon-of-choice to address such challenges at the enterprise scale. Microservices are independently deployable, bounded-scoped components that support interoperability by communicating through lightweight messages (often a HTTP API) [27]. In turn, microservice architecture is a style for engineering highly automated, evolvable software systems made up of capability-aligned microservices [27]. Each service also provides a physical module boundary, even allowing for different services to be written in different programming languages and be managed by different teams [26].

However, most of this definition applies to traditional SOAP-based or RESTful services as well, which feeds the debate regarding microservices and SOA. Although microservices can be seen as an evolution of SOA, they are inherently different regarding sharing and reuse. SOA is built on the idea of fostering reuse: a *share-as-much-as-possible* architecture style, whereas microservice architectures seconds the idea of a *share-as-little-as-possible* architecture style [33]: the goal became how to build systems that are *replaceable* while being *maintainable* [26]. Given that service reuse has often been less than expected [47], microservices should be "micro" enough to allow for the rapid development of new versions that can coexist, evolve, or even replace the previous one according to the business needs [19]. This is also possible thanks to continuous deployment techniques [2], such as canary deployment—pushing the new versions to a small number of end users to test changes in a real-world environment; and version concurrency—incrementally deploying new versions of a service, while both old and new versions of the service contract are running simultaneously for different clients. Thus, microservices fit well to scenarios with loose data integration and highly dynamic processes, bringing the opportunity to innovate quickly [25].

Undoubtedly, also microservices will be replaced by the next technological choice to implement the SOA architectural style. Thus, before moving to the challenges being faced nowadays by microservices (Sect. 3), we discuss one of the possible evolution paths for this architecture: functions-as-a-service (FaaS), also known as serverless computing. One should note that FaaS conveys the same design principles and benefits of microservices (isolation, interchangeability), but presents substantial differences to support such design at the technical and technological level, as we will see below.

2.4 *Upcoming Faasification*

A serverless architecture is a refined cloud computing model that processes requested functionality without pre-allocating any computing capability. Provider-managed containers are used to execute functions-as-a-service, which are event-triggered and ephemeral (may only last for one invocation) [35]. This approach allows one to write and deploy code without considering the runtime environment, resource allocation, load balancing, and scalability; all these aspects are handled by the provider.

Serverless represents a further evolution of the pay-per-use computing model: we started allocating and managing virtual machines (e.g., Amazon EC2) by the hour, then moved to containers (e.g., CS Docker Engine), and now we only allocate the resources (a container shared by several functions) for the time needed to carry out the computation—typically a few seconds or milliseconds.

The serverless architecture has many benefits with respect to more traditional, server-based approaches. Functions share the runtime environment (typically a pool of containers), and the code specific to a particular application is small and stateless by design. Hence, the deployment of a pool of shared containers (workers) on a machine (or a cluster of machines) and the execution of some code onto any of them become inexpensive, efficient, and completely handled by the cloud provider.

Horizontal scaling is completely automatic, elastic, and quick, allowing one to increase the number of workers against sudden spikes of traffic. The serverless model is much more reactive than the typical solutions of scaling virtual machines or spinning up containers against bursts in the workload [20]. Finally, the pay-per-use cost model is fine-grained, down to a 100 ms execution granularity for all the major vendors, in contrast to the "usual" hour/minute-based billing of virtual machines and containers. This allows companies to drastically reduce the cost of their infrastructures with respect to a typical monolithic architecture or even a microservice architecture [46].

Several cloud providers have developed serverless solutions recently that share those principles. AWS Lambda is the first and perhaps most popular one, followed by Azure Functions, Google Firebase, and IBM/Apache Openwhisk (the only open-source solution among the major vendors). A couple other promising open source alternatives are OpenFaaS (multilanguage FaaS upon Docker or Kubernetes) and Quarkus (heavily optimized for Java and Kubernetes).

Back to microservices, one of their main concerns is the effort required to deploy and scale each microservice in the cloud [46]. Although one can use automation tools such as Docker, Chef, Puppet, or cloud vendor-provided solutions, their adoption consumes time and resources. To address this concern, FaaS appears as a straightforward solution. Once deployed, functions can be scaled automatically, hiding the deployment, operation, and monitoring of load balancers or web servers. The per-request model helps reduce infrastructure costs because each function can be executed in computing environments adjusted to its requirements, and the customer pays only for each function execution, thus avoiding infrastructure payment when there is nothing to execute [46].

Thus, the way to go for microservices could be to become even more fine-grained, slayed into functions. For instance, given a RESTful microservice that implements an API with basic CRUD operations (GET, POST, PUT, DELETE), one might have a single function to represent each of these API methods and perform one process [41]. Furthermore, when CRUD microservices are not desirable,[2] event-driven or message-based microservices could still be represented as functions, tailored to the same events that the microservices listen(ed) to. Besides, serverless computing is stateless and event-based, so serverless microservices should be developed as such.

However, these new solutions bring together new challenges and opportunities.[3] For example, we still need to determine the sweet spots where running code in a FaaS environment can deliver economic benefits, automatically profile existing code to offload computation to serverless functions [4], bring adequate isolation among functions, determine the right granularity to exploit data and code locality, provide methods to handle state (given that functions are stateless by definition) [39], and finally increase the number of out-of-the-box tools to test and deploy functions locally. Additionally, going serverless is *not* recommended when one wants to [41]:

- Control their own infrastructure (due to regulations or company-wide policies)
- Implement a long-running server application (transactional or synchronous calls are the rule)

[2]https://www.ben-morris.com/entity-services-when-microservices-are-worse-than-monoliths/.

[3]https://blog.zhaw.ch/icclab/research-directions-for-faas/.

- Avoid vendor lock-in (given that each provider has its own set of serverless APIs and SDKs)
- Implement a shared infrastructure (as multi-tenancy is managed by the provider).

3 Challenges

The evolutionary view from early SOA to the advent of microservices helped us understand what is novel about microservices, and which concepts and principles of SOA still apply. In this section, we complement this evolutionary view with a discussion of the challenges still to face when adopting microservices.

The challenges presented throughout this section are the result of a literature review, following the guidelines for systematic literature review (SLR) proposed in [24]. Although a complete SLR is outside the scope of this work, this helped us organize the process of finding and classifying relevant literature. We considered research published up to the first quarter of 2017. This led us to a collection of 46 relevant works,[4] both primary (28) and secondary studies (18). Interested readers can refer to [15] for details on these studies.

Given the novelty of the topic, we enriched our results by comparing them with those of a recent gray literature review [38], which includes materials and research produced by organizations outside of the traditional academic publishing and distribution channels—such as reports, white papers, and working documents from industry [14]. Interestingly, academic and gray literature share common findings regarding open challenges in the microservice era, as we will see throughout this section. For the sake of organization, we divide such challenges regarding the lifecycle stages: Design (Sect. 3.1), Development (Sect. 3.2), and Operations (Sect. 3.3) and conclude with a discussion (Sect. 3.4).

3.1 Design Challenges

Despite the hype and the business push towards microservitization, there is still a lack of academic efforts regarding the design practices and patterns [19]. Design for failure and design patterns could allow to address challenges early as to bring responsiveness (e.g., by adopting "let-it-crash" models), fault tolerance, self-healing, and variability characteristics. Resilience patterns such as circuit-breaker and bulkhead seem to be key enablers in this direction. It is also interesting to understand whether the design using a stateless model based on serverless functions [20] can affect elasticity and scalability as well [8].

[4]Due to the space limit, the full list can be found at: https://goo.gl/j5ec4A.

Another problem at design time is *dimensioning* microservices—i.e., finding the right granularity level [38]. This obviously implies a trade-off between size and number of microservices [19]. Intuitively, the more microservices, the higher the isolation among business features, but at the price of increased network communications and distribution complexity. Additionally, the boundaries among the business capabilities of an application are usually not sharp. Addressing this trade-off systematically is essential for identifying the extent to which "splitting" is beneficial regarding the potential value of microservitization [3].

Security by design is also an open challenge, given the proliferation of endpoints in microservice ecosystems, which are only the surface of a myriad of small, distributed and conversational components. The attack surface to be secured is hence much larger with respect to classical SOA, as all the microservices are exposing remotely accessible APIs [38]. In this direction, access control is crucial, as the design of microservice-based applications should allow each component to quickly and consistently ascertain the provenance and authenticity of a request, which is challenging due to the high distribution [38].

3.2 Development Challenges

Most of today's microservices exploit RESTful HTTP communication [36]. Message queues are promising but not adopted as expected, in concordance with the lack of proposals for asynchronous interaction models [15]. As such, communications are purely based on remote invocations, where the API becomes a sort of contract between a microservice and its consumers. This generates coupling and directly impacts APIs' versioning, as new versions must always be retro-compatible to avoid violating the contracts among microservices, hence allowing them to continue to intercommunicate [38].

This suggests not only that microservices are being used in-house, with contracts negotiated between different teams/people inside the company, but also that their reuse should support concurrent versions and incremental releases: new versions can be (re)developed entirely to fulfill new requirements, while keeping old versions for other clients. The recent efforts on standardizing RESTful APIs through OpenAPI specifications[5] seem interesting and also applicable to specify microservices [3].

Another challenge comes from data persistency issues. A database can be part of the implementation of a microservice, so it cannot be accessed directly by others [34]. In this scenario, data consistency becomes difficult to achieve. Eventual consistency (the distributed database does not exhibit consistency immediately after a write, but at some later point) is an option, even if not always acceptable for any domain, and not easy to implement too. At the same time, this heavy distribution complicates distributed transactions and query execution (also because

[5]https://www.openapis.org/.

of the heterogeneity of the data stores to be queried). In this scenario, testing is also complex, as the business logic is partitioned over independently evolving services. Approaches that use/propose frameworks for resilience testing [21] or reusable acceptance tests [31] are highly required.

3.3 Operation Challenges

The primary challenge during the operation of microservice-based applications is given by their resource consumption. More services (with respect to traditional SOA) imply more runtime environments to be distributed, and remote API invocations. This increases consumption of computing and network resources [38]. However, there seems to be a mistrust regarding built-in solutions of cloud providers, which sometimes become too rigid [5] or cumbersome to configure and adjust [20]. In the meantime, cloud providers are growing in variety and usability (e.g., AWS has offered around 1000 new features per year[6]), and we believe that they will become the standard to deploy and manage cloud microservices in the near future [15].

Operational complexity also comes along with the distributed and dynamic nature of microservices. They could be flexibly scaled in and out, or migrated from one host to another. Moreover, they could be switched from the cloud to the edge of the network [6]. This, along with the huge number of microservices forming an application, makes it challenging to locate and coordinate their concrete instances. At the same time, distributed logging calls for aggregation approaches that help track the reasons behind issues/errors [38].

3.4 Discussion

The challenges of microservice-based applications are mainly due to their novelty and intrinsic complexity and distribution. Their design, development, and operation is hampered by the fact that the business logic in such applications is heavily distributed over many independent and asynchronously evolving microservices [38]. As a summary, Table 1 highlights the relationship among the usual steps of the development process (design, development, operation), the principles behind microservices (defined in the seminal book by Newman [28]), example features related to each principle extracted from the (academic and grey) literature review, and finally example tools or practices applicable to such a stage/principle. In this way, we pave the ground to the analysis of the microservices ecosystem on GitHub, presented in the next section.

[6]https://techcrunch.com/2016/12/02/aws-shoots-for-total-cloud-domination/.

Table 1 Relationship among microservices lifecycle stages, principles, features, and tools

Stage	Principle	Example features	Tools/practices
Design	Modeled around business domain	Contract, business, domain, functional, interfaces, bounded context, domain-driven design, single responsibility	Domain-driven design (DDD), bounded context
Design	Hide implementation details	Bounded contexts, REST, RESTful, hide databases, data pumps, event data pumps, technology-agnostic	OpenAPI, Swagger, Kafka, RabbitMQ, Spring Cloud Data Flow
Dev	Culture of automation	Automated, automatic, continuous*(deployment, integration, delivery), environment definitions, custom images, immutable servers	Travis-CI, Chef, Ansible, CI/CD
Dev	Decentralize all	DevOps, Governance, self-service, choreography, smart endpoints, dumb pipes, database-per-service, service discovery	Zookeper, Netflix Conductor
Dev/ Ops	Isolate failure	Design for failure, failure patterns, circuit-breaker, bulkhead, timeouts, availability, consistency, antifragility,	Hystrix, Simian Army, Chaos Monkey
Ops	Deploy independently	versioning, one-service-per-host, containers	Docker, Kubernetes, canary|A/B|blue/green testing
Ops	Highly observable	Monitoring, logging, analytics, statistics, aggregation	ELK, Elasticsearch, Logstash, Kibana

Recent implementations of microservices take the SOA idea to new limits, driven by the goals of rapid, interchangeable, easily adapted, and easily scaled components. As a cloud-native architecture, they play well on the basic functional features of cloud computing and its delivery capabilities [44]. The resulting factorization of workloads and incrementally scalable features of microservices provide a path by which SOA can be evolved from its previously rigid and overly formal implementation settings and be implemented in much less forbidding ways.

One consequence of this evolution is the development of new architectural patterns and the corresponding emergence and use of standards [37]. In that direction, we believe that open standard agreement is the basic prerequisite for achieving high interoperability and compatibility, being a key issue to be addressed [17]. The most clear example is a continued emphasis on the use and proper documentation of RESTful APIs, by means of Swagger/OpenAPI specifications [37]. A standardized service description and choreography approach can assure compatibility with any service, and achieve greater evolvability. Finally, standardized services in the surface can collaborate with partners for better data portability, collaborating to solve the challenges around distributed storage in microservices [38].

Finally, a few words about the organizational aspects that surround microservices. It is important to link more explicitly microservices with the DevOps (development plus operations as a single team) movement. DevOps seems to be a key factor in the success of this architectural style [1], by providing the necessary organizational shift to minimize coordination among the teams responsible for each component, and removing the barriers for an effective, reciprocal relationship between teams. DevOps implies an organizational rewiring (equivalent to, e.g., the adoption of agile methodologies) and certain key practices (e.g., continuous delivery, integration, management). As this organizational shift is not simple, the literature reports different sociotechnical patterns [43] to enable the transition towards microservices. For example, sociotechnical-risks engineering, where critical architecture elements remain tightly controlled by an organization and loosely coupled with respect to outsiders, or shift left, where organizational and operational concerns (e.g., DevOps team mixing) are addressed earlier ("left") in the lifecycle toward architecting and development, rather than implementation and runtime.

4 Microservices on GitHub

Given the open challenges discussed in the previous section, we are interested in how practitioners are addressing them in practice. To answer this, we delve into the current microservices landscape in the biggest source of software artifacts on the Web to date: GitHub.[7] Our main goal is to identify the actual incidence of microservices and related tooling in practice. We stated the following research questions (RQs):

- **RQ1**: What is the activity and relevance of microservices in open source public repositories?
- **RQ2**: What are the characteristics of microservices-related repositories?
- **RQ3**: How are these projects addressing the aforementioned open challenges?

4.1 Dataset Creation

We followed the guidelines for mining GitHub defined in the literature [23, 48], and considered the following information:

- *Releases* of a repository: Each release is a specially tagged push event, composed of several commits (at least one) to a stable repository branch.

[7]https://GitHub.com/.

- *Push events* to the master branch of a repository, as an indicator of repository *activity* (each push event is composed of one or more commits, and is triggered when a repository branch is pushed to).
- *Stars*, as an indicator of repository *relevance* for the GitHub community (starring a repository allows one to keep track of interesting projects).
- *Topics*, as an indicator of the repository *topics* (this allows one to describe, find, and relate repositories).

Then, we used GitHub Archive[8] as our datasource of GitHub events. GitHub Archive provides a daily dump of GitHub activity (around 2.5 Gb of events per day). Given its size, it is only accessible through Google Big Query,[9] a web service that allows one to perform SQL-like interactive analysis of massive datasets (billions of rows).

We started by looking for *active* repositories—those with a Push event to their *master* branch during the last month. The total amount of *active* projects during 2018 exceeds 1 million. Thus, we additionally filtered repositories corresponding to our research—i.e., those using the *topic* "microservice" or "microservices" or mentioning these terms in the repository description.

The total number of repositories related to microservices is around 36,000. However, when analyzing sample repositories at random, we noticed that some of them are personal or class projects that, although being active, are not relevant for the community. These repositories have only one contributor, zero forks, and low popularity. With this dataset as a starting point, we narrowed our scope to *active* repositories related to microservices. Then, we defined an additional criteria for *relevant* repositories as those with 10+ *stars* (equivalent to followers or level of popularity). This information is accessed through the GraphQL-based GitHubAPI.[10] All in all, the number of 2018's *relevant* and *active* microservices-related repositories on GitHub is 651,[11] roughly 2% of the total 36,000 repositories, excluding forks and duplicated.

4.2 Quantitative Analysis

From the dataset of 651 repositories extracted in the previous step, we performed an initial quantitative analysis with the goal of answering the research questions. We started by identifying their topics, languages used, and other metadata such as commits, stars, and forks. Table 2 presents a summary of the initial analysis and tries to answer RQ1: (*What is the activity and relevance of microservices in open source*

[8]https://www.GitHubarchive.org/.

[9]https://bigquery.cloud.google.com/.

[10]https://developer.GitHub.com/v4/.

[11]The full list can be found at: http://cor.to/Gvyp.

Table 2 Summary of Microservice Projects on GitHub (RQ1)

Metric	Total	Average	Median
Total microservices projects	~36,000	–	–
Active and relevant projects (+10 stars, PR in the last month)	651	–	–
Pull requests per project	–	128.7	17
Stars per project (average)	–	730.6	77
Watchers per project (average)	–	62.7	15

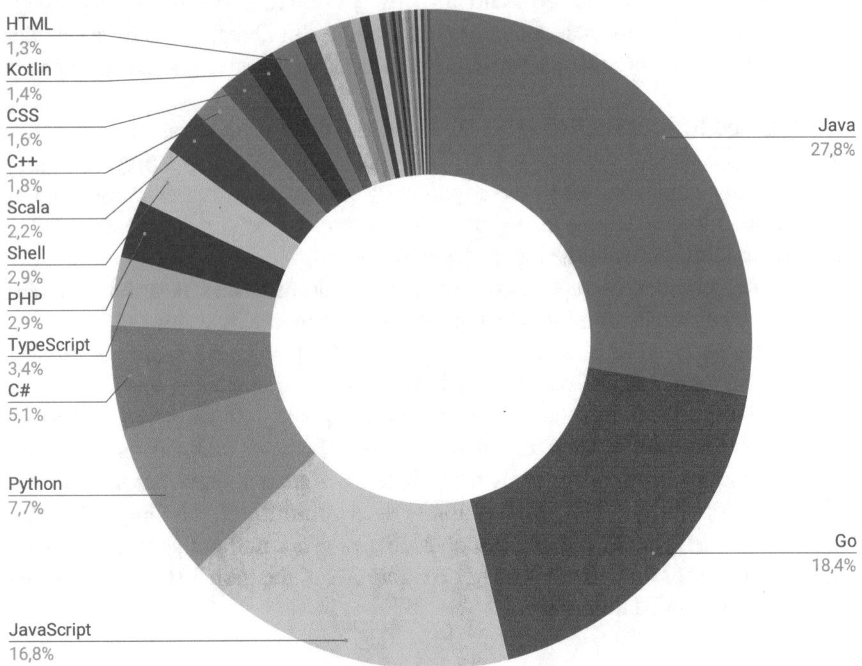

Fig. 1 Languages distribution of microservices projects (RQ2)

public repositories?). For brevity, raw data and the scripts and queries used to gather and analyze repositories metadata are accessible within our replication package.[12]

Moving to RQ2 (*What are the characteristics of the microservices-related repositories?*), Fig. 1 decomposes the use of programming languages in our dataset. Interestingly, Java is the most common language (27.8%), followed by Go (18.4%) and JavaScript (16.8%). Other languages show a narrower adoption, including Python, PHP, Typescrypt, and C#, among others. Given the polyglot nature of microservices, some of the repositories adopt various languages—we report the main language for each. Our results suggest that Java is still widely used [36] and,

[12]http://www.GitHub.com/webocs/mining-GitHub-microservices.

although it is perceived as an "old-fashioned" language, it can make microservices easier to adopt by Java developers, and also easier to integrate with legacy Java systems. Besides, microservices are commonly associated with lightweight, scripting languages such as JavaScript, which is reflected in practice—although we expected JavaScript to be the most popular language. Finally, Go is mostly a server-side language (developed by Google), mainly adopted for projects that provide support for microservices in the form of frameworks or middleware infrastructures.

As for RQ3, (*How are these projects addressing the aforementioned open challenges?*), we performed a topic ranking to grasp the underlying types of solutions and technologies used. Topics are labels that create subject-based connections between GitHub repositories and let one explore projects by, e.g., type, technology, or keyword.[13] Our ranking is summarized in Table 3. Note that microservices/microservice do not appear as a topic on all repositories, but it can be part of the description. Apart from those, the most popular languages: java, nodejs (javascript) and golang (go) appear among the top topics. The others are several tools for deploying and operating microservices such as docker (containers), kubernetes (a container orchestration tool) and spring-boot (spring "containers"), and cloud-related topics (cloud, spring-cloud). There are a few topics regarding specific solutions for microservices communication (rpc, grpc, REST, rabbitmq) and/or API design (API, REST, rest-api). Other challenges are underrepresented in the list of topics with quite small percentages.

Table 3 Main topics in microservices projects

Topic	Times	%	Topic	Times	%	Topic	Times	%
Microservices	270	41.47	API	31	4.76	Python	20	3.07
Microservice	222	34.10	Framework	30	4.61	Cloud	17	2.61
Java	88	13.52	Microservices-arch	28	4.30	Service-mesh	17	2.61
Docker	68	10.45	Distributed-systems	28	4.30	CQRS	16	2.46
Kubernetes	63	9.68	grpc	25	3.84	DevOps	16	2.46
Spring-boot	57	8.76	Rest	24	3.69	redis	16	2.46
Golang	52	7.99	API-gateway	23	3.53	http	16	2.46
Nodejs	51	7.83	Rest-API	21	3.23	Spring-cloud-core	16	2.46
Cloud-native	46	7.07	Containers	21	3.23	mongodb	15	2.30
Go	41	6.30	Serverless	20	3.07	Kafka	15	2.30
Spring-cloud	41	6.30	Service-discovery	20	3.07	DDD	15	2.30
Spring	41	6.30	Javascript	20	3.07	Proxy	14	2.15
rpc	33	5.07	Rabbitmq	20	3.07	Consul	13	2.00

[13]https://blog.GitHub.com/2017-01-31-introducing-topics/.

4.3 Qualitative Analysis

Continuing with RQ3, (*How are these projects addressing the aforementioned challenges?*), we performed a Qualitative analysis divided into two parts. First, we took a small sample (64 projects, 10% of the total) at random and analyzed it, which led to some preliminary insights. Support for the microservices lifecycle is the most common practice (44%), ranging from templates and boilerplate code for development to operational support in the form of containerization solutions, continuous integration, load-balancing, etc.—broadly speaking, DevOps practices—followed by specific solutions for communication among microservices (33%), implementing orchestration mechanisms, asynchronous communication, and API gateways. The rest of the projects actually implement microservices (23%), ranging from sample applications fully developed with several microservices to single or few microservices—e.g., for authentication or cryptography.

Interestingly, the focus is on supporting microservice architectures rather than on the development of microservices themselves. We believe that this is mainly due to two factors:

- A complexity shift: The claimed simplicity of microservices moves the complexity to their supporting systems [19].
- A different reuse perspective [33]: Instead of reusing existing microservices for new tasks or use cases, they should be small and independent enough to allow for rapidly developing a new one that can coexist, evolve, or replace the previous one according to the business needs [19].

Afterwards, we performed qualitative analysis on the whole dataset, organized around each stage of microservice lifecycle (recall Table 1). For doing this, we assessed the documentation of the repositories, in particular the *Readme* documents at the master branch. We crafted a dataset of 590 readme documents (90% of the total), given that some of the projects did not present their documentation in such a standard way.

We used the dataset (along with the metadata of repositories) to populate Apache Solr,[14] a search engine that features advanced matching capabilities including phrases, wildcards, and clustering. Solr makes use of Apache Lucene,[15] a well-known search library based on the TF.IDF model. This scoring model involves a number of scoring factors such as term frequency (the frequency with which a term appears in a document), inverse document frequency (the rarer a term is across all documents in the index, the higher its contribution to the score is) and other tuning factors such as coordination factor (the more query terms are found in a document, the higher its score is) and field length (the more words a field contains, the lower its score is). The exact scoring formula that brings these factors together is outside the

---

[14] http://lucene.apache.org/solr/.

[15] https://lucene.apache.org/.

scope of the present chapter, but a detailed explanation can be found in the Lucene documentation.[16]

Then, we built the queries accounting the different features and tools/practices presented in Table 1. The following discussion of obtained results is also organized around lifecycle steps, namely: design, development, and operation.

Table 4 shows the three queries related to the design stage, together with the total number of repositories found for each query, and the top 5 (most relevant) results. Clearly, the least addressed topic in the design of microservices is their modeling around the business domain, or domain-driven design, with only 29 repositories listed. As modeling is somewhat subjective, one may argue that tool support or examples may be scarce or not extrapolable to different domains. However, designing microservices and determining their granularity is still an open challenge [38], thus this may be a call for further efforts. Note that the most relevant repositories are sample applications and not supporting tools—with the exception of #4 (boilerplate architecture) and #5 (an opinionated framework for .NET).

Conversely, RESTful interfaces (specified through Swagger/OpenAPI) seem to be a widespread practice (208 repositories) in line with the perceived state-of-practice in industry [36]—#1 bringing together the most popular communication style (REST) with the most popular language (Java). Gaining traction, 147 repositories deal with asynchronous communication through messaging protocols such as RabbitMQ or Spring Cloud Stream for Java (#3).

Entering development stage (Table 5), the most addressed topic is automation (275 repositories) through continuous integration and deployment techniques (CI/CD), Travis being the weapon of choice, perhaps because of its easy integration with GitHub [48]. One may highlight #1 as it provides an interesting approach for managing multiple apps in a single (mono) repository.

Orchestration/choreography (41 repositories) are not so popular, as microservice integration so far has been usually ad hoc and in-house. The salient example is Netflix Conductor (#1), nowadays the most popular orchestrator for microservices. Somewhat service discovery (101 repositories) is more popular, although from a different perspective w.r.t. discovery in traditional SOA [18]. Nowadays, the problem is to find the "alive" endpoints among the multiple copies of a microservice at runtime [42], through tools such as Apache Zookeeper, etcd, Consul or VertX (#2). However, for large-scale microservice architectures, orchestration and choreography solutions are a must-have, although there is not a large number of these cases on GitHub. Technologies such as NGINX, AWS API gateways, or Kubernetes control plane are the alternatives for enterprise microservices management.

Finally, Table 6 summarizes results for the operation stage. Failure isolation patterns are not so common (54 repositories). Circuit-breaker is the only pattern that provides significant results, while others such as bulkheads or timeouts were not mentioned throughout our dataset. The first four repositories in the results are sample microservices applications that implement circuit-breakers: #5 is an

[16]http://lucene.apache.org/core/3_5_0/api/core/org/apache/lucene/search/Similarity.html.

Table 4 Repository analysis by design principles and query (total repos and top 5 per query)

#repos	Principle/repoId	Query/description
29	**Modeled around business domain**	*"bounded context" OR ddd OR "domain driven design"*
1st	EdwinVW/pitstop	This repo contains a sample application based on a garage management system for PitStop—a fictitious garage. The primary goal of this sample is to demonstrate several Web-scale architecture concerns…
2nd	banq/jdonframework	Domain Events Pub/Sub framework for DDD
3rd	idugalic/digital-restaurant	DDD. Event sourcing. CQRS. REST. Modular. Microservices. Kotlin. Spring. Axon platform. Apache Kafka. RabbitMQ
4th	ivanpaulovich/clean-architecture-manga	Clean architecture service template for your microservice with DDD, TDD and SOLID using .NET Core 2.0. The components are independent and testable, the architecture is evolutionary in multiple dimensions…
5th	volak/Aggregates.NET	.NET event sourced domain driven design model via NServiceBus and GetEventStore
208	**Hide implementation details**	*rest OR restful OR swagger OR openapi OR "api blueprint"*
1st	noboomu/proteus	High-Performance RESTful Java web and microservice framework
2nd	mfornos/awesome-microservices	A curated list of microservice architecture-related principles and technologies
3rd	banzaicloud/pipeline	Pipeline enables developers to go from commit to scale in minutes by turning Kubernetes into a feature-rich application platform integrating CI/CD, centralized logging, monitoring, enterprise-grade…
4th	benc-uk/smilr	Microservices reference app showcasing a range of technologies, platforms and methodologies
5th	rootsongjc/awesome-cloud-native	A curated list for awesome cloud native tools, software, and tutorials
147	**Hide implementation details**	*asynchronous OR "data pump" OR "event pump" OR messaging OR RabbitMQ OR Kafka*
1st	mfornos/awesome-microservices	A curated list of microservice architecture-related principles and technologies
2nd	binhnguyennus/awesome-scalability	Scalable, available, stable, performant, and intelligent system design patterns
3rd	hipster-labs/generator-jhipster-spring-cloud-stream	JHipster module for messaging microservices with Spring Cloud Stream
4th	SaifRehman/ICP-Airways	Cloud Native application based on microservice architecture, IBM Middlewares and following 12 factor practices
5th	idugalic/digital-restaurant	DDD. Event sourcing. CQRS. REST. Modular. Microservices. Kotlin. Spring. Axon platform. Apache Kafka. RabbitMQ

Table 5 Repository analysis by development principles and query (total repos and top 5 per query)

#repos	Principle/repoId	Query/description
275	**Culture of automation**	*travis OR ci OR cd*
1st	MozillaSecurity/orion	CI/CD pipeline for building and publishing multiple containers as microservices within a mono-repository
2nd	vietnam-devs/coolstore-microservices	A containerized polyglot service mesh based on .NET Core, Nodejs, Vuejs and more running on Istio
3rd	rootsongjc/awesome-cloud-native	A curated list for awesome cloud native tools, software, and tutorials.
4th	scalecube/scalecube-services	ScaleCube services is a broker-less reactive-microservices-mesh that features: API-gateways, service-discovery, service-load-balancing, the architecture supports plug-and-play service communication...
5th	banzaicloud/pipeline	Pipeline enables developers to go from commit to scale in minutes by turning Kubernetes into a feature-rich application platform integrating CI/CD, centralized logging, monitoring, enterprise-grade...
41	**Decentralize all**	*orchestration OR choreography OR "netflix conductor"*
1st	Netflix/conductor	Conductor is a microservices orchestration engine
2nd	rootsongjc/awesome-cloud-native	A curated list for awesome cloud native tools, software, and tutorials
3rd	taimos/dvalin	Taimos microservices framework.
4th	InVisionApp/go-health	Library for enabling asynchronous health checks in your service
5th	Sharding-sphere/sharding-sphere	Distributed database middleware
101	**Decentralize all**	*"service discovery" OR zookeeper OR consul*
1st	smallnest/rpcx	Faster multilanguage bidirectional RPC framework in Go, like alibaba Dubbo and weibo Motan in Java, but with more features, scale easily
2nd	vert-x3/vertx-service-discovery	Some tools one can use for doing microservices with Vert.x
3rd	rootsongjc/awesome-cloud-native	A curated list for awesome cloud native tools, software, and tutorials
4th	senecajs/seneca-mesh	Mesh your Seneca.js microservices together—no more service discovery
5th	containous/traefik	The cloud native edge router

interesting framework that actually supports circuit-breakers out of the box (through the Netflix Hystrix library).

Following the "deploy independently" principle, the most popular practice overall, along with CI/CD (Table 5), is containerization, achieved mainly through docker (274 repositories). An important number of sample microservices or sidecar libraries is containerized. Interestingly, #5 combines microservices, mobile devices, and blockchain.

Table 6 Repository analysis by operation principles and query (total repos and top 5 per query)

#repos	Principle/repoId	Query/description
54	**Isolate failure**	*"circuit breaker" OR hystrix*
1st	sqshq/PiggyMetrics	Microservice architecture with Spring Boot, Spring Cloud and Docker
2nd	ERS-HCL/nxplorerjs-microservice-starter	Node JS, Typescript, Express based reactive microservice starter project for REST and GraphQL APIs
3rd	raycad/go-microservices	Golang Microservices Example
4th	spring-petclinic/spring-petclinic-microservices	Distributed version of Spring Petclinic built with Spring Cloud
5th	wso2/msf4j	WSO2 Microservices Framework for Java (MSF4J)
274	**Deploy independently**	*docker OR containers OR kubernetes*
1st	rootsongjc/awesome-cloud-native	A curated list for awesome cloud native tools, software, and tutorials
2nd	benc-uk/smilr	Microservices reference app showcasing a range of technologies, platforms, and methodologies
3rd	dotnet-architecture/eShopOnContainers	Easy to get started sample reference microservice- and container-based application. Cross-platform on Linux and Windows Docker Containers, powered by .NET Core 2.1, Docker engine and optionally Azure...
4th	IF1007/if1007	Desenvolvimento de Aplicaes com Arquitetura Baseada em Microservices
5th	IBM/android-kubernetes-blockchain	Build a blockchain-enabled health and fitness app with Android and Kubernetes
81	**Highly observable**	*monitoring OR logging OR elk*
1st	slanatech/swagger-stats	API telemetry and APM
2nd	hootsuite/health-checks-api	Standardize the way services and applications expose their status in a distributed application
3rd	banzaicloud/pipeline	Pipeline enables developers to go from commit to scale in minutes by turning Kubernetes into a feature-rich application platform integrating CI/CD, centralized logging, monitoring, enterprise-grade...
4th	wso2/msf4j	WSO2 Microservices Framework for Java (MSF4J)
5th	mfornos/awesome-microservices	A curated list of microservice architecture related principles and technologies

The last principle (highly observable) is mainly represented by monitoring and logging techniques (81 repositories), while other practices and technologies (e.g., correlation IDs, analytics, and specific libraries) are not relevant. #1 is a monitoring tool for RESTful APIs (i.e., for most microservices), while #2 and #3 are comprehensive frameworks that include monitoring facilities, among others.

To conclude, let us recap on RQ3, (*How are these projects addressing the aforementioned challenges*?). From our analysis, it can be highlighted that both containerization and CI/CD are the most widespread practices in the microservice ecosystem, followed closely by RESTful specifications. Those correspond to three principles: deploy independently, culture of automation, and hide implementation details, respectively. Mild attention is put on asynchronous communication, service discovery, and monitoring. Finally, the least discussed issues in the GitHub microservice landscape are failure isolation patterns (mostly synonyms with circuit-breakers), orchestration/choreography, and an alarming lack of modeling (DDD, bounded context, etc.) support.

As *threats to validity* of our qualitative assessment, one may note that: (1) queries are not representative of all the keywords and their combinations in Table 2 and (2) queries are constructed using terms related to each other (e.g., REST and OpenAPI/Swagger). This was done to increase the accuracy of results according to the Solr underlying matching mechanisms. We first excluded terms that are not relevant for the queries—i.e., they return (almost) all of the documents as a result, or the inverse (none). Then, we grouped only similar terms (according to their topics) in the same query. This prevents retrieving only general-purpose repositories (e.g., awesome lists[17]) and not the specific, relevant ones for the query at hand—a bias introduced by the coordination factor of TF.IDF weighting [12]. We acknowledge the importance of such lists, but in our case they introduce noise by biasing towards listed tools/frameworks/libraries. Additionally, we are not taking into account historical data of repositories, which may help us track certain behaviors—e.g., the periodicity of releases before/after implementing CI/CD tools, or the impact of containerization in the popularity of a given repository. Besides, this is an ongoing work and performing more comprehensive analysis through, e.g., clustering techniques or topic modeling is the subject of future work.

4.3.1 The Serverless Panorama

Finally, we discuss the current tendencies of serverless microservices (Table 7). We found 35 repositories mentioning serverless (5% of the microservices-related repositories), showing that this technology is still in the early stages of adoption. Through a detailed analysis, one can find example apps using recent serverless platforms—in this case IBM/Apache Openwhisk, but there are others for Google Cloud and Azure functions. Two frameworks to handle the serverless functions' lifecycle, with special focus on deployment, are the serverless framework and UP. Finally, a representative of the event-oriented nature of functions: flogo, and the usual awesome list of serverless solutions.

The most popular languages (when applicable) are JavaScript (mostly for examples, tutorials, and boilerplate applications) and Go (for deployment frameworks such as UP). Popular topics are straightforward: *serverless* and its variety of vendor flavors (Google functions, Azure functions, IBM Openwhisk, AWS Lambda). Apart from that, other popular topics are: *deployment*, since functions involve yet more moving parts than microservices, making deployment even more complex; *Apis*

[17]A common type of curated lists of entries within a given topic—https://GitHub.com/sindresorhus/awesome.

Table 7 Serverless repositories analysis, total and top 5

#repos	Principle/repoId	Query/description
35	**Serverless**	*serverless OR faas*
1st	serverless/serverless	Serverless framework—build web, mobile, and IoT applications with serverless architectures using AWS Lambda, Azure functions, Google CloudFunctions
2nd	anaibol/awesome-serverless	A curated list of awesome services, solutions, and resources for serverless/no-backend applications
3rd	apex/up	Deploy infinitely scalable serverless apps, apis, and sites in seconds to AWS
4th	TIBCOSoftware/flogo	An open source ecosystem of opinionated event-driven capabilities to simplify building efficient and modern serverless functions, microservices, and edge apps
5th	IBM/spring-boot-microservices-on-kubernetes	In this code we demonstrate how a simple Spring Boot application can be deployed on top of Kubernetes

and *integration*, since functions are typically used to generate "entry points" for systems and architectures, probably relying on traditional servers for more complex processing, and finally *events* and *messages* platforms such as Kafka or Mqtt, as functions are typically event driven.

From this analysis, we derive the following challenges and opportunities. First, support for *FaaSification* [39] (i.e., splitting into functions) of legacy or microservices code. Then, tool support for creating and managing complex functions. Usually, functions are used for simple tasks, although they can encapsulate complex microservices such as image recognition [4, 6] or model checking [45], as demonstrated in our previous work. However, this involves trial and error and significant effort, which implies an opportunity to develop supporting techniques, frameworks, and tools. For example, to embed custom languages (e.g., OCAML), improve long-running algorithms, or exploit opportunistic container reuse of the underlying platform as a cache of sorts.

Additionally, some aspects that may not arise from the state of the art should be mentioned here. Serverless is being pushed forward by major vendors, beyond the traditional use cases of short computation as lambda functions.[18] For example, through AWS Fargate for long running functions, or AWS step functions to define complex serverless workflows. Furthermore, solutions such as OpenFaaS and Kubernetes as managed service are blurring the frontier between lightweight containers and serverless functions. The industry tendency is that of starting with containerized microservices (from scratch or from a monolith) and then migrate key features to FaaS to exploit its unique capabilities.

[18] https://aws.amazon.com/en/serverless/serverlessrepo/.

5 Conclusions

This chapter presented an evolutionary perspective that captures the fundamental understanding of microservice architectures, encompassing their whole lifecycle. This is necessary to enable effective exploration, understanding, assessing, comparison, and selection of microservice-based models, languages, techniques, platforms, and tools.

Microservice architectures are fairly new, but their hype and success is undeniable, as big IT companies have chosen them to deliver their business, with Amazon, Netflix, Spotify, and Twitter among those. Due to this traction, the industrial state of practice on microservices has surpassed academic research efforts, which are still at an earlier stage [38]. This resulted in a sort of gap between academic state of the art and industrial state of practice, confirmed by our literature review, which also provides a panorama of available solutions and current and future challenges. Among them are the early use of resilience patterns to design fault-tolerant microservice solutions, the standardization of their interfaces [37], and the development of asynchronous microservices. Special attention should be given to the latent use of the serverless model (FaaS) to design, deploy, and manage microservices. FaaS has the potential to become the next evolution of microservices [9] as event-driven, asynchronous functions, because the underlying constraints have changed, costs have reduced, and radical improvements in time to value are possible.

Finally, we present an analysis of microservices-related repositories on GitHub, which confirmed our findings regarding open challenges, in particular those related to microservices design and modeling (granularity, DDD, and bounded context). This is an on-going work with the main goal of understanding how, and to which degree, software developers are embracing microservice architectures in practice, and which tools and practices are available to overcome their challenges. Our current work encompasses automating the repository analysis through a mining tool, capturing and processing additional metadata, mainly regarding the history of releases, issues, etc. Then, applying natural language processing techniques to infer information (features, topics) from repositories' documentation. Finally we would like to combine this analysis with developers' feedback to understand their vision regarding microservice architectures.

Acknowledgements This work has been partially supported by the GAUSS national research project, which has been funded by the MIUR under the PRIN 2015 program (Contract 2015-KWREMX); and by the grant ANPCyT PICT-2017-1725.

References

1. A. Balalaie, A. Heydarnoori, P. Jamshidi, Microservices architecture enables DevOps: migration to a cloud-native architecture. IEEE Softw. **33**(3), 42–52 (2016)
2. A. Balalaie, A. Heydarnoori, P. Jamshidi, D.A. Tamburri, T. Lynn, Microservices migration patterns. Softw. Pract. Experience **48**(11), 2019–2042 (2018)
3. L. Baresi, M. Garriga, A. De Renzis, Microservices identification through interface analysis, in *European Conference on Service-Oriented and Cloud Computing (ESOCC)* (Springer, Berlin, 2017)
4. L. Baresi, D.F. Mendonça, M. Garriga, Empowering low-latency applications through a serverless edge computing architecture, in *European Conference on Service-Oriented and Cloud Computing* (Springer, Berlin, 2017), pp. 196–210
5. L. Baresi, S. Guinea, A. Leva, G. Quattrocchi, A discrete-time feedback controller for containerized cloud applications, in *ACM Sigsoft International Symposium on the Foundations of Software Engineering (FSE)* (ACM, New York, 2016)
6. L. Baresi, D.F. Mendonça, M. Garriga, S. Guinea, G. Quattrocchi, A unified model for the mobile-edge-cloud continuum. ACM Trans. Internet Technol. **19**(2), 29:1–29:21 (2019). https://doi.org/10.1145/3226644
7. D. Box, D. Ehnebuske, G. Kakivaya, A. Layman, N. Mendelsohn, H.F. Nielsen, S. Thatte, D. Winer, Simple Object Access Protocol (SOAP) 1.1 (2000). W3C Recommendation
8. G. Casale, C. Chesta, P. Deussen, E. Di Nitto, P. Gouvas, S. Koussouris, V. Stankovski, A. Symeonidis, V. Vlassiou, A. Zafeiropoulos, et al., Current and future challenges of software engineering for services and applications. Proc. Comput. Sci. **97**, 34–42 (2016)
9. A. Cockroft, Evolution of business logic from monoliths through microservices, to functions (2017). https://goo.gl/H6zKMn
10. N. Dragoni, S. Giallorenzo, A.L. Lafuente, M. Mazzara, F. Montesi, R. Mustafin, L. Safina, Microservices: yesterday, today, and tomorrow, in *Present and Ulterior Software Engineering* (Springer, Cham 2017), pp. 195–216
11. J. Erickson, K. Siau, Web service, service-oriented computing, and service-oriented architecture: separating hype from reality. J. BD Manage. **19**(3), 42–54 (2008)
12. C. Fautsch, J. Savoy, Adapting the TF IDF vector-space model to domain specific information retrieval, in *Proceedings of the 2010 ACM Symposium on Applied Computing* (ACM, New York, 2010), pp. 1708–1712. https://doi.org/10.1145/1774088.1774454
13. R.T. Fielding, R.N. Taylor, Architectural styles and the design of network-based software architectures, vol. 7. (University of California, Irvine, 2000)
14. V. Garousi, M. Felderer, M.V. Mäntylä, Guidelines for including grey literature and conducting multivocal literature reviews in software engineering. Inf. Softw. Technol. **106**, 101–121 (2019)
15. M. Garriga, Towards a taxonomy of microservices architectures, in *International Conference on Software Engineering and Formal Methods* (Springer, Berlin, 2017), pp. 203–218
16. M. Garriga, A. Flores, A. Cechich, A. Zunino, Web services composition mechanisms: a review. IETE Tech. Rev. **32**(5), 376–383 (2015)
17. M. Garriga, C. Mateos, A. Flores, A. Cechich, A. Zunino, Restful service composition at a glance: a survey. J. Netw. Comput. Appl. **60**, 32–53 (2016)
18. M. Garriga, A.D. Renzis, I. Lizarralde, A. Flores, C. Mateos, A. Cechich, A. Zunino, A structural-semantic web service selection approach to improve retrievability of web services. Inf. Syst. Front. **20**(6), 1319–1344 (2018). https://doi.org/10.1007/s10796-016-9731-1
19. S. Hassan, R. Bahsoon, Microservices and their design trade-offs: a self-adaptive roadmap, in *IEEE International Conference on Services Computing (SCC)* (IEEE, Piscataway, 2016), pp. 813–818
20. S. Hendrickson, S. Sturdevant, T. Harter, V. Venkataramani, A.C. Arpaci-Dusseau, R.H. Arpaci-Dusseau, Serverless computation with openlambda. Elastic **60**, 80 (2016)

21. V. Heorhiadi, S. Rajagopalan, H. Jamjoom, M.K. Reiter, V. Sekar, Gremlin: systematic resilience testing of microservices, in *2016 IEEE 36th International Conference on Distributed Computing Systems (ICDCS)* (IEEE, Piscataway, 2016), pp. 57–66
22. V. Issarny, N. Georgantas, S. Hachem, A. Zarras, P. Vassiliadist, M. Autili, M.A. Gerosa, A.B. Hamida, Service-oriented middleware for the future internet: state of the art and research directions. J. Internet Services Appl. **2**(1), 23–45 (2011)
23. E. Kalliamvakou, G. Gousios, K. Blincoe, L. Singer, D.M. German, D. Damian, The promises and perils of mining github, in *Proceedings of the 11th Working Conference on Mining Software Repositories* (ACM, New York, 2014), pp. 92–101
24. B. Kitchenham, Guidelines for performing systematic literature reviews in software engineering. Technical report, ver. 2.3 EBSE Technical Report. EBSE. sn (2007)
25. P. Lemberger, M. Morel, *Why Has SOA Failed So Often?* (Wiley, London, 2013), pp. 207–218. https://doi.org/10.1002/9781118562017.app3
26. J. Lewis, M. Fowler, Microservices (2014). http://martinfowler.com/articles/microservices.html
27. I. Nadareishvili, R. Mitra, M. McLarty, M. Amundsen, *Microservice Architecture: Aligning Principles, Practices, and Culture* (O'Reilly Media, Sebastopol, 2016)
28. S. Newman, *Building Microservices* (O'Reilly Media, Sebastopol, 2015)
29. M.P. Papazoglou, P. Traverso, S. Dustdar, F. Leymann, Service-oriented computing: a research roadmap. Int. J. Coop. Inf. Syst. **17**(02), 223–255 (2008)
30. C. Pautasso, O. Zimmermann, F. Leymann, Restful web services vs. "big" web services: making the right architectural decision, in *17th International Conference on World Wide Web* (ACM Press, New York, 2008), pp. 805–814
31. M. Rahman, J. Gao, A reusable automated acceptance testing architecture for microservices in behavior-driven development, in *2015 IEEE Symposium on Service-Oriented System Engineering (SOSE)* (IEEE, Piscataway, 2015), pp. 321–325
32. J. Rao, X. Su, A survey of automated web service composition methods, in *International Workshop on Semantic Web Services and Web Process Composition* (Springer, Berlin, 2004), pp. 43–54
33. M. Richards, *Microservices vs. Service-Oriented Architecture* (O'Reilly Media, Sebastopol, 2015)
34. C. Richardson, Microservices architecture (2014). http://microservices.io/
35. M. Roberts, Serverless architectures (2016). http://martinfowler.com/articles/serverless.html
36. G. Schermann, J. Cito, P. Leitner, All the services large and micro: revisiting industrial practice in services computing, in *International Conference on Service-Oriented Computing (ICSOC)* (Springer, Berlin, 2015), pp. 36–47
37. A. Sill, The design and architecture of microservices. IEEE Cloud Comput. **3**(5), 76–80 (2016)
38. J. Soldani, D. Tamburri, W.J. Van Den Heuvel, The pains and gains of microservices: a systematic grey literature review. J. Syst. Softw. **146**, 215–232 (2018). https://doi.org/10.1016/j.jss.2018.09.082
39. J. Spillner, C. Mateos, D.A. Monge, Faaster, better, cheaper: the prospect of serverless scientific computing and HPC, in *Latin American High Performance Computing Conference* (Springer, Berlin, 2017), pp. 154–168
40. B. Srivastava, J. Koehler, Web service composition-current solutions and open problems, in *ICAPS 2003 Workshop on Planning for Web Services*, vol. 35 (2003), pp. 28–35
41. M. Stigler, Understanding serverless computing, in *Beginning Serverless Computing* (Springer, Berlin, 2018), pp. 1–14
42. J. Stubbs, W. Moreira, R. Dooley, Distributed systems of microservices using docker and serfnode, in *International Workshop on Science Gateways (IWSG)* (IEEE, Piscataway, 2015), pp. 34–39
43. D.A. Tamburri, R. Kazman, H. Fahimi, The architect's role in community shepherding. IEEE Softw. **33**(6), 70–79 (2016). https://doi.org/10.1109/MS.2016.144

44. G. Toffetti, S. Brunner, S., M. Blöchlinger, J. Spillner, T.M. Bohnert, Self-managing cloud-native applications: design, implementation, and experience. Futur. Gener. Comput. Syst. **72**, 165–179 (2017). https://doi.org/10.1016/j.future.2016.09.002.
45. C. Tsigkanos, M. Garriga, L. Baresi, C. Ghezzi, Cloud deployment tradeoffs for the analysis of spatially-distributed systems of internet-of-things. Technical Report, Politecnico di Milano (2019)
46. M. Villamizar, O. Garcés, L. Ochoa, H. Castro, L. Salamanca, M. Verano, R. Casallas, S. Gil, C. Valencia, A. Zambrano, et al., Infrastructure cost comparison of running web applications in the cloud using AWS Lambda and monolithic and microservice architectures, in *2016 16th IEEE/ACM International Symposium on Cluster, Cloud and Grid Computing (CCGrid)* (IEEE, Piscataway, 2016), pp. 179–182
47. N. Wilde, B. Gonen, E. El-Sheik, A. Zimmermann, *Emerging Trends in the Evolution of Service-Oriented and Enterprise Architectures, chap. Approaches to the Evolution of SOA Systems.* Intelligent Systems Reference Library (Springer, Berlin, 2016)
48. F. Zampetti, S. Scalabrino, R. Oliveto, G. Canfora, M. Di Penta, How open source projects use static code analysis tools in continuous integration pipelines, in *2017 IEEE/ACM 14th International Conference on Mining Software Repositories (MSR)* (IEEE, Piscataway, 2017), pp. 334–344
49. O. Zimmermann, Do microservices pass the same old architecture test? Or: SOA is not dead–long live (micro-) services, in *Microservices Workshop at SATURN Conference* (Software Engineering Institute SEI, Carnegie Mellon University, 2015)

Size Matters: Microservices Research and Applications

Manuel Mazzara, Antonio Bucchiarone, Nicola Dragoni, and Victor Rivera

Abstract In this chapter we offer an overview of microservices providing the introductory information that a reader should know before continuing reading this book. We introduce the idea of microservices and we discuss some of the current research challenges and real-life software applications where the microservice paradigm plays a key role. We have identified a set of areas where both researcher and developer can propose new ideas and technical solutions.

1 The Shift Towards Distribution

History of programming languages, paradigms, and software architectures have been characterized in the last few decades by a progressive shift towards distribution, modularization, and loose coupling. The purpose is to increase code reuse and robustness [13, 26], ultimately a necessity dictated by the need of increasing software quality, not only in safety- and financial-critical applications [42], but also in more common off-the-shelf software packages. The two directions of *modularization*[1] (code reuse and solid design) and *robustness* (software quality and formal methods: verification/correctness-by-construction) advanced to some extent

[1] https://www.oreilly.com/ideas/modules-vs-microservices.

A. Bucchiarone
Distributed Adaptive Systems (DAS) Research Unit, Fondazione Bruno Kessler, Trento, Italy
e-mail: bucchiarone@fbk.eu

M. Mazzara (✉) · V. Rivera
Innopolis University, Innopolis, Russian Federation
e-mail: m.mazzara@innopolis.ru; v.rivera@innopolis.ru

N. Dragoni
DTU Compute, Technical University of Denmark, Kongens Lyngby, Denmark

Centre for Applied Autonomous Sensor Systems, Orebro University, Orebro, Sweden
e-mail: ndra@dtu.dk

A. Bucchiarone et al. (eds.), *Microservices*,
https://doi.org/10.1007/978-3-030-31646-4_2

independently and pushed by different communities, although with a nonempty overlap.

Object-oriented technologies are prominent in software development [52], with specific instances of languages incorporating both the aspects aforementioned (modularity and correctness). A notable example is the Eiffel programming language [44], incorporating solid principles of object-oriented-programming (OOP) within a programming framework coordinated by the idea of *design-by-contract*, which aims at correctness-by-construction. None of these technologies can nevertheless rule out the need for testing, which robustly remains a pillar of the software development lifecycle.

Other examples exist of languages having a strong emphasis on correctness, both from the architectural viewpoint and in terms of meeting functional requirements [37]. However, until recently, not much attention was dedicated to integrating these principles into a distributed setting winning out properties such as easiness of deployment, a lightweight design and development phase, and minimal need for integration testing. The idea of microservices [16, 26] and DevOps [1, 2, 41] stem out exactly from this widespread and recognized need.

Chapter Outline and Contribution The contribution of the chapter is twofold, and thus organized in two main sections. Section 2 overviews the essential concepts characterizing the microservices paradigm, thus serving as an introduction for the entire book. Section 3 instead highlights some key research areas in which microservices applications have gained particular interest and showed some research progress. Conclusions and future works are summed up in Sect. 4.

2 Microservices

Microservices [16, 20, 26, 47] is an architectural style stemming from service-oriented architectures (SOAs) [35, 54]. According to this architectural style, a system is structured by small independent building blocks—the *microservices*—communicating only via message passing. The main idea is to move *in the small* (within an application) some of the concepts that worked *in the large*, i.e., for cross-organization business-to-business workflow, which makes use of orchestration engines such as WS-BPEL (in turn inheriting some of the functional principles from concurrency theory [34]). The characteristic differentiating the new style from monolithic architectures and classic service-oriented architectures is the emphasis on *scalability*, *independence*, and *semantic cohesiveness* of each unit constituting the system. In its fundamental essence, the microservices architecture [16] is built on a few very simple principles:

- *Bounded Context*. First introduced in [18], this concept captures one of the key properties of microservices architecture: focus on business capabilities. Related functionalities are combined into a single business capability which is then implemented as a service.

- *Size*. Size is a crucial concept for microservices and brings major benefits in terms of service maintainability and extendibility. The idiomatic use of microservices architecture suggests that if a service is too large, it should be refined into two or more services, thus preserving granularity and maintaining focus on providing only a single business capability.
- *Independency*. This concept encourages loose coupling and high cohesion by stating that each service in microservices architectures is operationally independent from others, and the only form of communication between services is through their published interfaces.

2.1 *Microservices vs. Monolith*

All the programming languages for development of server-side applications provide abstractions to break down the complexity of programs into modules or components [9, 23, 49]. However, these languages are designed for the creation of single executable artifacts. In monolithic architectures, the modularization abstractions rely on the sharing of resources such as memory, databases, and files of the same machine. The components are therefore not independently executable. Figure 1 (reproduced from [43]) shows the classic monolithic organization: the different layers of the system (interface/presentation, internal business logic, and persistence tools) are here split in terms of responsibilities between different modules (the vertical split with numbers from 1 to 4). In fact, each module may take part in

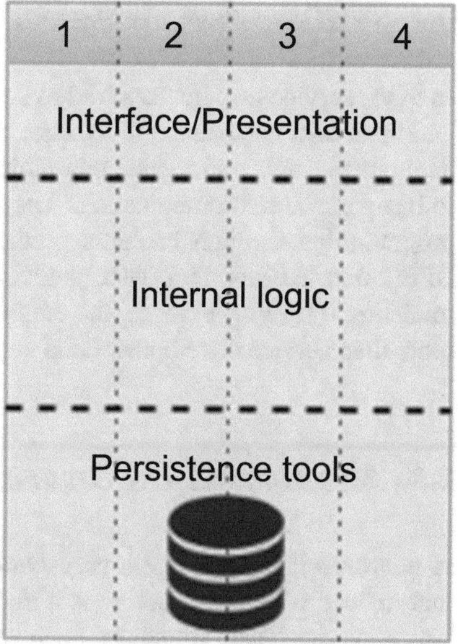

Fig. 1 Monolith architecture

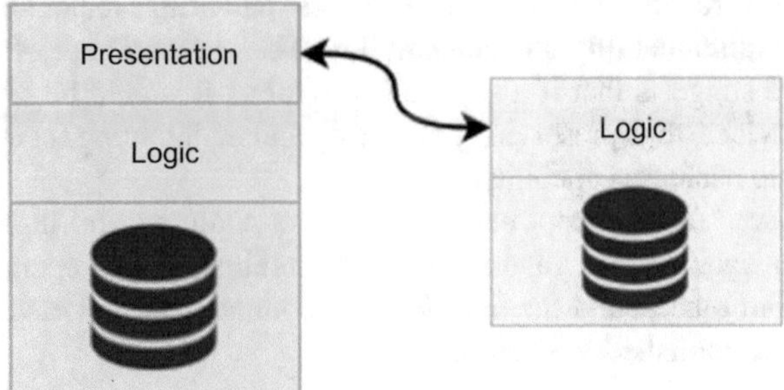

Fig. 2 Microservices architecture

the implementation of functionalities related to each layer, the database is common, and so the access to other resources, such as memory.

Figure 2 (reproduced from [43]) shows the componentization in a microservices architecture. Each service has its own dedicated persistence tool and communication with each other is through lightweight mechanisms without a need for centralized control [56]. With this organization there is no vertical split through all the system layers, and the deployment is independent. The complexity is moved to the level of coordination of services (often called orchestration [38]). Moreover, a number of additional problems need to be addressed due to the distributed nature of the microservices approach (e.g., trust and certification [12, 14]).

2.2 *Microservices vs. SOA*

In SOA, services are not required to be self-contained with data and User Interface, and their own persistence tools, e.g., database. SOA has no focus on independent deployment units and related consequences, it is simply an approach for business-to-business intercommunication. The idea of SOA was to enable business-level programming through business processing engines and languages such as WS-BPEL and BPMN that were built on top of the vast literature on business modeling [60]. Furthermore, the emphasis was all on *service composition* [17, 33] more than service development and deployment.

2.3 *Size Matters: The Organization of Teams*

A microservice is not just a *very small service*. There is no predefined size limit that defines whether a service is a microservice or not. From this angle, the term "microservice" can somehow be misleading. Each microservice is expected to implement a single *business capability*, in fact a very limited system functionality, bringing benefits in terms of service maintainability and extendibility. Since each microservice represents a single business capability, which is delivered and updated independently, discovering bugs or adding minor improvements does not have any impact on other services and on their releases. In common practice, it is also expected that a single service can be developed and managed by a single team [16].

In order to build a system with a modular and loosely coupled design, it is necessary to pay attention to the organization structure and the communication patterns. These patterns directly impact the produced design (Conway's law [10]). If a structure is based on the idea that each team work on a single service, then the communication will be more efficient at the team level and in the entire organization. This will lead to an improved design in terms of modularity. Microservices' approach is to keep teams small and communications efficient by creating small cross-functional (DevOps) teams that are able to continuously work on the same service and to be fully responsible for it ("you build it, you run it" principle [22]).

The teams are organized around services, which in turn are organized around business capabilities [20]. The optimal team size for microservices is best described by Jeff Bezos' famous "two pizza team" rule, which suggests that the size of a team should be no larger than what two pizzas can feed. The rule itself does not give an exact number; however, it is possible to estimate it to be around 6–8 people. The drawback of such an approach is that it is not always practical from the financial point of view to maintain a dedicated team of developers for a single service as it may lead to high development/maintenance costs [27]. Furthermore, one should be careful when designing the high-level structure of the organization using microservices—increasing the number of services might negatively impact the overall organization efficiency, if no further actions are taken.

3 Research and Applications

Microservices have recently seen a dramatic growth in popularity and in concrete applications [47]. The shift towards microservices is seeing several companies involved in a major refactoring of their back-end systems to accommodate the new paradigm [7, 42]. Other companies just start their business model developing software following the microservice paradigm since day one. We are in the middle of a major change in the view in which software is intended, and in the way in which capabilities are organized into components, and industrial systems are conceived. In this section we describe recent research progress done in the context of microservices-based applications [43]. We have identified the following research areas that we analyse separately in the next sections:

- Programming languages
- Type checker
- Migration from monoliths
- Education in DevOps
- Modeling and self-adaptability
- Real-life software applications with microservices

3.1 Programming Languages

Microservice systems are currently developed using mostly general-purpose programming languages that do not provide dedicated abstractions for service composition. Current practice is indeed focused on the deployment aspects of microservices, in particular by using containerization. We investigated this issue and made a case for a language-based approach to the engineering of microservices architectures. We believe that this approach is complementary to current practice. In [24], we discussed the approach in general, and we instantiate it in terms of the Jolie programming language; however, the concept is independent from the specific technical solution adopted. Four important concepts have been identified to be first-class entities in the programming language in order to address the microservices architecture:

1. *Interfaces*: To support modular programming, services have to be deployed as *black boxes*. In order to compose services in larger systems, interfaces have to describe the provided functionalities and those required from the environment.
2. *Ports*: Since a microservice interacts with other services, a communication port describes how its functionalities are made available to the network (interface, communication technology, and data protocol). Ports should be specified separately from the implementation of a service. Input ports describe the functionalities that the service provides to the rest of the system, while output ports describe the functionalities that the service requires from the rest of the system.
3. *Workflows*: Structured protocols appear repeatedly in microservices and they are not natively supported by mainstream languages. All possible operations are always enabled (e.g., in object-oriented programming). Causal dependencies are programmed using a book-keeping variable, which is error prone, and it does not scale when the number of causality links increases. A microservice language should provide abstractions for programming workflows.
4. *Processes*: Workflows define the blueprint of the behavior of a service. At runtime a service may interact with multiple clients and other external services, therefore there is a need to support multiple concurrent executions of its workflow. A process is a running instance of a workflow, and a service may include many processes executing concurrently. Each process runs independently of the others, to avoid interference, and has its own private state.

3.2 Type Checker

Static type checking is generally desirable for programming languages improving software quality, lowering the number of bugs, and preventing avoidable errors [25, 31]. The idea is to allow compilers to identify as many issues as possible before actually running the program, and therefore avoid a vast number of trivial bugs, catching them at a very early stage. Despite the fact that in the general case interesting properties of programs are undecidable [51], static type checking, within its limits, is an effective and well-established technique of program verification. If a compiler can prove that a program is well typed, then it does not need to perform dynamic safety checks, allowing the resulting compiled binary to run faster.

In [46] we described and prototyped the Jolie Static Type Checker (JSTC), a static type checker for the Jolie programming language which natively supports microservices. The static type system for the language was exhaustively and formally defined on paper [48], but needed implementation. The type checker prototype consists of a set of rules for the type system expressed in SMT Lib language. The actual implementation covers operations such as assignments, logical statements, conditions, literals, and comparisons.

In [57] we integrated dynamic and static type checking with the introduction of refinement types, verified via an SMT solver. The integration of the two aspects allows a scenario where the static verification of internal services and the dynamic verification of (potentially malicious) external services cooperate in order to reduce testing effort and enhance security.

3.3 Migration from Monoliths

Several companies are evaluating the pros and cons of migrating to microservices (e.g., [55]). Financial institutions are positioned in a difficult situation due to the economic climate and the appearance of small players that grew big fast in recent times, such as alternative payment systems, that can also navigate in a more flexible (and less regulated) legal framework and started their business since day one with more agile architectures and without being bounded to outdated technological standard. We worked closely with Danske Bank, the largest bank in Denmark and one of the leading financial institutions in Northern Europe, to demonstrate how scalability is positively affected by reimplementing a monolithic architecture into a microservices one [7].

Evolution is necessary to stay competitive. When compared to companies (such as PayPal) that started their activities using innovative technologies as a business foundation, in order to scale and deliver value, old banking institutions appear outdated with regards to technology standards. We worked on the *FX Core* system, a mission-critical system of Danske Bank's software. A key outcome of our research has been the identification of a repeatable migration process that can be used to convert a real-world monolithic architecture into a microservices one in the specific setting of a financial system, which is typically characterized by legacy systems and batch-based processing on heterogeneous data sources [42].

3.4 Education in DevOps

DevOps is a natural evolution of the agile approaches [1, 30] from the software itself to the overall infrastructure and operations. This evolution was made possible by the spread of cloud-based technologies and the everything-as-a-service approaches. Adopting the DevOps paradigm helps software teams to release applications faster and with more quality. DevOps and microservice architecture appear to be an indivisible pair for organizations aiming at delivering applications and services at high velocity. Investing in DevOps is a good idea in general, and after migration to microservices it is typically crucial.

As DevOps becomes a widespread philosophy, the necessity for education in the field becomes increasingly important, from both the technical and organizational points of view [8]. The DevOps philosophy may be introduced in companies with adequate training, but only if certain technological, organizational, and cultural prerequisites are present. If not, the prerequisites should be developed. We have been deeply involved in recent years in teaching both undergraduate and graduate students at university, and junior/senior professional developers in industry. We have also been working often with management [2, 41].

3.5 Modeling and Self-Adaptability

Innovative engineering is always looking for adequate tools to model and verify software systems, as well as support developers in deploying correct software. Microservices is an effective paradigm to cope with scalability; however, the paradigm still misses a *conceptual model* able to support engineers since the early phases of development. To make the engineering process of a microservices-based application efficient, we need a *uniform way to model autonomous and heterogeneous microservices*, at a level of abstraction that allows for easy interconnection through dynamic relations. Each microservice must have a partial view on the surrounding operational environment (i.e., system knowledge) and at the same time must be able to be specialized/refined and adapted to face different requirements, user needs, context-changes, and missing functionalities.

To be robust, each microservice must be able to dynamically adapt its behavior and its goals to changes in the environment but also to collaborative interactions with other microservices during their composition/orchestration. At the same time the adaptation must not be controlled centrally and imposed by the system but must be administrated in a decentralized fashion among the microservices.

An important feature of dynamic and context-aware service-based systems is the possibility of handling at runtime extraordinary/improbable situations (e.g., context changes, availability of functionalities, trust negotiation), instead of analyzing such situations at design time and pre-embedding the corresponding recovery activities. The intrinsic characteristics of microservice architectures make possible to nicely model runtime dependability concepts, such as "self-protecting" and "self-healing" systems [14]. To make this feasible, we should enable microservices to monitor their operational environment and trigger adaptation needs each time a specific system property is violated. To cover the aforementioned research challenges, we already started to define a roadmap [45] that includes an initial investigation on how domain objects [5] could be an adequate formalism both to capture the peculiarity of MSA and to support the software development since the early stages.

3.6 *Real-Life Software Applications with Microservices*

3.6.1 Smart Buildings

Smart buildings represent a key example of application domain where properties like scalability, minimality, and cohesiveness play a key role. As a result, smart buildings are an ideal application scenario for the microservices paradigm. This domain has been investigated with an outlook on Internet-of-Things (IoT) technologies and smart cities [40]. In [53] and [28], it has been shown how rooms of a building can be equipped with devices and sensors in order to capture the fundamental parameters determining well-being and livability of humans, such as temperature, humidity, and illumination. This solution allows to monitor an equipped area and therefore collect data that can be mined and analyzed for specific purposes. The nodes used in this system consist of Raspberry Pi microcomputers [50], Texas Instruments Sensor Tags [58], door sensor, and web camera. Currently, this system is able to collect and analyze room temperature, pressure, and illumination level. It is also able to distinguish and count people located in the covered area. The purpose is to monitor and optimize working conditions. The software infrastructure, tightly connected to the hardware, makes use of microservices to achieve the desired level of scalability, minimality, and cohesiveness. Sensors and actuators are connected to a central control panel that is responsible to manage them. At the same time, an automatic personal assistant has been designed. It is capable to observe data, learn about different users preferences, and adapt the room conditions accordingly for the different phases of his/her work [29].

3.6.2 Smart Mobility

Organizing and managing the mobility services within a city, meeting traveler's expectations, and properly exploiting the available transport resources are becoming more and more complex tasks. The inadequacy of traditional transportation models is proven by the proliferation of alternative, social, and grassroots initiatives aiming at a more flexible, customized, and collective way of organizing transport (e.g., carpooling, ride and park sharing services, flexi-buses) [11, 19, 21]. Some of these attempts have been very successful (e.g., Uber), even if in most cases these are seen as isolated solutions targeting specific mobility target groups and are not part of the city mobility ecosystem, mainly based on traditional public and private transport facilities.

An attempt of rethinking the way mobility is managed and offered is represented by the mobility as a service (MaaS) model. MaaS solutions (e.g., MaaS Global: http://maas.global) aim at arranging the most suitable transport solution for their customers thanks to cost-effective integrated offer of different multi-modal means of transportation. MaaS also foresees radical changes in the business landscape, with a new generation of mobility operators emerging as key actors to manage the increased flexibility and dynamism offered by this new concept of mobility.

People need to travel quickly and conveniently between locations at different scales, ranging from a trip of a few blocks to a journey across town or further. Each trip has its set of requirements. Time may be of the essence. Cost may be paramount, and the convenience of door-to-door travel may be important. In each case, the transportation infrastructure should seamlessly provide the best option. A modern city needs to flexibly integrate transportation options, including buses, trains, taxis, autonomous vehicles, bicycles, and private cars.

Before changing communities to support what is believed the future transportation will look like and behave, it is necessary to develop mechanisms that allow planners of these localities to model, analyze, and present these possible configurations in ways that the citizens of the communities can understand and participate in.

Coordination for mobility as a service can be implemented on a spectrum, ranging from independent services communicating exclusively through market exchanges to hybrid market/hierarchy approaches for fixed hierarchical control systems.

Every transportation mean does not need to be an individual competing across multiple markets, but neither should there be only one rigid hierarchy. *"Diversity"* and *"distributed"* selection of the appropriate mean (or a combination of means) is the right compromise respect to say that if one is better than the other, we "kill" the other.

To realize such a *"dynamic"* and *"emergent"* behavior in transportation systems needs a new way for developing their supporting software systems. In the last years, collective adaptive systems (CAS) have been introduced and studied by many researchers in different application domains (i.e., Industry 4.0, logistics, smart cities and mobility, energy, biology, etc.).[2] CAS consists of diverse heterogeneous entities composing a sociotechnical system. Individual entities "opportunistically" enter a system and self-adapt in order to leverage other entities' resources and services to perform their task more efficiently and effectively. At the same time, also collections of entities, called ensembles, must be able to self-adapt simultaneously to preserve the collaboration and benefits of the system (or subsystem) they are within.

[2]http://www.focas.eu/focas-manifesto.pdf.

In this very dynamic and rapidly evolving setting, microservices have the potential of offering the right concepts for modeling and for programming smart mobility solutions. Coordination for mobility as a services (MaaS) is a mandatory requirement to maintain a certain level of city sustainability (i.e., less CO2 emission, more citizen participation and satisfaction, etc.). It can be implemented on a spectrum, ranging from independent agents communicating exclusively through market exchanges to hybrid market/hierarchy approaches fixed hierarchical control systems. Our opinion is that instead of implementing a selfish mobility we see the need to realize a collective and cooperative mobility where each MaaS provider sees in every competitor a partner and not an enemy [4]. This domain opens new challenges in how distributed microservices, provided by different mobility entities, can be composed dynamically to provide real-time and continuous answers to citizens in a smart city.

4 Conclusions

The microservice architecture is a style that is increasingly gaining popularity, both in academia and in the industry. Even though it is likely to conduct to a paradigm shift and a dramatic change in perception, it does not build on vacuum, and instead relates to well-established paradigms such as OO and SOA. In [16] a comprehensive survey on recent developments of microservices architecture is presented with focus on the *evolutionary* aspects more than the *revolutionary* ones. The presentation there is intended to help the reader in understanding the distinguishing characteristics of microservices.

We have a long experience in the field of services and business processes [6, 32, 36, 59, 60], including workflows and their reconfiguration [3, 15, 39]. We built on top of this expertise to focus on the active research field of microservices, and summarized our work in this chapter.

The future will see a growing attention regarding the matters discussed in this chapter, and the development of new programming languages intended to address the microservice paradigm [24]. Object-oriented programming brought fresh ideas in the last decades, and the expectation is that a comparable shift may be just ahead of us. Holding onto optimism, the future is certainly not challenge free. The security of the microservice paradigm is an issue almost completely untouched [16]. Commercial-level quality packages for development are still far to come, despite the acceleration in the interest regarding the matter. Fully verified software is an open problem the same way it is for more traditional development models. That said, several research centers around the world have addressed and are addressing all these issues in an attempt to ride the wave and make the new generation of distributed systems a reality.

References

1. L. Bass, I. Weber, L. Zhu, *DevOps: A Software Architect's Perspective*, 1st edn. (Addison-Wesley, Reading, 2015)
2. E. Bobrov, A. Bucchiarone, A. Capozucca, N. Guelfi, M. Mazzara, S. Masyagin, Teaching DevOps in academia and industry: reflections and vision, in *Software Engineering Aspects of Continuous Development and New Paradigms of Software Production and Deployment—Second International Workshop, DEVOPS 2019* (Chateau de Villebrumier, 2019)
3. A. Bucchiarone, A. Marconi, M. Pistore, H. Raik, Dynamic adaptation of fragment-based and context-aware business processes, in *ICWS* (IEEE Computer Society, Silver Spring, 2012), pp. 33–41
4. A. Bucchiarone, M. De Sanctis, A. Marconi, Decentralized dynamic adaptation for service-based collective adaptive systems, in *ICSOC Workshops*. Lecture Notes in Computer Science, vol. 10380 (Springer, Berlin, 2016), pp. 5–20
5. A. Bucchiarone, M. De Sanctis, A. Marconi, M. Pistore, P. Traverso, Incremental composition for adaptive by-design service based systems, in *IEEE ICWS, 2016* (San Francisco, 2016), pp. 236–243
6. A. Bucchiarone, A. Marconi, M. Pistore, H. Raik, A context-aware framework for dynamic composition of process fragments in the internet of services. J. Internet Services Appl. **8**(1), 6:1–6:23 (2017)
7. A. Bucchiarone, N. Dragoni, S. Dustdar, S.T. Larsen, M. Mazzara, From monolithic to microservices: an experience report from the banking domain. IEEE Softw. **35**(3), 50–55 (2018)
8. I. Bucena, M. Kirikova, Simplifying the DevOps adoption process, in *Joint Proceedings of the BIR 2017 pre-BIR Forum, Workshops and Doctoral Consortium co-located with 16th International Conference on Perspectives in Business Informatics Research (BIR 2017)* (Copenhagen, 2017)
9. J. Clark, C. Clarke, S. De Panfilis, A. Sillitti, G. Succi, T. Vernazza, Selecting components in large COTS repositories. J. Syst. Softw. **73**(2), 323–331
10. M.E. Conway, How do committees invent. Datamation **14**(4), 28–31 (1968)
11. O. Dakroub, C.M. Boukhater, F. Lahoud, M. Awad, H. Artail, An intelligent carpooling app for a green social solution to traffic and parking congestions, in *16th International IEEE Conference on Intelligent Transportation Systems, ITSC 2013* (The Hague, 2013), pp. 2401–2408
12. E. Damiani, N. El Ioini, A. Sillitti, G. Succi, WS-certificate, in *2009 IEEE International Workshop on Web Services Security Management* (IEEE, Piscataway, 2009)
13. E.S. de Almeida, A. Alvaro, D. Lucrédio, V.C. Garcia, S.R. de Lemos Meira, Rise project: towards a robust framework for software reuse. In *Proceedings of the 2004 IEEE International Conference on Information Reuse and Integration, IRI - 2004* (Las Vegas, 2004), pp. 48–53
14. N. Dragoni, F. Massacci, A. Saidane, A self-protecting and self-healing framework for negotiating services and trust in autonomic communication systems. Comput. Netw. **53**(10), 1628–1648 (2009)
15. N. Dragoni, M. Zhou, M. Mazzara, Dependable workflow reconfiguration in WS-BPEL, in *Proceedings of the 5th Nordic Workshop on Dependability and Security* (2011)
16. N. Dragoni, S. Giallorenzo, A. Lluch-Lafuente, M. Mazzara, F. Montesi, R. Mustafin, L. Safina, Microservices: yesterday, today, and tomorrow, in *Present and Ulterior Software Engineering* (Springer, Berlin, 2017), pp. 195–216
17. S. Dustdar, W. Schreiner, A survey on web services composition. IJWGS **1**(1), 1–30 (2005)
18. E. Evans, *Domain-Driven Design: Tackling Complexity in the Heart of Software* (Addison-Wesley, Reading, 2004)
19. D. Fagnant, K. Kockelman, Dynamic ride-sharing and fleet sizing for a system of shared autonomous vehicles in Austin, Texas. Transportation **45**, 28–46 (2016)
20. M. Fowler, J. Lewis, *Microservices* (ThoughtWorks, Chicago, 2014)

21. M. Furuhata, M. Dessouky, F. Ordóñez, M.-E. Brunet, X. Wang, S. Koenig, Ridesharing: the state-of-the-art and future directions. Transp. Res. B Methodol. **57**, 28–46 (2013)
22. J. Gray, A conversation with Werner Vogels. ACM Queue **4**(4), 14–22 (2006)
23. H.G. Gross, M. Melideo, A. Sillitti, Self-certification and trust in component procurement. J. Sci. Comput. Program. **56**(1–2), 141–156 (2005)
24. C. Guidi, I. Lanese, M. Mazzara, F. Montesi, *Microservices: A Language-Based Approach* (Springer, Cham, 2017), pp. 217–225
25. S. Hanenberg, S. Kleinschmager, R. Robbes, É. Tanter, A. Stefik, An empirical study on the impact of static typing on software maintainability. Empir. Softw. Eng. **19**(5), 1335–1382 (2014)
26. P. Jamshidi, C. Pahl, N.C. Mendonça, J. Lewis, S. Tilkov, Microservices: the journey so far and challenges ahead. IEEE Softw. **35**(3), 24–35 (2018)
27. S. Jones, Microservices is SOA, for those who know what SOA is (2014). http://service-architecture.blogspot.co.uk/2014/03/microservices-is-soa-for-those-who-know.html
28. K. Khanda, D. Salikhov, K. Gusmanov, M. Mazzara, N. Mavridis, Microservice-based IoT for smart buildings, in *2017 31st International Conference on Advanced Information Networking and Applications Workshops (WAINA)* (IEEE, Piscataway, 2017), pp. 302–308
29. A. Khusnutdinov, D. Usachev, M. Mazzara, A. Khan, I. Panchenko, Open source platform digital personal assistant, in *32nd International Conference on Advanced Information Networking and Applications Workshops, AINA 2018 Workshops* (Krakow, 2018), pp. 45–50
30. G. Kim, P. Debois, J. Willis, J. Humble, *The DevOps Handbook: How to Create World-Class Agility, Reliability, and Security in Technology Organizations* (IT Revolution Press, Portland, 2016)
31. S. Kleinschmager, R. Robbes, A. Stefik, S. Hanenberg, E. Tanter, Do static type systems improve the maintainability of software systems? An empirical study, in *2012 20th IEEE International Conference on Program Comprehension (ICPC)* (IEEE, Piscataway, 2012), pp. 153–162
32. S. Lane, A. Bucchiarone, I. Richardson, SOAdapt: a process reference model for developing adaptable service-based applications. Inf. Softw. Technol. **54**(3), 299–316 (2012)
33. A.L. Lemos, F. Daniel, B. Benatallah, Web service composition: a survey of techniques and tools. ACM Comput. Surv. **48**(3), 33:1–33:41 (2016)
34. R. Lucchi, M. Mazzara, A Pi-calculus based semantics for WS-BPEL. J. Log. Algebr. Program. **70**(1), 96–118 (2007)
35. C.M. MacKenzie, K. Laskey, F. McCabe, P.F. Brown, R. Metz, B.A. Hamilton, Reference model for service oriented architecture 1.0. OASIS Standard **12** (2006)
36. M. Mazzara, Towards abstractions for web services composition. Ph.D. thesis, University of Bologna, 2006
37. M. Mazzara, Deriving specifications of dependable systems: toward a method (2010). arXiv preprint arXiv:1009.3911
38. M. Mazzara, S. Govoni, *A Case Study of Web Services Orchestration* (Springer, Berlin, 2005), pp. 1–16
39. M. Mazzara, F. Abouzaid, N. Dragoni, A. Bhattacharyya, Toward design, modelling and analysis of dynamic workflow reconfigurations—a process algebra perspective, in *8th International Workshop on Web Services and Formal Methods WS-FM* (2011), pp. 64–78
40. M. Mazzara, I. Afanasyev, S.R. Sarangi, S. Distefano, V. Kumar, A reference architecture for smart and software-defined buildings (2019). arXiv preprint arXiv:1902.09464
41. M. Mazzara, A. Naumchev, L. Safina, A. Sillitti, K. Urysov, Teaching DevOps in corporate environments—an experience report, in *First International Workshop on Software Engineering Aspects of Continuous Development and New Paradigms of Software Production and Deployment, DEVOPS 2018*, Revised selected papers (Chateau de Villebrumier, France, 2018), pp. 100–111
42. M. Mazzara, N. Dragoni, A. Bucchiarone, A. Giaretta, S.T. Larsen, S. Dustdar, Microservices: migration of a mission critical system. IEEE Trans. Services Comput. (2019). https://doi.org/10.1109/TSC.2018.2889087

43. M. Mazzara, K. Khanda, R. Mustafin, V. Rivera, L. Safina, A. Sillitti, Microservices science and engineering, in *Proceedings of 5th International Conference in Software Engineering for Defence Applications*, ed. by P. Ciancarini, S. Litvinov, A. Messina, A. Sillitti, G. Succi (Springer, Cham, 2018), pp. 11–20
44. B. Meyer, *Object-Oriented Software Construction*, 1st edn. (Prentice-Hall, Englewood Cliffs, 1988)
45. K. Mikhail, A. Bucchiarone, M. Mazzara, L. Safina, V. Rivera, Domain objects and microservices for systems development: a roadmap, in *Proceedings of 5th International Conference in Software Engineering for Defence Applications* (2017)
46. B. Mingela, L. Safina, A. Tchitchigin, N. Troshkov, D. de Carvalho, M. Mazzara, Jolie static type checker: a prototype. Model. Anal. Inf. Syst. **24**(6), 704–717 (2017)
47. S. Newman, *Building Microservices* (O'Reilly Media, Sebastopol, 2015)
48. J.M. Nielsen, A type system for the Jolie language. Master's thesis, Technical University of Denmark, 2013
49. P. Predonzani, A. Sillitti, T. Vernazza, Components and data-flow applied to the integration of web services, in *The 27th Annual Conference of the IEEE Industrial Electronics Society (IECON01)* (2001)
50. Raspberry PI foundation, Raspberri Pi official site. https://www.raspberrypi.org/. Accessed June 2017
51. H.G. Rice, Classes of recursively enumerable sets and their decision problems. Trans. Am. Math. Soc. **74**, 358–366 (1953)
52. J. Rumbaugh, M. Blaha, W. Premerlani, F. Eddy, W.E. Lorensen, et al., *Object-Oriented Modeling and Design*, vol. 199 (Prentice-Hall, Englewood Cliffs, 1991)
53. D. Salikhov, K. Khanda, K. Gusmanov, M. Mazzara, N. Mavridis, Jolie good buildings: internet of things for smart building infrastructure supporting concurrent apps utilizing distributed microservices, in *Proceedings of the 1st International conference on Convergent Cognitive Information Technologies* (2016), pp. 48–53
54. A. Sillitti, T. Vernazza, G. Succi, Service oriented programming: a new paradigm of software reuse, in *7th International Conference on Software Reuse*. Lecture Notes in Computer Science vol. 2319 (Springer, Berlin, 2002), pp. 269–280
55. D. Taibi, V. Lenarduzzi, C. Pahl, Processes, motivations, and issues for migrating to microservices architectures: an empirical investigation. IEEE Cloud Comput. **4**(5), 22–32 (2017)
56. D. Taibi, V. Lenarduzzi, C. Pahl, Architectural patterns for microservices: a systematic mapping study, in *Proceedings of the 8th International Conference on Cloud Computing and Services Science—volume 1*, CLOSER, INSTICC (SciTePress, 2018), pp. 221–232
57. A. Tchitchigin, L. Safina, M. Mazzara, M. Elwakil, F. Montesi, V. Rivera, Refinement types in Jolie. Proc. Inst. Syst. Program. **28**, 33–44 (2016)
58. Texas Instruments, Texas instruments sensor tag official site. http://www.ti.com/tools-software/sensortag.html. Accessed June 2017
59. Z. Yan, E. Cimpian, M. Zaremba, M. Mazzara, BPMO: semantic business process modeling and WSMO extension, in *2007 IEEE International Conference on Web Services (ICWS 2007)* (Salt Lake City, 2007), pp. 1185–1186
60. Z. Yan, M. Mazzara, E. Cimpian, A. Urbanec, Business process modeling: classifications and perspectives, in *1st International Working Conference on Business Process and Services Computing, BPSC 2007* (Leipzig, 2007), p. 222

Part II
Migration

Migrating to Microservices

Alexis Henry and Youssef Ridene

Abstract Microservice is an architectural pattern which has risen based on the success of Amazon, Netflix, and other digital-native companies. Designing such architecture requires understanding your business goals and creating a balance between microservices benefits and associated drawbacks. This trade-off is essential in order to successfully migrate your business applications toward microservices. In this chapter we aim to drive you through this journey by presenting a roadmap and methodology which has been used successfully in several projects. We guide you through the typical microservice migration project by using migration patterns for managing service decomposition and data isolation and replication. Those patterns may be used iteratively and in any order, therefore we will define a reference architecture to sequence the building of your microservice architecture. Eventually we conclude with a use case from the real world.

1 Modernization Challenges

Modernizing a monolith toward microservice architecture is not necessarily an easy journey. This is due to multiple factors, not all of them being technical. First of all there is no "one size fits all" microservice architecture; therefore each microservice architecture should be designed specifically to the needs of the applications it will support. As such, microservice architects in charge of migration must have a broad understanding of what microservices are, well above the usual list of expected benefits and key prerequisites. A deep understanding of key aspects such as data consistency, dependency analysis, and continuous automation is required. Eventually it must be clear that migration toward microservices is a decision to take when other architecture styles do not help achieve the objectives (scalability objectives, software distribution objective, partial deployment objectives, etc.).

A. Henry (✉) · Y. Ridene
Blu Age R&D Department, Netfective Technology, Pessac, France
e-mail: a.henry@netfective.com; y.ridene@netfective.com
http://www.bluage.com

A. Bucchiarone et al. (eds.), *Microservices*,
https://doi.org/10.1007/978-3-030-31646-4_3

Often, microservice architecture is compared to SOA, thus software architects could believe it is SOA done right. But microservice architecture [1] is about designing isolated services with a strong focus on data isolation. Microservice architecture aims at isolating features so that they can be freely deployed, independently from each other, onto a distributed architecture. Therefore, migrating an existing application to such a "share as little as possible" [2] architecture is not about splitting an application into pieces, it is about extracting features out of an existing code base which is organized with a different design. In this first section we will go into some analysis of the state of the art and return of experience from early adopters, then based on their feedback we will dive into the transformation methodology. This step is important to understand the key elements the code will use to resist change. For more details refer to the "Assessing Your Migration" chapter in this book.

1.1 Reason for Change and Traps Along the Journey

Migrating to microservices is expected to provide benefits to your application life cycle [3, 4]. Because not all decision-makers fully understand that microservice architecture is a compromise—complexity never disappear—we analyzed microservices adopters experience. The outcome of existing surveys [5] provide us with interesting information. For instance, the main reasons why organizations choose microservices are (Fig. 1):

– To make an application scalable
– To enable a fast partial deployment

Value	Percent	Responses
Management requested that we do so	12.0%	43
To improve quality by having teams focus on just one piece of an app	50.1%	179
To make applications easily scalable	80.7%	288
To improve quality by narrowing down the source of failures to a particular piece of an app	40.9%	146
To enable faster deployments to just one part of an application	69.5%	248
To experiment with the architecture	24.4%	87
Flexibility to chose different tools or languages for each service	35.6%	127
Other - Write in (click to view)	3.9%	14

Fig. 1 Microservices: reasons for it [5]

Value	Percent	Responses
Finding where to break up monolithic components	50.0%	313
Overcoming tight coupling	49.7%	311
Incorporating other technologies (containerization, etc.)	23.6%	148
Testing	30.8%	193
Time investment	38.5%	241
Other-Write In (click to view)	2.9%	18
Not applicable	21.2%	133

Fig. 2 Microservices migration: main difficulties [5]

– To improve quality by segmenting code
– To reduce cognitive load by having a dedicated programmers team per feature
– To use polyglot architecture [6, 7] (architecture may be different for each service)

However the focus on scalability (80% of answers) is double the interest for isolating features (a rough 40%), and for partial availability (individual service availability). This is a first evidence of a potential misunderstanding of microservice architecture. This also shows that decoupling features may be underestimated both in complexity and effort. Figure 2 confirms this and identifies two main reasons for migration issues:

– Finding where to split monolith into pieces
– To do the split by creating loosely coupled services

Clearly the most complex task when migrating to a microservice architecture is to overcome tight coupling. This task is difficult because traps may be hidden inside every line of code. The required code refactoring is complex and global (scope of refactoring may go beyond procedure scope) but must be achieved to perform service decomposition and uncoupling. An additional cause for complexity comes from isolation of distributed services. Services must be stateless (not depend on shared memory) and each service must own its own data store and forbid direct access to it from the outside (database per service pattern [8]) [9]. Furthermore global transactions are no longer available and are replaced by eventual consistency [10].

As such, service decomposition must focus on:

– Decouple code/data access: refactoring calls between procedures, removing shared instances/variables, replacing transactions with raw persistence, and synchronizing data across various data storage…
– Creating meaningful business services

The first task is significantly more complex than most would think. Indeed any medium size software is made of millions of lines of code. That is more than the number of gears from a disassembled Airbus plane. Many organizations underestimate "Business" applications complexity, but they are large and complex engineered systems. For this reason the analysis of an existing system is difficult to achieve and will require both methodology and tooling. Furthermore most legacy systems which candidate for microservice transformation are business-critical applications which were built long ago. Many candidates are mainframe-based applications, written in legacy languages such as Cobol or RPG. Therefore we designed a methodology that suits either modern or legacy monolith applications.

The second task is difficult as well because most legacy software are not made of business rules. While from a distance many decision-makers see applications as a set of logical rules, this is not exactly true. Applications are made of programs that work as expected at runtime, or more simply said they produce the expected data with the right inputs. Unfortunately software are not designed like this. A feature may and will be implemented through many programs. Those programs most probably implement other features as well. Coding practices that were used to design monoliths do not follow rules which allow to split business features apart in a simple way. Therefore untangling an existing software to isolate business features while removing technical dependencies is a real challenge.

The second reason for complexity is related to the difficulties of implementing microservices. Figure 3 allows to group microservice implementation difficulties into two distinct groups:

– **Technical complexity**: Microservice relies on service distribution and data isolation. Operating such architecture is more difficult, because distribution introduces new weaknesses and because debugging distributed API calls is

Value	Percent	Responses
Monitoring	46.6%	292
Service discovery	21.7%	136
App/service stability	26.8%	168
App/service security	27.2%	170
Deploying apps or services	25.4%	159
Changing culture to be open to microservices	38.2%	239
Other-Write In (click to view)	5.1%	32
Not applicable	17.6%	110

Fig. 3 Microservices migration: main difficulties [5]

complex. Monitoring, deployment, and stability are clearly being identified as more difficult compared with monolith. This comes from the fact that a distributed system depends on underlying infrastructure and that any network delay or outage will cause problems. And all distributed systems experience networking issues at some point; it will happen whatever the quality of design and operation excellence. So, those systems must be designed to be self-healing and capable of working partially (meaning individual services may work, either fully or partially, when other services are not available from their standpoint) to avoid single point of failure. Typically a robust service discovery mechanism is mandatory to achieve this. Unfortunately this is not a well-known design pattern and most programmers do not design it properly when building a microservice application. Creating a well-defined service discovery and a robust distributed application using eventual consistency is something difficult and unknown to most programmers in the industry. While this type of design is becoming more popular as microservice architecture is growing, every organization planning to migrate to microservice must take ensure good software practices for distributed programming and database per service. Moreover such practices must cover both the development side and the operational side. For instance, microservice architecture must automatically manage its underlying infrastructure to detect failure, react automatically, spawn new instances, reroute traffic, and inform the monitoring system while your IP addresses have changed.

- **Cultural change**: Cultural change may be the most difficult part because it can't be solved technically; it's all about people. Indeed, microservices are about building teams which rule their business features with full autonomy. Not all organizations are ready to reorganize themselves; not every manager is ready to accept the new organization and give full autonomy to a team of programmers. Organizations must adopt decentralized governance to be successful in their microservice journey [11]. On the contrary, they must be careful to not make microservice architecture a global solution to software engineering and must resist the microservice envy [12]. Not every application has a fit for microservices and not every block of code should become a business feature. For instance nanoservices are an antipattern and must be avoided not to fall into the law of the instrument [13, 14].

The last difficulty we will cover in this chapter is the fact that there is no microservice reference architecture. Figure 4 highlights some of the suggested design patterns used to build microservice applications. They are numerous and not unique to each problem they solve, therefore deciding which one to use and for what reason is a key principle before coding. Furthermore each part of the architecture may be implemented using various architectural patterns. The reason is that each pattern has its benefits and drawbacks. Thus designing microservice architecture is always an opinioned trade-off. For instance, service discovery may be done *server side* or *client side*. *API composition* [16] and *CQRS* [17] are both valid options depending on the context, so are *Saga* [9] and *Event Sourcing* [9]. In all these cases, the design is derived from the business features that must be enabled

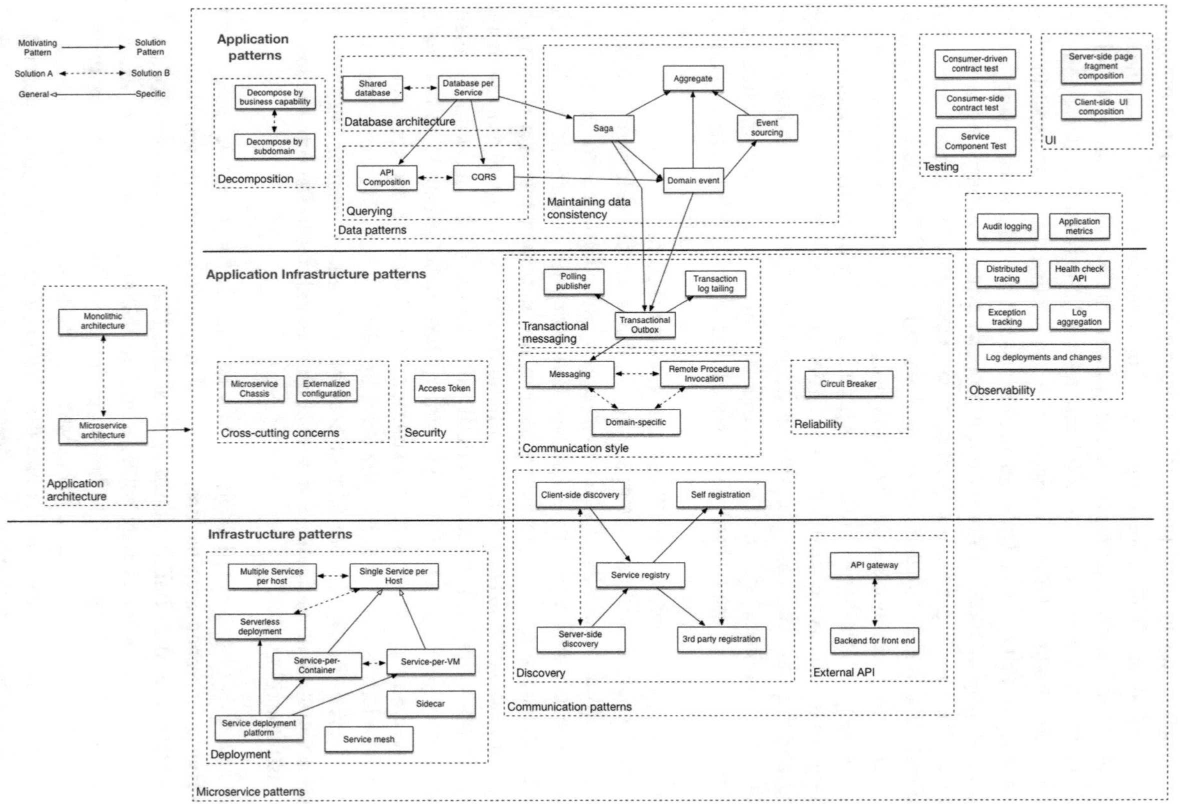

Fig. 4 Microservices patterns: build your own architecture [15]. Copyright ©2018. Chris Richardson Consulting, Inc. All right reserved. http://microservices.io

through microservice architecture. Of course not all patterns have the same technical capabilities; for instance, Saga is not a valid option for batches due to associated latency. The key is to come up with a strategy according to the business features to enable and protect for failure.

For this reason we advise not to try building a long-lasting universal microservice architecture. Instead, design an architecture with agility and changeability in mind. The objective is to constantly react to changes, new feature requests, and onboard game changing technology to promote change and control technical debt. microservice architecture may vary per application in order to bring more benefits for each. Furthermore new technology may unbalance choices, for instance, service mesh, API gateway, and serverless frameworks may be considered and to enable the architecture to evolve. Therefore the upcoming section will cover how to incrementally make an architecture grow by choosing patterns and to benefit from evolutionary architecture [18].

2 Transformation

2.1 Warm-Up and Scale Operations

The first step is to identify and migrate a first and easy microservice candidate. This can be either a subsystem of a larger application or a smaller application to transform into a single microservice. While doing so, the operational maturity is assessed. Test automation, DevOps readiness, and continuous integration are evaluated and improved to the right level. Because distributed systems are more difficult to manage at scale it is essential to build up a strong infrastructure and application life cycle automation [19, 20].

The burden of deploying services and managing scalability must be simplified using abstraction level from regular infrastructure. If public cloud deployment is the target then we will benefit from additional compute abstraction with managed services, serverless computing, and all integrated container orchestration. Otherwise containerization must be implemented as a prerequisite because virtual machines do not bring required deployment capabilities [21]. Only lightweight execution platform can deploy fast enough to support microservice architectures at scale. Containers, container orchestration, and serverless frameworks are de facto standards [5] because they provide fast startup, without the need to manage operating system, and are well suited to distribute application parts.

Because of this, the first step is to improve automation by building development pipeline and implement a continuous deployment solution. Automation applies to packaging, testing, versioning, tagging, and deployment of microservices. At this stage new releases will not automatically be deployed to production. Instead the focus is on producing container images that are ready to be deployed at will. Releases should be tagged with versioning information and any metadata information which helps manage deployment environment. For instance, the versioning objective is to know which features are embedded in a release, while tagging is to be used to add information to the benefit of monitoring and service location.

At this stage it is important not to rush out to use more complex and powerful middleware such as API gateways and service mesh. Scaling and availability should be guaranteed using application load balancers with autoscaling and/or container orchestration. Only organizations with an established Kubernetes practice may be more ambitious and anticipate API routing but we would recommend to scale operations and application design approximately at the same pace. Operations must be ready to receive applications based on powerful architecture design.

Microservice architecture is always distributed, therefore the use of log aggregation framework and real time APIs monitoring solution is mandatory. Tracing how APIs call each other is important to replicate bugs and solve potential issues. Serializing input and output of stateless services may be a valid choice to replicate real-life scenarios.

Once the infrastructure is in place, the first feature can be migrated. The first candidate must be an easy one, the potential failure of which will not harm business operations. Such a service is an edge service with limited or no user facing logic, not using a datastore or only with isolated data at this stage. We will address data dependencies later on.

For instance, an authentication service or a rewards service from an online shop are good candidates because they are based exclusively on user information. We recommend to select a service which does not perform updates on the database and which does not call other services (Fig. 5).

For a while we will only migrate and operate edge services because at this stage the biggest risk is failing to operate the microservices properly. Indeed each team is fully responsible and autonomous of the infrastructure and associated management technology. It is therefore crucial to let complexity increase only when teams are ready to manage more complex distributed architectures. Once perfectly skilled with container orchestration, autoscaling, and version tracking, then it is time for splitting the monolith to remove deeply embedded features.

2.2 *Release Data as Soon as Possible*

The main driver for decoupling capabilities out of a monolith is to be able to release them independently. To be fully autonomous we need to solve data dependencies and make databases private to their micro services. Every time we will detach a feature from a monolith to make it a microservice we will have to make sure we isolate associated data and migrate them as well. This principle should guide every decision to perform the decoupling.

Unfortunately this is not always programmers' or decision-makers' choice. Because monolithic systems are made of tightly integrated layers—or multiple subsystems that need to be released together—most microservice migration projects

Fig. 5 Candidate edge service: reward service

are initiated by removing technical layers and more often the user interface. The typical monolith is similar to an online retail system. It is composed of one or multiple customers facing applications relying on a back-end system implementing many business capabilities and using a central data store to hold state for the entire system.

Because of this, most decoupling attempts start with extracting user facing components and by adding a few facade services to provide developer friendly APIs for the modern UIs. When doing this the data remains locked in one schema and storage system. It is not rare from then to see a data lake project be initiated to expose data in a different way and to see a new project spawning to be built using the data lake. Though this approach gives some quick wins when it comes to core capabilities the delivery teams can only move as fast as the slowest part: the monolith and its monolithic data store. Simply put, without decoupling the data, the architecture is not microservices. Keeping all the data in the same data store is counter to the decentralized data management characteristic of microservices. As such it will not promote nor leverage decoupling between teams, and micro services cannot evolve independently from each other.

To avoid this we will use the three following patterns to release data early depending on the type of coupling and consistency we need to keep in your individual services.

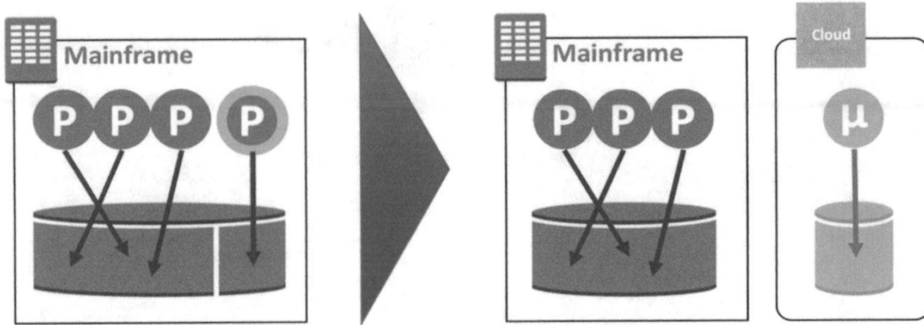

Fig. 6 Data-independent services [22]

Peel with Data-Independent Services This is a favorable pattern where the extracted service and monolith have independent data dependencies. Programs are grouped into a domain, forming boundaries of the microservice. Domain boundaries are defined around low coupled interfaces, such as file transfer, message queuing, reports, and business intelligence queries. The data model is strictly consistent within each domain, within the remaining monolith data store, and within the microservice data store. One data-independent microservice is extracted and moved to the cloud or containerized environment (Fig. 6).

Peel with Data Eventual Consistency This is a pattern where there are data dependencies between the extracted service and monolith. Data is replicated across the former system and the new environment. Both environments may not be located closely, which is typical for a migration from on premise toward cloud. Doing so avoids network latency or jitter, which would be unmanageable for typical I/O-intensive batch programs, or detrimental to high-throughput online backend transactions. One data-dependent service is extracted and moved to the microservice architecture, and dependent data is asynchronously replicated both ways in real time. Because of the bidirectional asynchronous replication, there is data eventual consistency. For conflict resolution, based on workload analysis and access types, strategies such as mainframe-as-a-reference or Last Write Win can be adopted (Fig. 7).

Group Then Peel with Strict Consistency When there are too many write dependencies or strong transactionality requirements, eventual consistency can become a challenge. In this pattern, groups of programs and their data dependencies are moved altogether in order to preserve strict consistency. Data-dependent programs are grouped into data-independent groups. One data-independent group is extracted and moved to your microservice architecture with a shared data store. Eventually, individual microservices may benefit from a separate deployment stack or data store (Fig. 8).

The following table is an overview of the balance between patterns and consistency model (Fig. 9):

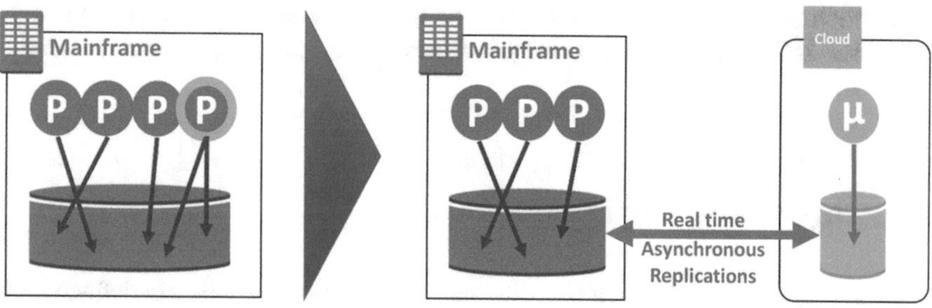

Fig. 7 Eventual consistency with real-time replication [22]

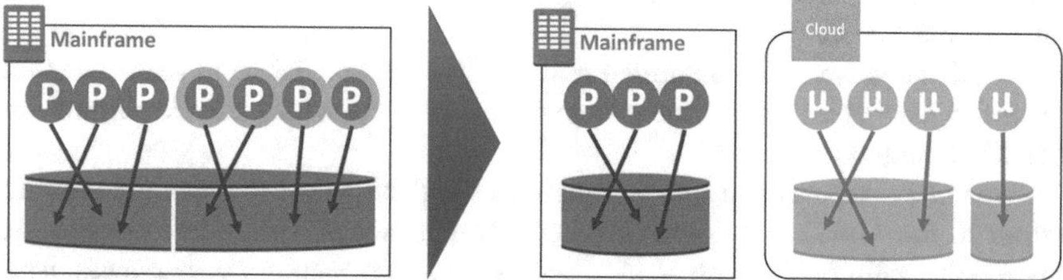

Fig. 8 Group then peel with strict consistency [22]

Data Pattern	Database Pattern	Peeling Pattern	Application-level Consistency Model	Application-level Transaction Support
Independent data	Database per domain	Peel with data-independent services	Strict consistency	Yes
Shared data	Shared database	Group then Peel with data strict consistency	Strict consistency	Yes
Shared data	Database per domain with API composition	Peel with data eventual consistency	Eventual consistency	No
Shared data	Database per domain with data synchronization	Peel with data eventual consistency	Eventual consistency	No

Fig. 9 Consistency and transaction support per peeling pattern

2.3 Release Quick Win as Soon as Possible

Fortunately there are cases where splitting is easy, typically when a set of features/programs/classes all rely on the same data and do not share those with other services. Services using only transient data or those using a given set of tables clearly go into this group.

In this case the group of services can instantly be removed from the monolith and resulting computing can be sent back to caller in the monolith, and detached services are fully independent from the remaining monolith and are a very good candidates for (or multiple once further divided) microservices.

Furthermore the dependency is from the monolith toward the microservice. As such there is no way by which a change to the monolith can impact the microservice behavior and design.

2.4 Dig Vertically and Isolate Writes

The strategy is to move out capabilities vertically. To do so we clearly define which business features we want to move out of the monolith. We identify associated entry points, users, batches, and data exchange which implement the features in the software. We use static analysis tools to dig vertically and go down call trees until we reach data.

At this stage we have identified how capabilities are linked to data. We have identified what other parts of the system use the same data, how they do so, and how the data is stored.

Eventually we may run into complex decisions because too many components writes to the same shared data. Furthermore the monolith may be very old, for instance, a mainframe using VSAM file system, that taking the data away from it will overcomplicate both the data migration and data synchronization that any distributed system must manage.

The delivery teams need to incorporate a data migration strategy that suits their environment depending on whether they are able to redirect and migrate all the data readers/writers at the same time or not.

If the migration data is too much of a challenge you may decide to apply three patterns:

- **Stepped database per pattern**: There are a few different ways to keep data private. A simple one is to keep a relational database and to split table and schema away from each other gradually. The following are a good way to simplify your migration strategy and data synchronization between microservices:
  - Private-tables-per-service—each service owns a set of tables that must only be accessed by that service (Fig. 10).
  - Schema-per-service—each service has a database schema that is private to that service (Fig. 11).
  - Database-server-per-service—each service has its own database server (Fig. 12).
- **Macro then micro**:
  - In this case the strategy is to split the monolith into coarse-grain services which will later split into smaller piece. This approach does not target optimized microservice definition at first, but brings early loose coupling benefits. For instance, we can decompose a software into 6 large domains which do not interfere by writing in the same data. In this case the data

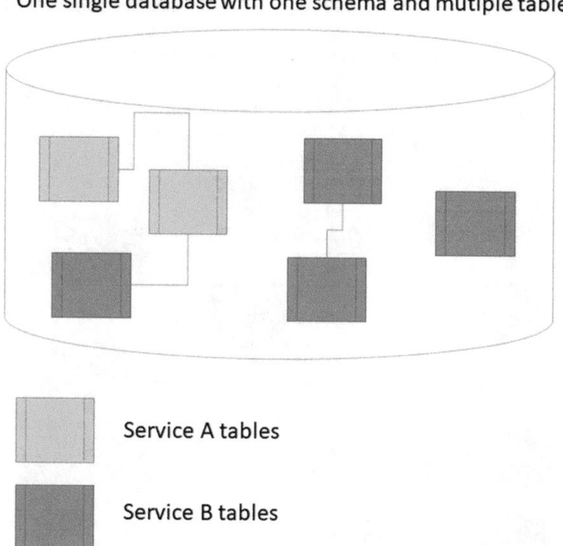

Fig. 10 Tables duplication

migration is way easier and the synchronization less critical because using distributed in memory caches is favorable for read only common data.

- When we are done with the first step we may decide to decompose to finer grain to produce more specialized and independent microservices. One advantage is that this strategy may only be applied to the most business-critical and changing part of your system while other macro microservices will just do well remaining 'Big' (Fig. 13).

– **Merge then split**:

- "Merge then split" aims at grouping microservice candidate prior to migrating them to the new platform. Once migrated to that platform they will be decomposed into fine-grained microservices. This happens when too many data dependencies tie services. In order to avoid multiple data synchronization across very different infrastructure we will migrate a bigger part and then simplify data dependencies once in the new target architecture. This applies well when migrating away from mainframe toward distributed systems. The difference with "macro then micro" is that we apply "merge then split" only on key microservices. For instance, we may decide to migrate "pricing" and "promotion" services all together but without the "buy" microservice. Doing so allows to automatically isolate data access, specifically for write accesses which may create data consistency issues (Fig. 14).

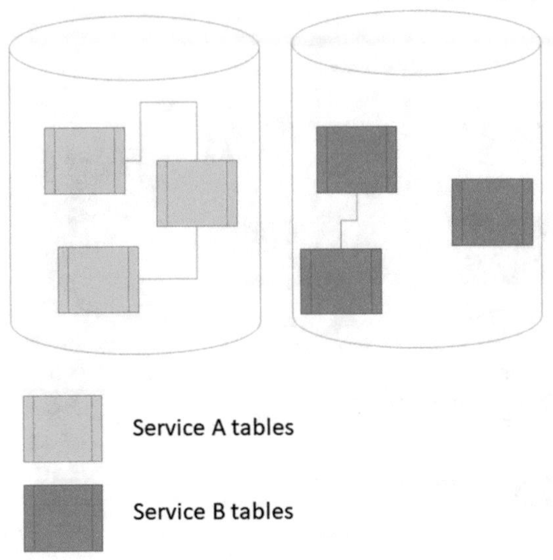

Fig. 11 Collocated schemas

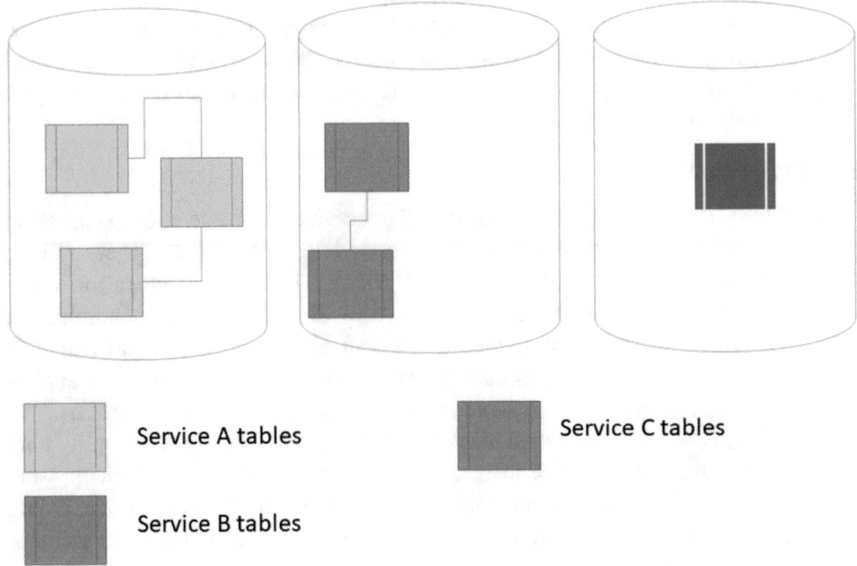

Fig. 12 Database server per domain

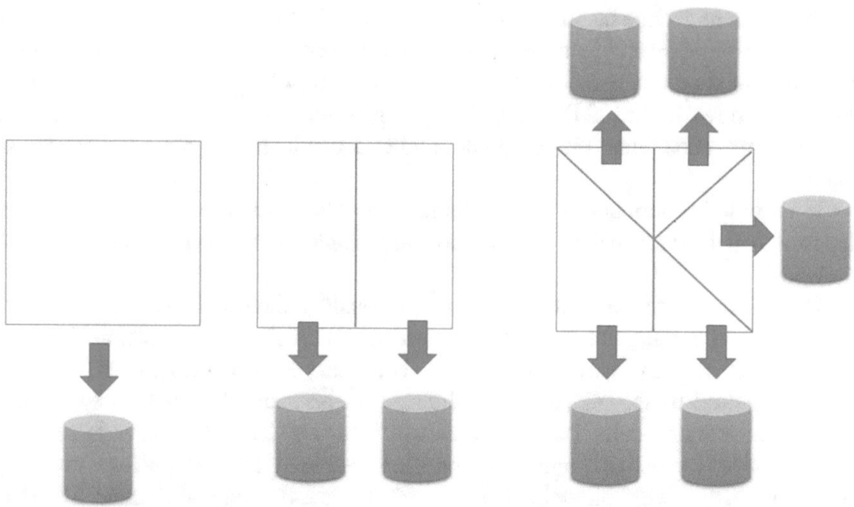

Fig. 13 Iteratively split the database

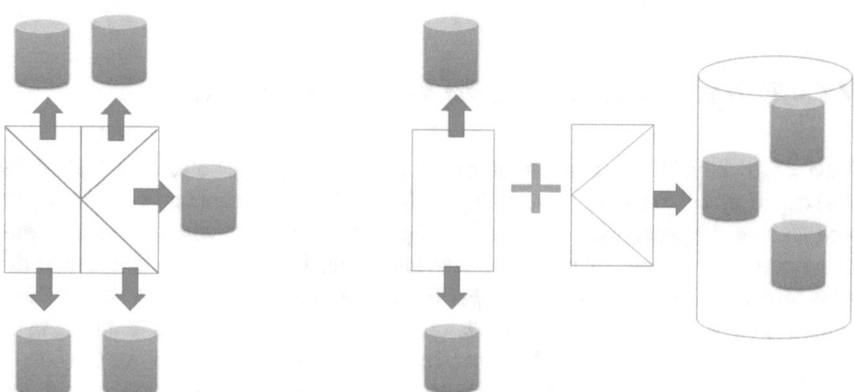

Fig. 14 Merge domains and split macro domains first

2.5 Domain Boundaries Are Not Data Access

Finding the domain boundaries in a legacy monolith is of course related to data. But there are no established rules and we should not drive our strategy by analyzing the data schema and individual data access within code. It is and will remain an art and a science. Microservice architecture relies on bounded context, therefore defining boundaries with domain-driven design [23] is a good start. However, we must resist the urge to design really small services inspired by the current normalized view of the data. This approach to identifying service boundaries almost always leads to an explosion of a large number of CRUD microservices and nanoservices [24]. First of all this does not isolate business nor bring it agility. Then your API composition will become a nightmare and your system may become very slow. Service decomposition must be based on business features isolation, starting with finding entry points and then going down to find all the data. Then going bottom-up to see what other features buried in the code share the same data allows for adjusting domain boundaries if need be.

If boundaries are not properly defined then we will create a high friction environment that ultimately fails release independence and correct execution of services.

Furthermore there are other elements to consider than technical ones. Indeed whatever the automation level that is reached with CI/CD microservice architecture design must fit with team skill and size. There are some heuristics [25] on how "micro" should be the microservice: the size of the team, the time to rewrite the service, how much behavior it must encapsulate, etc. The size depends on how many services the delivery and operation teams can independently release, monitor, and operate. We will start with larger services around a logical domain concept, and break the service down into multiple services when the teams are operationally ready with macro-then-micro or merge-then-split.

2.6 Start with What Brings the Most Business Value

Decoupling capabilities from the monolith is not an easy task and it requires skills and experience. Extracting a capability involves carefully extracting the data, logic, and user facing components and redirecting them to the new service. Because this is a nontrivial amount of work, the developers need to continuously evaluate the cost of decoupling against the benefits (going faster or growing in scale). If there is no payback because the cost for doing the migration is too high, then we must think wisely. There is absolutely no need to migrate all of a monolith; we can keep a core system as is. A good strategy is to identify the business features which are under constant change and which bring the more value when isolated from the monolith. You may identify the associated code by conducting workshop, static code analysis, or by analyzing the log files of your change management system or source repository. Jira and Git can easily be analyzed to identify what code changes the most, what code is error prone or subject to change request. Doing so, the delivery teams can analyze the code commit patterns to find out what has historically changed the most. By comparing with the product roadmap it is possible to identify the most desired capabilities which will require intensive code change in the near future. Interacting with the business owners and product managers to understand the differentiating capabilities is crucial. For instance, in Fig. 15 the monolith was split in order to remove all data from customer profile in memory and have stateless services to all features related to selling, shipping, and ordering services.

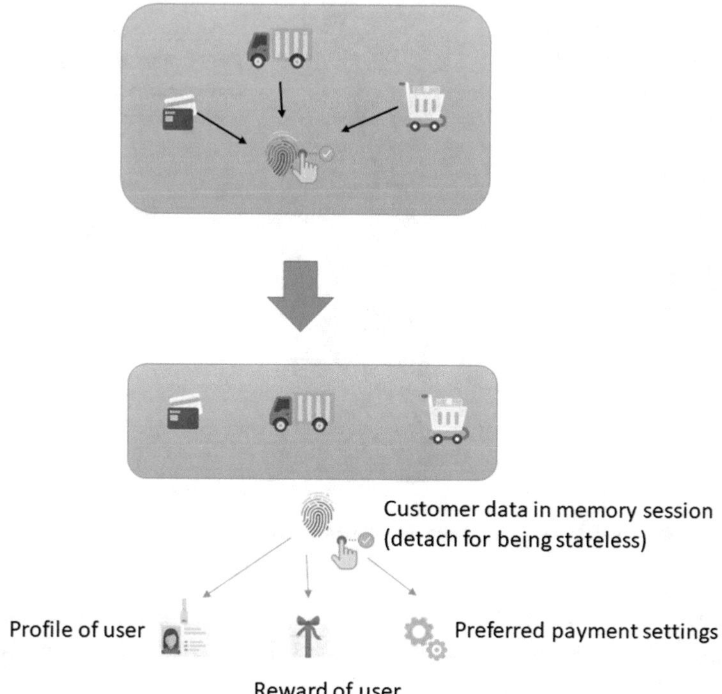

Fig. 15 Make important features stateless and make them microservices

2.7 Minimize Dependencies Back to the Monolith ... If You Can

As a founding principle, the delivery teams need to minimize the dependencies of newly formed microservices to the monolith. A major benefit of microservices is to have a fast and independent release cycle. Having dependencies to the monolith—data, logic, APIs—couples the service to the monolith's release cycle, prohibiting this benefit.

The prime motivation for moving away from monoliths is the slow pace of change of the current system. It is expected that uncoupling critical and changing capabilities from the monolith allows for fast change due to data autonomy, autonomous packaging, and automatic testing and deployment. This will be true if the externalized microservice truly is autonomous, and as such the business logic within the microservice shall not depend upon API calls back to the monolith.

While we recommend starting the migration process with edge services, there may be little of those. Initially they are helpful because migrating those first allows for getting ready for more critical and larger microservices.

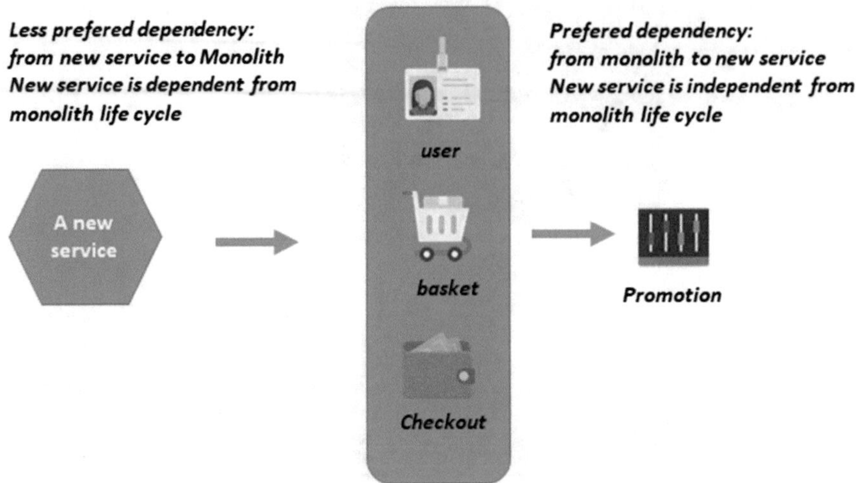

Fig. 16 Inverse dependencies: from monolith to new microservices

However, it is not a valid option to peel a monolith like an onion because the migration process will create dependencies in the reverse direction, from the monolith to the services (Fig. 16).

Therefore, once we are ready and used to operate microservices, we will have to dig vertically the core features out of the monolith. This is the desired dependency direction as it does not slow down the pace of change for new services.

To illustrate this we will consider a retail online system, where buy and promotions are core capabilities. Buy uses promotions during the checkout process to offer the customers the best promotions that they qualify for, given the items they are buying. If we need to decide which of these two capabilities to decouple next, we suggest starting with decoupling promotions first and then "buy". Because in this order we reduce the dependencies back to the monolith. In this order buy first remains locked in the monolith with a dependency out to the new promotions microservice.

While this guideline is very efficient when modernizing a relatively young monolith it may prove much more difficult when modernizing very old applications coming from mid-range or mainframe. Indeed, programming language capabilities and middleware/operating systems are not in favor of having the monolith depend upon external capabilities. When facing such systems we will have to balance the current guideline with merge-then-split and macro-then-micro, which may offer better decentralized management and lesser complexity.

We may as well expose a new API from the monolith (if the monolith's underlying infrastructure and programing language allows for that) and to access the API through an anticorruption layer [26] in the new service to make sure that the monolith concepts do not leak out. We must strive to define the API that reflects well-defined domain concepts and structures, even though the monolith's internal

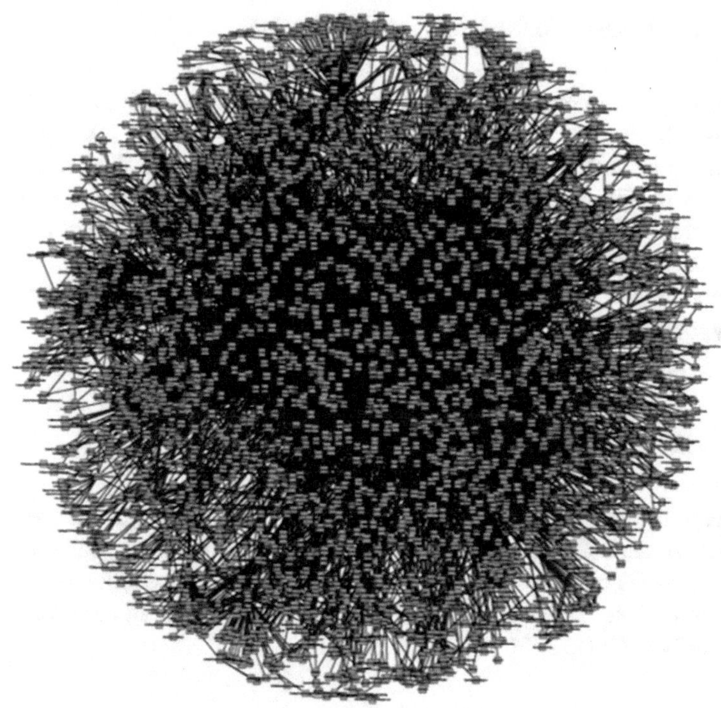

Fig. 17 The API tangle: use API gateways when coordination becomes a challenge

implementation may be otherwise. In this unfortunate case, we will be bearing the cost and difficulty of changing the monolith, testing and releasing the new services coupled with the monolith release.

An API's first design becomes difficult to operate when too many inbound and outbound dependencies exist. Figure 17 illustrates this by displaying API endpoints and calls between deployed microservices at Amazon. In such a complex scenario the use of external configuration to manage dependency complexity will be required. For this current issue the use of API gateway will be required and API coordination will make sense. However this feature is useful in an evolutionary architecture when you are ready to use it (see below), based on the payback for the extra complexity management.

3 Analysis Use Case: Blu Age Analyzer

A microservice architecture decomposes applications into loosely coupled business domains. The idea is that any team responsible for a domain may change how things are done inside the domain without impacting other application domains it interacts with. When peeling a monolith, one must identify the various domains and associated boundaries. Blu Age Analyzer relies on the preceding patterns to define the microservices decomposition.

In this section, we will describe the steps taken with Blu Age Analyzer [27] to identify microservice domains.

3.1 Step 1: Vertical Analysis

Blu Age Analyzer automatically identifies all entry points into the system and organizes the dependencies into concentric rings. Microservices appear as local trees starting from the outside. At this stage, there are still some coupling elements that appear in the inner layers identified by the green zone in the figure. This analysis stage is fully automated (Fig. 18).

3.2 Business Domains Definition

During this step, dependencies to core programs are solved and individual domain boundaries are finalized. It leads to a starfish collaboration where few central domains (programs with very little code) contain utility programs and satellite domains contain the business logic. Satellite domains use central domains and collaborate directly with other satellite domains as well (Fig. 19).

Domain decomposition and boundary detection is made by analyzing both caller/callee relationships, data access type, and data formats. The example in Fig. 20 shows for a given program tree the data dependencies according to their data formats. It highlights the virtual storage access method (VSAM) and DB2 access types.

At this stage, a Blu Age Analyzer user may choose to alter boundary definitions. Typically, s/he can adjust a domain based on business enhancements or to optimize API composition and data synchronization. This is common for microservices definition where boundaries are optimized through iterations.

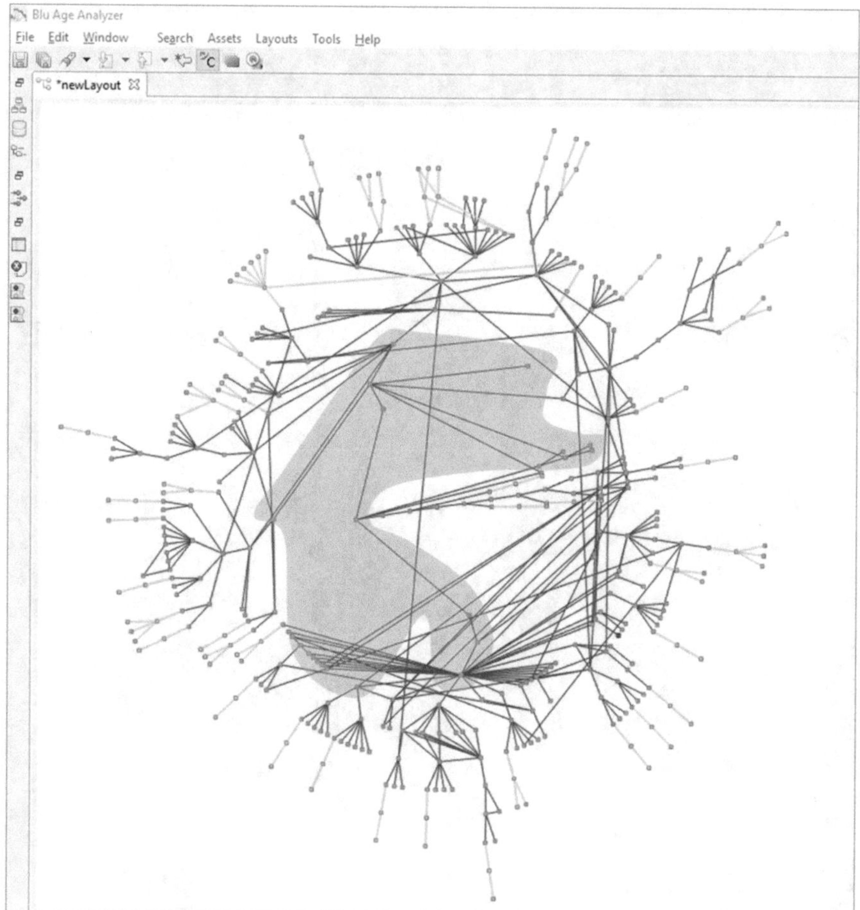

Fig. 18 Vertical analysis using Blu Age Analyzer

Blu Age Analyzer facilitates this task using tags annotation. Domain boundaries adjustment effort is typically 1/2 man-day per million lines of code.

3.3 Utility Domains Definition

Users must then decide to include the central utility domains as libraries within microservices or as real microservices of their own. These central domains usually

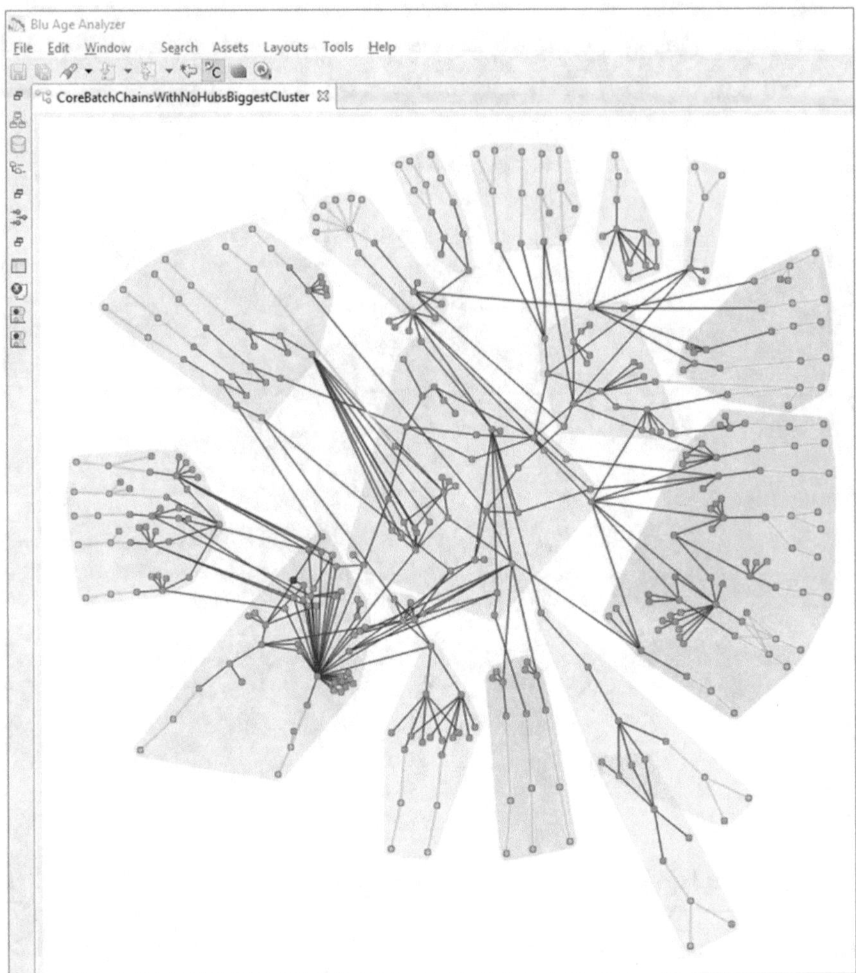

Fig. 19 Domain definition using Blu Age Analyzer

become libraries since they usually do no I/O and contain only utility programs, which would likely be replaced by off-the-shelf frameworks when modernized.

Figure 21 shows the final decomposition with connections between domains with a single orange arrow per domain collaboration.

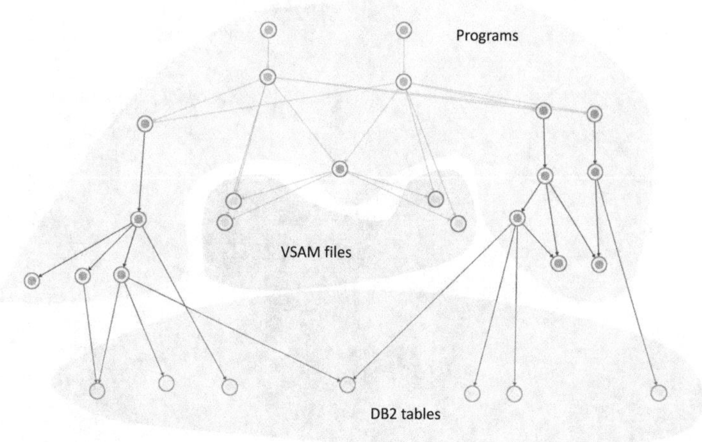

Fig. 20 Data dependencies analysis using Blu Age Analyzer

4 Reference Roadmap

4.1 Step Your Architecture and Go the Right Pace

Any seasoned engineer can share stories of legacy migration and modernization attempts that got planned and initiated with over-optimism of total completion, and at best got abandoned at a good enough point in time.

Long-term plans of such endeavors get abandoned because the conditions change: the program runs out of money, the organization pivots its focus to something else, or leadership in support of it leaves.

So this reality should be designed to get regular valuable benefits. Do not try to get directly to the perfect architecture nor to get huge savings and business agility benefit in the long run.

It is essential to plan the journey to sell constant payback in a way which is clear to upper management.

Our advice is to go fast, to define an architecture evolution roadmap and to be ready to adapt it to changing conditions. Furthermore, a given microservice architecture is not necessarily a global solution that can be used for all microservice projects, and a business application may rely on different patterns per microservice. Microservice decomposition must not be based once and then delivered with an immutable plan because unexpected refactoring will be required and constantly readjusting a global strategy will take too long. Each microservice is a unit of its own and we must use this to our advantage to go fast and show results.

Within each microservice create a microservice roadmap which lets you go through more advanced technology over time. Below is an example of an incremental roadmap, prior to changing conditions. The roadmap is as follows:

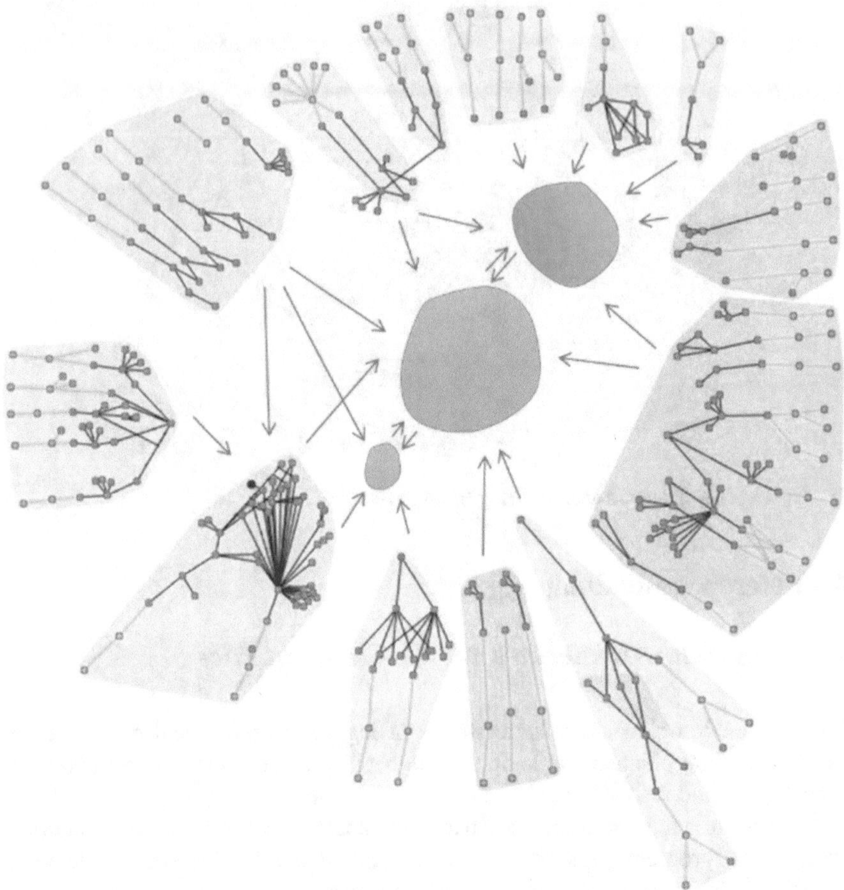

Fig. 21 Final microservice decomposition

- **Stage 1: Ready to operate** The first stage is about being ready to operate microservices by automating testing, release forging, and deployment. Data becomes distributed, service discovery is in place and so is monitoring. Therefore the following must be ready and well used:
  - CI/CD to automate all the release management and deployment
  - Database per service. This pattern should be stepped with the following roadmap:

    Tables per service: We keep a single database layer but isolate tables within the same instance. This is a single schema but denormalized to split apart data. Data are virtually disconnected.

Schema per service: We keep the same underlying technology but dedicate schema and instances of databases per service. Each schema is private per microservice.

Database per service: each microservice uses its own database technology which may be relational, key/value, column based, graph based, etc.

- Service discovery: Doing API composition requires service discovery. A modern microservice-based application usually runs in a virtualized or containerized environment where the number of instances of a service and their locations change dynamically. As such we must rely on service discovery: client side discovery [28], server side discovery [28], and service registry.
- Monitoring: we need to be able to track a minimum of elements:

Machines, virtual machines, containers are up and running and application does respond to API request (health check API).

We must be able to track APIs versioning and where they are deployed to be able to debug.

We have centralized log management.

– **Stage 2: Scale and enhance**

- Enhance release management: At this stage, automation allows to convert any GIT commit into a machine image or a container image. Microservice images are stored individually, versioned, and ready to deploy in seconds.
- Enhance deployment target: We no longer rely on host nor virtual machines. We use only containers and container orchestration. Container images are automatically built and stored ahead of time for on-demand deployment. Container orchestration makes us ready for adaptive scaling and fast deployment.
- Load balancing and autoscaling: We have enough underlying infrastructure to enable auto scaling. Containers will be deployed and removed based on monitoring events, such as unavailability of service, poor response time, or overconsumption of CPU/RAM. We enable load balancing to enforce performance and availability, be free to deploy at various places, and to ease service discovery.
- Canary deployment: Service discovery is used to manage deployment of different versions of service and to route API request to incrementally roll out to the newer versions. We will use load balancing and service registry to route request per criteria like geolocation, user id, etc.
- Consider private versus public cloud in case of tremendous success of public APIs. Indeed it may prove impossible to scale the physical infrastructure fast enough to serve increasing traffic and API queries. Furthermore, services may be required to be distributed all around the world to serve local users, which is a significant challenge. Another challenge is to deal with services with varying compute power which cannot be predicted (online bets, for instance). In which case you will want to quit on premise architecture to go to public cloud and go with on demand and pay as you go.

- **Stage 3: Optimize and be an API provider**
  - API Gateway will allow to provide advance routing and service location capabilities. They can be used to filter and secure traffic as well. Use API gateway:

    When APIs go public
    To monetize APIs with usage control
    To handle huge API request and to simplify load balancing, service location, and API routing
    To do API composition at the gateway level

  - ServiceMesh [29]: This is a network communication infrastructure which allows to decouple and offload most of the application network functions from service code. Hence service-to-service communication does not need to implement resilient communication patterns such as circuit breakers nor timeouts in your services code. Similarly, service mesh provides other features such as service discovery, observability, etc. There is a balance [30] to define between API gateway and service mesh.
  - Serverless is the next stage beyond containers. In this case, there is nothing to provision and manage. Scalability is virtually without limits and brings extra cost savings. Serverless is way faster than containers (typically an instance is up and running in 120 ms) but requires more discipline because they must be stateless or with minimal data serialization. However serverless, and more specifically Function as a Service, is perfect for API first design and have a natural fit with API gateways.
  - Backend for front end [31, 32] will be used for multichannel APIs. For instance, mobile devices will want to make different calls, fewer calls, and will want to display different (and probably less) data than their desktop counterparts. This means that we need to add additional functionality to our API backend to support mobile interfaces.

5 Conclusions

This chapter presented a methodology for successfully migrating monolith application toward microservice architecture. Based on survey [5] results and return of experience from real projects, we identified key issues typically faced during migrating. Typically five main risk factors have been identified and solved, namely:

- Difficulties for doing microservice decomposition and getting rid of tight coupling
- Underestimating the consequences of service isolation and database per service
- Difficulties in operating microservice architecture
- Assessing the readiness for change
- Focusing too much on technology and less on design and migration patterns.

Fig. 22 Evolutionary architecture

Furthermore we highlighted that most migration projects start by designing a "perfect" microservice architecture while it is counterproductive. As explained, microservice architecture is a trade-off between individual design patterns, therefore the architecture design depends upon the application features to migrate. Moreover, each pattern has operational consequences and a microservice architecture must be built with operation excellence because distributed systems are more difficult to manage.

Based on this analysis we detailed both a methodology and a roadmap to help build microservice applications.

The key principle of the methodology is to build an evolutionary architecture. This starts by learning how to do microservice decomposition while jointly creating the basis for operation excellence and associated automation. Then we introduce more migration patterns to manage data uncoupling, minimize dependencies, and manage APIs.

Then we went through a service decomposition from a real large system. We also went into differentiating between microservice candidates versus common components which shall be deployed into all services. By doing this we will avoid creating nanoservices and the consequences of the *law of the instrument*.

Finally we proposed a reference roadmap to build a microservice ecosystem based on operational readiness (Fig. 22):

- Ready to operate
- Scale and enhance
- Optimize and become an API provider.

References

1. M. Fowler, Microservices, a definition of this new architectural term (2011), https://martinfowler.com/articles/microservices.html
2. S. Tuli, Microservices vs SOA: what's the difference? (2018), https://dzone.com/articles/microservices-vs-soa-whats-the-difference
3. W.K. Loo W.Y. Tham Y.B. Leau, S.F. Tan, Software development life cycle agile vs traditional approaches, in *International Conference on Information and Network Technology (ICINT 2012)*, vol. 37 (ICINT, IACSIT Press, Singapore, 2012)
4. P.M. Clarke, R.V. O'Connor, P. Elger, *Continuous Software Engineering: A Microservices Architecture Perspective* (Wiley, London, 2017)
5. A.M. Glen, Microservices priorities and trends (2018), https://dzone.com/articles/dzone-research-microservices-priorities-and-trends
6. B.J. Evans, *The Well-Grounded Java Developer: Vital Techniques of Java 7 and Polyglot Programming* (Manning Publications, Shelter Island, 2012)
7. R.V. Rajesh, *Spring 5.0 Microservices*, 2nd edn. (Packt, Birmingham, 2017)
8. C. Richardson, *Database Per Service* (2018)
9. C. Richardson, *Microservice Patterns, with Examples in Java* (Manning, Shelter Island, 2018)
10. W. Vogels, Eventually consistent. Commun. ACM **52**(1), 40–44 (2009)
11. M. Conway, Conway's law. https://en.wikipedia.org/wiki/conway%27s_law
12. ThoughtWorks, *Microservice Envy* (2018)
13. A. Maslow, *The Psychology of Science* (Harper & Row, New York, 1966)
14. A. Maslow, Law of the instrument. https://en.wikipedia.org/wiki/law_of_the_instrument
15. C. Richardson, Microservice architecture patterns (2018), https://microservices.io/patterns/index.html
16. S. Newman, *Building Microservices* (O'Reilly, Sebastopol, 2015)
17. Martin Fowler. CQRS pattern (2011), https://martinfowler.com/bliki/cqrs.html
18. P. Kua, N. Ford, R. Parsons, *Building Evolutionary Architectures* (O'Reilly, Sebastopol, 2017)
19. P. Jamshidi, A. Balalaie, A. Heydarnoori, *Microservices Architecture Enables DevOps: Migration to a Cloud-Native Architecture*, vol. 33 (IEEE Software, 2016)
20. J. Gao, M. Rahman, *A Reusable Automated Acceptance Testing Architecture for Microservices in Behavior-Driven Development* (IEEE, Piscataway, 2015)
21. B. Golden, 3 reasons why you should always run microservices apps in containers. https://techbeacon.com/app-dev-testing/3-reasons-why-you-should-always-run-microservices-apps-containers.
22. A. Henry, How to peel mainframe monoliths for AWS microservices with Blu Age (2018), https://aws.amazon.com/fr/blogs/apn/how-to-peel-mainframe-monoliths-for-aws-microservices-with-blu-age/
23. E. Evans, *Domain-Driven Design: Tackling Complexity in the Heart of Software* (Addison Wesley, Reading, 2003)
24. gpestana, https://www.gpestana.com/blog/data-microservices/
25. M. Mclarty, M. Amundsen, *Microservice Architecture: Aligning Principles, Practices, and Culture* (O'Reilly, Sebastopol, 2016)
26. E. Evans, *Domain-Driven Design: Tackling Complexity in the Heart of Software* (Addison Wesley, Reading, 2003)
27. A. Henry, https://www.bluage.com/products/blu-age-analyzer
28. C. Richardson, Server side discovery (2018), https://microservices.io/patterns/server-side-discovery.html
29. R. Parsons, Servicemesh, 2019
30. K. Indrasiri, Service mesh vs API gateway, 2017
31. S. Newman, *Monolith to Microservices* (O'Reilly, Sebastopol, 2019)
32. S. Newman, Pattern: Backends for frontends (2015), https://samnewman.io/patterns/architectural/bff/

Assessing Your Microservice Migration

Alexis Henry and Youssef Ridene

Abstract Microservice is an architectural pattern that has risen based on the success of Amazon, Netflix, and other digital-native companies. Designing such an architecture requires understanding your business goals and creating a balance between microservices benefits and associated drawbacks. This trade-off is essential in order to successfully migrate your business applications to microservices. In this chapter we aim to drive you through assessing your readiness to microservice and migration to microservice. We will first start by highlighting key microservice concepts and their impact on both your coding and operations practices and your organization. Then we will investigate further to identify how to establish a trade-off between microservices benefits and associated drawbacks. Database per service, API first design, readiness to operate and NoOps on public cloud will be investigated so that you can clearly establish your own design and strategy in adopting a microservice architecture.

1 Principles

1.1 Mimicking Internet Giants and Unicorns

We are living in a digital world that is driven by data and software innovation. Every day we hear stories of a start-up that turned into an industry giant. The reason of their success is clear: direct access to consumers, innovation to enhance user experience, quality, constant deployment of new features, scalability up to billions of users, and an always-on architecture.

Technically speaking, the success of Netflix, Amazon, and most Unicorns [1] is based on technology which allows scaling to serve millions and even billions of

A. Henry (✉) · Y. Ridene
Blu Age R&D Department, Netfective Technology, Pessac, France
e-mail: a.henry@netfective.com; y.ridene@netfective.com
http://www.bluage.com

A. Bucchiarone et al. (eds.), *Microservices*,
https://doi.org/10.1007/978-3-030-31646-4_4

Fig. 1 Microservices let you change things easily and fast

users at the same time. This was achieved by adopting microservice architecture, in order to isolate individual business services and to organize their software development department into autonomous units. Therefore, they can innovate faster than any competitors, choosing the technology most appropriate for each service. Consequently, they constantly release new features that keep consumers attracted to them (Fig. 1).

We now see older organizations involved in migrating to a microservice architecture. They have been surveyed [2] about their microservice architecture strategy, objectives, and return of experience:

- Only 24% have deployed microservices into their production environment (Fig. 2).
- Four out five respondents stated microservice architecture makes their job easier (Fig. 5). Surprisingly only 177 respondents are using microservices in

Value	Percent	Responses
Yes, in development	24.7%	181
Yes, in production	24.2%	177
No, but we're considering them	38.7%	283
We've tried them and decided not to use them	0.8%	6
No, and we're not considering them	11.6%	85
		Totals: 732

Fig. 2 Adoption of microservices [2]

Value	Percent	Responses
Management requested that we do so	12.0%	43
To improve quality by having teams focus on just one piece of an app	50.1%	179
To make applications easily scalable	80.7%	288
To improve quality by narrowing down the source of failures to a particular piece of an app	40.9%	146
To enable faster deployments to just one part of an application	69.5%	248
To experiment with the architecture	24.4%	87
Flexibility to chose different tools or languages for each service	35.6%	127
Other - Write In (click to view)	3.9%	14

Fig. 3 Reasons for adopting microservices [2]

Value	Percent	Responses
Lack of training	24.4%	22
Lack of time to train developers	6.7%	6
Lack of time to refactor existing applictions	22.2%	20
Lack of knowledge on the subject	37.8%	34
Lack of applicable use case	38.9%	35
Other - Write In (click to view)	8.9%	8

Fig. 4 Reasons for not adopting microservices [2]

production, which is significantly less than the number of respondents benefiting from microservice architecture (286).

- The two main reasons for adopting microservice architecture are faster partial deployment (69.5%) and scalability (80%) (Fig. 3).
- The main reason for not adopting microservice architecture is the lack of knowledge and know-how (68.9% when summing need for training, no time for training, and lack of knowledge). Then more than one third of the respondents consider they do not have applicable use case (Fig. 4).

An early conclusion would be that nearly all adopters do benefit from microservice architecture, with a rather narrow focus on the performance of distributed components. The reason for not adopting it is more a readiness assessment rather than a lack of interest or a fear it would not work (Fig. 5).

Value	Percent	Responses
Yes	80.1%	286
No	19.9%	71
		Totals: 357

Fig. 5 Are microservices beneficial to your organization? [2]

However many returns of experience [3–6] from the industry speak about complexity of microservices architecture, and there are still many debates on microservice design patterns. Is reality different or is microservice a complex topic that needs deep technical expertise in order to bring benefits?

1.2 Where Is the Complexity?

Isolation is at the core of microservice architecture. While SOA was designed in order to reuse existing services, microservice architecture was designed to create loosely coupled services. However, this goes further: data are not shared between services, each microservice is managed by only one team that is fully autonomous, and service may be reused but implementation is stateless and hidden from consumer services. Microservice architecture is polyglot; each microservice may be implemented with a different programming language or database technology, there is no global design or technical architecture. This is the reason it is often qualified as the "share as little as possible" architecture.

But distributed systems are more difficult to manage, due to CAP theorem, and complexity will arise because of decentralized data management. As a consequence of isolation and distribution, trade-off needs to be established between benefits and drawbacks of microservice architecture [7]. Microservice architecture pioneers still describe it as both powerful and complex and do not consider it a general all-purpose architecture principle [8].

Analyzing respondents' answers highlight some of the drawbacks of migrating to microservice architecture:

- Many adopters consider microservice architecture as a technical architecture, thus limiting the design to include only microservice technology and tools.
- The complexity of uncoupling element is usually underestimated.
- Complexity never disappears, microservice requires DevOps maturity and significant automation of application life cycle.

Indeed, most survey respondents have chosen the same technical architecture, Java (80%) with either Java EE and/or SpringBoot (total is 77.1%), and most of them deploy to containers [2] (Figs. 6 and 7).

Value	Percent	Responses
Java	80.2%	528
C/C++	8.4%	55
C#	17.5%	115
Python	28.4%	187
JavaScript	27.7%	182
PHP	10.6%	70
Ruby	8.8%	58
Go	12.0%	79
Node.js	34.3%	226
.NET	12.6%	83
Other - Write In (click to view)	6.5%	43

Fig. 6 Microservices: preferred programming languages [2]

Value	Percent	Responses
Spring Boot	48.6%	319
Java EE	28.5%	187
Hystrix	7.6%	50
Prometheus	3.8%	25
AWS Lambda	15.5%	102
Azure Functions	9.6%	63
MicroProfile	1.8%	12
Google Cloud Functions	6.8%	45
Akka	5.9%	39
Other - Write In (click to view)	7.8%	51

Fig. 7 Microservices: preferred frameworks [2]

Nevertheless, from Figs. 8 and 9 we clearly see monitoring is a problem for one out of two adopters and that more than a third of adopters experience issues because microservice architecture requires a culture change. Furthermore, when migrating a monolith, half of the respondents were not able to identify where to break up the original system. Finally half of the respondents were not able to decouple identify services to peel off the monolith.

In fact, what is not well understood is that there is no such thing as a reference microservice architecture. Microservice is not about selecting technology nor deploying containers. Above all, microservice architecture is about business

Value	Percent	Responses
Finding where to break up monolithic components	50.0%	313
Overcoming tight coupling	49.7%	311
Incorporating other technologies (containerization, etc.)	23.6%	148
Testing	30.8%	193
Time investment	38.5%	241
Other - Write In (click to view)	2.9%	18
Not applicable	21.2%	133

Fig. 8 Microservices are difficult to identify and isolate [2]

Value	Percent	Responses
Monitoring	46.6%	292
Service discovery	21.7%	136
App/service stability	26.8%	168
App/service security	27.2%	170
Deploying apps or services	25.4%	159
Changing culture to be open to microservices	38.2%	239
Other - Write In (click to view)	5.1%	32
Not applicable	17.6%	110

Fig. 9 Deploying and managing is not that easy [2]

product and autonomous teams. Each team has full responsibility and autonomy to manage technical choices, release cycles, deployment to production, and underlying infrastructure. Each team is responsible for isolated business features that they make available to other teams as black boxes via APIs. Each database is private to the microservice it belongs to, which allows each microservice to make any change at any time without affecting dependencies of other microservices.

Consequently, the design and the management of your architecture is very different, and so is data consistency. Unfortunately, there is little chance that an existing monolith complies to this prior to its migration toward the new architecture model.

In order to be successful with the migration, the following changes must be made:

- Focus on business and users: You must consider your microservices as business parts. Your sole objective when creating/upgrading a microservice is to deliver a business case.
- Autonomy, uncoupling, and API first design: Microservices are parts. Parts may be replaced and upgraded at any time without affecting other services. As such, all microservices are managed by dedicated teams that are black boxes to other microservices. Each team has full autonomy over implementation choices. They communicate with the outside world only with APIs.
- You build it, you run it: Each team is responsible for design, implementation, maintenance, and operation of their microservices. You can't delegate to another team to operate your application and software infrastructure. This does not mean you can't share choices and design principles with other teams but no external team shall have any impact on your choices. Furthermore keeping your application scalable, available, and consistent is your duty.
- Local data consistency: Each microservice runs its own private datastore. Data consistency exists only within a microservice. There is no such thing as coordinated transaction among microservices. Data state is local to individual microservices. When performing service composition you will not and can't have strict consistency. A data replication mechanism must be implemented so that denormalized data is synchronized. As such, at API coordination level you have only weak consistency, most probably eventual consistency.

The last item is very restrictive and is the one that is mostly demanding for a balance between gains and drawbacks. Indeed you get benefits by isolating and decoupling business components. Each may change for any reason, in any way, without affecting other business processes. However, doing so with scalability, performance, and individual availability of services forbid strict data consistency (more details on this later in this chapter). Therefore, the balance is between the consistency model, the business agility it brings, and the associated limits on the coding style.

2 Why Microservice Architecture Is Different

2.1 A Zoom-In on Key Characteristics

In order to assess the capability of building and operating microservices, each organization must have a deep understanding of the key characteristics of such an architecture. Indeed local consistency, data isolation, and API first design significantly affect the life cycle of microservices with regards to other programming styles.

Because the system is distributed [9–12], a balance must be established between availability, performance, and consistency. For this reason, we will further investigate microservice architecture characteristics.

2.1.1 Business Modules

Each microservice is a runnable unit that delivers a business service. Microservices should not be technical components, common utilities, or shared services. Each business module must be self-contained. Typically a *stock management* service should not be responsible for *pricing* or *promotion* (Fig. 10).

Dependencies must be managed so that those other two services use "stock management" in order to vary pricing by triggering specific promotions when stock is too high or increase prices for rare items (Fig. 11).

Business modules must be considered as a product you could buy from a third party without knowing its internals. They are applications of their own. They can grow both in size of code and engineering team. Keeping this in mind is important because microservice is an ambiguous name which could create an impression that microservices must be small. However, microservice architecture is not about cutting your monolith in small services, it is about slicing your software into independent business parts that can be upgraded, extended, and replaced as long as you preserve their public APIs (Fig. 12).

Over time, a successful microservice may grow big, implemented by 15–20 people. A significant microservice can grow bigger than many existing applications

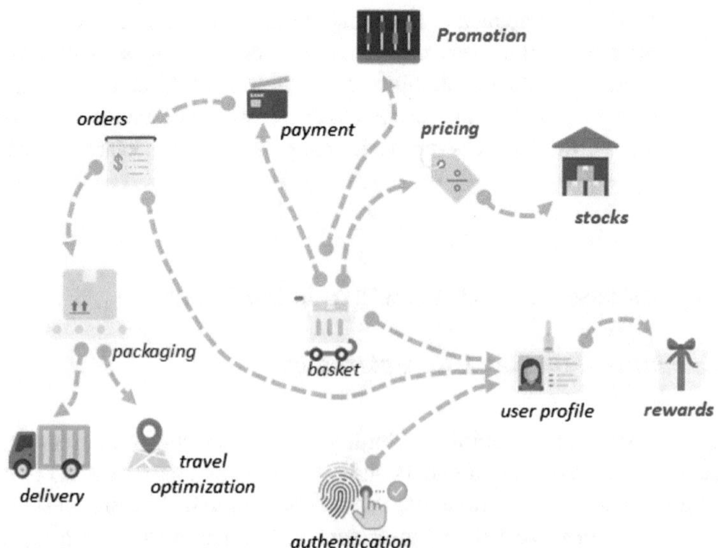

Fig. 10 Collaboration of individual services within a user process

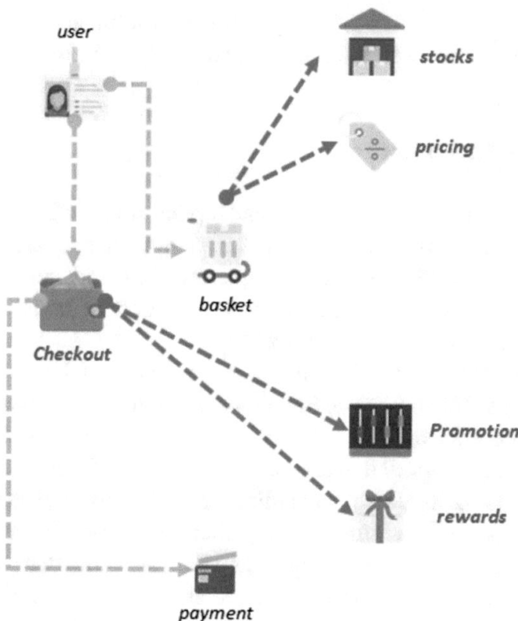

Fig. 11 Focus on customer *promotion* business use case, i.e., a microservice candidate

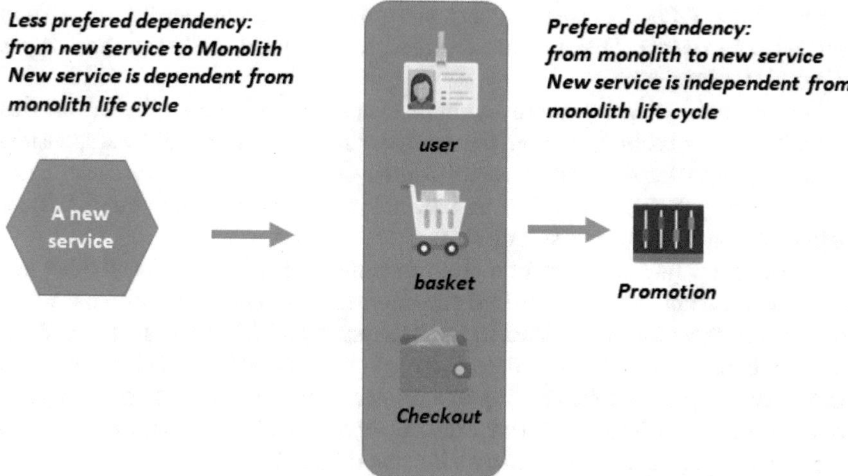

Fig. 12 Preferred dependencies when isolating microservices

within your organization and be perfectly designed, useful, and easy to maintain and evolve. Only when a microservice is too big shall it be split into smaller services.

2.1.2 Database Per Service

This design pattern is at the core of microservice architecture [13] to uncouple different services. An organization may have implemented the perfect software with the most brilliant SOA design, using event bus and queuing, have perfect loose coupling to manage calls between procedures and methods, and yet be tightly coupled because of the application database.

Indeed if that software is fast changing it will require schema updates, a newer configuration of its ORM (Object-Relational Mapping), or require new database features. Once the data definition has been modified, all components using the former structure are impacted and must be updated. Data structure change is always cascading globally within an application if there is no data isolation design. Furthermore, changing data structure may alter transaction management and will require update of all components using shared data structure definition.

As a result, all of the software is impacted and because many different components must be updated, each change cascades into more code adaptations.

To solve data coupling, each microservice owns privately its datastore [14]. Data sharing is forbidden and data is exchanged only through API composition and automatic data synchronization.

Distributed APIs are used to query and return application-level objects from isolated components. Data is decentralized, denormalized, and replicated across microservice boundaries.

For instance, when designing an online shop, there will be an "order" service and a "customer profile" service. The *customer profile* service will be responsible for managing customer record structure. Moreover, all updates on records attributes will be done by that service. However, the *order* service does not know the structure of that table and cannot access it directly.

So when creating an order for a given customer the *customer-ID* and other key profile information are denormalized and duplicated into the order records. When the customer records are updated in the "customer profile" database, the updates must be replicated into denormalized records in the order service. This allows each microservice team to make any required change to the data design and associated technical choices without affecting external services as long as interfaces remain stable and data synchronization is working fine (Fig. 13).

2.1.3 API First Design

Each microservice publishes APIs so that all use cases are done through API Composition. Typically, when buying from an online store the *buying* service will

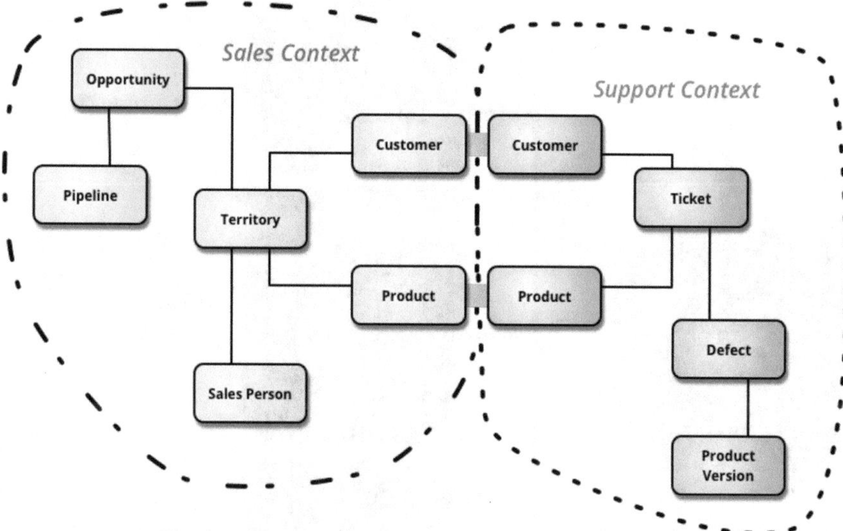

Fig. 13 Record duplication and denormalized schemas (customer and product) [13]

coordinate all actions by consuming the *customer profile*, *promotions*, *payment*, *stock management*, and *pricing modules*.

This principle allows deployment and configuration of distributed elements at will. Creating new services is done via service composition of autonomous services. Implementation is hidden from other services and can evolve as often as needed with no impact on API consumers.

Whenever an API is not available (due to an outage, unavailable network device, unreliable network delay, etc.) the coordinating service can chose to deliver the most important services while postponing other actions. Unreachable services will be activated later on without blocking the entire process.

A typical scenario is buying from an online shop while the "stock management" service is over-flooded and cannot serve all incoming requests. The Buying service will perform all actions that are available—send order to Shipping, process Payment—and will manage the stock update asynchronously.

This is an example of trade-off that must happen to make microservices efficient: We must be ready to sacrifice stocks consistency to the benefit of the Buying microservice. There is no global transaction, and global data consistency is not strict. However, the most important services are always up and scalable even if the other parts do not behave as expected. A monolith is a single part that is either doing well or bad. Microservice architecture allows for splitting responsibilities and operational states (Fig. 14).

For that reason, API first design makes real use of cloud capabilities. Indeed, modules are distributed in various places. Different versions of the same service may be deployed and active at the same time. This allows features to be seen as a

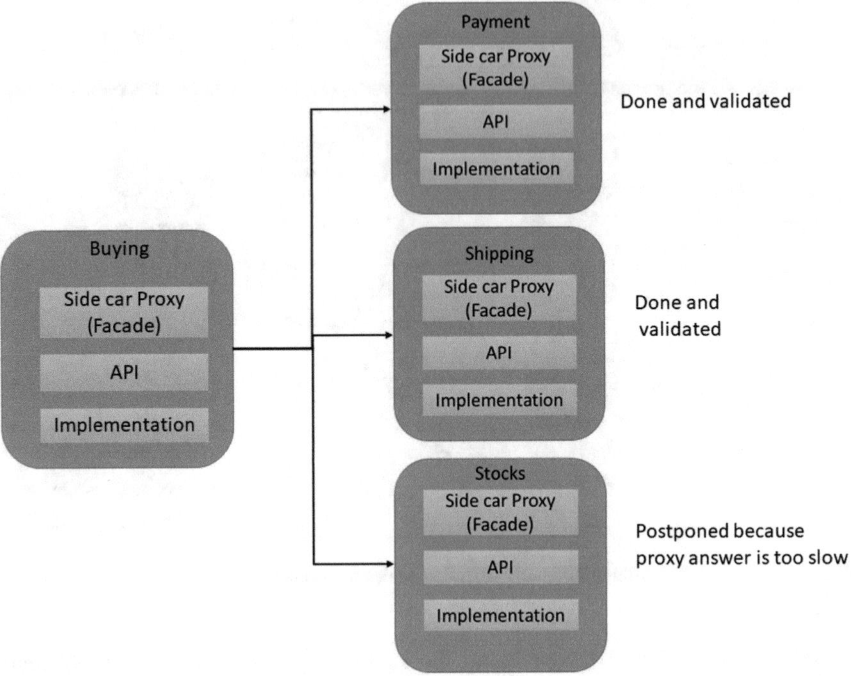

Fig. 14 Managing remote services availability and network latency

global application which cannot fail. Typically, API gateway and load balancer make distributed architecture extremely reliable and resilient to varying load stresses and unexpected failure scenarios.

2.1.4 Polyglot Architecture

Microservices do not expose their implementation, only their public API are visible. This black box approach allows selecting the technical stack for each service independently [13] of other services. For instance, a crime scene investigation software (CSI system) that helps the police will require features such as (Fig. 15):

- A very good geolocation service to help spot and chase suspects
- Advanced analysis capabilities to establish connection between suspects
- A video recording service that streams and saves recordings of police action and keeps track of evidence

A polyglot architecture allows choosing a different database system (a GIS database for the first service, a graph database for the second, and a streaming middleware for the last one) per microservice. Polyglot architecture is not limited to database but extends to programming languages and associated frameworks as well.

Fig. 15 CSI software services

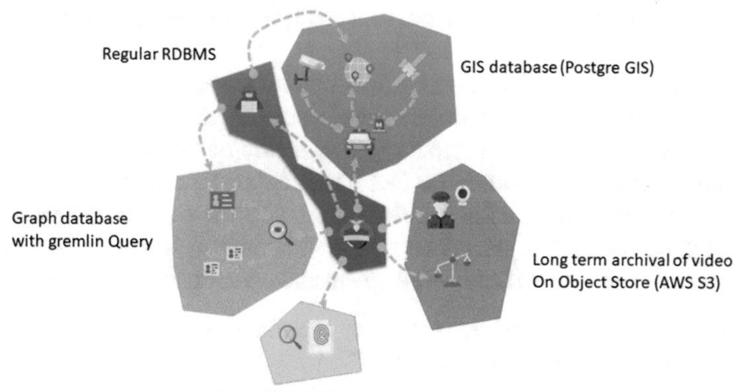

Fig. 16 Database choices may differ for each microservice

For instance, Groovy and Gremlin are good for doing graph transformation on top of a graph database. Therefore, a geolocation service is probably best implemented with angular for the frontend and Java and PostgreSQL for the backend. This is one of the reasons loosely coupled distributed services allow choosing the right technical stack according to required features and user experience (Fig. 16).

As seen previously, microservices benefits come from isolation and uncoupling. When doing greenfield development, this approach adds workload to the initial development phase because establishing microservices boundaries is not that easy. Furthermore, refactoring across microservices is complex. However, once boundaries are stable, microservice design is extremely beneficial.

Yet, this adds complexity when migrating. Indeed most existing monoliths rely on transactions, rollback, and sharing data in memory. Refactoring data scope, replacing transactions, and developing your own rollback services is complex. Another constraint adds further complexity: Microservices must be business components; therefore features must be identified within the code.

Unfortunately, it is very unlikely that the existing code base is made of isolated code block per feature. Most classes/programs will be part of multiple features that require to be distributed apart in the future. That issue is not limited to block of code, and queries to database tables and shared objects in memory will have to be refactored as well.

Because of this, each coupling type must be well understood and managed specifically:

- **Data coupling**: Each microservice owns its datastore and does not share its data schema nor allows direct access to persisted records. This allows decoupling at the data definition level. Consequently, data is denormalized and the information is distributed over multiple databases and partitions. Therefore data (records or information stored into records) must be replicated. However, replication takes time and may fail (due to outage, congestion, or availability issues) ACID transactions and strong consistency is not guaranteed.
- **Module/routine call coupling**: Code is compiled/packaged per microservice, deployed on multiple containers/machine instances and call are remote (not in the same virtual machine, without memory sharing and most probably rely on network infrastructure). Routines that were formerly running within the same compute unit are now running in different remote environments. Data in memory can no longer be shared, and networking makes routine communication slow and error prone. This creates both development and operational consequences:
  - Remote calls are slower, performance management, load balancing, and automatic deployment are a must.
  - Remote calls are not reliable, therefore monitoring, auto health check and automatic redeployment is a must.
  - Refactoring of code across microservices boundaries is much more difficult than with a monolith. Testing and debugging become more difficult as well.
  - Deployment of services is not predictive as it may be done automatically to support automatic scaling and load balancing or because a newer service version has been published and automatically deployed. As organization skill increases, it will raise the automation level to get more agility. Eventually every code commit may be automatically compiled, tested, versioned, and deployed into a canary deployment with automatic load balancing configuration. Such an objective requires a strong discipline to enforce version management and deployment management. A strong CI/CD (continuous integration, continuous deployment) automation is necessary in this case, otherwise the infrastructure will turn to chaos.

- **Transaction coupling**:
  - This is one limitation not usually well understood at first. In monoliths, data consistency is achieved using transactions. This allows for controlling the state of data in the following two scenarios:

    Service updating data in multiple databases simultaneously
    Multiple services collaborate to update multiple tables in a database
  - Monolith has safe transactions because they rely on the following:

    ACID and rollback capabilities from RDBMS
    Transaction at programming level to trigger global rollback or global commit
    Two phase commit to coordinate the two above on distributed datastores
  - Unfortunately, programmers must do without transactions when using Microservice. Strong consistency is difficult to manage on distributed systems. The more you split your monolith the more you distribute your system. Transactions on such systems would become harder and harder to coordinate and would involve significant delay (time for coordinating confirmation between datastore) and multiple rollbacks (because one single point of failure causes a complete rollback). This is the reason microservices are said to be consistent only within themselves. Their private database can be consistent, but the replication with the databases of other services is only eventually consistent because of decentralized data and the need for synchronization. Furthermore, there are technical issues coming from technology stack used in microservices:

    Database per design: Many modern NoSQL databases do not support two-phase commit. Many are not ACID compliant.
    API composition: REST is not compliant with distributed transactions and prevents coordinated services to behave as a global transaction.
  - As such when choosing a microservice architecture, it is key to have a very good understanding of eventual consistency. BASE databases favor availability and performance at the expense of consistency. If at least one partition of the database is up and running then the system is considered available. Furthermore there is no transaction atomicity (atomicity is at the record level) which means that rollback must be managed at the application level. Finally, data are in a soft state, meaning that they can change even without new inputs. Data state can be guaranteed only if in no updates happen during a long enough time, in order for the database to reach a stable state. Managing all of this at the application level is complex, so this type of consistency model should be chosen wisely.
- **Temporal coupling**: Temporal coupling comes from changes to code over time. Indeed, it is not possible to predict how microservices will be deployed while consumed by other services. Microservice architecture enables partial deploy-

ment and as such each microservice can be deployed with full autonomy. There is no need, technically, to coordinate global release cycles as such microservices are deployed automatically based on infrastructure events: performance threshold alarm that triggers a new deployment to scale up, a GIT commit to deploy a code update specific to the legislation of a given country, plus the configuration to route incoming http requests from that country to that new version of the microservice. Furthermore, microservices may be deployed on different technical architectures, such as virtual machines, containers, and function as a service frameworks, depending on the type of computation. Therefore, temporal coupling must be managed by using automated service discovery mechanism with a strong deployment automation process in a CI/CD environment. Furthermore, the deployment process must add metadata to deployed services so that monitoring may deliver business-oriented information (hostname, IP addresses, and the like are of no use to understand the impact of the failure of a running unit in microservice architecture).

As already stated by Martin Fowler, microservice architecture is a trade-off [7]. On one side, we have loose coupling, ease of deployment, and technology diversity per microservice. On the other, we have to deal with eventual consistency, failure management, and operational complexity.

While microservice architecture is often qualified "0 dependency architecture" a better name is "share as little as possible and optimize trade-off" architecture. The core of microservice architecture relies on loose coupling with no cascading of data structure changes. Data structure updates are defined at the microservice level and is not known to other microservices because they do not consume the data schema. Therefore, there is true data change isolation between microservices. Each microservice owns its own copy of decentralized data and informs other microservice of data updates. Other microservices subscribe to the data synchronization channel and react to it with their own private method. However, call dependencies are still here and they come with additional challenges that require a much stronger operational discipline.

2.2 *What Level of Microservice Design Do We Need ?*

Assessing organization readiness or defining the path to be ready is the first and most important step when migrating a monolith toward microservices. We must question your teams to make sure we have the required skills to deal with microservices drawbacks, needs for operational automation, and excellence. We must also make sure microservice is the right architecture for the business application features.

Next chapter will illustrate tools and define a methodology that will help define precisely the journey and the expected benefits.

2.3 *Is a Monolith Too Complex and Too Big?*

The following questions are assessment tools that should be used to qualify the real needs of a microservice architecture. Answering these questions will help define which characteristics will be beneficial, thus allowing to define the technical architecture depending on each feature needs.

This is an important step to consider in order not to solve a problem that does not exist. Again, it is important to keep in mind that most organizations can perfectly do well with a monolith, and most applications that do well are monoliths and will remain so. Moreover, you do not need to go to microservices to benefit from a technology or to update your technical stack. It is important to resist the urge to copy success stories if the use case is not the same.

Today when discussing with organizations considering migrating monoliths to microservice architecture, the most common drivers for microservice migration are going to API first design or to monetize APIs to generate revenue. However, microservice architecture is not the only way to achieve this.

You should go to microservice when your overall system has become too big and too complex and with components coupled so tightly that the pace of change slows down your business. If splitting a system into independent subcomponents is the best way to break complexity down to manageable units then microservice is most probably a good solution.

If migrating some services outside the monolith brings more agility then microservices is a valuable target. If we have a team of 50 people to manage an application and that an update requires all 50 persons to coordinate for days and weeks before releasing a version then microservice is a good choice. However, if a 10-person team manages a business-critical application and can deliver update and release on a daily basis using CI/CD, then there is probably no need to migrate to microservices.

2.3.1 Do We Need Five Releases Per Day?

Continuous integration and continuous deployment allow for building, testing, and deploying software releases faster and better [15, 16].

Netflix gives full autonomy to developers [17] and they do automatically push code commits to production. They potentially deploy microservices hundreds of times per day. They get huge benefits in doing this. Indeed they have a very resilient architecture, and customers always get access to their streaming in seconds. Sometimes the streaming fails, starts with low quality, or we may have to wait for our Netflix client to relaunch the video. This is perfectly fine from a user standpoint, we are happy with the service level and we do prefer the movie to start fast rather than waiting multiple minutes to have high quality.

However, not everybody is Netflix and the feature we deliver to our customers may be too important to allow for reduced quality. A financial transaction can't be approximately correct, a stock exchange order must be on time, and a life-saving system must preserve integrity at all times and always be available and consistent. The release cycle must be defined according to the risk associated to push an incorrect code or a code that is not fully battle tested. .

Microservice deployment is not about how many times you will deploy per day. It is about deploying fast when needed and deploying well what is required. Because not all of us work at Netflix or Amazon we have to choose a deployment strategy which fits our business priorities and DevOps capabilities, including unit testing automation, code coverage, and nonregression testing.

Microservice architecture was designed to control cost of failures and to be capable of solving issues fast and well. Therefore, the main problem probably is not deploying speed but the right trade-off between deployment speed, capacity management, and data integrity.

For most organization, the main reason for a deployment to production is more about releasing a new feature update or pushing a patch. Therefore, the key point from that perspective is the capability to deploy on demand and within minutes.

It is important not to confuse test automation with test excellence. It is difficult to reach 100% code coverage even with a CI/CD. However, unless this is achieved, it is best to keep some control over automatic deployment.

Furthermore, a monolith usually relies on simple infrastructure, mostly physical servers or virtual machines and dedicated centralized database. This architecture is much more dynamic and heterogeneous with microservices. It is based on a variety of containers being deployed automatically, new machines being spawned based on performance threshold, need for managing concurrently multiple versions of APIs, and routing traffic for canary [18]-based deployment. Deploying too fast and without control may become a problem when there is a need for debugging in production.

Release deployment should scale based on DevOps maturity and on the cost associated with potential production issues.

It is by scaling, in an iterative manner, the following capabilities will an organization be able to constantly increase its ability to automatically deploy new features directly from code to production environment:

- Continuous delivery
- Quick provisioning of virtual machines and containers
- Automatic scalability up and down
- Traceability of deployed services with versioning
- Monitoring capabilities
- Application level routing for Canary deployment
- DevOps culture [19]

There is no need to build all of this prior to any microservice migration. However, microservice architecture grows by increasing automation of DevOps tasks.

2.3.2 Is Eventual Consistency a Problem?

Because microservice architecture relies on distribution, failure will happen. It can be the unavailability of an API, a time out due to lack or performance, a slowdown of data synchronization between microservices, or duplicated synchronization messages that require data correction. In this case, the system operates with incorrect data state until it is solved. Under such circumstances, data synchronization may take time.

This is quite the opposite to how software have been designed and operated for the last 20–40 years. Programmers have been using ACID databases [20], transactions relying on a single central database (thus away from CAP theorem [9–12]). Dealing with distributed data was not a problem, operations are not used to solve related synchronization and rollback issues, and they did not have to consider the business consequences of such a scenario.

Unfortunately, the now famous *"Starbucks does not do two-phase commit"* [21, 22] and the success of Netflix microservice architecture have been doing too well at showing good principles and success. Unfortunately such references do not clearly state they are based on eventual consistency.

Starbucks does not mind replacing a coffee, associated cost is nothing compared to customer satisfaction. Similarly, there is no real impact to Google if results are not always the same on the first page. Netflix reduces streaming quality to favor quick start time if need be. However, what is the use case we are interested in will not do with approximate results, quality decrease, and refunding? Typically, a batch processing millions of records, a stock exchange order with prices changing every one tenth of a second do not fit into the Starbuck's metaphor.

Internet giants' main concern is to serve as much users as possible per second. Their business model is based on having their number one service always up and running, with limitless scalability, even if it means that a percentage of API calls fail and that the system ends up with inconsistent data, which means incorrect and partial results to the service consumer.

It is key to understand that microservice architecture means eventual consistency and partial transactions. Not all monoliths benefit from microservice migration, not as a whole at least. A safe decision can be to split between the core and satellites. Satellites will be migrated as microservices while key transactional processes remain in a reduced core with full consistency.

Some large organizations or historical businesses have been running extremely critical and safe business software without many production issues for years. They consider themselves IT leaders and are right to think so, as key players in their business and very strong IT practitioners. They can consider that they are capable performing as Netflix or Twitter, and of course, replicating is always less difficult than creating a new architecture.

However, we must always make sure we do not lose more than a tweet or coffee when things go wrong when we consider microservices and database per service.

3 Plan Your Journey

In the previous section, we identified why microservice architecture requires specific design. Using this knowledge and real migration projects return of experience, we have built a methodology to help adopt microservice architecture and migrate existing monoliths. In the upcoming paragraphs, we will go into explaining a methodology to safely strangle your existing monolith and turn it into a microservice-based application. We will highlight key elements by describing microservice-related tools and frameworks when they are of interest.

Generally speaking, the methodology is based on a few key concepts:

- **(R)Evolutionary architecture**: Microservice architecture is a revolution to application development practice, operational methods, and architecture design. It affects the structure of organizations, the way people work, and how teams work. The definition and implementation of a microservice architecture should happen step by step as the number of microservices grow and based on return of experience in order to improve and adjust the design over time. The architecture must be designed to be flexible not to be perfect (evolutionary [23] architecture). The objective must not be to start a project only when the architecture is perfectly defined. Furthermore, the goal is not to make a technical revolution by designing everything ahead. Always keep in mind that we are not looking for architectural perfection, we are looking for a pragmatic constant enhancement to boost the agility of our organization to support and favor constantly changing business. The right architecture mutates to accommodate changes.
- **Current and future architecture**: There may be a significant gap between the current technical architecture and the target architecture. Polyglot architecture and Database per service make the new ecosystem protean and multidimensional. The architecture must evolve step by step, each step defined as per the benefit it brings. This can be new architectural features to be able to take a service out of the monolith, better automation for testing and release management, or increase scalability of a business features that will do well with eventual consistency. While peeling the monolith the architecture must be able to manage the communication between the old and the new components. Old platform, such as mainframe, or old programming languages with limited interfaces can prove difficult to interact with, data synchronization may prove difficult (VSAM files, for instance, CODASYL database, CICS transactions). Therefore, the target architecture must be clearly defined and its characteristics must be defined based on the existing system technical limits and new platform capabilities. Fitness function is a good tool to assess the required characteristics of an architecture. By defining a fitness function, it is possible to control the convergence of an architecture to the desired final state we want to reach.

  Be sure to define your target architecture characteristics with a fitness function you can assess in detail (scalability, rich user interface, consistency model, configurability, automatic testing capability, monitorability, etc.) and a compliance function to measure and fill the gap between old and new architecture. This will

be even truer if your monolith is a mainframe monolith, in which case you will have to go through different scenario and intermediate architecture steps (partial migration, data synchronization, specific data storage format and technologies, programming languages barriers, etc.) to adapt to mainframe capabilities to support data synchronization and to execute transactions with both external and internal programs.

– **Macro then micro**: Defining boundaries in a business application is not an easy task and is better done iteratively. Code of features is usually more tightly coupled than expected and code/data dependencies within the monolith must be analyzed and solved.

  Going directly to a fine-grained definition may require post migration refactoring of microservices. This could be a problem because it is always much simpler to refactor within a module than across distributed modules. Indeed, distributed modules do not execute in the same environment, thus former common variables and shared memory must be removed. Method calls will be affected as well to support remote call, transaction boundaries and new scope of objects.

  When transforming a monolith we must take time to analyze dependencies between the microservices boundaries to be. Anytime decomposition is too complex, we advise to start with a macro microservice that will later be decomposed into smaller parts.

  Furthermore going macro-then-micro will allow restoring knowledge that is buried into a 40-year-old code and technology. Which such strategy the microservice definition is based on reliable knowledge, this simplify complex refactoring which could unbalance the service decomposition.

– **Automate, automate, automate**: Microservices are more complex to operate than regular applications. The more they are deployed the more the need for operational maturity and automation. Specific testing practice and methodology [24, 25] is required and some prerequisites are mandatory [26]:

  • Automating product making with continuous integration and continuous deployment in order to deploy any service update at any time while keeping track of deployed services and versions.
  • Automate infrastructure management to deploy hundreds and thousands of IT components (code, containers, container orchestration, load balancers, API gateways for traffic routing, monitoring, external partner entry points, and ACL). Public cloud should be considered to benefit from on-demand and self-service IaaS and PaaS for scalability reasons and automation capabilities. Public cloud can't be matched to provision machines and containers versus on-premise infrastructure.
  • Automate static code analysis to support domain definition from legacy applications. Many older systems are gigantic (50 million lines of code, 10,000 tables), while knowledge is gone. Such systems were built 30–50 years ago and people in charge long retired. It is therefore difficult to derive from workshops and business information how the logic is distributed into the code base and databases. Moreover, the monolith may rely on technologies which

operate differently from modern languages and you may make mistakes if you do not use appropriate tools. This is typical to mainframe modernization when modernizing stacks, such as CICS, VSAM, RPG 4000, and the like. Advanced and accurate Static Analysis is a strong asset in such cases.
- Automate transformation when coming from Mainframe. Surprisingly, Cobol applications have a natural fit for microservices on some topics. Indeed they are made of run units, basically a group of programs compiled and bundled in small runnable units. From a compilation standpoint, mainframe applications are a collection of smaller executables. This gives room for automating analysis, transformations, and automatic code migration [27].

– **Eventually, it is all about organization readiness**: Technology is important but in the end the human factor is prime, and three criteria must be assessed. The first one is the skill of the development and operation teams. The second one is the organization capability to fully embrace DevOps culture. The third is to accept to organize microservice teams as fully autonomous cross-functional units (including the full range of skills required for the development: user-experience, database, and project management) in order not to fall into Conwayss law [28].

  Therefore, the migration strategy has to be planed and done as per the team capabilities to make sure they can go through the appropriate learning curve to reach operational excellence. Each team needs to fully embrace DevOps culture and given more freedom. They must be fully responsible for their scope and be ready to manage application and associated middleware from A to Z. In all cases, the mantra must be *"You do it, you take it."*

4 Defining Your Architecture

4.1 Microservice Patterns

As said before there is nothing as the reference architecture for microservice. Instead, many patterns can be used to build a microservice architecture. Furthermore, microservice architecture is still evolving, typically service mesh is emerging as a pattern to consider when deploying many services. Service mesh makes splitting control plane from data plane better. We will not go into the analysis of each pattern in this chapter but we will go into illustrating some that are beneficial to migration (Fig. 17).

4.2 Fitness Function and Architecture Definition

Fitness function was introduced by Neal Ford, Rebecca Parsons, Patrick Kua in “Building Evolutionary Architecture” [23].

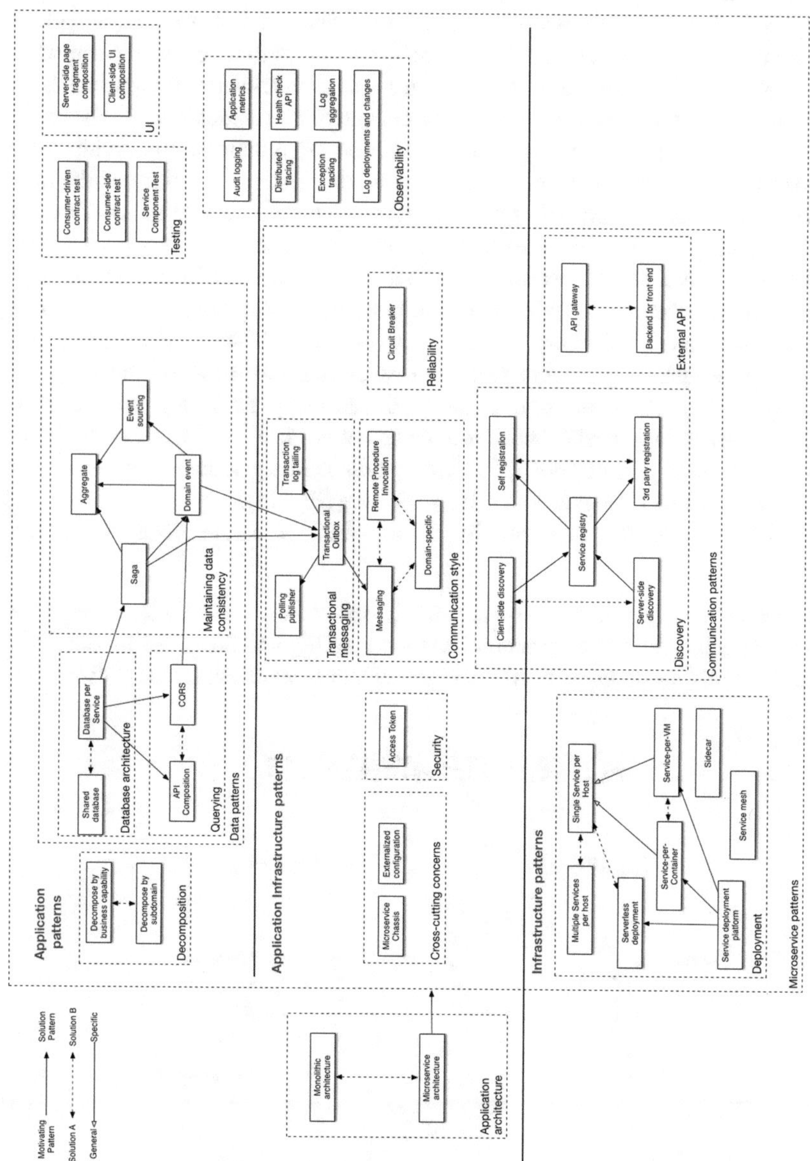

Fig. 17 Some microservice design patterns [29]. Copyright ©2018. Chris Richardson Consulting, Inc. All right reserved. http://microservices.io

The authors borrow a concept from evolutionary computing called *"fitness functions"* used in genetic algorithm design to define success. Evolutionary computing includes a number of mechanisms that allow a solution to gradually emerge via small changes in each generation of the software. At each generation of the solution, the engineer assesses the current state: Is it closer to or further away from the ultimate goal? Architects define a fitness function to explain what better is and to help measure when the goal is met. In software, fitness functions check that developers preserve important architectural characteristics. By using fitness functions, organizations can successfully describe their current architecture characteristics, decide which to keep, and define the desired capability of the new architecture. Fitness function must be defined for each microservice to benefit from polyglot architecture and to ensure that each microservice relies on its own trade-off.

It is recommendable to describe a number of effective and helpful stacks and architectural principles you either want or must have. You will have to balance between what new architecture can bring to you (scalability, performance) and how their drawback may prevent you from executing your business properly. As illustrated before, sacrificing transactions in finance may not be a good idea even though you want to execute faster and scale better. The below fitness function highlights some key indicators to control when defining a target microservice architecture and how to step its evolution over time (Fig. 18).

We will now describe three simplified use cases and create associated fitness functions:

- **Insurance**: This type of business constantly adds new compute rules to promote new contracts to attract customers; increasing agility and doing partial development is clearly a valuable objective. Negotiating a contract takes time, this is not a

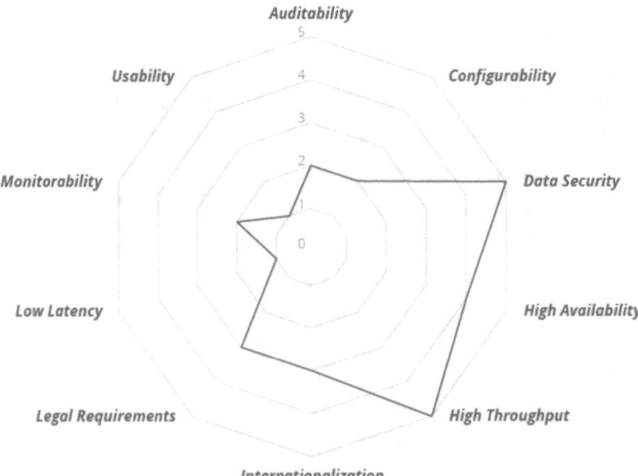

Fig. 18 Example of fitness function definition

real-time system. There is limited chance that concurrent update happens to your records. Therefore, eventual consistency is not a problem. Usually, insurance can easily be decomposed into business-oriented features: life insurance, non-life insurance, risk analysis module, pricing module, and so on. Microservice architecture is a good fit for this type of use case.

- **Stock Exchange**: This is a perfect example of a critical transactional system. Business transactions may group different orders and you may need to execute all or none. The cost for operational failure or partial transactions may be extremely high (multiple millions of dollars) so savings on the development and infrastructure may not be worth the risk of changing the architecture. However, there may be a need for extreme scalability due to the amount of order to be processed per day. Such a use case is more about scalability than isolation and agility. A serverless approach or a regular distributed system with message queuing is most probably a better solution than a microservice architecture.
- **CIS: Crime Investigation Software**: This is a use case which can easily be decomposed into different features: geolocation of the person of interest, video streaming while pursuing or arresting a criminal, DNA sequencing and comparison, expert system to establish relationships based on cellphone information. We can easily see how different technologies would help, for instance, a postGIS database would be very helpful for geolocation, while a graph database associated with the Gremlin programming language would allow for extremely simple and powerful relationship graph analysis (Figs. 19 and 20).

Each fitness function helps analyze the business domain to be implemented based on individual characteristics: data isolation, eventual consistency, real time processing, scalability, streaming capability, cost for automation, cost for failure. etc.

Nevertheless, in the end, your fitness function must be evaluated in order to better your business and not to implement a technology you believe is valuable. We strongly advise to share and look for architecture and frameworks feedback; technology radar [30] exists to review and share return of experienced in a structured manner. As the number of microservice grows so does the number of autonomous teams; radars are good to promote feedback and advises as microservice architecture becomes successful.

4.3 Static Analysis: Purpose and Key Features

Once fitness functions are defined, it is possible to guide the migration. Each microservice candidate migration will be managed using this technique and gradually its underlying architecture will converge to the final target. However, this does not allow for analyzing with details how the current system is made. That information is within the code base and there may be specific constructs in legacy systems that make them difficult to migrate from a technical perspective.

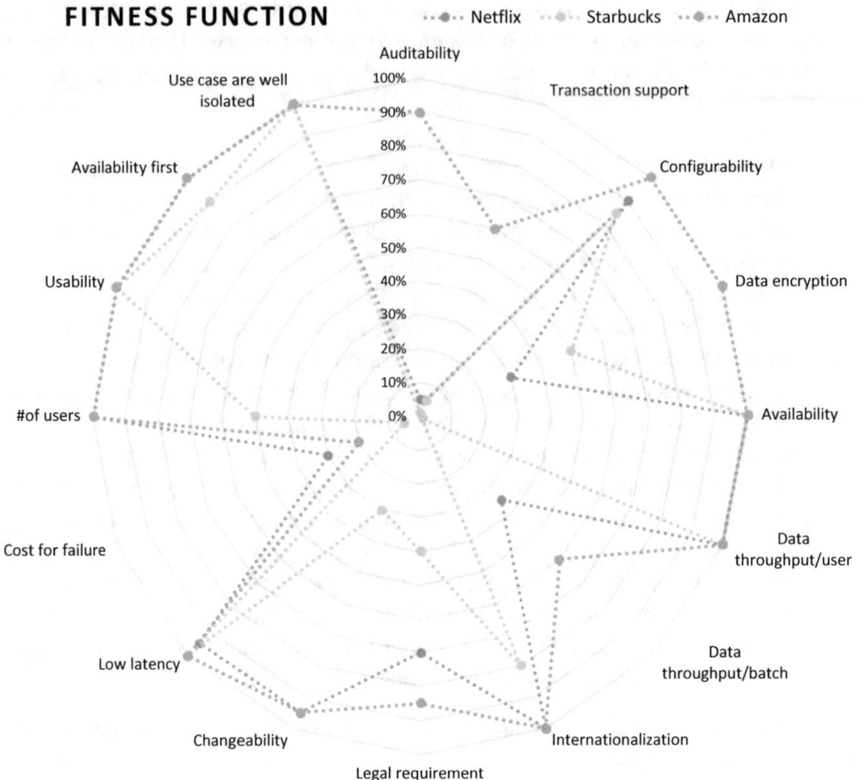

Fig. 19 Examples of fitness functions

Unfortunately, monoliths—and more specifically mainframe monoliths—have grown over the years with overwhelming complexity. They often mix different languages and datastores with various interfaces, evolving coding standards, online and batch, and millions of lines of code.

A deep understanding of the legacy assets to transform is one of the key steps for building a successful migration strategy. However, analyzing millions of lines of code written in various legacy languages is a long and tedious task. Cobol, Pacbase, PL1, and even Java are not point-and-click technologies. Software architects have to identify the application architecture, entry points (start of transactions, batch chains), direct and indirect dependencies through data calls, main programs, isolated programs, dead code, static and dynamic calls, etc. Therefore, there is a need for performing fine-grained code analysis to identify dependencies on large heterogeneous software.

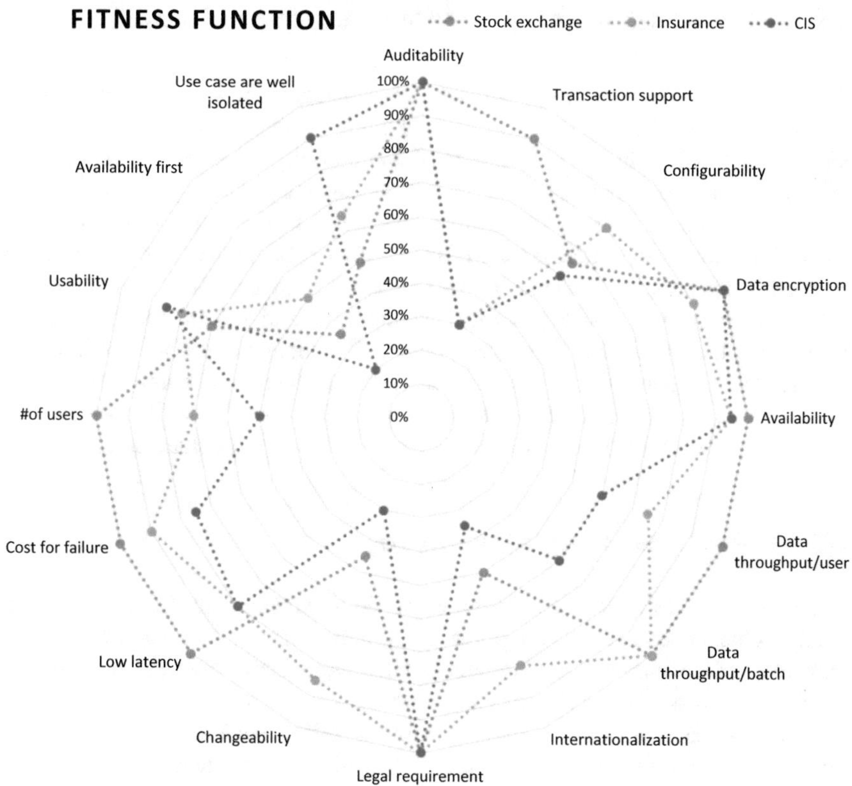

Fig. 20 Examples of fitness functions

First, dependencies must be analyzed and solved. Only programs that satisfy with all dependencies solving are grouped and then transformed into microservices. However, satisfying all may create huge components. The following kinds of dependencies must be solved:

- Method call dependencies
- Local data access dependencies (to files, for instance)
- In memory data dependencies (singleton in memory, for instance)
- Containment dependencies (encapsulation, association, aggregation, composition)
- Inheritance dependencies (plus interface dependencies)
- Type dependencies

In addition, dependencies may be direct (A depends on B) or indirect (B depends on C, A depends on B, therefore A depends on C).

4.4 Analysis: Methodology for Managing Dependencies

One difficulty when performing service decomposition for a microservice architecture is the fact that each microservice is going to be executed on a distributed network and will rely on a topology of middleware components, ecosystems, and, in general, dependencies. This means that memory cannot be shared among deployed services and that any resource access and method call is done over the network. Because each microservice is deployed as a standalone product, packages from other microservices cannot be included at deployment time. Therefore, all dependencies between packages must be removed and remote resource access must be implemented. This makes the slicing—the context boundary definition—a complex task. Depending on the workload or monolith size and complexity, one or multiple patterns can be combined to cover most situations. Therefore, the peeling strategy must be derived from how groups of related programs share data.

4.4.1 Peel with Data-Independent Services

This is a favorable pattern where the extracted service and monolith have independent data dependencies. Programs are grouped into a domain, forming the boundaries of the microservice. Domain boundaries are defined around low coupling interfaces, such as file transfer, message queuing, reports, and business intelligence queries. The data model is strictly consistent within each domain, within the remaining monolith data store, and within the microservice data store. One data-independent microservice is extracted and moved to your cloud or containerized environment (Fig. 21).

4.4.2 Peel with Data Eventual Consistency

This is a pattern where there are data dependencies between the extracted service and monolith. Data is replicated across the mainframe and your selected cloud.

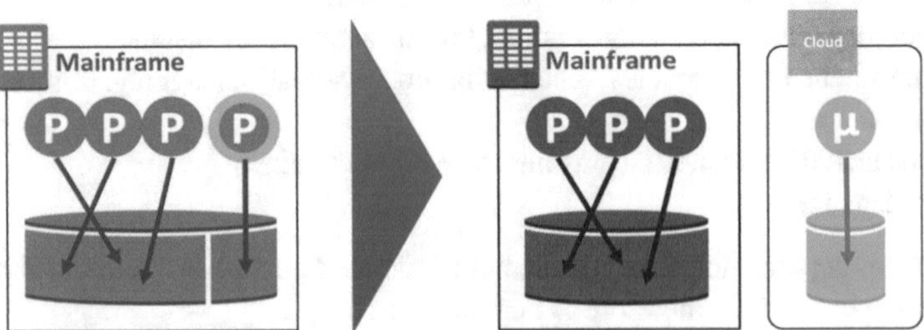

Fig. 21 Data-independent services

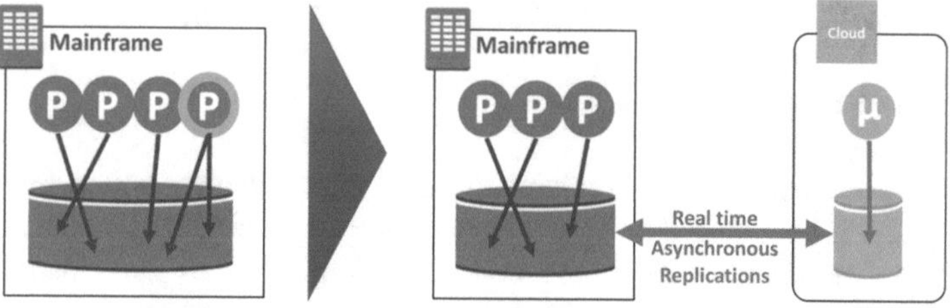

Fig. 22 Eventual consistency with real-time replication

It avoids network latency or jitter, which would be unmanageable for typical I/O-intensive mainframe batch programs, or detrimental to high-throughput online backend transactions. One data-dependent service is extracted and moved to your selected cloud, and dependent data is asynchronously replicated both ways in real-time. Because of the bidirectional asynchronous replication, there is data eventual consistency. For conflict resolution, based on workload analysis and access types, strategies such as mainframe-as-a-reference or Last Write Win can be adopted (Fig. 22).

4.4.3 Group Then Peel with Strict Consistency

When there are too many write dependencies or strong transactionality requirements, eventual consistency can become a challenge. In this pattern, groups of programs and their data dependencies are moved altogether in order to preserve strict consistency. Data-dependent programs are grouped in data-independent groups. One data-independent group is extracted and moved to AWS microservices with a shared datastore. Eventually, individual microservices may benefit from a separate deployment stack or datastore (Fig. 23).

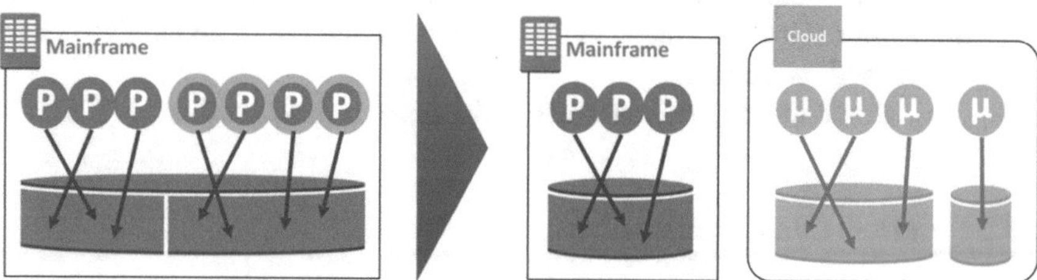

Fig. 23 Group then peel with strict consistency

4.5 *Domain Boundaries and Deployment Schedule*

4.5.1 Guarantee Data Consistency

Data adds complexity because microservices are atomic only within themselves, meaning that if an external service orchestrates using multiple microservices then there is no global transaction atomicity. This can lead to data inconsistency. Therefore, when splitting a monolith into individual microservices, one must decide which strategies are valid with regard to the underlying use cases. The choice of target design patterns impacts how a monolith splits into microservices and what are the microservices data consistency capabilities. Here are the various options concerning transaction atomicity and data consistency:

- At first we suggest not to use a database per domain pattern [31] and keep a central database with ACID [20] capabilities. This decision can be made globally or for collaborating services which require data consistency.
- At this stage keep technology which allows preserving 2PC [32–34] (two-phase commit) when you must guarantee transactions atomicity.
- Favor availability over consistency for use cases which do well with a potential delay for synchronization.
- When using a database per domain and eventual consistency, then rollback and transactions scope no longer exists. Make sure the architecture relies on design patterns that increase the robustness of data state across service boundaries. Try-cancel/confirm (TCC) [35] patterns and message queuing with data retention should be included in the underlying architecture to simplify service choreography failure management.
- In all cases where BASE [36] is favored over 2PC (two-phase commit) and ACID, the system must be designed for failure: Service choreography will occasionally fail and data will be inconsistent. We suggest proceeding as follows to support BASE systems:
    - Spread the architecture with redundancy and canary/blue-green deployment.
    - Test your production environment to see how it would react to failure. (Netflix even stresses its live production by creating failure to ensure the live system is designed for failure.)
    - Build data fixing algorithms to detect discrepancies and fix it.

4.5.2 Address Configuration Management Issues

As microservices grow, more and more containers (or virtual instances or server instances or serverless processes) will be deployed. Due to microservice design for failure, multiple instances of microservices will be deployed: different versions as per canary design pattern, different locations for redundancy, on the fly deployment for performance, or last minute release push due to business reasons.

Software architects should consider that the microservice architecture is a hive, it is a live thing, in perpetual change. Containers are spawned, retired, moved, versioned, copied, changed, reconfigured, redeployed. All of this happens fast and automatically to serve new connections. Very soon, the configuration management may become a nightmare that results in loss of all benefits of microservice. Therefore, all of the following must be automated with full traceability:

- What is deployed, from which code version, using which compile and packaging scripts?
- Where are microservices deployed?
- Which compute configuration? Load balanced, clustered, serverless, container? Which container configuration?
- Which middleware and service choreography? Using API gateway? Which configuration of API gateway?
- We need to remove all 1.5 versions of microservice A, how do we do this? We want to update 30% of version 2.0 of the same microservice to version 2.5, how do we do this? How can we make sure that new connections are balanced so that only 25% of new users connect to updated services?
- We have a failure, how can we make sure to what feature this component is contributing?

When designing, building, compiling, and deploying microservices, all elements must be tagged to enable traceability in order for configuration management and monitoring tools to use tag information. Only full continuous integration and automation may satisfy this constraint.

4.5.3 Database Patterns Pros and Cons

One key decision to make when designing microservices is to choose the database pattern based on data consistency requirements. Financial systems or lifesaving systems typically require the strongest consistency model. Other systems may accept eventual consistency to favor performance, lower coupling, and promote business efficiency.

The following table details what consistency support is associated with database and peeling patterns (Fig. 24).

Strict consistency and ACID (atomicity, consistency, isolation, durability) transaction support provide automatic transaction rollback in case of failure. The database and transaction servers of the application perform it transparently.

On the contrary, eventual consistency cannot use such transaction feature and requires additional application code or mechanisms to manage failure. For example, with API composition the try-cancel/confirm (TCC) [35] pattern or saga [37] pattern may be implemented to remediate failures. With data synchronization, replication retry and conflict resolution strategies may be implemented.

The shared database pattern preserves strict consistency and transaction support. It is therefore appealing when transitioning from mainframe to AWS in hybrid

Data Pattern	Database Pattern	Peeling Pattern	Application-level Consistency Model	Application-level Transaction Support
Independent data	Database per domain	Peel with data-independent services	Strict consistency	Yes
Shared data	Shared database	Group then Peel with data strict consistency	Strict consistency	Yes
Shared data	Database per domain with API composition	Peel with data eventual consistency	Eventual consistency	No
Shared data	Database per domain with data synchronization	Peel with data eventual consistency	Eventual consistency	No

Fig. 24 Consistency and transaction support per peeling pattern

mode. This mitigates the need for manual code changes and advantages refactoring automation well, which is the reason it often reduces risks to first use the shared database pattern and then move on to using the database per domain pattern if needed.

The database-per-domain patterns require explicit domain boundaries. These are typically defined iteratively with complex manual refactoring until boundaries are eventually stable. Usually, the data synchronization pattern is preferred over API composition, as it provides better performance, agility, and accommodates mainframe workload batches.

4.6 *Operating Microservices*

4.6.1 Ops, DevOps, NoOps

Operating microservices is different from operating monoliths. We have explained the need for automation and autonomy. DevOps techniques have a natural fit with microservice architecture but you should not consider this as the end of your DevOps journey.

Indeed DevOps and automation still rely on system administrators and developers. For instance, if an organization is using Docker containers with Kafka (for the communication layer), Cassandra (for the database), and Nginx (for load balancing), it still requires a lot of configuration and most probably a lot of effort when failure happens. Furthermore, this does not solve the communication problem when debugging is required to solve a complex and critical failure in production.

In such cases, the next step is NoOps. NoOps is based on a self-service "infrastructure" and advanced cloud services such as managed services and serverless frameworks. Doing so a microservice architecture relies on self-managed, auto-scalable and autohealing software services which do not require developers to manage the underlying infrastructure. Indeed the cloud provider manage all of this and whatever the number of underlying devices we do not have to worry for this and we do not even see them. Only coding the application is required. Scaling is automatic and guaranteed. Unscaling as well and so do availability.

Managed databases such as Dynamo DB, distributed messaging such as KMS and Kinesis, managed service mesh, and API gateway are standard services of public cloud vendors. On top of this, serverless platforms allow complete disappearance of the infrastructure. It is now possible to create technical architecture that do not require a split between operations and developers.

This was clearly foreseen by Netflix as early as 2012: There is no ops organization involved in running our cloud, no need for the developers to interact with ops people to get things done, and less time spent actually doing ops tasks than developers would spend explaining what needed to be done to someone else [38].

4.6.2 Consider Public Cloud and Managed Services

Previous perspectives on NoOps led us to the role public cloud may play in your microservices. For quite long, public cloud providers have been seen as IaaS only, meaning providing raw infrastructure for an optimized price/performance ratio.

However, this is very far from what public cloud providers bring to the table for your microservice architecture. Indeed be it AWS, Azure, or Google, they all provide high-level managed services and serverless platforms. It is key to understand what benefit this has for you. Typically Kafka Managed Service (AWS MSk for instance) AWS Kinesis, Azure Functions, AWS Aurora make most, if not all, of your operational goals disappear. All of availability, up/down scalability, pay per use, and self-healing are automated and guaranteed by your providers.

Of course organization could decide to buy tons of servers, create their perfect Kubernetes clusters, manage ten different Kafka and ZooKeeper services on their own. But this is a very significant upfront investment and a perpetual cost (for human resources, sourcing machines, etc.) and it will take time to create this. Moreover, and more importantly, they will never reach the quality and operational excellence provided by AWS, Azure, Google, and others.

This is key because microservice is about being prime and fast. If you are the first to provide a new feature and if you continue to innovate faster you will attract and keep customers to yourself. If you decide to copy Google or AWS, then by the time you are ready the game is over and the new kids on the block have become the true leaders.

In the past, most organizations were afraid of public cloud, considering them proprietary. However, this is clearly not true. For instance, if we do not wish to rely on AWS Kinesis then we can go for AWS MSK, which is a fully Kafka-compliant service. We can always choose between the native Managed service and the open source managed service; cloud vendors take care of this. Vendor native services will give additional benefits and optimization, while open source managed services allow to change provider or in-source at any time!

This is true for managed database, communication middleware, container orchestrators, service mesh, and even serverless platforms.

Organizations that wish to get all benefits (first to innovate, faster to release new services, best price/performance ratio) should consider to go direct to public cloud providers.

5 Conclusion

In this chapter, we aimed at illustrating why assessing microservice readiness is important and why it is not limited to choosing technology.

Because microservice architecture comes from isolation and shares as little concepts as possible, we established the need to create a balance between microservice architecture benefits and drawbacks.

Then we explained the need for automation and eventual consistency. With the support of fitness function, we investigated theoretical use cases to establish when Microservice architecture is a benefit and when it should be avoided.

Then we concluded with introducing NoOps model and the advantages of deploying it to managed services provided by public cloud vendors.

This chapter can be read standalone but is also an introduction to "Migrating to Microservice" chapter that specifically focuses on migration strategy.

References

1. A. Lee. Unicorn (finance) (2018). https://en.wikipedia.org/wiki/unicorn_(finance)
2. A.M. Glen, Microservices priorities and trends (2018), https://dzone.com/articles/dzone-research-microservices-priorities-and-trends
3. M. Feathers, Microservice mistakes—complexity as a service (2015), https://iasaglobal.org/microservice-mistakes-complexity-as-a-service/
4. N. Bohorquez, The complexity of scaling a microservices architecture (2018), https://thenewstack.io/the-complexity-of-scaling-a-microservices-architecture/
5. D. Kerr, The death of microservice madness in 2018 (2018), https://dwmkerr.com/the-death-of-microservice-madness-in-2018/
6. C. Posta, The hardest part about microservices: your data (2016), https://blog.christianposta.com/microservices/the-hardest-part-about-microservices-data/
7. M. Fowler, Microservice trade-offs (2014), https://martinfowler.com/articles/microservice-trade-offs.html
8. R. Parsons, Microservice in adopt, 2019
9. Cap Theorem, https://en.wikipedia.org/wiki/cap_theorem
10. L. Nicolas, The confusing cap and acid wording (2019), http://blog.thislongrun.com/2015/03/the-confusing-cap-and-acid-wording.html
11. S. Gilbert, N. Lynch, *Brewer's Conjecture and the Feasibility of Consistent, Available, Partition-Tolerant Web Services*, vol. 33 (ACM SIGACT News, 2002)
12. E. Brewer, *CAP Twelve Years Later: How the 'rules' Have Changed*, vol. 45 (Computer 2012)
13. M. Fowler, Microservices, a definition of this new architectural term (2014), https://martinfowler.com/articles/microservices.html
14. C. Richardson, *Microservices Patterns* (Manning, Shelter Island, 2018)
15. A. Maslow, *The Psychology of Science* (Harper & Row, New York, 1966)

16. A. Maslow, The law of the instrument. https://en.wikipedia.org/wiki/law_of_the_instrument
17. M.M. Ed Bukoski, B. Moyles, How we build code at Netflix (2016), https://medium.com/netflix-techblog/how-we-build-code-at-netflix-c5d9bd727f15
18. D. Sato, Canary release (2014), https://martinfowler.com/bliki
19. R. Wilsenach, DevOps culture (2015), https://martinfowler.com/bliki/devopsculture.html
20. A. Reuter, T. Haerder, Principles of transaction-oriented database recovery. ACM Comput. Surv. **15**(4), 287–317 (1983)
21. G. Hohpe, Your coffee shop doesn't use two-phase commit (2015), https://www.enterpriseintegrationpatterns.com/docs/ieee_software_design_2pc.pdf
22. W. Labaj, What starbucks can teach us about software scalability (2016), https://dzone.com/articles/what-starbucks-can-teach-us-about-software-scalabi
23. P. Kua, N. Ford, R. Parsons, *Building Evolutionary Architectures* (O'Reilly, Sebastopol, 2017)
24. T. Clemson, Microservice testing (2014), https://martinfowler.com/articles/microservice-testing/
25. S. Newman, *Building Microservices* (O'Reilly, Sebastopol, 2015)
26. M. Fowler, Microservice prerequesites, 2014
27. A. Henry, Mainframe batch to microservice (2018), https://aws.amazon.com/fr/blogs/apn/how-to-migrate-mainframe-batch-to-cloud-microservices-with-blu-age-and-aws/
28. M. Conway, Conway's law. https://en.wikipedia.org/wiki/conway%27s_law
29. C. Richardson, Micro service design patterns (2018), https://microservices.io/patterns/index.html
30. Thoughtworks, Technology radar. https://www.thoughtworks.com/radar
31. C. Richardson, Database per service pattern (2018), https://microservices.io/patterns/data/database-per-service.html
32. Two phase commit protocol. https://en.wikipedia.org/wiki/two-phase_commit_protocol
33. N. Goodman, P.A. Bernstein, V. Hadzilacos, *Concurrency Control and Recovery in Database Systems* (Addison Wesley, Reading, 1987)
34. E. Newcomer, P.A. Bernstein, *Principles of Transaction Processing*, 2nd edn. (Morgan Kaufmann, Los Altos, 2009)
35. G. Pardon, Transaction management for rest api (2014), https://www.atomikos.com/blog/transactionmanagementapiforresttcc
36. Base vs. acid, https://www.johndcook.com/blog/2009/07/06/brewer-cap-theorem-base/
37. C. Richardson, Saga pattern. http://microservices.io/patterns/data/saga.html
38. A. Cockcroft, Ops and DevOps at Netflix (2012), http://perfcap.blogspot.com/2012/03/ops-devops-and-noops-at-netflix.html

Part III
Modeling

Microservices Anti-patterns: A Taxonomy

Davide Taibi, Valentina Lenarduzzi, and Claus Pahl

Abstract Several companies are rearchitecting their monolithic information systems with microservices. However, many companies migrate to microservices without experience, mainly learning how to migrate from books or from practitioners' blogs. Because of the novelty of the topic, practitioners and consultancies are learning by doing how to migrate, thus facing several issues but also several benefits. In this chapter, we introduce a catalog and a taxonomy of the most common microservices anti-patterns in order to identify common problems. Our anti-pattern catalog is based on the experience summarized by different practitioners we interviewed in the last 3 years. We identified a taxonomy of 20 anti-patterns, including organizational (team oriented and technology/tool oriented) anti-patterns and technical (internal and communication) anti-patterns. The results can be useful to practitioners to avoid experiencing the same difficult situations in the systems they develop. Moreover, researchers can benefit from this catalog and further validate the harmfulness of the anti-patterns identified.

1 Introduction

Microservices are increasing in popularity, being adopted by several companies, including SMEs, but also big players such as Amazon, LinkedIn, Netflix, and Spotify.

Microservices are small and autonomous services deployed independently, with a single and clearly defined purpose [11, 14]. Microservices propose to vertically decompose the applications into a subset of business-driven independent services.

D. Taibi (✉) · V. Lenarduzzi
Tampere University, Tampere, Finland
e-mail: davide.taibi@tuni.fi; valentina.lenarduzzi@tuni.fi

C. Pahl
Free University of Bozen-Bolzano, Bolzano, Italy
e-mail: claus.pahl@unibz.it

A. Bucchiarone et al. (eds.), *Microservices*,
https://doi.org/10.1007/978-3-030-31646-4_5

Every service can be developed, deployed, and tested independently by different development teams, and by means of different technology stacks. Microservices have a lot of advantages. They can be developed in different programming languages, they can scale independently from other services, and they can be deployed on the hardware that best suits their needs. Moreover, because of their size, they are easier to maintain and more fault-tolerant since the failure of one service may not break the whole system, which could happen in a monolithic system.

However, the migration to microservice is not an easy task [17, 19, 22, 27]. Companies commonly start the migration without experience with microservices, only in a few cases hiring a consultant to support them during the migration [22, 27]. Therefore, companies often face common problems, which are mainly due to their lack of knowledge regarding bad practices and patterns [4, 17, 22, 27].

In this chapter, we provide a taxonomy of architectural and organizational anti-patterns specific to microservices-based systems, together with possible solutions to overcome them. To produce this catalog, we adopted a mixed research method, combining industrial survey, literature review, and interviews. We replicated and extended our previous industrial surveys [24, 27] also considering the bad practices proposed by practitioners (Table 7). We surveyed and interviewed 27 experienced developers in 2018, focusing on bad practices they found during the development of microservices-based systems and the solutions they adopted to overcame them. The interviews were based on the same questionnaire we adopted in [27], with the addition of a section where we asked the interviewees if they experienced some of the anti-patterns proposed by practitioners (Table 7). We proposed a taxonomy of 20 microservices-specific anti-patterns, by applying an open and selective coding [23] procedure to derive the anti-pattern catalog from the practitioners' answers.

The goal of this work is to help practitioners avoid these bad practices altogether or deal with them more efficiently when developing or migrating monoliths to microservices-based systems.

The remainder of this chapter is structured as follows. Section 2 describes the empirical study we carried out. Section 3 reports results. Section 4 describes the background on microservices and related works, while Sect. 5 draws conclusions.

2 The Empirical Study

As reported in the introduction, the goal of this work is to provide a taxonomy of anti-patterns specific for microservices.

We first collected the anti-patterns by means of a survey among experienced developers, collecting bad practices in microservices architectures and how they overcame them. Then, we classified the anti-patterns and proposed a taxonomy. Therefore, we formulated our research questions as:

RQ1 What anti-patterns have been experienced by practitioners when using microservices?
In this RQ, we aim at understanding if practitioners experienced some anti-patterns, including these proposed in previous works (Table 7), which problem the anti-pattern caused, and how they overcame the problem they caused.

RQ2 What type of anti-patterns have been identified by practitioners?
In this RQ, we aim at classify the different anti-patterns identified by means of a taxonomy.

2.1 Study Design

We designed the survey with semistructured interviews, both in a structured fashion, via a questionnaire with closed answers, and in a less structured way, by asking the interviewees open-answer questions to elicit additional relevant information (such as possible issues when migrating to microservices). One of the most important goals of the questionnaire was to understand which bad practices have the greatest impact on system development and which solutions are being applied by practitioners to overcome them.

Thus, we asked the interviewees to rank every bad practice on a scale from 0 to 10, where 0 meant "the bad practice is not harmful" and 10 meant "the bad practice is exceedingly harmful." Moreover, we clarified that only the ranking of the bad practices has real meaning. As an example, a value of 7 for the "hardcoded IPs" bad practice and 5 for "shared persistence" shows that hardcoded IPs is believed to be more harmful than shared persistence, but the individual values of 7 and 5 have no meaning in themselves. Harmful practice refers to a practice that has created some issue for the practitioner, such as increasing maintenance effort, reducing code understandability, increasing faultiness, or some other issue.

The interviews were based on a questionnaire organized into four sections, according to the information we aimed to collect:

- Personal and company information: interviewee's role and company's application domain.
- Experience in developing microservices-based systems: number of years of experience in developing microservices. This question was asked to ensure that data was collected only from experienced developers.
- Microservices bad practices harmfulness: List of the practices that created some issues during the development and maintenance of microservices-based applications ranked according to their harmfulness on a 10-point Likert scale. Moreover, for each practice, we asked to report which problem was generated and why they considered it harmful. For this answer, the interviewer did not provide

any hints, letting the participants report the bad practices they had faced while developing or maintaining microservices-based systems. Moreover, in order to avoid influencing the interviewees, we asked them to list their own bad practices, without providing them with a list of pitfalls previously identified by practitioners [1, 5, 20, 21, 27].

- Bad practices solutions: For each bad practice identified, we asked the participants to report how they overcame it.
- Rank the harmfulness of the bad practices previously identified in previous study [27] and those identified by practitioners (Table 7): After the open questions, for each of the bad practices reported we asked (1) if they ever experienced that issue and (2) in case they did, to rank the harmfulness on a 10-point Likert scale. We decided to ask interviewees to ranking the harmfulness of the bad practices proposed in the literature after the open questions, to avoid bias based on results of the previous questionnaire. While ranking the bad practices proposed in the literature, practitioners also noted if some of the bad practices they specified in the open questions had the same meaning as those reported in the literature, thus reducing the risk of misinterpretation of their classification.

We are aware that the structure of this questionnaire increased the collection time, but helped us to increase the quality of the answers, avoiding bias among participants with a preselected set of answers.

2.2 Study Execution

All interviews were conducted in person. An online questionnaire might have yielded a larger set of answers, but we believe that face-to-face interviews are more reliable for collecting unstructured information, as they allow establishing a more effective communication channel with the interviewees and make it easier to interpret open answers.

The interviewees were asked to provide individual answers, even if they worked in the same group. This allowed us to get a better understanding of different points of view, and not only the company's point of view.

We selected the participants from the attendees of two practitioner events. We interviewed 14 participants of the O'Reilly Software Architecture Conference in London (October 2018) and 13 participants of the international DevOps conference in Helsinki (December 2018). During the interviews, we first introduced our goals to the participants and then asked them if they had at least 2 years of experience in developing microservices-based systems, so as to save time and avoid including nonexperienced practitioners.

2.3 *Data Analysis*

We partitioned the responses into homogeneous subgroups based on demographic information in order to compare the responses obtained from all the participants with the different subgroups separately.

Ordinal data, such as 10-point Likert scales, were not converted into numerical equivalents, since using a conversion from ordinal to numerical data entails the risk that subsequent analysis will give misleading results if the equidistance between the values cannot be guaranteed. Moreover, analyzing each value of the scale allows us to better identify the possible distribution of the answers. The harmfulness of the bad practices was analyzed calculating the medians, as customarily done for ordinal ranges.

Open questions were analyzed via open and selective coding [23]. In addition, practitioners were asked to report if some of the bad practices they reported in the first section of the questionnaire were related to some of the anti-patterns reported in Table 7, some practitioners proposed a set of bad practices not directly related to the existing anti-patterns. Therefore, for these cases, we extracted codes from the answers provided by the participants and answers were grouped into different anti-patterns. Answers were interpreted extracting concrete sets of similar answers and grouping them based on their perceived similarity. The qualitative data analysis was conducted individually by two authors. Moreover, in order to get a fair/good agreement on the first iteration of this process, pairwise inter-rater reliability was measured across the three sets of decisions. Based on the disagreements, we clarified possible discrepancies and different classifications. A second iteration resulted in 100% agreement among all the authors.

The taxonomy was then proposed by two of the authors that grouped different set of anti-patterns into homogeneous categories and then was validated by the third author.

3 The Study Results

We conducted 27 interviews with participants belonging to 27 different organizations. No unexperienced participants such as students, academics, or non-industrial practitioners were considered for the interviews. Thirty-six percent of our participants were software architects, 19% project managers, 38% experienced developers, and 7% agile coaches. All the interviewees had at least 4 years of experience in software development. Of our interviewees 28.57% worked for software development companies, 28.57% for companies that produce and sell only their own software as a service (e.g., website builders, mobile app generators, and others), and 9.52% in banks/insurances. Seventeen percent had adopted microservices for more than 5 years, 60% had adopted them for 3 to 4 years, and the remaining 23% for 2 to 3 years.

On top of the proposed bad practices identified in [27] and in (Table 7), the practitioners reported a total of nine different bad practices together with the solutions they had applied to overcome them. Two authors of this paper grouped similar practices (considering both the description and the justification of the harmfulness provided by the participants) by means of open and selective coding [23]. In cases where they interpreted the descriptions differently, they discussed incongruities so as to achieve agreement on similar issues.

3.1 Data Analysis and Interpretation

The answers were mainly analyzed using descriptive statistics. No noticeable differences emerged among different roles or domains. As reported in Table 1, eight anti-patterns proposed by practitioners have never been experienced by the interviewees while four new ones were introduced. Wrong cuts, cyclic dependencies, hardcoded endpoints, and shared persistency are still considered the most harmful issues.

Different from our previous study, more organizational issues are now playing an important role during migration to microservices. Participants considered very important the alignment between the organization structure and the system architecture. Moreover, they also highlighted the importance of having a fully functional DevOps tools pipeline, including continuous testing, integration, and delivery.

However, not all the anti-patterns proposed by practitioners turned out to be harmful. For example, the shared ownership of several microservices from one time is not considered as very important.

Table 1 lists the microservices anti-patterns together with the number and percentage of practitioners who mentioned them (column Answer # and %) and the median of the perceived harmfulness reported.

We identify the taxonomy classifying the anti-patterns experienced by our interviewees into two groups: technical and organizational anti-patterns. Figure 1 depicts the proposed classification. For the purpose of completeness, we report (underlined) the anti-patterns proposed by the practitioners (Table 7) but never experienced by our interviewees. In Tables 2, 3, and 4 we describe the technical anti-patterns that have been reported by our interviewees, and the solutions they adopted to overcome the issues they generated. In Tables 5 and 6 we describe the organizational anti-patterns identified. The results of this work are subject to some threats to validity, mainly due to the selection of the survey participants and to the data interpretation phase. Different respondents might have provided a different set of answers. To mitigate this threat, we selected a relatively large set of participants

Table 1 The microservices anti-patterns identified in the survey

Microservices anti-pattern	Also proposed by	Answers		Perceived harmfulness (0–10)
		#	%	
Hardcoded endpoints	[20, 27]	10	37	8
Wrong cuts	[27]	15	56	8
Cyclic dependency	[27]	5	19	7
API versioning	[16, 20]	6	22	6.05
Shared persistence	[5, 21, 27]	10	37	6.05
ESB usage	[27]	2	7	6
Legacy organization	[18]	2	7	6
Local logging	NEW	17	63	6
Megaservice	[21]	5	19	6
Inappropriate service intimacy	[27]	5	19	5
Lack of monitoring	NEW	3	11	5
No API-gateway	[1, 27]	4	15	5
Shared libraries	[16, 27]	8	30	4
Too many technologies	[7, 18, 27]	3	11	4
Lack of microservice skeleton	NEW	9	33	3.05
Microservice greedy	[7, 18, 27]	4	15	3
Focus on latest technologies	[18]	2	7	2.05
Common ownership	[7]	4	15	2
No DevOps tools	NEW	2	7	2
Non-homogeneous adoption	[18]	2	7	2
Lack of service abstraction	[21]	0		
Magic Pixie dust	[18]	0		
Microservices as the goal	[18]	0		
Pride	[7]	0		
Sloth	[7]	0		
Timeout	[16, 20]	0		
Try to fly before you can walk	[18]	0		

Harmfulness was measured on a 10-point Likert scale, 0 means “the bad practice is not harmful” and 10 means “the bad practice is extremely harmful”

- Technical
  - Internal: Anti-patterns that impact the individual microservice.
    - API Versioning
    - Hardcoded Endpoints
    - Inappropriate Service Intimacy
    - Megaservice
    - Local Logging
    - Lack of service abstraction
  - Communication: Anti-patterns related to the communication between microservices
    - Cyclic Dependency
    - ESB Usage
    - No API-Gateway
    - Shared Libraries
    - Timeout
  - Others
    - Lack of Monitoring
    - Shared Persistence
    - Wrong Cuts
- Organizational
  - Team-Oriented: Anti-patterns related to the team's dynamics.
    - Legacy Organization
    - Non-homogeneous adoption
    - Common Ownership
    - Microservice Greedy
    - Magic Pixie Dust
    - Microservice as the goal
    - Pride
    - Sloth
  - Technology and Tool Oriented
    - Focus on latest technologies
    - Lack of Microservice Skeleton
    - No DevOps tools

Fig. 1 The proposed microservice anti-pattern taxonomy. The anti-patterns underlined were proposed by the practitioners (Table 7) but never experienced by our interviewees

working in different companies and different domains. During the survey, we did not propose a predefined set of bad practices to the participants so as to not bias their answers based on the results of previous works. However, as the surveys were carried out during public events, we are aware that some participants may have shared some opinions with others during breaks and therefore some answers might have been partially influenced by previous discussions. Finally, the answers were aggregated independently by the two authors by means of open and selective coding [23].

Table 2 Internal anti-patterns

Microservices anti-pattern	Description (Desc)/Detection (Det)	Problem it may cause (P)/Adopted solutions (S)
API versioning	**Desc:** APIs are not semantically versioned	**P:** In the case of new versions of nonsemantically versioned APIs, API consumers may face connection issues. For example, the returning data might be different or might need to be called differently
	Det: Lack of semantic versions in APIs (e.g., v1.1, 1.2)	**S:** APIs need to be semantically versioned to allow services to know whether they are communicating with the right version of the service or whether they need to adapt their communication to a new contract
	Also proposed as "Static Contract Pitfall" by Richards [16] and Saleh [20]	
Hardcoded endpoints	**Desc/Det:** Hardcoded IP addresses and ports of the services between connected microservices	**P:** Microservices connected with hardcoded endpoints lead to problems when their locations need to be changed
	Also proposed by Saleh [20] as "Hardcoded IPs and Ports"	**S:** Adoption of a service discovery approach
Inappropriate service intimacy	**Desc:** The microservice keeps on connecting to private data from other services instead of dealing with its own data	**P:** Connecting to private data of other microservices increases coupling between microservices. The problem could be related to a mistake made while modeling the data
	Det: Request of private data of other microservices. Direct connection to other microservices databases	**S:** Consider merging the microservices
Megaservice	**Desc:** A service that does a lot of things. A monolith	**P:** The same problem of a monolithic system
	Det: Several business processes implemented in the same service. Service composed by several modules, and developed by several developers, or several teams	**S:** Decompose the megaservice into smaller microservices
Local Logging	**Desc/Det:** Logs are stored locally in each microservice, instead of using a distributed logging system	**P:** Errors and microservices information are hidden inside each microservice container. The adoption of a distributed logging system eases the monitoring of the overall system

Table 3 Communications anti-patterns

Microservices anti-pattern	Description (Desc)/detection (Det)	Problem it may cause (P)/adopted solutions (S)
Cyclic dependency	**Desc:** A cyclic chain of calls between microservices	**P:** Microservices involved in a cyclic dependency can be hard to maintain or reuse in isolation
	Det: Existence of cycles of calls between microservices. E.g., A calls B, B calls C, and C calls back A	**S:** Refinement of the cycles according to their shape [15] and application of an API-Gateway pattern [14]
ESB usage	**Desc/Det:** The microservices communicate via an enterprise service bus (ESB)	**P:** ESB adds complexities for registering and de-registering services on the ESB
	Usage of ESB for connecting microservices	**S:** Adopt a lightweight message bus instead of the ESB
No API gateway	**Desc:** Microservices communicate directly with each other. In the worst case, the service consumers also communicate directly with each microservice, increasing the complexity of the system and decreasing its ease of maintenance	**P:** Our interviewees reported being able to work with systems consisting of 50 interconnected microservices; however, if the number was higher, they started facing communication and maintenance issues
	Det: Direct communication between microservices	**S:** Application of an API gateway pattern [14] to reduce the communication complexity between microservices
	Also proposed by Alagarasan [1] as "Not having an API-Gateway."	
Shared libraries	**Desc/Det:** Usage of shared libraries between different microservices	**P:** Tightly coupled microservices together, leading to a loss of independence between them. Moreover, teams need to coordinate with each other when they need to modify the shared library
	Also named "I was taught to share" by Richards [16]	**S:** Two possible solutions: (1) accept the redundancy to increase dependency among teams; (2) extract the library to a new shared service that can be deployed and developed independently by the connected microservices

4 Background and Related Works

Microservices are relatively small and autonomous services deployed independently, with a single and clearly defined purpose [11]. Because of their independent deployment, they have a lot of advantages. They can be developed in different

Table 4 Other technical anti-patterns

Microservices anti-pattern	Description (Desc)/detection (Det)	Problem it may cause (P)/adopted solutions (S)
Lack of monitoring	**Desc/Det:** Lack of usage of monitoring systems, including systems to monitor if a service is alive or if it responds correctly	**P:** A service could be offline, and developers could not realize it without continuous manual checks
		S: Adoption of a monitoring system
Shared persistence	**Desc/Det:** Different microservices access the same relational database. In the worst case, different services access the same entities of the same relational database	**P:** This anti-pattern highly couples the microservices connected to the same data, reducing team and service independence
	Also proposed by Bogard as "data ownership" [5]	**S:** Three possible solutions for this anti-pattern are: use (1) independent databases for each service, (2) a shared database with a set of private tables for each service that can be accessed only by that service, and (3) a private database schema for each service
Wrong cuts	**Desc:** Microservices should be split based on business capabilities, not on technical layers (presentation, business, data layers)	**P:** Wrong separation of concerns, increased data-splitting complexity
		S: Clear analysis of business processes and the need for resources

programming languages, they can scale independently from other services, and they can be deployed on the hardware that best suits their needs. Moreover, because of their size, they are easier to maintain and more fault-tolerant since a failure of one service will not break the whole system, which could happen in a monolithic system. Since every microservice has its own context and set of code, each microservice can change its entire logic from the inside, but from the outside it still does the same thing, reducing the need for interaction between teams [30, 31].

Different microservice patterns have been proposed by practitioners [33] and researchers [32]. Zimmerman et al. [33] proposed a joint collaboration between academia and industry to collect microservices patterns. However, all these works focus on patterns that companies should follow when implementing microservices-based systems instead of anti-patterns and bad smells to avoid. Balalaie [4] also conducted an industrial survey to understand how companies migrated to microservices, obtaining 15 migration patterns.

As for anti-patterns, several generic architectural anti-pattern have been defined in the last years in different research works [8, 12, 13, 26] and different tools

Table 5 Organizational (team-oriented) anti-patterns

Microservices anti-pattern	Description (Desc)/detection (Det)	Problem it may cause (P)/adopted solutions (S)
Legacy organization	**Desc:** The company still work without changing their processes and policies. For example, with independent Dev and Ops teams, manual testing and scheduling common releases	**P:** Developers are bound to the traditional process, they cannot benefit from most of the outcomes of microservices
	Also proposed as "Red Flag" by Richardson [18]	
Nonhomogeneous adoption	**Desc/Det:** Only a few teams migrated to microservices, and the decision to migrate or not is delegated to the teams	**P:** Duplication of effort. E.g., effort for building the infrastructure, deployment pipelines...
	Also defined as "scattershot adoption" by Richardson [18]	
Common ownership	**Desc/Det:** One team owns all the microservices	**P:** Each microservice will be developed in pipeline, and the company is not benefiting from the development independency
Microservice greedy	**Desc:** Teams tend to create new microservices for each feature, even when they are not needed. Common examples are microservices created to serve only one or two static HTML pages	**P:** This anti-pattern can generate an explosion in the number of microservices composing a system, resulting in a huge, useless system that will easily become unmaintainable because of its size. Companies should carefully consider whether the new microservice is needed
	Det: Microservices with very limited functionalities (e.g., a microservice serving only one static HTML page)	

have been proposed both from industry and from researchers to detect them [2, 3, 9, 10, 29]. However, to the best of our knowledge, no peer-reviewed work and, in particular, only few empirical studies have proposed bad practices, anti-patterns, or smells specifically concerning microservices. On the other side, practitioners proposed several anti-patterns, mainly by means of talks in technical events.

As for research works, Bogner et al. [6] reviewed microservices bad smells and anti-patterns proposed in the literature, extracting 36 anti-patterns from 14 peer-reviewed publications. Their survey includes the vast majority of anti-patterns and bad smells highlighted also by practitioners. However, they did not report or classify their harmfulness.

Table 6 Organizational (technology- and tool-oriented) anti-patterns

Microservices anti-pattern	Description (Desc)/detection (Det)	Problem it may cause (P)/adopted solutions (S)
Focus on latest technologies	**Desc:** The migration is focused on the adoption of the newest and coolest technologies, instead of based on real needs. The decomposition is based on the needs of the different technologies aimed to adopt	**P:** The development is not solving existing problems but is mainly following the technology vendor recommendations
	Also proposed as "Focusing on Technology" by Richardson [18]	
Lack of microservice skeleton	**Desc/Det:** Each team develops microservices from scratch, without the benefit of a shared skeleton that would speed up the connection to the shared infrastructure (e.g., connection to the API Gateway)	**P:** Developers have to redevelop the skeleton from scratch every time, wasting time and increasing the risk of errors
		S: Introduction of a common code boilerplate
No DevOps tools	**Desc:** The company does not employ CD/CI tools and developers need to manually test and deploy the system	P: Slower productivity, possible deployment errors due to lack of automation
Too many technologies	**Desc/Det:** Usage of different technologies, including development languages, protocols, frameworks...	**P:** The company does not define a common policy. Although microservices allow the use of different technologies, adopting too many different technologies can be a problem in companies, especially in the event of developer turnover
	Also proposed by Bryant [7] as "Lust" and "Gluttony"	Companies should carefully consider the adoption of different standards for different microservices, without following new hypes

In our previous study [27], we performed an industrial survey investigating the migration processes adopted by companies to migrate to microservice. One of the side results was that practitioners are not aware of the patterns they should adopt and anti-patterns to avoid. In another work we investigated the most used architectural patterns [32], while finally in our latest work [24, 28] we investigated "bad smells" of microservices, specific to systems developed using a microservice architectural style, together with possible solutions to overcome these smells. We identified 20 microservice-specific organizational and technical anti-patterns, bad practices that

Table 7 The main pitfalls proposed in non-peer-reviewed literature and practitioner talks

Bad practice	Description
Timeout (Richards [16]) Dogpiles (Saleh [20])	Management of remote process availability and responsiveness. Richards recommends using a timeout value for service responsiveness or sharing the availability and the unavailability of each service through a message bus, so as to avoid useless calls and potential timeout due to service unresponsiveness
I was taught to share (Richards [16])	Sharing modules and custom libraries between microservices
Static contract pitfall (Richards [16], Saleh [20])	Microservices API are not versioned and therefore service consumers may connect to older versions of the services
Mega-service (Shoup [21])	A service that is responsible for many functionalities and should be decomposed into separated microservices
Shared persistence (Shoup [21]) Data ownership (Bogard [5])	Usage of shared data among services that access the same database. Microservices should own only the data they need and possibly share them via APIs
Leak of service abstraction (Shoup [21])	Service interfaces designed for generic purposes and not specifically designed for each service
Hardcoded IPs and ports (Saleh [20])	Hardcoding the IP address and ports of communicating services, therefore making it harder to change the service location afterwards
Not having an API-Gateway (Alagarasan [1])	Exposing services through an API gateway layer and not connecting them directly so as to simplify the connection, supporting monitoring and delegating authorization issues to the API gateway. Moreover, changes to the API contract can be easily managed by the API gateway, which is responsible for serving the content to different consumers, providing only the data they need
Lust (Bryant [7]) Focus on technology (Richardson [15])	Usage of the latest technologies
Gluttony (Bryant [7])	Usage of too many different communication protocols such as HTTP, ProtoBuffs, Thrift, etc.
Greed (Bryant [7])	All the services belong to the same team
Sloth (Bryant [7])	Creation of a distributed monolith due to the lack of independence of microservices
Wrath (Bryant [7]) Magic pixie dust (Richardson [15])	Believing a sprinkle of microservices will solve the development problems
Microservices as the goal (Richardson [15])	Migrating to microservices because everybody does it, and not because the company needs it
Scattershot adoption (Richardson [15])	Multiple teams independently adopting microservices without coordination
Envy (Bryant [7]) The more the merrier (Richardson [15])	Creating as many microservices as possible
Trying to fly before you can walk (Richardson [15])	Migrating to microservices while lacking the key skills, e.g., clean code, object-oriented design, automated testing
Pride (Bryant [7])	Testing in the world of transience
Red flag law (Richardson [15])	Adopting microservices without changing process, policies, and organization

practitioners found during the development of microservice-based systems, and we highlighted how practitioners overcame them by interviewing 72 experienced developers. Our results [24] are also confirmed by a recent industrial survey performed by Soldani et al. [22]. They identified, and taxonomically classified and compared the existing gray literature on pains and gains of microservices, from their design to their development, among 51 industrial studies. Based on the results, they prepared a catalog of migration and rearchitecting patterns, in order to facilitate rearchitecting non-cloud-native architectures during migration to a cloud-native microservices-based architectures. In another study [25] we proposed a decomposition framework to decompose monolithic systems into microservices, where one of the most important steps is the investigation and removal of possible microservices anti-patterns.

Balalaie [4] also performed an industrial survey proposing a set of 15 migration patterns to understand how companies migrated to microservices. However, they did not report bad practices or anti-patterns. Practitioners have started to discuss bad practices in microservices in recent years. In his eBook [16], Richards introduced three main pitfalls: "Timeout," "I Was Taught to Share," and "Static Contract Pitfall." Moreover, in the last 2 years, practitioners have given technical talks about bad practices they experienced when building microservices. In Table 7, we summarize the main bad practices presented in these works. Chris Richardson recently gave a talk on microservices anti-patterns [18] proposing six organizational anti-patterns based on his consultancy experience.

Unlike these works, we identified a set of microservices anti-patterns based on bad practices reported by the 72 participants of our previous survey [27] and on the 27 participants of this current study. In the Results Section, we map our set of microservices anti-pattern to the bad practices identified in Table 7.

5 Conclusion

In this work, we identified a set of 20 microservices anti-patterns based on bad practices experienced by practitioners while developing microservices-based systems. This review, based partly on earlier work, has resulted as a consequence of the additional surveys in a significantly more comprehensive and up-to-date catalog of patterns. Furthermore, we identified change in perception over the years that the microservice architectural style is in use.

The results show that splitting a monolith, including splitting the connected data and libraries, is the most critical issue, resulting in potential maintenance issues when the cuts are not done properly. Moreover, the complexity of a distributed system increases the system complexity, especially when dealing with connected services that need to be highly decoupled from any point of view, including communication and architecture (hardcoded endpoints, No API gateway, inappropriate service intimacy, cyclic dependency).

This work resulted in the following four lessons learned:

- **Lesson learned 1**: Besides traditional anti-patterns, microservices-specific anti-patterns can also be problematic for the development and maintenance of microservices-based systems. Developers can already benefit from our catalog by learning how to avoid experiencing the related bad practices from an organizational and an architectural point of view.
- **Lesson learned 2**: Splitting a monolith into microservices is about identifying independent business processes that can be isolated from the monolith and not only about extracting features in different web services.
- **Lesson learned 3**: The connections between microservices, including the connections to private data and shared libraries, must be carefully analyzed.
- **Lesson learned 4**: As a general rule, developers should be alerted if they need to have a deep knowledge of the internal details of other services or if changes in a microservice require changes in another microservice.

The proposed taxonomy of anti-patterns can be used by practitioners as a guideline to avoid the same problems happening to them as faced by our interviewees. Moreover, the catalog is also a starting point for additional research on microservices. It is important to note that, even though the identified anti-patterns reflect the opinion of the interviewed developers, the rating of the harmfulness of the reported anti-patterns is only based on the perception of the practitioners and needs to be empirically validated.

Microservice is still a very recent technology and future, long-term investigation will be needed to evaluate the harmfulness and the comprehensiveness of our catalog. This, together with more in-depth empirical studies (such as controlled experiments), will be part of our future work.

References

1. V. Alagarasan (Asurion), *Microservices Antipatterns* (Microservices-Summit, New York, 2016)
2. F. Arcelli Fontana, V. Lenarduzzi, R. Roveda, D. Taibi, Are architectural smells independent from code smells? An empirical study. J. Syst. Softw. **154**, 139–156 (2019)
3. U. Azadi, F. Arcelli Fontana, D. Taibi, Architectural smells detected by tools: a catalogue proposal, in *International Conference on Technical Debt (TechDebt 2019)* (2019)
4. A. Balalaie, A. Heydarnoori, P. Jamshidi, D.A. Tamburri, T. Lynn Microservices migration patterns. Softw. Pract. Exp. **48**(11), 2019–2042 (2018)
5. J. Bogard, Avoiding microservices megadisaster, in *NDC-Conference London* (2017)
6. J. Bogner, T. Boceck, M. Popp, D. Tschechlov, S. Wagner, A. Zimmermann, Towards a collaborative repository for the documentation of service-based antipatterns and bad smells. *IEEE International Conference on Software Architecture Companion (ICSA-C)* (2019)
7. D. Bryant (SpectoLabs), *The Seven (more) Deadly Sins of Microservices* (O'Reilly OSCON, London, 2016)

8. J. Garcia, D. Popescu, G. Edwards, N. Medvidovic, Identifying architectural bad smells, in *2009 13th European Conference on Software Maintenance and Reengineering, Kaiserslautern* (2009), pp. 255–258
9. V. Lenarduzzi, A. Sillitti, D. Taibi, Analyzing forty years of software maintenance models, in *International Conference on Software Engineering (ICSE)* (2017)
10. V. Lenarduzzi, A. Sillitti, D. Taibi, A survey on code analysis tools for software maintenance prediction, in *International Conference in Software Engineering for Defence Applications (SEDA)* (2018)
11. J. Lewis, M. Fowler, *Microservices* (2014). www.martinfowler.com/articles/microservices.html. Accessed July 2017
12. I. Macia, J. Garcia, D. Popescu, A. Garcia, N. Medvidovic, A. von Staa, Are automatically-detected code anomalies relevant to architectural modularity? an exploratory analysis of evolving systems, in *International Conference on Aspect-Oriented Software Development (AOSD '12)* (2012), pp. 167–178
13. N. Moha, Y.G. Gueheneuc, L. Duchien, A.F. Le Meur, DECOR: a method for the specification and detection of code and design smells. IEEE Trans. Softw. Eng. **36**(1), 20–36 (2010)
14. S. Newman, *Building Microservices* (O'Reilly, Sebastopol, 2015)
15. C. Pahl, P. Jamshidi, Microservices: a systematic mapping study, in *Proceedings of the 6th International Conference on Cloud Computing and Services Science—CLOSER* (2018)
16. M. Richards, *Microservices AntiPatterns and Pitfalls* (O'Reilly eBooks, Sebastopol, 2016)
17. C. Richardson, *Microservice Patterns* (Manning Publications, Shelter Island, 2017)
18. C. Richardson, Potholes in the road from monolithic hell: microservices adoption anti-patterns, in *O'Really Software Architecture Conference*, London (2018)
19. N. Saarimäki, F. Lomio, V. Lenarduzzi, D. Taibi, Does migrate a monolithic system to microservices decrease the technical debt? CoRR, abs/1902.06282, 2019. [Online]. http://arxiv.org/abs/1902.06282
20. T. Saleh, *Microservices Antipatterns* (QCon, London, 2016)
21. R. Shoup, *From the Monolith to Microservices: Lessons from Google and eBay*. Craft-Con April 24th, 2015.
22. J. Soldani, D.A.Tamburri, W. van den Heuvel. The pains and gains of microservices: a systematic grey literature review. J. Syst. Softw. **146**, 215–232 (2018)
23. A.L. Strauss, J. Corbin, *Basics of Qualitative Research: Techniques and Procedures for Developing Grounded Theory* (SAGE Publications, Thousand Oaks, 2008)
24. D. Taibi, V. Lenarduzzi, On the definition of microservice bad smells. IEEE Softw. **35**(3), 56–62 (2018)
25. D. Taibi, K. Systa, From monolithic systems to microservices: a decomposition framework based on process mining, in *8th International Conference on Cloud Computing and Services Science, CLOSER 2019* (2019)
26. D. Taibi, A. Janes, V. Lenarduzzi, How developers perceive smells in source code: a replicated study. Inf. Softw. Technol. **92**, 223–235 (2017). https://doi.org/10.1016/j.infsof.2017.08.008
27. D. Taibi, V. Lenarduzzi, C. Pahl, Processes, motivations and issues for migrating to microservices architectures: an empirical investigation. IEEE Cloud Comput. **4**(5), 22–32 (2017). https://doi.org/10.1109/MCC.2017.42509312017
28. D. Taibi, V. Lenarduzzi, C. Pahl, A. Janes, in *Microservices in Agile Software Development: A Workshop-Based Study into Issues, Advantages, and Disadvantages" XP '17 Workshops*, Cologne (2017)
29. D. Taibi, V. Lenarduzzi, P. Diebold, I. Lunesu, Operationalizing the experience factory for effort estimation in agile processes, in *International Conference on Evaluation and Assessment in Software Engineering (EASE2017)* (2017)
30. D. Taibi, V. Lenarduzzi, M.O. Ahmad, K. Liukkunen, Comparing communication effort within the scrum, scrum with kanban, XP, and banana development processes, in *Proceedings of the 21st International Conference on Evaluation and Assessment in Software Engineering, EASE17* (2017)

31. D. Taibi, V. Lenarduzzi, A. Janes, K. Liukkunen, M.O. Ahmad, Comparing requirements decomposition within the scrum, scrum with kanban, XP, and banana development processes, in *Agile Processes in Software Engineering and Extreme Programming* (2017)
32. D. Taibi, V. Lenarduzzi, C. Pahl, Architectural patterns for microservices: a systematic mapping study, in *Proceedings of the 8th International Conference on Cloud Computing and Services Science—CLOSER* (2018)
33. O. Zimmermann, M. Stocker, U. Zdun, D. Lubke, C. Pautasso, *Microservice API Patterns* (2018). https://microservice-api-patterns.org. Accessed 5 June 2019

Modeling Microservice Conversations with RESTalk

Ana Ivanchikj and Cesare Pautasso

Abstract Microservices are characterized by their small size and low degree of coupling. As a consequence, building microservice architectures requires composing multiple microservices and determine how they interact to achieve a given client's goal. In this chapter we introduce the concept of RESTful conversation, whereby clients or API gateways perform multiple basic HTTP request/response interactions with one or more microservice APIs. To represent possible sequences of interactions, we introduce the RESTalk visual notation, as well as its textual DSL, and the corresponding metamodel, and show how it can be used to complement existing structural approaches to represent RESTful APIs, such as the OpenAPI Specification. To reveal the degree of coupling between clients and microservices, the language supports the concept of hyperlink flow, showing whether, within a conversation, the links embedded into responses provided by a microservice are used by the client/API gateway to form the subsequent requests.

1 Introduction

Splitting up a monolith into smaller scalable, loosely-coupled microservices [35] requires defining an efficient way of communication between the newly created services. This is because, microservices are required to be technically self-contained, but not functionally self-contained, as they may interact with other microservices to provide their business functions [23]. Different integration technologies between microservices can be used [8], some supporting synchronous request-response interactions, some asynchronous event-based interactions, and some using a mix of both [6]. The best approach depends on the use case [25], but in this chapter we will focus on the lightweight synchronous interactions built in accordance

---

A. Ivanchikj (✉) · C. Pautasso
Software Institute, Università della Svizzera italiana (USI), Lugano, Switzerland
e-mail: Ana.Ivanchikj@usi.ch; Cesare.Pautasso@usi.ch

A. Bucchiarone et al. (eds.), *Microservices*,
https://doi.org/10.1007/978-3-030-31646-4_6

with the representational state transfer (REST) architectural style [31]. Such synchronous communication frequently requires an orchestrated approach for driving the communication between the client and the microservices, seen as a conversation composed of multiple basic HTTP request-response interactions. One such orchestration approach is implemented by using the API gateway pattern [28]. An API gateway is a single entry point that provides access to different microservices [20]. It simplifies the client by moving the logic for calling multiple microservices from the client to the API gateway [24]. Namely, the API gateway can be in charge, among other things, for service discovery, and thus act as a router and decide which resources of the microservices to access based on the nature of the client (e.g., mobile or desktop) and the received call (e.g., retrieving data, creating data, etc.) [6]. This decision can be rather simple when the microservices are independent from each other and thus they can all be called at the same time upon the request of the external client. So in this case the API gateway simply fans out the requests to the related microservices. However, in real-world microservice architectures this is rarely the case, as frequently data provided from one microservice is needed to make the request to another microservice, thus requiring a predefined sequence of interactions. This emphasizes the importance of knowledge gathering and documentation of such sequences of calls to the microservices, which are necessary to achieve a given client's goal.

Big e-commerce companies are known for their microservice architecture [22, 28], and they do use tools to facilitate the design and documentation of that architecture. For instance, as eBay was restructuring its existing APIs into microservices, it adopted the OpenAPI specification for documenting the structure of the RESTful APIs.[1] Namely, at the end of 2015 the OpenAPI initiative[2] was launched to promote the effort of standardizing the description of the structure of RESTful APIs. The Swagger 2.0 specification has become the basis for the proposed standard Open API specification (OAS). OAS is a vendor-neutral, portable and open specification using a YAML/JSON-based format for the API description. The specification is both human and machine readable.

However, while the OAS structural API documentation enumerates all possible operations (combinations of resource path and method) provided to clients, it lacks a description of which are the meaningful sequences of API interactions that can be followed by clients to achieve their goals. Such behavioral aspects, i.e., the dynamic interactions between the client and the API, or between the API gateway and the microservices, are not always evident in large and complex systems. The latest version of OAS, 3.0, has added a new component to the specification, called `links`, which serves to describe how various parameter values returned by one operation can be used as input for other operations. Thus, API description documents using OAS 3.0 potentially can contain behavioral information; however, their format is

[1] https://www.openapis.org/blog/2018/08/14/ebay-provides-openapi-specification-oas-for-all-its-restful-public-apis.

[2] https://www.openapis.org.

not user friendly for those who need to traverse the links to get a general image of the API behavior, as no visualization of the same is available as part of the standard.

A complete documentation integrating both the static structure and the dynamic behavior of microservice APIs is crucial for the maintenance and extension of such systems. While, as mentioned, documentation of the static structure is already covered with the Open API standard, such standard is lacking for documentation of the dynamic interactions and data exchanges between the microservices. To that end we have designed RESTalk [15, 19], a Domain Specific Language (DSL) for visualizing the behavior, i.e., the sequences of HTTP interactions between clients and servers. In this chapter we show how RESTalk can be useful for understanding and documenting the interactions between different microservices in the context of a microservice architecture. We argue that visualizing the inter-dependencies between the microservices requires the system designers to actively think about them, both when designing and when extending the system, and empowers a discussion regarding the same with the interested parties, for instance, the developers of the individual microservices. Having a DSL for the visualization helps to capture all relevant, REST-specific details about the interactions. These REST-specific details supported by RESTalk are evident in its metamodel presented in this chapter. To fit different preferences we envision two types of representation of the DSL, a graphical representation and a textual log-like representation which allows mining user-specified interactions to discover any divergence/convergence in the communication flow.

The chapter is structured as follows. In Sect. 2 we define and discuss the characteristics of RESTful conversations, so that we can continue with presenting RESTalk, the DSL for modeling the RESTful conversations, and its metamodel in Sect. 3, as well as the components of its visual and textual representations in Sect. 4. In Sect. 5 we model an example of the possible interactions in a microservice architecture of an e-commerce system using RESTalk, and discuss the benefits of the same in Sect. 6. Before we conclude in Sect. 8, we present in Sect. 7 the work related to what is presented in this chapter.

2 Modeling Microservice APIs and RESTful Conversations

Although microservice interfaces can be exposed using solutions different from RESTful APIs, the loose coupling and lightweight communication promoted by the REST architectural style [31] blends well with the microservices doctrine. One of the main principles of REST is known as the *Hypertext as the Engine of Application State (HATEOAS)*, and it requires RESTful API clients to simply follow hyperlinks [2] provided in server's responses, without making any assumptions about the URI's structure [30]. URI stands for *Uniform Resource Identifier*, which is a pointer used to globally address an API *resource*. In the microservices context, each microservice can be considered a resource, as resources in general terms are conceptual abstractions of any information or service that can be named. It is also possible that a microservice is comprised of multiple resources. What is important is that the server can create different *representations* of the same resource depending on the received request [25] and thus serve different clients differently. The format of the representation can be different, with JSON and XML being the most frequently used ones. The server does not need to remember the session state of the request, as each request contains all the necessary information in order to be processed by the server. This REST principle is known as *statelessness* and as a consequence every request can be treated independently from the previous ones. Last but not least, REST as an architectural style provides for standardization of the communication between the client and the server, due to the principle of *uniform interface*, i.e., the calls to RESTful resources are made using HTTP standard methods applied to a resource addressed by its URI. The semantics of each of the methods (GET, POST, PUT, DELETE) is strictly defined in the HTTP protocol, as are the status codes that can be sent as a response. As mentioned previously, hyperlinks are an important REST tenet. Depending on the state of the requested resource, server's responses can contain from zero to many links. The server might also send parametrized links based on which the client can dynamically construct the URI for the next request by providing the required parameter(s)' values. As the client is following links, the RESTful API can be seen as a navigation graph-like structure of resources connected by hyperlinks [13].

The term conversation [3, 14] has been long used in the field of web services indicating richer forms of interactions [34]. In the context of the REST architectural style, we define a RESTful conversation [17], i.e., a model of all possible sequences of HTTP request-response interactions between clients and servers—or between microservices in this book's setting—which allow them to achieve different goals. Different runtime instances of a given RESTful conversation can take different paths in the conversation model as different clients might have different goals to achieve, or may take different paths to reach the same goal. Due to the fine-grained nature of RESTful APIs [29], a single client-server interaction is not always sufficient to achieve the client's goals, which leads us to the notion of a conversation which is comprised of multiple interactions.

3 RESTalk Meta-Model

RESTalk is a domain-specific language for modeling and visualization of RESTful conversations. Its constructs have been designed with the main REST architectural style constraints in mind, while borrowing and adapting a subset of the visualization elements from the BPMN standard [21]. Thus, the meta-model of RESTalk is based on the meta-model of the OpenAPI Specification [9], which focuses on the description of the structure of the API, and also on part of the BPMN meta-model [21], used to depict the behavioral aspect of the API where different paths can be taken. RESTalk's meta-model is presented in Fig. 1. The classes colored in green are the ones based on the BPMN meta-model, while the ones in blue are

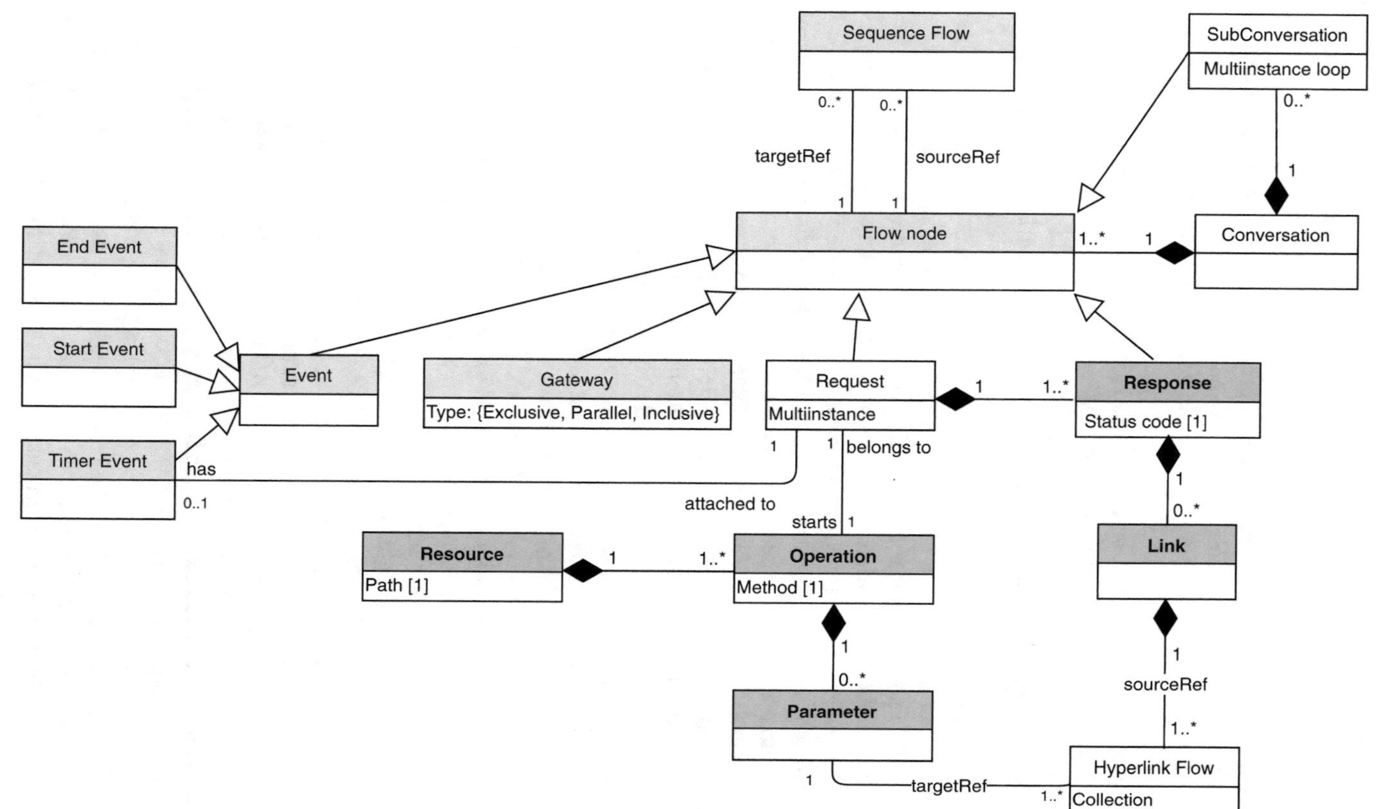

Fig. 1 RESTalk core constructs meta-model

based on the Open API Specification meta-model. The remaining white classes are specific to RESTalk.

The semantical meaning of each class in the domain specific language meta-model is the following:

1. The *Conversation* refers to the diagram representing all the possible sequences of HTTP request-response interactions between one client and multiple microservice APIs. As such, it can have multiple flow nodes, but each flow node belongs to just one conversation.
2. *Subconversations* have the same characteristics as conversations, i.e., they can also contain multiple flow nodes. The difference is that they are a flow node themselves and as such are contained inside a conversation. A conversation can, but does not have to, contain subconversations. A subconversation can be used to delimit logical groups of interactions, e.g., groups of interactions executed in a *multi-instance loop* iterating over a given array parameter found in a previous response. For each element of the array the same subconversation is executed.
3. An *event* is something that happens that impacts the normal request-response sequence of the conversation. A *start event* marks the beginning of the conversation. An *end event* marks the end of the conversation, when the API client or API gateway stops sending further requests as it has achieved its goal. A *timer event* shows alternative paths to be taken in case the server/microservice takes too long to respond to the request. The alternative path can lead to resending the request, if the response is crucial for the conversation, or it can simply continue to the next request. The timer event element is used attached to the request element to show its interrupting nature [21, pg.342] that breaks the normal request-response sequence and introduces a request-timeout-request sequence.
4. In a normal conversation execution, without timeouts, each *request* is followed by at least one *response*. The request corresponds to exactly one operation in OAS terminology which contains the REST method (GET, POST, PUT, DELETE) that can be called on the *resource* that the request refers to. The resource is identified by its URI, i.e., its *path*. As resources can be called with different methods, each resource can have one or more operations.
5. The *hyperlink flow* highlights the usage of resource identifiers discovered from previous responses. It acts as an edge whose source reference is a *link* that is found in a response. The link can be a hyperlink or a reference to a link parameter defined in the OAS documentation. The parameter can have one value or can provide a *collection* of values. The target reference of the hyperlink flow is a *parameter* that needs to be added in the path of the next request to be made or even multiple parameters, depending on the URI template [11]. If in the previous response a full hyperlink was provided, then the target reference is the full resource path. When the source reference of the hyperlink flow provides a collection of parameter values, the request whose URI path contains the target reference parameter has to be inside a loop or has to have the multi-instance marker, as it will need to be executed for each of the parameter values provided from the source reference.

6. *Gateways* show control flow divergence or convergence [21, p.287] in the conversation which can be due to client's decisions, e.g., to navigate to a given resource or to end the conversation, or due to different alternative responses that can be sent by the server. Three types of gateways are used in RESTalk: XOR—exclusive gateway that allows only one of the outgoing paths to be taken. This is the gateway type that must be used when modeling alternative server responses; OR—inclusive gateway that allows one, some or all of the outgoing paths to be taken; AND—parallel gateway that requires all outgoing paths to be taken. Similar logic is used when the gateways are used to converge the flow. Namely, in order to continue the conversation after an XOR—exclusive join gateway, the request from only one of the incoming flows has to be received; for OR—inclusive join gateway, the requests from all paths that have been activated with an inclusive split need to be received; for AND—parallel join gateway, the requests from all concurrent paths need to be received.
7. *Flow node* is any node in the RESTalk graph and as such can be a source or a target of a *sequence flow* which represents an edge in the RESTalk graph. Some types of flow nodes, such as the start event, can only be a source reference of a sequence flow, while the end event type of flow node on the other hand can only be the target reference of a sequence flow. Requests, responses, and subconversations are the source reference of exactly one sequence flow and the target reference of a different sequence flow. Gateways are the only type of flow nodes that can be the source or the target of multiple sequence flows depending on whether they act as a split or a join.

4 RESTalk: Visual and Textual DSL

RESTalk supports both visual and textual modeling of RESTful APIs behavior. As mentioned earlier, the visual constructs have been adopted from the BPMN standard and are specified in [15, 19]. In Fig. 2 we present the core visual constructs of the language, the semantics of which have been defined in Sect. 3.

The textual DSL on the other hand represents the possible conversation instances between microservices in the form of logs, from which the visual conversation diagram is meant to be obtained by using process mining techniques [18, 33]. Each

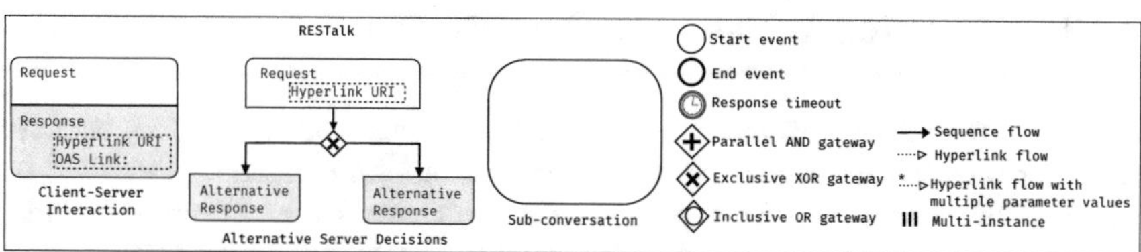

Fig. 2 RESTalk core visual constructs

log entry represents a single request-response interaction, stating the method, the resource URI, the name of the microservice acting as a server (optional), response status code, and any links provided in the response.

As mentioned in Sect. 3, the response can contain a link to a parameter defined in the OAS documentation, in which case the provided parameter is stated in square brackets (e.g., [userId]). If the response provides a collection of values for the parameter which are relevant for the rest of the flow, a range can be stated (e.g., [userIds=[1...4]]) or a list of values can be stated (e.g., [userIds = [1,3,5]]). The values of the parameter in the collection can then be used in the URI of subsequent requests so that the mining algorithm can discover the hyperlink flows in the conversation. The mining algorithm would recognize that the link is an OAS link if it is included in square parenthesis (e.g., [x]), otherwise if it starts with a backslash (e.g., /x) it will know that it is a hyperlink.

Unlike in real API access logs, no time-stamp is needed, but it is assumed that the order in which the interactions are stated is the order in which they would be executed. There is no need to explicitly state the control flow elements, such as gateways and start and end events, as they are deduced based on the mining of the log-like input provided by the user [16]. For instance, if two different requests never appear together in the same conversation instance, the miner will deduce that an exclusive gateway needs to be visualized before reaching these requests; if they appear together in some conversation instances but not in others, an inclusive gateway would be visualized; if they appear together in all conversation instances, regardless of in which order, then parallelism will be deduced. Different conversation instances are separated by an empty line. In order to produce a complete diagram of the RESTful conversation, all the possible conversation instances need to be stated. The advantage of using this approach in the textual DSL is that it can help developers capture different user stories, an approach frequently used to gather requirements during software design [5]. Each usage scenario of the API is represented with a different sequence of interactions. The RESTalk visual model for the whole API is obtained by merging all different scenarios together.

Different mining algorithms can be used on top of the above-described textual DSL. They can be built from scratch for the RESTalk purposes or they can be adapted from other fields, such as business process mining, where substantial work has been done on the matter [33].

5 RESTalk Model Example in E-commerce

Due to the frequent use of microservices in e-commerce companies [22], we have opted for this domain to provide an example of the use of RESTalk inspired by Amazon. In our example we assume that the microservice architecture includes an API gateway, which means that the client makes a call to the API Gateway

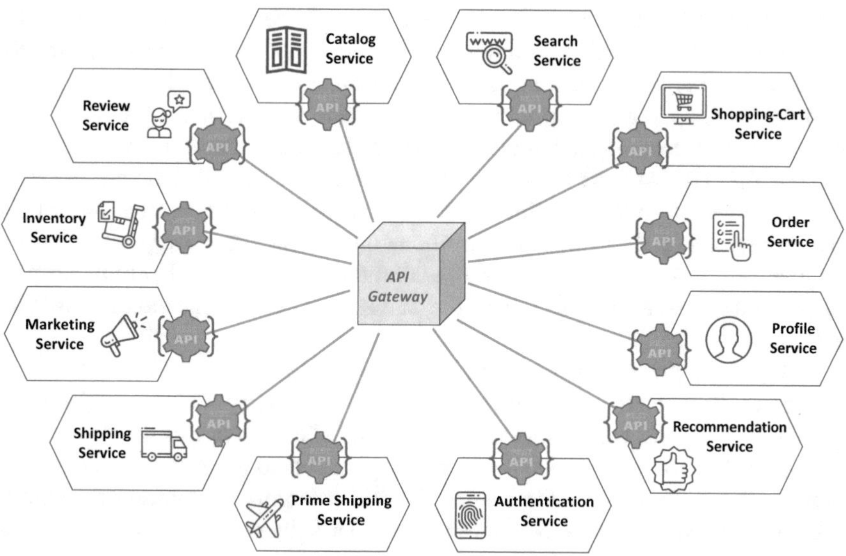

Fig. 3 Microservice architecture of the example e-commerce company

which in turn makes different calls to all of the relevant microservices. In Fig. 3 we show a possible microservice architecture of an e-commerce solution. As users can create their profiles for faster and more personalized shopping experience, the *profile service* stores all the relevant user data, such as addresses, contact details, the type of user, etc. User's authentication, log-in credentials, and validity of the access token are controlled by the *authentication service*. User's orders are managed by the *order service*, while draft orders, which have not been submitted yet, are managed by the *shopping cart service* to which items can be added both by logged-in and non-logged-in users. The shipping of ordered items is managed by a call to an external provider noted as the *shipping service* for nonprime users and *prime shipping service* for prime users. Frequent users may also receive special discounts and promotions, which are managed by the *marketing service*. The *search service* provides the searching functionality and stores session IDs and product IDs related to the session to later be used by the *recommendation service* which provides the business logic over recommending certain products over others. All the details about a product, including its characteristics and price, are stored in the *catalog service*, while the *inventory service* handles the up-to-date information about the available quantity of a given product. Last but not least, the *review service* stores and aggregates customer's reviews about a given product.

In a microservice architecture using an API gateway there are two layers of communication. In the first layer there is the communication between the client and the API gateway, abstracting from the existence of microservices, as the client would make the same calls also in the case of a monolith application. In the e-commerce example, this would refer to a conversation between the client and the server which includes searching the website, looking at the products, and adding them to the shopping cart up until the placing and modification of an order. The second layer of communication refers to the interactions between the API Gateway and the RESTful APIs of the microservices, triggered by a specific client call in the first layer of communication. RESTalk can be used to represent any of the layers; however, given the focus of this book on microservices, we present a visual diagram of the conversation occurring within the second layer of communication. An example of conversations within the first layer of communication is presented in [15].

In Fig. 4 we present the conversation that is triggered by the API Gateway as soon as a call for rendering a specific product item's web page is made, which in the e-commerce context happens as soon as the user clicks on one of the items in the search results. We assume that when entering the home page of the e-commerce website, the system stores the session ID and performs a geolocation query to determine the country based on the IP address. Thus, these two parameters, session ID and country, are already known when making the call for rendering the product item's web page. The input provided by the user when making this call is the product ID and optionally the access token. When there is no access token it means that the user is not logged in, thus only the left part of the conversation diagram will be executed.

Most of the microservices can be called in parallel, as they only require the parameters that are already available at the start of the conversation. This is the case with the catalog service, inventory service, and review service, which only require the product ID. Note that these services will be executed even if the user is logged in as they are on the outgoing path of the inclusive gateway split which has a condition that is always true. The IDs of the best seller products provided by the Recommendation service will also be retrieved in parallel with the above-mentioned microservices as no parameter is required for the call. For each of the best seller product IDs, the inventory service will need to be called to check whether the product is available, and the catalog service to check its price, before they can be rendered on the web page. The same sequence needs to be followed when generating the recommendations based on the search chronology for the user who is not logged in, or based on the order history, for the user who is logged in. This is why the parallel calls to the catalog service and the inventory service are visually represented as subconversations which are called for each product ID generated by any of the resources of the recommendation service, as evident from the hyperlink flow visual construct.

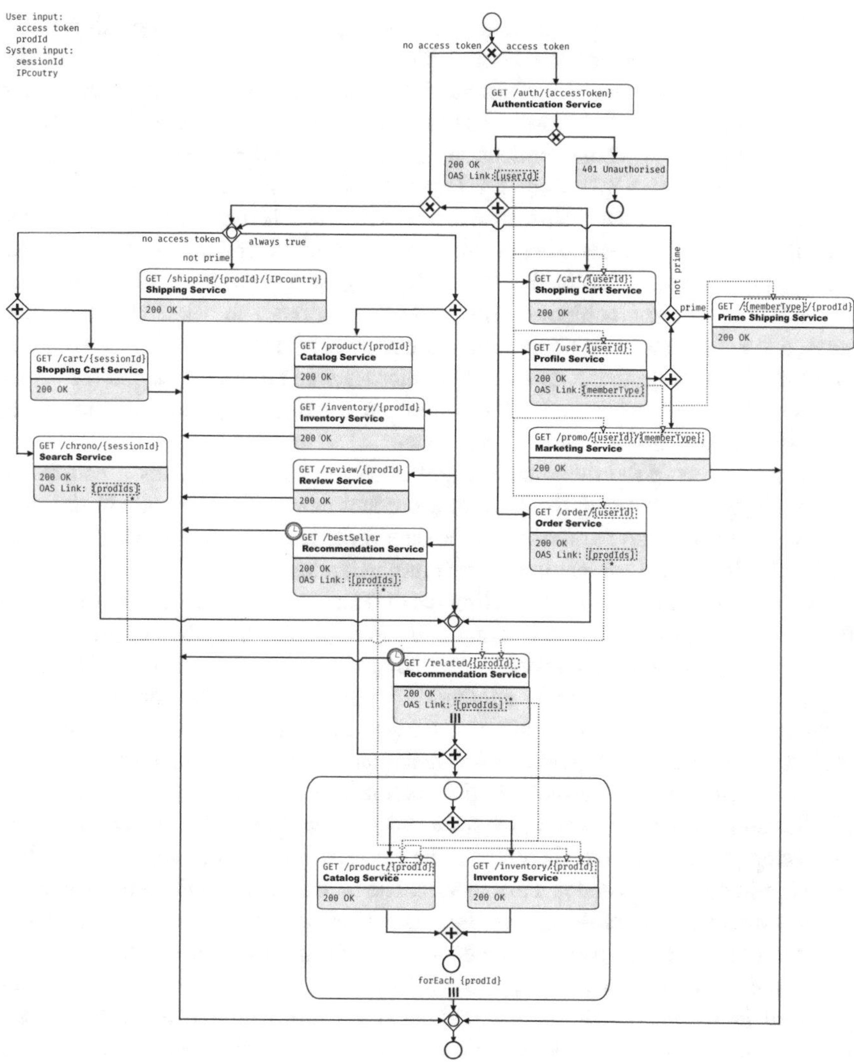

Fig. 4 RESTful conversation for rendering a product item page

The timer event on all the calls to the different resources of the recommendation service will ensure that at least all the page data, except for the recommended products, is rendered in case the recommendation service is slow (or down), as the recommendation service just provides added value for the users, but is not crucial for the users to continue with their order.

The shopping cart service is called for both logged-in and non-logged-in users, using different parameters: the session ID for a non-logged-in user, and the user ID for a logged-in user. While the session ID is available from the start of the conversation, the hyperlink flow visual construct shows that the user ID is obtained from the response of the authentication service. This service, based on the validity of the provided access token, can send the user ID or a 401 status code if the token is no longer valid. As the profile service stores the durable user data, when provided with the user ID it reveals whether the user is a prime member, and thus whether the shipping microservice or the Prime shipping microservice should be invoked to render the estimated shipping time and price on the web page. The marketing service also uses the user ID and the membership type data to calculate different promotions available to the user. As this microservice requires data obtained from the authentication service and the Profile service, it cannot be called before receiving the response from both of these microservices.

As evident from the diagram in Fig. 4 each time a client makes a call to the API gateway for rendering the page of a product item, at least 5 calls to different microservices are made to render all the data for a non-logged-in user, plus all the optional calls needed for making the recommendations.

As mentioned in Sect. 4, for creating the diagram in Fig. 4, we currently envision two possible approaches. One is using a visual modeler where the designer is able to drag&drop the desired constructs and connect them as best seen fit. The other approach is a textual editor to enumerate possible user stories, or conversation instance examples, written by one or more API designers or developers which are then aggregated using a process mining technique to create the diagram.

For our e-commerce example, in this section two of the user stories would look like those in Listing 1. The two user stories, or conversation instances, are separated by an empty line. The first one refers to the conversation instance when the user has valid log-in credentials and is a prime user. The second conversation instance refers to the user story of a non-logged-in user. The other possible conversation instances that need to be stated in order to generate the diagram in Fig. 4, are not shown due to their length. However, they would follow the same syntax as the examples provided in Listing 1. The textual editor would run a mining algorithm in the background which, e.g., would infer the existence of parallelism between the calls to the catalog service and the inventory service, since in the first conversation instance first the catalog service is called and then the inventory service, while in the second conversation instance the inventory service is called before the catalog service. More user stories would be needed to discover all of the different calls which can be performed in parallel. The mining algorithm would use the parameter name, userId, to discover the hyperlink flow between the response of the authentication service and the request URI of the profile service. It would use the values of the collection parameters in the response of the recommendation service to discover the loops to gather the information regarding the recommended products.

Listing 1 Example of a user story for the e-commerce use case in Fig. 4 written in RESTalk's textual DSL

```
GET /auth/{accessToken} Authentication Service 200 [userId]
GET /product/{prodId} Catalog Service 200
GET /user/{userId} Profile Service 200 [memberType=prime]
GET /promo/{userId}/{memberType=prime} Marketing Service 200
GET /{memberType=prime}/{prodId} Prime Shipping Service 200
GET /inventory/{prodId} Inventory Service 200
GET /order/{userId} Order Service 200 [prodIds=[a,b]]
GET /review/{prodId} Review Service 200
GET /cart/{userId} Shopping Cart Service 200
GET /bestSeller Recommendation Service 200 [prodIds=[1,2]]
GET /product/{prodId=1} Catalog Service 200
GET /inventory/{prodId=1} Inventory Service 200
GET /product/{prodId=2} Catalog Service 200
GET /inventory/{prodId=2} Inventory Service 200
GET /related/{prodId=a} Recommendation Service 200 [prodIds=[3,4]]
GET /related/{prodId=b} Recommendation Service 200 [prodIds=[5,6]]
GET /product/{prodId=3} Catalog Service 200
GET /product/{prodId=4} Catalog Service 200
GET /inventory/{prodId=3} Inventory Service 200
GET /inventory/{prodId=4} Inventory Service 200
GET /inventory/{prodId=5} Inventory Service 200
GET /product/{prodId=5} Catalog Service 200
GET /product/{prodId=6} Catalog Service 200
GET /inventory/{prodId=6} Inventory Service 200

GET /cart/{sessionId} Shopping Cart Service 200
GET /shipping/{prodId}/{IPcountry} Shipping Service 200
GET /inventory/{prodId} Inventory Service 200
GET /product/{prodId} Catalog Service 200
GET /chrono/{sessionId} Search Service 200 [prodIds=[x,y]]
GET /related/{prodId=x} Recommendation Service 200 [prodIds=[1]]
GET /review/{prodId} Review Service 200
GET /inventory/{prodId=1} Inventory Service 200
GET /product/{prodId=1} Catalog Service 200
GET /related/{prodId=y} Recommendation Service 200 [prodIds=[2,3]]
GET /product/{prodId=2} Catalog Service 200
GET /product/{prodId=3} Catalog Service 200
GET /inventory/{prodId=2} Inventory Service 200
GET /inventory/{prodId=3} Inventory Service 200
GET /bestSeller Recommendation Service 200 [prodIds=[4,5]]
GET /inventory/{prodId=4} Inventory Service 200
GET /product/{prodId=4} Catalog Service 200
GET /product/{prodId=5} Catalog Service 200
GET /inventory/{prodId=5} Inventory Service 200
```

6 Discussion

In microservice architectures, it might be easy to reason about the behavior of each individual component, but understanding the behavior of the entire system can become rather complex [6]. That said, visualizing the communication flow between the microservices makes it possible to explain their mutual dependencies and interactions to newbie developers, and helps developers document the interactions in the existing architecture from a behavioral viewpoint. While a RESTful conversation model complements existing structural models, together they can be used to discuss any possible extensions in terms of additional API usage scenarios. Furthermore, structured knowledge about the interdependencies between microservices can help identify patterns and anti-patterns in this relatively new architectural style which still faces the issue of communication optimization [1]. On another note, having a precise communication model is a needed step for building automatic testing frameworks that test the communication behavior of microservices [8].

Although some existing general modeling languages, such as UML activity or sequence diagrams or BPMN choreographies, could be used for modeling the communication behavior, when the microservices expose RESTful APIs, having a domain-specific language, such as RESTalk, facilitates capturing important RESTful facets, such as the request-response behavior, the method and status codes combinations and the use of hyperlinks. In standard languages, such as UML or BPMN, these would need to be captured by adding domain-specific semantics to model annotations and comments [12, 26], thus cluttering the readability of the diagram and hindering the interoperation with other RESTful API modeling tools.

Researchers have been working on textual support for general modeling languages in order to facilitate the adoption of those languages, as developers seem to be more inclined to use textual editors as opposed to graphical editors. The reason behind that is the long tradition of using textual, general-purpose programming languages, which reduce the learning curve [4] for the textual DSLs. There are different textual editors for UML, such as ZenUML,[3] PlantUML,[4] WebsequenceDiagrams,[5] etc. However, they use either natural language like syntax or programming language like syntax. In our approach for the textual DSL for RESTalk, we have decided to let the user describe the user story, a common practice in software engineering [5]. The goal of classical user stories is for the software user to describe the desired functionalities of the software to be developed. Classical user stories have a predefined content structure to facilitate understanding, but are written in natural language. In the case of microservices and RESTalk, the purpose of the user stories is to describe how the functionality of the system (i.e., the goal of the conversation) is mapped to interdependencies and sequences of interactions

[3]https://app.zenuml.com/.

[4]https://www.planttext.com/.

[5]https://www.websequencediagrams.com.

between microservices (i.e., the conversation instance). It can be challenging for one person to know all the different data that needs to be exchanged between the microservices and the order in which it has to be done. This can be facilitated by having the possibility for all the involved developers to simply state the logic and communication that they have been implementing or designing in the form of logs, which can then be mined to generate the RESTalk diagram aggregating all usage scenarios.

7 Related Work

Most of the works which mention the challenge of microservice communication and integration focus on microservice architecture in general and only touch upon the communication challenge as evident from the literature survey conducted by Alshuqayran et al. in [1]. The authors in the same work also provide a survey of the different approaches used to model different aspects of the microservice architecture. They have discovered that the most frequently used diagrams are component diagrams to show the static interdependencies between microservices. Some researchers have also used UML sequence diagrams, use case diagrams, or class diagrams to depict different viewpoints of the microservice architecture. Srikanta et al. [27] use UML sequence diagrams to describe the communication flow in the microservice architecture that they propose for dynamic rating, charging, and billing for cloud service providers. The microservices in their reference architecture are RESTful; however, their use case is more simplistic then ours as it uses just three microservices which communicate among each other in a sequential flow, with no control flow divergence. Toffetti et al. [32], in the context of cloud resources deployment, use a type graph to represent the needed cloud resources and the connections between them together with their cardinality, and an instance graph to show the actual deployment of the resources, visualized by square nodes and undirected edges. They propose using the same type of graphs for microservice-based applications as well. De Lange et al. [7], in their Community Application Editor, built to support model driven web engineering, include the modeling of microservices as part of the server-side modeling view. They have RESTful resources as the central entity of their microservice view meta-model, together with their HTTP methods and responses. The communication dependencies between the microservices, or between a microservice and the front-end components, are drawn automatically by the tool in the communications view based on the data entered in the other views. In the communications view, the microservice is visualized as a node, but the microservice call is also visualized as a node. Contrary to our approach, no control flow divergence/convergence constructs are available, and the hyperlink flow is also not visualized.

Granchelli et al. [10] use a model reverse engineering approach in their tool MicroART to recover the microservice architecture of a system which is available on Github. They use the communication logs to discover the interdependencies between the microservices. The automatically generated links between the microservices can be edited and refined by a knowledgeable human using the graphical editor of the tool. One refinement that they propose is to resolve the interfaces referring to what they call the service discovery service (e.g., an API gateway), which masks the real resource dependencies. Thus, the human should remove the API gateway from the microservice architecture visual diagram, and reestablish the links (the calls) directly between the microservices. Contrary to our approach, where we only focus on the communication aspect, in their visual model, they also include information about the teams and the developers working on each of the microservices. As they group together all the resources belonging to a discovered microservice, their approach only reveals the resource URI and the microservice it belongs to, but not the method calls and the hyperlinks flow, i.e., the diagram contains directed edges to show the static dependencies between the different resources, but they do not show the dynamic interaction behavior that can be followed at execution time.

8 Conclusion

In this chapter we have shown how to use RESTalk, a domain-specific language for modeling RESTful conversations and to visualize RESTful conversations, i.e., models of all possible HTTP interaction sequences between a client and a RESTful API, in the context of a microservice architecture where different microservices need to communicate in order to achieve client's goal. To describe RESTalk, we have presented its meta-model and the two types of editing modalities that we envision for the language, a graphical editor using the drag&drop functionality to add constructs to the diagram, and a textual editor using a mining algorithm to deduce the RESTalk diagram from a log-like user input. As microservice architecture is frequently found in e-commerce application, we showcase a RESTalk model which visualizes what happens behind the scenes when a human user clicks on a shop item to see its details. The goal of the example is to show the expressiveness of RESTalk and its semantics, but also to facilitate the discussion of the potential benefits of visualizing the dynamic microservice communication. Namely, in the name of achieving better scalability, performance, and maintainability, the microservice architecture introduces complexity in terms of microservices communication compared to a monolith architecture. Encoding the knowledge about such—unavoidable by design—interactions between the microservices helps in sharing that knowledge and leveraging it to induce the discussion and application of best practices. Although this knowledge could be visualized and encoded also in existing general-purpose languages, such as UML, using a domain-specific language, such as RESTalk, helps to emphasize important facets of REST and the underlying HTTP protocol in the visualization.

References

1. N. Alshuqayran, N. Ali, R. Evans, A systematic mapping study in microservice architecture, in *2016 IEEE 9th International Conference on Service-Oriented Computing and Applications (SOCA)* (IEEE, Piscataway, 2016), pp. 44–51
2. M. Amundsen, *Building Hypermedia APIs with HTML5 and Node* (O'Reilly, Beijing, 2011)
3. B. Benatallah, F. Casati, F. Toumani, Web service conversation modeling: a cornerstone for e-business automation. IEEE Internet Comput. **8**(1), 46–54 (2004)
4. M. Brambilla, J. Cabot, M. Wimmer, *Model-Driven Software Engineering in Practice* (Morgan & Claypool Publishers, San Rafael, 2017)
5. M. Cohn, *User Stories Applied: For Agile Software Development* (Addison-Wesley Professional, Boston, 2004)
6. S. Daya, N. Van Duy, K. Eati, C.M. Ferreira, D. Glozic, V. Gucer, M. Gupta, S. Joshi, V. Lampkin, M. Martins, et al. *Microservices from Theory to Practice: Creating Applications in IBM Bluemix Using the Microservices Approach* (IBM Redbooks, Poughkeepsie, 2016)
7. P. de Lange, P. Nicolaescu, R. Klamma, M. Jarke, Engineering web applications using real-time collaborative modeling, in *CYTED-RITOS International Workshop on Groupware* (Springer, Berlin, 2017), pp. 213–228
8. N. Dragoni, S. Giallorenzo, A.L. Lafuente, M. Mazzara, F. Montesi, R. Mustafin, L. Safina, Microservices: yesterday, today, and tomorrow, in *Present and Ulterior Software Engineering* (Springer, Berlin, 2017), pp. 195–216
9. H. Ed-Douibi, J.L. Cánovas Izquierdo, J. Cabot, Example-driven web api specification discovery, in *European Conference on Modelling Foundations and Applications* (Springer, Berlin, 2017), pp. 267–284
10. G. Granchelli, M. Cardarelli, P. Di Francesco, I. Malavolta, L. Iovino, A. Di Salle, Towards recovering the software architecture of microservice-based systems, in *2017 IEEE International Conference on Software Architecture Workshops (ICSAW)* (IEEE, Piscataway, 2017), pp. 46–53
11. J. Gregorio, R. Fielding, M. Hadley, M. Nottingham, D. Orchard, *URI Template* (2012). Request for Comments: 6570
12. F. Haupt, F. Leymann, C. Pautasso, A conversation based approach for modeling REST APIs, in *Proceeding of the 12th Working IEEE/IFIP Conference on Software Architecture (WICSA 2015)*, Montreal, Canada (2015)
13. F. Haupt, F. Leymann, K. Vukojevic-Haupt, API governance support through the structural analysis of rest APIS. Comput. Sci. Res. Dev. **33**(3), 291–303 (2018)
14. G. Hohpe, Let's have a conversation. IEEE Internet Comput. **11**(3), 78–81 (2007)
15. A. Ivanchikj, RESTful conversation with RESTalk -the use case of doodle-, in *Proceedings of the International Conference on Web Engineering (ICWE'16)* (Springer, Berlin, 2016), pp. 583–587
16. A. Ivanchikj, C. Pautasso, Sketching process models by mining participant stories, in *International Conference on Business Process Management* (Springer, Berlin, 2019), pp. 3–19
17. A. Ivanchikj, C. Pautasso, S. Schreier, Visual modeling of restful conversations with restalk. J. Softw. Syst. Model. **17**, 1–21 (2016)
18. A. Ivanchikj, I. Gjorgjiev, C. Pautasso, Restalk miner: mining restful conversations, pattern discovery and matching, in *International Conference on Service-Oriented Computing* (Springer, Berlin, 2018), pp. 470–475
19. A. Ivanchikj, C. Pautasso, S. Schreier, Visual modeling of RESTful conversations with RESTalk. Softw. Syst. Model. **17**(3), 1031–1051 (2018)
20. P. Jamshidi, C. Pahl, N.C. Mendonça, J. Lewis, S. Tilkov, Microservices: the journey so far and challenges ahead. IEEE Softw. **35**(3), 24–35 (2018)
21. D. Jordan, J. Evdemon, *Business Process Model and Notation Version 2.0* (OMG, Needham, 2011). http://www.omg.org/spec/BPMN/2.0/

22. P. Karwatka, M. Gil, M. Grabowski, A. Graf, P. Jedrzejewski, M. Kurzeja, A. Orfin, B. Picho, *Microsevice Architecture for eCommerce* (2017). https://divante.co/books/PDFy/microservices-architecture-for-ecommerce.pdf
23. H. Knoche, W. Hasselbring, Drivers and barriers for microservice adoption–a survey among professionals in germany. Enterp. Model. Inf. Syst. Archit. (EMISAJ) **14**, 1–1 (2019)
24. D. Malavalli, S. Sathappan, Scalable microservice based architecture for enabling DMTF profiles, in *2015 11th International Conference on Network and Service Management (CNSM)* (IEEE, Piscataway, 2015), pp. 428–432
25. S. Newman, *Building Microservices* (O'Reilly, Sebastopol, 2015)
26. A. Nikaj, S. Mandal, C. Pautasso, M. Weske, From choreography diagrams to RESTful interactions, in *Proceeding of the 11th International Workshop on Engineering Service-Oriented Applications (WESOA)* (2015), pp. 3–14
27. S. Patanjali, B. Truninger, P. Harsh, T.M. Bohnert, Cyclops: a micro service based approach for dynamic rating, charging & billing for cloud, in *2015 13th International Conference on Telecommunications (ConTEL)* (IEEE, Piscataway, 2015), pp. 1–8
28. C. Richardson, *Microservices Patterns: With Examples in Java* (Manning, Shelter Island, 2018)
29. L. Richardson, M. Amundsen, S. Ruby, *RESTful Web APIs* (O'Reilly, Sebastopol, 2013)
30. T. Steiner, J. Algermissen, Fulfilling the Hypermedia constraint via HTTP OPTIONS, the HTTP vocabulary in RDF, and link headers, in *Proceedings of the Second International Workshop on RESTful Design* (ACM, New York, 2011), pp. 11–14
31. R. Thomas Fielding, *Architectural Styles and the Design of Network-based Software Architectures*, PhD thesis, University of California, Irvine, 2000
32. G. Toffetti, S. Brunner, M. Blöchlinger, F. Dudouet, A. Edmonds, An architecture for self-managing microservices, in *Proceedings of the 1st International Workshop on Automated Incident Management in Cloud* (ACM, New York, 2015), pp. 19–24
33. W. van der Aalst, *Process Mining: Discovery, Conformance and Enhancement of Business Processes* (Springer, Berlin, 2011)
34. M. Völter, M. Kircher, U. Zdun, *Remoting Patterns: Foundations of Enterprise, Internet and Realtime Distributed Object Middleware* (Wiley, Hoboken, 2013)
35. O. Zimmermann, Microservices tenets. Comput. Sci. Res. Dev. **32**(3), 301–310 (2017)

Graphical and Textual Model-Driven Microservice Development

Florian Rademacher, Jonas Sorgalla, Philip Wizenty, Sabine Sachweh, and Albert Zündorf

Abstract Model-driven development (MDD) is an approach to software engineering that aims to enable analysis, validation, and code generation of software on the basis of models expressed with dedicated modeling languages. MDD is particularly useful in the engineering of complex, possibly distributed software systems. It is therefore sensible to investigate the adoption of MDD to support and facilitate the engineering of distributed software systems based on microservice architecture (MSA).

This chapter presents recent insights from studying and developing two approaches for employing MDD in MSA engineering. The first approach uses a graphical notation to model the topology and interactions of MSA-based software systems. The second approach emerged from the first one and exploits viewpoint-based modeling to better cope with MSA's inherent complexity. It also considers the distributed nature of MSA teams, as well as the technology heterogeneity introduced by MSA adoption. Both approaches are illustrated and discussed in the context of a case study. Moreover, we present a catalog of research questions for subsequent investigation of employing MDD to support and facilitate MSA engineering.

1 Introduction

Microservice architecture (MSA) is a novel approach towards developing and deploying distributed software systems [23]. It relies on *services* as architectural building blocks, i.e., software components that (1) are loosely coupled to minimize

F. Rademacher (✉) · J. Sorgalla · P. Wizenty · S. Sachweh
IDiAL Institute, University of Applied Sciences and Arts Dortmund, Dortmund, Germany
e-mail: florian.rademacher@fh-dortmund.de; jonas.sorgalla@fh-dortmund.de; philipnils.wizenty@fh-dortmund.de; sabine.sachweh@fh-dortmund.de

A. Zündorf
Department of Computer Science and Electrical Engineering, University of Kassel, Kassel, Germany
e-mail: zuendorf@uni-kassel.de

A. Bucchiarone et al. (eds.), *Microservices*,
https://doi.org/10.1007/978-3-030-31646-4_7

dependencies on other components, (2) agree on *contracts* as predefined specifications of communication relationships and interact via *interfaces*, (3) encapsulate reusable business or infrastructure logic, and (4) can be composed to coordinately accomplish coarse-grained tasks [9]. MSA promotes tailoring of services along domain-specific functional and technical infrastructure capabilities [23]. Each microservice is responsible for providing exactly one, distinct capability to the architecture. It is *owned* by a single team that accounts for the service's design, development, deployment, operation, and maintenance [22].

The adoption of MSA increases the degree of *service-specific independence* which is considered to result in several benefits. First, the system's scalability is expected to increase. A microservice can be deployed and scaled separately [23]. Second, the system's resilience is expected to increase, because failures need to be expected at any point in runtime [16]. Thus, each service needs to be as robust as possible to prevent failure cascades [2]. Third, team productivity is expected to increase. MSA favors small team sizes and directed, efficient communication along service boundaries [22]. Moreover, MSA teams are free to choose arbitrary technologies for service implementation, provided that service interfaces comply with consumers' expectations. For instance, teams can align technology choices to (1) performance requirements [17]; (2) implementation requirements [7]; and (3) further technical requirements related to, e.g., the deployment infrastructure [2].

Model-Driven Development (MDD) [6] is a supportive approach for engineering complex, distributed architectures like those of MSA-based software systems. MDD leverages *models* as means of abstraction throughout the software engineering process, which is expected to (1) facilitate reasoning about a software's architecture by omitting technical details, (2) enable analysis by formalizing specific parts of a software system, and (3) increase development productivity by generating code from models [6]. This chapter explores the applicability of MDD to MSA for a graphical and a textual modeling approach. It discusses the strengths and weaknesses of each approach in the light of a case study from the electromobility domain and derives research questions to further investigate the usage of MDD in MSA engineering.

The remainder of the chapter is organized as follows. Section 2 presents background information on MDD in general and in the context of MSA. Section 3 introduces the case study. Section 4 presents and discusses AjiL [36], a graphical approach towards model-driven MSA engineering. Section 5 presents and discusses a textual modeling approach for MSA. It was developed based on our experiences with using AjiL in complex modeling scenarios and is centered around a workflow for model-driven MSA engineering that considers the different stakeholder roles of distributed, DevOps-based MSA teams. Section 5 also comprises a catalog of research questions on enabling MDD of MSA. Section 6 gives an overview of related work and Sect. 7 concludes the chapter with an outlook on future works.

2 Background

This section provides background information on MDD in general (cf. Sect. 2.1) and presents benefits of employing MDD in MSA engineering (cf. Sect. 2.2).

2.1 *Model-Driven Development*

MDD is an approach to software engineering that uses models as first-class citizens throughout the engineering process [6]. A *model* can be distinguished from other software engineering artifacts on the basis of three *model criteria* [19]. First, there must be an original that is mapped to the model (*mapping criterion*). Second, a model is a reduction of the original that intentionally drops selected properties of the original (*reduction criterion*). Third, a model must be able to replace the original for a given purpose (*pragmatic criterion*). A model is thus a means to capture certain parts and aspects of a software system at an appropriate level of abstraction [6].

Employing models in software engineering yields several benefits [6]. Basically, reasoning about a software architecture is facilitated when details at lower levels of abstraction are omitted in models (mapping and reduction criteria). Such details may be components' inner structures or behaviors in order to only show the overall topology of the architecture [3]. A second benefit of MDD is the enabling of an architecture's analysis, simulation, and testing prior to its implementation [6].

Furthermore, models may be (semi)automatically transformed to other models or source code (pragmatic criterion) [6]. *Code generation* is one of the key enablers for adopting MDD in software engineering practice as it may increase developer productivity by up to 30% [40]. Additionally, *model-to-model transformations* contribute to increasing models' value by deriving further artifacts from them [18]. For example, submodels may be automatically extracted from larger models to facilitate reasoning about isolated system parts. Another use case for model-to-model transformations is *model refinement*, where a generic model is transformed into more concrete models. In the context of MSA, the derivation of service models from underspecified domain models can be considered a refinement action [29].

Next to model transformation, *modeling languages* are a pivotal element of MDD pragmatics [6]. A modeling language's syntax imposes structural and semantic constraints on models. It restricts the set of expressible models to those that adhere to the constraints and can thus be considered *correct*. A modeling language's syntax consists of the abstract syntax and one or more concrete syntaxes [6]. The *abstract syntax* defines the available modeling concepts, their structures, and relationships. It may be enriched with semantic constraints, e.g., in the form of OCL invariants [25]. The abstract syntax is captured in *metamodels* and typically expressed in object-oriented representations, e.g., UML class diagrams [6]. Each class then corresponds to a modeling concept, and its attributes and associations represent the concept's structure and relationships. A modeling language's *concrete syntax* specifies a notation for modelers to construct models. It may be, e.g., graphical or textual [6].

The development of a modeling language may follow an iterative process. It starts with the definition or refinement of the metamodel [6]. Next, a concrete syntax for the metamodel is derived or refined. Finally, the language semantics are integrated or refined. When following such a "metamodel-first approach" to language development, the metamodel typically also defines the Abstract Syntax Tree (AST). That is, a bidirectional mapping between metamodel concepts and grammar rules of the concrete syntax is specified, which also enables the automatic derivation of language-specific editors and parsers [6]. A model that conforms to a metamodel and is expressed in a concrete syntax for the metamodel is then parsed to an AST instance which also conforms to the metamodel. One benefit of this approach is that the metamodel is reusable across concrete syntaxes.

Figure 1 illustrates the relationship between metamodel and modeling language with an example of a trivial modeling language for specifying microservices.

Figure 1a shows the metamodel in an object-oriented notation based on UML class diagrams [6]. It specifies the `Microservice` concept for modeling microservices. Each microservice has at least one `Interface`, which comprises at least one `Operation`. An operation may be composed of a set of named and primitively typed `Parameters`. Moreover, an operation may have a `returnType` or no return type at all when `voidReturnType` is set to "true."

Figure 1b shows the metamodel from Fig. 1a in Xcore,[1] a textual language for metamodel specification from the Eclipse Modeling Framework (EMF) [37]. The metamodel contains all concepts from Fig. 1a and an additional concept `ServiceModel` to cluster all `Microservice` instances.

Figure 1c contains the grammar of the modeling language. It is expressed in the grammar language of Xtext,[2] an EMF-based framework for developing textual languages. The grammar defines a rule for each metamodel concept in Fig. 1b. The bidirectional mappings between grammar rules and metamodel concepts (see above) are established by the `returns` keyword.

Figure 1d shows an example model that is expressed in the concrete syntax defined in Fig. 1c. Because the grammar is based on the metamodel in Fig. 1b, the model adheres to the structure and hence constitutes an instance of the metamodel.

2.2 *Model-Driven Development for Microservice Architecture*

Employing MDD is particularly beneficial in the engineering of complex software systems, because of the problem-oriented abstractions provided by models and modeling languages [11]. Sophisticated MDD techniques like model checking,

[1] https://wiki.eclipse.org/Xcore.

[2] https://www.eclipse.org/Xtext.

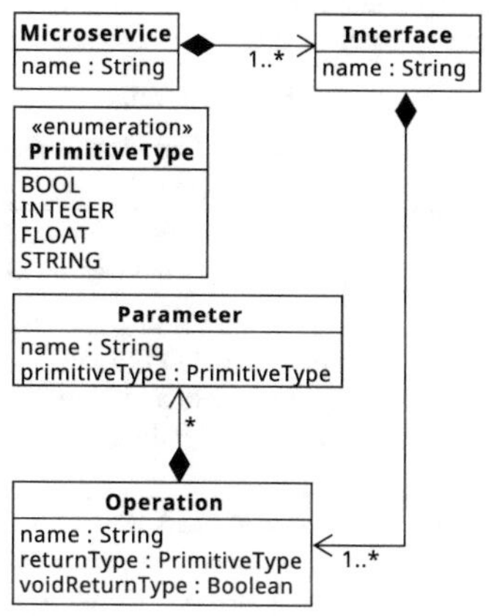

a

```
enum PrimitiveType { BOOL, INTEGER,
  FLOAT, STRING }
class ServiceModel {
  contains Microservice[] microservices
}
class Microservice {
  String name
  contains Interface[1..*] interfaces }
class Interface {
  String name
  contains Operation[1..*] operations }
class Operation {
  String name
  PrimitiveType returnType
  boolean voidReturnType
  contains Parameter[] parameters }
class Parameter {
  String name
  PrimitiveType primitiveType }
```

b

```
enum PrimitiveType
  returns PrimitiveType:
  BOOL='bool' | INTEGER ='int' |
  FLOAT='float' | STRING = 'string';
ServiceModel returns ServiceModel:
  microservices+=Microservice+;
Microservice returns Microservice:
  'microservice' name=ID '{'
  interfaces+=Interface+ '}';
Interface returns Interface:
  'interface' name=ID '{'
  operations+=Operation+'}';
Operation returns Operation:
  (returnType=PrimitiveType |
  voidReturnType?='void')
  name=ID '('
  (parameters+=Parameter
  (',' parameters+=Parameter)*)?')';
Parameter returns Parameter:
  primitiveType=PrimitiveType name=ID;
```

c

```
microservice AddressBookService {
  interface AddressBook {
    int addEntry(
      int addressBookId,
      string name,
      string address
    )
    string getFormattedEntry(
      int addressBookId,
      int entryId
    )
    void deleteEntry(
      int addressBookId,
      int entryId
    )
    float getQuota(
      int addressBookId
    )
  }
}
```

d

Fig. 1 Example of a metamodel-first approach to modeling language development. (**a**) and (**b**) show the metamodel of the modeling language. (**c**) depicts the grammar of a textual concrete syntax for the metamodel. (**d**) comprises an example model expressed in the concrete syntax

simulation, and transformation additionally increase models' value. Given their distributed nature, service-based software systems are inherently complex [27]. Thus, we consider it sensible in general to investigate the application of MDD in MSA engineering.

In addition, MSA exhibits certain characteristics, which further strengthen our conviction that reasoning about MDD approaches for MSA engineering will be worthwhile. Table 1 lists such characteristics according to Newman [23] and correlates them with MDD means that are likely to be supportive in their context

Table 1 Overview of MSA characteristics and supportive MDD means [30]

MSA characteristic	Supportive MDD means	Summary of means application	Expected benefits
Service identification	Model transformation	Refinement of domain models towards implementation	Increase of efficiency and domain models' value
Technology heterogeneity	Abstraction	Concise, viewpoint-specific documentation of the software architecture	Cost reduction of architecture definition and enabling of model reuse
Technology heterogeneity	Code generation	Transformation of architecture models to, e.g., microservice implementation stubs	Increase of developer productivity and reduction of service migration costs
Organizational alignment	Modeling languages	Provisioning of modeling languages with, e.g., DevOps-aware modeling viewpoints	Concise MSA modeling with reduced conceptual clutter and reuse of viewpoint models

[30]. The MDD approaches described in Sects. 4 and 5 particularly address the listed MSA characteristics.

In the following, we describe the application of the supportive MDD means listed in Table 1 as well as the potential benefits per MSA characteristic.

2.2.1 Service Identification

Domain-driven design (DDD) [10] is a methodology to capture domain knowledge in *domain models*. They result from collaborative modeling of domain experts and software engineers. Newman proposes to use DDD to determine the boundaries of microservice candidates [23]. However, DDD-based domain models are, by intent, expressed as underspecified UML class diagrams [29]. Thus, they commonly only serve as documentation artifacts and "implementation templates" [10]. While documentation is a benefit of models that pays off in the long run [40], refinement model transformations (cf. Sect. 2.1) could help to directly increase domain models' value. Therefore, they could automatically be transformed to more implementation-specific models for subsequent modeling steps [29] (cf. Sect. 5.6.1).

2.2.2 Technology Heterogeneity

Technology heterogeneity [23] results from MSA teams being free in their technology choices. It leads to additional costs when new members join a team and also need to learn its technologies, or when services are migrated to other technologies [38].

As models abstract from selected details (cf. Sect. 2.1), they can support the induction of new team members, e.g., by presenting the microservice architecture's topology in a technology-agnostic way [3]. In addition, code generation helps to decrease costs that emerge when migrating a service to another technology. Technology-agnostic architecture models can be reused across technology-specific code generators to produce, e.g., boilerplate code (cf. Sect. 5.1).

2.2.3 Organizational Alignment

MSA promotes to align software architecture and team structure to increase communication efficiency, and also fosters DevOps [22]. Thus, a microservice may be maintained by a team whose members have heterogeneous technical backgrounds and roles. While service developers are responsible for the implementation of microservices, service operators focus on their deployment and operation (cf. Sect. 5.1).

MDD supports collaboration of different stakeholder roles with *modeling viewpoints* [24]. A viewpoint model captures only those parts of a system that concern certain stakeholder roles. This approach is particularly useful when engineering complex systems with many cross-cutting concerns, because modeling viewpoints decompose the overall system's complexity into specialized concern-specific modeling tasks [11]. Models of different viewpoints can then be composed to reason about coherent system parts or reuse modeled elements across model transformations.

In the following, we present two approaches for graphical and textual model-driven MSA engineering. They are discussed w.r.t. the described MSA characteristics and their supportive MDD means (cf. Table 1). Furthermore, we reason about open questions concerning the limitations and constraints of employing MDD to MSA.

However, before we present the modeling approaches in detail in Sects. 4 and 5, we first introduce the case study of an MSA-based software system in Sect. 3. It will be used as a running example throughout Sects. 4 and 5 in order to facilitate the understanding of the underlying principles of the presented modeling approaches.

3 Case Study

This section introduces an MSA-based software system that will act as a case study for Sects. 4 and 5. Sections 3.1 and 3.2 describe its context and architecture.

3.1 Context

The case study application is located in the electromobility domain. It constitutes an MSA-based software system that enables its users to rent their electric vehicles'

Table 2 Selected functionalities of the case study application

#	Title	Category	Description
F1	Point sharing	Charging point management	Users must be able to offer their charging point to drivers of electric vehicles and configure a price for its usage
F2	Status query	Charging point management	The application allows for querying a charging point's status, e.g., if it is in use and how long a vehicle parks in front of it
F3	Parking space search	Charging point management	The application provides users with a function to search for free parking spaces with charging points in a given quarter
F4	Point booking	Payment	Users can book shared charging points. The application also handles the related payment processes
F5	Environmental data query	Environment monitoring	Charging points integrate sensors for environmental data like fine dust concentration. Authorized users can query that data

charging points to other electric vehicle drivers. Moreover, the application aims to foster the reuse of parking spaces and the reduction of fine dust emissions in populous city quarters. Therefore, it facilitates the finding of free parking spaces for electric vehicles and gathers environmental data from sensors built into charging points.

The application provides its users with capabilities to offer, search, and book private charging stations, pay for their usage, and monitor environmental data. It also communicates with charging points to activate and deactivate charging processes, and determines if a vehicle arrived at or left a parking space with a charging point. Table 2 shows an overview of selected functionalities of the case study application. They are structured in three categories, depending on whether they address the management of charging points, payment processes, or the monitoring of environmental data. Each functional category is then mapped to a microservice in Sect. 3.2.

3.2 *Case Study Architecture*

Figure 2 shows the architecture of the case study application. Each category from Table 2 is realized by a specific functional microservice.

The "ChargingService" implements functionalities F1 to F3 (cf. Table 2). The payment processing for functionality F4 is realized by the "PaymentService." It is isolated from the "ChargingService" due to security requirements. The "EnvironmentService" provides functionality F5, i.e., the querying of environmental data. Functionalities related to user interaction are realized in a specialized "UIService."

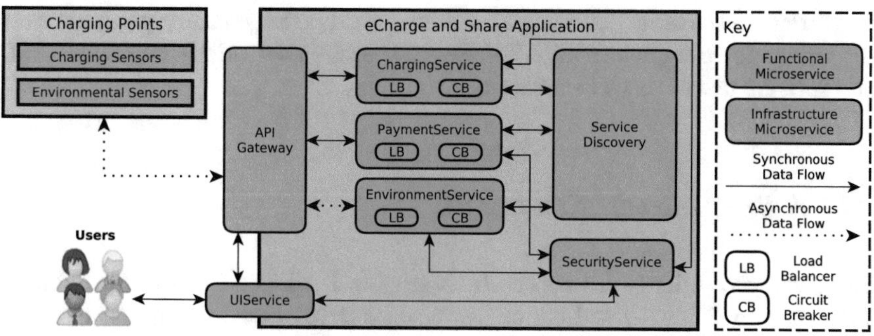

Fig. 2 Architecture overview of the case study

Next to functional microservices, the application consists of microservices that provide the architecture with infrastructure capabilities (cf. Fig. 2). The "ServiceDiscovery" is an architecture-internal registry for every microservice instance [2]. The "APIGateway" provides external service consumers with a uniform interface to exposed functionalities. For instance, it receives sensor data from charging points and forwards them to the services. Together with the "SecurityService," the "APIGateway" realizes a Single-Sign-On gateway, i.e., consumers do not need to reauthenticate for every service interaction. Instead, the "SecurityService" issues a unique security token to identify consumers and their access rights based on the authentication credentials they sent to the "APIGateway."

Each microservice encapsulates a circuit breaker (CB) and load balancer (LB) [2] (cf. Fig. 2). The CB prevents failure cascades in that it blocks periodically failing service interactions. The LB realizes client-side load balancing within services.

The case study application was realized with Spring Cloud.[3] Most services interact synchronously (cf. Fig. 2) and therefore employ REST with JSON as data format. However, interactions between "Charging Points," "APIGateway," and "EnvironmentService" instances happen asynchronously via MQTT.[4] Environmental data can thus efficiently be processed as a continuous stream of measuring points.

4 AjiL—A Graphical Approach Towards Model-Driven Microservice Development

AjiL [36] is a graphical language and toolkit for model-driven MSA engineering. It comprises concepts to specify functional microservices, REST-based interfaces, service security, and deployment. Moreover, it allows for declaring API gateways

[3]http://www.spring.io/projects/spring-cloud.

[4]http://www.mqtt.org.

and service discoveries (cf. Sect. 3). An integrated code generator produces stubs for service logic implementation (cf. Sect. 2). Section 4.1 briefly introduces AjiL, and Sect. 4.2 discusses its benefits and drawbacks.

4.1 A Brief Introduction to AjiL

We developed AjiL as an approach to graphical MDD of MSA. Therefore, it comprises an Eclipse-based editor that enables developers to construct diagrams of an intended microservice architecture. From the diagrams, an integrated code generator produces boilerplate code for subsequent service implementation. To this end, we chose Java and Spring Cloud as target technologies, because they are widely used in MSA practice due to their maturity, good developer availability, and tool support [5].

AjiL's abstract syntax (cf. Sect. 2.1) was derived in a bottom-up approach from the target technologies. That is, we analyzed several MSA implementations relying on Java and Spring Cloud, and designed the metamodel accordingly [36]. However, basic modeling concepts, e.g., for services and interfaces, are kept technology-agnostic by decomposing the metamodel into two hierarchical packages. The first package contains the basic concepts. The second package extends them with technology-specific information for code generation.

AjiL's concrete syntax (cf. Sect. 2.1) consists of two types of *box-and-line diagrams* [6, 36]. The *overview diagram* focuses on expressing the architecture's topology. Figure 3a shows the AjiL overview diagram for the case study (cf. Fig. 2).

Microservices are displayed as cubes and a cube's color identifies the respective service's type (cf. Fig. 3a). For instance, yellow cubes represent security services and blue cubes correspond to functional microservices like the "PaymentService" from the case study (cf. Sect. 3). The interface of a microservice is modeled as a bordered circle next to the service cube. Outgoing service interactions are expressed in the form of edges that start at the outgoing service's interface circle and end at the receiving service's cube. Service-specific properties like endpoints or interface names are specified textually in the properties tab below the diagram editor.

AjiL's second diagram type is the *detailed diagram* [36]. It exists for every functional microservice in an overview diagram and defines a service's integral components, i.e., its interface and data entities. Figure 3b shows a detailed AjiL diagram for the case study's "PaymentService" (cf. Fig. 2). Data entities are depicted as blue boxes with two compartments. The first compartment stores the entity's name and the second compartment clusters its attributes. Black arrows represent associations between entities. Entities can be assigned to a *data model* (displayed as a gray circle) to reflect semantic coherence. Detailed diagrams also model service interfaces. An interface is depicted as a green box that holds a set of operations (displayed as gray boxes). An operation processes instances of the data entities being assigned to it via black arrows. For example, in Fig. 3b the "getInvoice" operation of the "InvoiceInterface" processes the "Invoice" entity of the "Payment" data model.

a

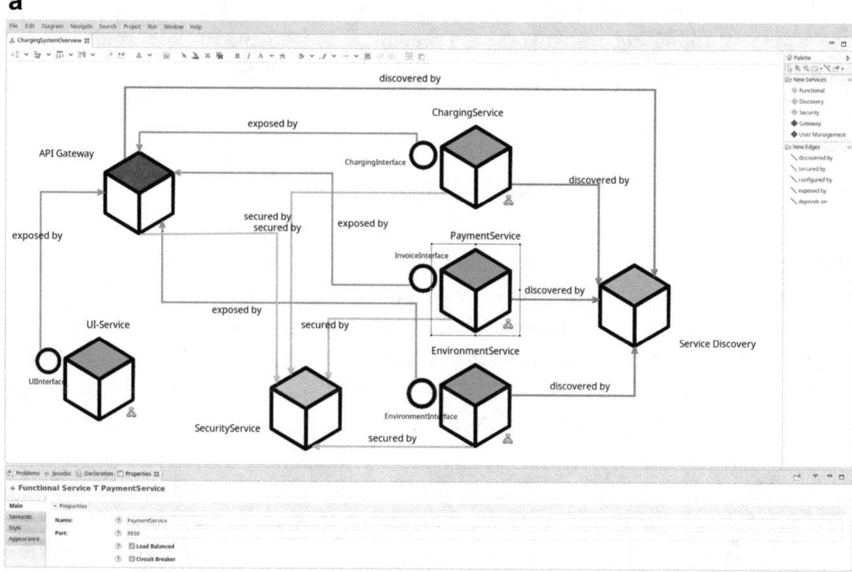

b

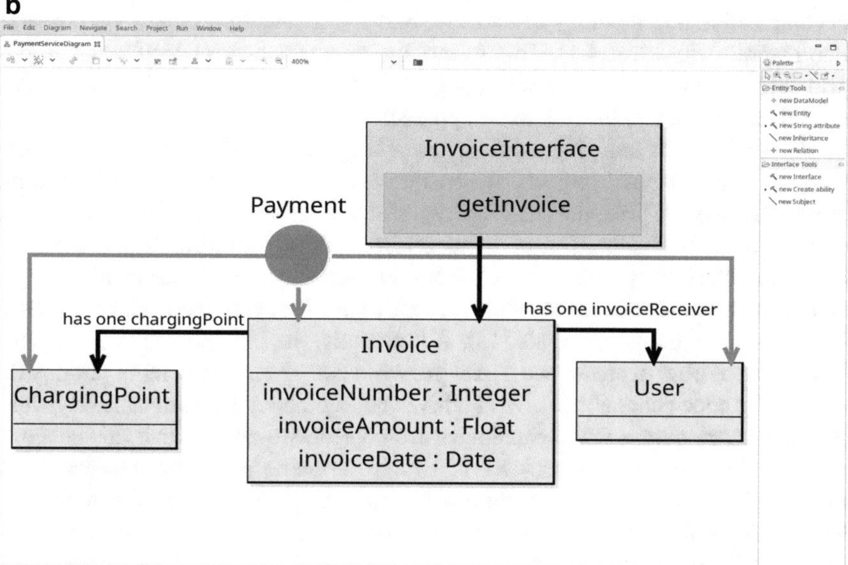

Fig. 3 (**a**) AjiL overview diagram for the case study (cf. Sect. 3) in Eclipse. (**b**) AjiL detailed diagram for the "PaymentService" (cf. Sect. 3) in Eclipse

AjiL was realized with EMF (cf. Sect. 2.1). More specifically, we used Sirius[5] as the graphical modeling framework and Acceleo[6] to implement the template-based code generation [6]. AjiL is available on GitHub[7] as an Eclipse plugin.

4.2 Benefits and Drawbacks of AjiL

We employed AjiL in teaching and application-oriented research projects. In the teaching case, our main focus was on explaining the building blocks and topology of MSA-based software systems to undergraduates. In this context, AjiL's graphical notation facilitated the students' structural understanding of microservice architectures. Moreover, the relationship between models and derived code was directly obvious, because AjiL allows for selective generation of microservices' boilerplate code.

In general, graphical notations for the programming of computer systems are considered to be more accessible than textual notations, because they map better with the way people think [28]. Also, they tend to have a higher level of abstraction. AjiL reflects these characteristics in the form that it clearly shows the functional decomposition and topology of an MSA-based software architecture via box-and-line diagrams (cf. Sect. 4.1). This fosters the understanding of MSA's underlying principle of autonomous, loosely coupled services and makes AjiL particularly suitable to get started with the MSA approach as such.

However, when applying AjiL in research projects, which are usually more complex than students' projects, we encountered several drawbacks related to the graphical notation. First, the graphical representations need a lot of on-screen space as illustrated in Fig. 3a. Ten or more services already exacerbate the overview diagrams' clarity significantly. Moreover, the graphical arrangement of a bigger amount of microservices is too slow for experienced programmers who are used to textual programming languages [13]. Additionally, the high degree of abstraction is limiting AjiL's expressiveness and forces a lot of assumptions regarding the underlying code generator [6]. While this is not a problem for comparatively small projects where only a few technologies are present, we noticed that this becomes an issue for larger MSA projects in which the same modeling concepts need to be realized with different technologies depending on services and teams (cf. Sect. 2.2.2). AjiL lacks the possibility to express this heterogeneity in the realization. Finally, AjiL does not support MSA's organizational alignment characteristic (cf. Sect. 2.2.3). Instead, it focuses on providing a coherently accessible view on an MSA-based software system. The distribution of diagram parts over MSA teams and their subsequent consolidation is out of AjiL's scope [36].

[5] https://www.eclipse.org/sirius.

[6] https://www.eclipse.org/acceleo.

[7] https://www.github.com/SeelabFhdo/AjiL.

In summary, based on the successful application of AjiL in teaching as well as for designing MSA-based software systems that are small in both the number of services and teams, we are certain that graphical notations are a promising way to explain and understand MSA. However, while graphical representations tend to be attractive to the human reader, they may lack the necessary precision and expressiveness [20]. In particular, we experienced this issue with AjiL when modeling complex microservice architectures and their organizational environments. Thus, we shifted our focus on developing a more efficient MDD approach for the engineering of real-world MSA-based software systems, which exhibit a significant number of services, distributed teams, and technologies being used.

5 Viewpoint-Specific Model-Driven Microservice Development with Textual Modeling Languages

This section presents our second approach towards model-driven MSA engineering [33]. It differs from AjiL (cf. Sect. 4) in that it aims to (1) consider technology heterogeneity of microservices (cf. Sect. 2.2.2), (2) reduce modeling complexity via viewpoints (cf. Sect. 2.2.3), (3) scale with team distribution, and (4) increase modeling conciseness and efficiency by employing a textual notation.

The section first introduces a workflow for distributed, viewpoint-specific MSA modeling (cf. Sect. 5.1). Sections 5.2–5.4 present the modeling languages for each viewpoint in the workflow. Section 5.5 outlines their implementation. Section 5.6 discusses the approach and derives subsequent research questions.

5.1 Modeling Viewpoints and Workflow

The viewpoint-specific modeling approach addresses DevOps-based MSA teams and involves domain experts to cope with MSA's domain-driven "Service Identification" characteristic (cf. Sect. 2.2.1). Table 3 lists the considered stakeholder roles.

The viewpoint-specific MSA modeling approach is based on a workflow for model-driven MSA engineering [32], which involves the stakeholder roles in Table 3. Figure 4 presents a methodological overview of the workflow.

The workflow in Fig. 4 considers MSA's technology heterogeneity (cf. Sect. 2.2.2) twofoldly. First, teams are free to employ MDD for their services' implementation and operation. Second, teams can independently decide upon the used technologies. In Fig. 4, each model-driven team uses a different technology for their services' implementation, i.e., "T1" and "T3." These could, for instance, refer to different programming languages. Both teams, however, employ the same

Table 3 Considered stakeholder roles in the viewpoint-specific MSA modeling approach

Role	Description
Domain expert	Domain experts have a deep knowledge of the domain being addressed by an MSA-based software system. Their primary interest is to obtain a system that sufficiently fits their needs and expectations. They collaborate with service developers to iteratively capture relevant domain knowledge (cf. Sect. 5.2)
Service developer	Service developers are concerned with building a software system that fulfills the functional, quality, and technical requirements of domain experts and other stakeholders. Service developers have the technical knowledge for this task. They are familiar with, e.g., programming and specification languages, and can support domain experts in expressing their domain knowledge in a modeling language. Additionally, they are aware of the conceptual and technical building blocks of MSA (cf. Sect. 5.3)
Service operator	Service operators are familiar with languages used to construct software systems. Moreover, they are aware of the concerns related to microservice deployment and operation. Therefore, they can coordinate with service developers on a technical level (cf. Sect. 5.4). The distinction between service developers and operators allows for flexibility regarding the composition of MSA teams. It supports DevOps strategies in which developers and operators are different persons, as well as strategies in which developers are also responsible for operation concerns

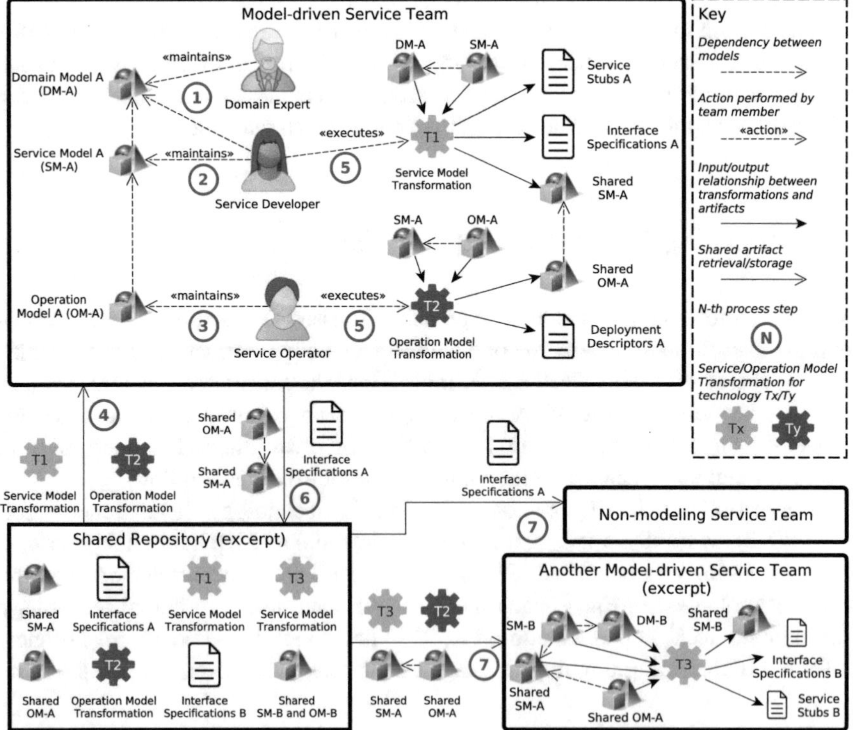

Fig. 4 Workflow for distributed, model-driven MSA engineering [32]

technology "T2" for service operation. In practice, this could be a container platform like Docker.[8] The workflow's methodology consists of seven steps (cf. Fig. 4)[9]:

S.1 *Domain Data Modeling*

In the first step, domain experts and service developers collaboratively construct and maintain a domain model (DM; cf. Sect. 2.2.1). It comprises the domain concepts, their structures, and relationships.

S.2 *Service Modeling*

From the DM, a service model (SM) is derived by a service developer. It clusters microservices, their interfaces, and operations.

S.3 *Operation Modeling*

Based on the SM, an operation model (OM) is constructed and maintained by the service operator. It specifies deployments and other operation-related information for the microservices in the SM.

S.4 *Model Transformation Retrieval*

After creation or refinement of an SM and OM, service developers and operators apply model transformations to derive artifacts from the models (cf. Sect. 2.1). The transformations are retrieved as executable applications from the shared repository that also hosts the *shared libraries* [23]. Separate service and operation model transformations (SMT and OMT) exist for different technologies, e.g., an SMT for "T1" and an OMT for "T2" (cf. Fig. 4).

S.5 *Model Transformation Execution*

The retrieved model transformations are now executed on input models. SMTs transform input SMs together with the DMs they refer to (cf. Sect. 5.3) into service stubs, interface specifications, and shared SMs. Service stubs comprise generated boilerplate code for subsequent service implementation. Interface specifications encapsulate the description of service interfaces in a technology-agnostic format, e.g., OpenAPI.[10] They can be shared with teams that do not employ MDD (cf. Fig. 4). Shared SMs, on the other hand, can directly be used by model-driven teams. A shared SM contains information extracted from SMT input models, which were specified as being visible to other MSA teams or service consumers (cf. Sect. 5.3). Shared models enable model-driven teams to also use their MDD tools to express dependencies to services of other teams.

OMTs work analogously to SMTs. They use operation and referred service models as inputs (cf. Sect. 5.4). The produced artifacts comprise deployment descriptors, e.g., Dockerfiles, and shared OMs.

---

[8]https://www.docker.com.

[9]The steps are sequentially described, but may be continuously executed, e.g., domain models could be refined iteratively. Furthermore, there is only one entity shown per model type and stakeholder representative, but teams are free to construct more models per type as deemed sensible.

[10]https://www.github.com/OAI/OpenAPI-Specification.

A central requirement for SMTs and OMTs is that they do not overwrite custom, service-specific code in repeated executions on evolved input models. In combination with a versioning shared repository this supports iterative *model refinement* [6], continuous delivery, and agile DevOps [22].

S.6 *Propagation of Shared Artifacts*

This step comprises the transmission of shared artifacts to the shared repository.

S.7 *Shared Artifact Retrieval and Application*

From the shared repository, the shared artifacts are available to other teams. Nonmodeling teams retrieve, e.g., interface specifications from it (cf. Fig. 4) to develop microservices that can interact with those of other teams. Conversely, model-driven teams can also acquire shared models from the repository to refer to the services of other model-driven teams directly in their own models. Thus they can, e.g., execute SMTs to generate artifacts that automatically reflect the dependencies of their microservices to those of other model-driven teams.

For each stakeholder role in Table 3 and Fig. 4, a dedicated modeling language was derived to enable the construction of models from the respective modeling viewpoint. Figure 5 details the relationships between the viewpoint-specific model types depicted in Fig. 4. Additionally, Fig. 5 shows on which elements the relationship is based. For instance, a service model refers to domain concepts in a domain model.

Sections 5.2–5.4 present the modeling languages with which each stakeholder role can construct the viewpoint-specific model types depicted in Fig. 5.

5.2 Domain Data Modeling Language

The domain data modeling language enables domain experts and service developers to express static domain knowledge about an MSA-based software system [29, 33] (cf. Sect. 5.1). Figure 6 shows the metamodel of the language (cf. Sect. 2.1).

The domain data modeling language defines the type system for the modeling languages of the viewpoint-specific modeling approach (cf. Fig. 5). The central modeling concept of the built-in type system is `PrimitiveType` (cf. Fig. 6) and each concrete primitive type is a specialization of it. The specializations are,

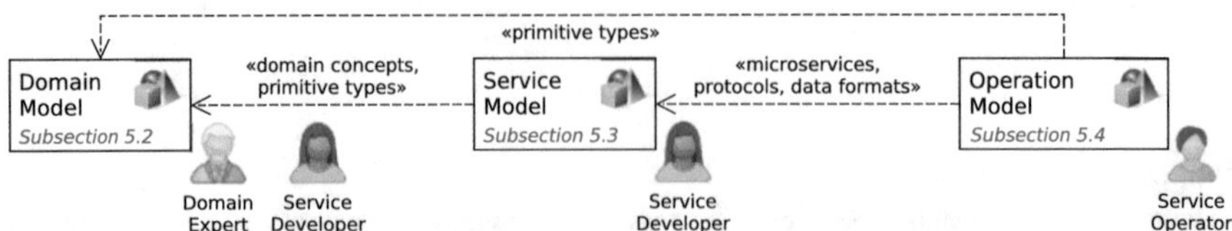

Fig. 5 Overview of relationships between viewpoint-specific model types. Arrows correspond to the semantics of UML dependency associations. The modeling concepts being shared between model types are depicted as association stereotypes

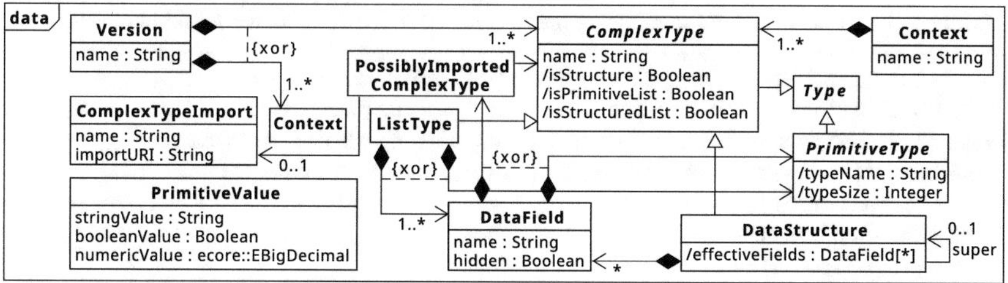

Fig. 6 Metamodel of the domain data modeling language

however, omitted in Fig. 6 for brevity. The primitive types of the type system comprise the eight primitive types of Java, i.e., boolean, byte, character, double, float, integer, long, and short [14]. Furthermore, Date and String primitive types exist to natively express points in time and character sequences, respectively. The `PrimitiveValue` concept (cf. Fig. 6) provides the modeling languages with a means to express instances of primitive types (cf. Sect. 5.4). The conversion rules of the type system observe Java's *widening primitive conversion* mechanism [14], i.e., smaller types can be converted to greater types without losing information.

The metamodel supports the definition of `DataStructures` and `ListTypes` (cf. Fig. 6). A data structure is a named `ComplexType` that is composed of `DataFields`. A data field has a name and a primitive or complex type. The latter type may be defined in the same domain model as the data field or be imported from another domain model. The `ComplexTypeImport` concept enables such imports by referring to the model file that contains the domain model to import (`importURI` property) and assigning an alias (`name`) to it. The alias acts as a shorthand reference for the imported file. Basically, the import mechanism is pivotal for establishing relationships between viewpoint models of the same or different types (cf. Fig. 5).

The domain data modeling language supports inheritance of data fields between data structures (`super` property of `DataStructure` in Fig. 6). All data fields that are not marked as being `hidden` are inherited. The derived property `effectiveFields` of `DataStructure` determines local as well as inherited fields of a data structure. Moreover, the `ListType` concept enables domain modelers to express sequences of primitive values or data fields.

The conversion rules for complex types build upon the conversion rules for primitive types. A data structure is convertible to another if all of its primitively typed effective fields are convertible. Complex typed effective fields are then recursively checked for convertibility. In the process of checking the conversion compatibility of two data structures, the ordering of their data fields is ignored. This follows the tolerant reader pattern [23], which is common in MSA, i.e., a microservice that receives data structure instances is responsible for their restructuring if necessary. List types also follow this logic in case they encapsulate data fields (cf. Fig. 6). For lists of primitive values, Java's widening primitive conversion is applied.

Listing 1 Example of a domain model expressed with the domain data modeling language

```
1 /* Excerpt of domain model file "payment.data" */
2 import datatypes from "common.data" as commonData
3 import datatypes from "charging.data" as chargingData
4 version v01 { context Payment { structure Invoice {
5   int invoiceNumber,
6   float invoiceAmount,
7   date invoiceDate,
8   commonData::v01.Common.User invoiceReceiver,
9   chargingData::v01.Charging.ChargingPoint chargingPoint } } }
```

The domain data modeling language also defines concepts for namespaces. `Versions` (cf. Fig. 6) can be used to organize evolving domain models. `Contexts` provide a means to organize parts of a domain model that share a semantic domain. Conceptually, they correspond to DDD's bounded context pattern [10].

To demonstrate the usage of the domain data modeling language, Listing 1 shows an excerpt of the domain model of the case study's "PaymentService" (cf. Sect. 3). The model is expressed in the language's concrete textual syntax (cf. Sect. 2.1).

Lines 2 and 3 comprise two instances of the `ComplexTypeImport` modeling concept (cf. Fig. 6). The domain models with the `importURIs` "common.data" and "charging.data" are imported under the aliases "commonData" and "chargingData". In line 4, a `Version` (cf. Fig. 6) with `name` "v01" is created. It clusters a `Context` called "Payment", which itself defines a `DataStructure` "Invoice". This data structure models invoices that are created by the "PaymentService" (cf. Sects. 3 and 4.1). In lines 5 to 7, three `DataFields` that represent an invoice's number, amount, and date are defined for the structure (cf. Fig. 6). They exhibit the built-in, concrete `PrimitiveTypes` "int", "float", and "date". Furthermore, the structure encapsulates two data fields that are typed with imported complex types (lines 8 and 9). The first field, "invoiceReceiver", identifies the user to whom the invoice was issued. The corresponding "User" data structure is defined in the imported domain model with the alias "commonData". The second complex typed field "chargingPoint" represents the charging point, which the user activated to charge her electric vehicle (cf. Sect. 3). The referenced data structure "ChargingPoint" originates from the imported domain model with the alias "chargingData".

5.3 Service Modeling Language

The service modeling language addresses the modeling needs of service developers (cf. Sect. 5.1) with concepts to express microservices, their interfaces, and operations [33]. It allows for importing domain models which were constructed with the domain data modeling language (cf. Sect. 5.2). Figure 7 shows the metamodel of the

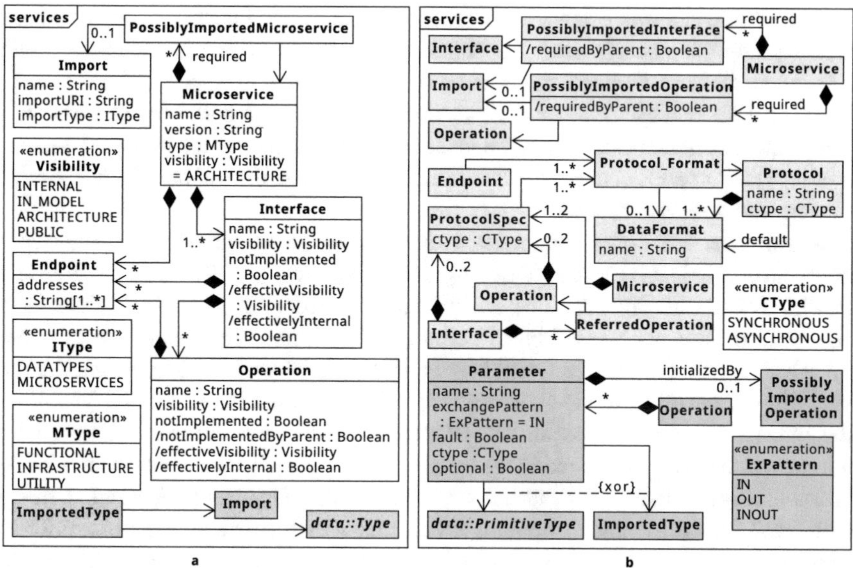

Fig. 7 Metamodel of the service modeling language. Coherent concept structures are colored uniformly

service modeling language, which, due to its complexity, has been divided into two parts. Coherent concept structures are colored uniformly.

The metamodel is centered around the `Microservice` concept (cf. Fig. 7a). A microservice has a `name` and a `version`. It may be of a functional, infrastructure, or utility `type`. A functional microservice realizes a business function and an infrastructure microservice provides technical capabilities to other services [34]. Utility microservices cluster generic functions, e.g., the resolution of geolocations.

A microservice exhibits a `visibility` (cf. Fig. 7a). The default `ARCHITECTURE` visibility makes the service discoverable for all microservices of the architecture. With a `PUBLIC` visibility, a service is additionally invokable by architecture-external consumers. An `INTERNAL` visibility prevents access to the microservice from other teams' services, e.g., to restrict the invocation of team-internal utility services.

A microservice has at least one `ProtocolSpec` that determines its default protocol and possibly data format for a given communication type (`Protocol_Format` concept and `CType` enumeration in Fig. 7b). If a `Protocol_Format` instance lacks a `DataFormat`, the default format of the `Protocol` is implicitly considered.

A microservice may have several `Endpoints` (cf. Fig. 7a). An endpoint associates addresses with protocols and data formats (`Protocol_Format` concept in Fig. 7b). Endpoint addresses are logical, e.g., they represent the path segments of a URI. Physical address parts, e.g., scheme and authority of a URI, are determined in operation models (cf. Sect. 5.4).

A microservice may depend on other services, their interfaces, or operations (see below). To specify such dependencies, a microservice is associated with a `PossiblyImportedMicroservice` (cf. Fig. 7a), `PossiblyImported-Interface` (cf. Fig. 7b), or `PossiblyImportedOperation` (cf. Fig. 7b). The required element can be defined either in the same or an imported service model. The `Import` concept depicted in Fig. 7a enables the import of other service models into a service model.

A microservice comprises at least one `Interface` (cf. Fig. 7a). Interfaces may have a `visibility`, whereby the semantics of `ARCHITECTURE` and `PUBLIC` visibility are the same as for microservices. An `INTERNAL` interface, however, is only visible within its defining microservice and cannot be required by other microservices. If no visibility is specified for an interface, it inherits the visibility of its microservice. In case the microservice has an internal visibility, the interface implicitly has an `IN_MODEL` visibility and can be referenced by microservices being contained in the same service model. This enables the modeling of internal interfaces of, e.g., utility services. An interface can be marked as being `notImplemented` and hence not invokable, which provides the possibility to iteratively design APIs until they are stable, or to subsequently deactivate deprecated interfaces. Like microservices, interfaces may have explicit endpoints and protocol specifications assigned (cf. Fig. 7a, b).

An interface clusters at least one `Operation` or `ReferredOperation` (cf. Fig. 7a, b). Operations have a `name`, a `visibility`, and may be `notImple-mented` like interfaces. Operations can have several named, possibly `optional` `Parameters` (cf. Fig. 7b). A parameter has a built-in primitive type (cf. Sect. 5.2) or a complex type being imported from a domain model (`ImportedType` concept in Fig. 7a). The import of domain-specific types realizes the relationship between domain and service models (cf. Fig. 5), and hence between the domain and service viewpoint.

A parameter may be incoming, outgoing, or both (`ExPattern` enumeration in Fig. 7b). If an operation has several outgoing parameters, they are returned to the service consumer as fields of a consolidating data structure. Outgoing parameters may also be used to signal failures to callers (`fault` property of `Parameter`). For each parameter, its communication type (`ctype`) must be specified. In combination with the optional flag and exchange pattern, the communication type determines the parameter's and thus the operation's calling behavior. Operations may only be invoked, if all their nonoptional, synchronously incoming parameters receive a value. During processing, an operation may expect incoming asynchronous parameters and yield results in the form of outgoing asynchronous parameters. Callers can expect to receive nonoptional outgoing synchronous parameters after processing. A parameter may be modeled as being `initializedBy` a required operation (see above). If an initialization relationship between a parameter and an operation exists, type checking is performed on all outgoing parameters of the operation and the modeler is warned if none of them is compatible with the parameter (cf. Sect. 5.2).

Listing 2 Example of a service model expressed with the service modeling language

```
1  /* Excerpt of service model file "payment.services" */
2  import datatypes from "payment.data" as paymentData
3  protocols {
4    sync rest data formats json default with format json;
5    async mqtt data formats json default with format json; }
6  @sync(protocols.rest) @async(protocols.mqtt)
7  functional microservice org.example.PaymentService {
8    @endpoints(protocols.rest : "/invoice";)
9    public interface InvoiceInterface {
10     @endpoints(protocols.rest : "/{invoiceNumber}";)
11     getInvoice(sync in invoiceNumber : int,
12       sync out invoice : paymentData::v01.Payment.Invoice); } }
```

Interfaces can comprise `ReferredOperations` (cf. Fig. 7b). They enable compositions of interfaces in that invocations of referred operations are forwarded to their actual implementations in their defining interfaces.

Listing 2 shows an excerpt of the service model for the case study's "PaymentService" (cf. Sects. 3 and 4.1) in the service modeling language.

Line 2 comprises an instance of the `Import` modeling concept for the `DATATYPES` import type (cf. Fig. 7a). It results in the data structures and list types that are defined in the domain model of the case study's "PaymentService" (cf. Listing 1), to be available in the service model under the alias "paymentData". In lines 3 to 5, two `ProtocolSpec` instances are declared (cf. Fig. 7b). They define the `Protocol` and `DataFormat` combinations "rest/json" and "mqtt/json" for synchronous and asynchronous communication within the case study (cf. Sect. 3). Both protocol specifications are assigned to the "PaymentService" in line 6, which results in all instances of the `Parameter` modeling concept to implicitly rely on them for the respective communication type (cf. Fig. 7b). The "PaymentService" is modeled as a `Microservice` instance (cf. Fig. 7a) in lines 7 to 12. It comprises the `Interface` "InvoiceInterface" with a dedicated `Endpoint` for the "rest" `Protocol`. The interface defines the "getInvoice" `Operation` to enable consumers to retrieve a created invoice. Therefore, the operation has to be invoked synchronously with the "invoiceNumber" `Parameter` (cf. Fig. 7b). The corresponding invoice is then returned via REST in the JSON data format within the outgoing synchronous parameter "invoice". Its type is the "Invoice" data structure being imported from Listing 1.

5.4 Operation Modeling Language

The operation modeling language is used by service operators to specify the deployment and operation of microservices being imported from service models

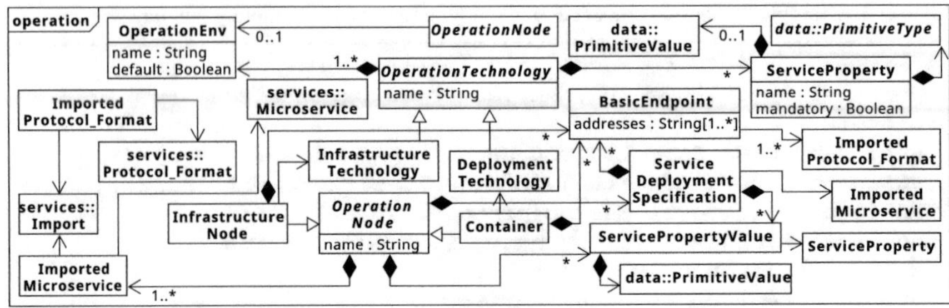

Fig. 8 Metamodel of the operation modeling language

[33] (cf. Sects. 5.1 and 5.3). Figure 8 shows the metamodel of the operation modeling language (cf. Sect. 2.1).

The central concept of the metamodel is `OperationNode` (cf. Fig. 8). It represents a computing node to which microservices can be assigned. Therefore, microservices are imported from service models with the `ImportedMicroservice` concept. An operation node may be associated with an `OperationEnv` to specify the technology that runs on the node, e.g., a Docker image. In the case a node does not refer to an operation environment, the `default` environment is used.

`Containers` and `InfrastructureNodes` refine the semantics of an operation node (cf. Fig. 8). Containers model microservice deployments, while infrastructure nodes provide technical capabilities to assigned microservices, e.g., for service discovery [2]. The technology of a container or infrastructure node, e.g., Docker or Eureka,[11] is specified with an instance of the `OperationTechnology` modeling concept. Operation technologies may also predefine a `ServiceProperty` set. A service property can, for instance, refer to a configuration parameter of a Dockerfile. The `ServicePropertyValue` concept allows for assigning a concrete, primitive value to a predefined property, either as default value on an operation node or specifically per deployed service (see below).

The assignment of a microservice to an operation node may be substantiated via `ServiceDeploymentSpecifications` (cf. Fig. 8). They enable the specification of physical `BasicEndpoints` for services, e.g., the scheme and authority of a URI (cf. Sect. 5.3). The association between `ServiceDeploymentSpecification` and `ServicePropertyValue` (cf. Fig. 8) provides a means to assign a value to a predefined operation technology's property for a specific service.

Listing 3 shows an excerpt of the operation model for the case study's "PaymentService" (cf. Sect. 3) in the concrete syntax of the Operation Modeling Language.

[11] https://www.github.com/Netflix/eureka.

Listing 3 Example of an operation model expressed with the operation modeling language

```
1 /* Excerpt of operation model file "payment.operation" */
2 import microservices from "payment.services" as paymentserv
3 deployment technologies { docker { operation environments = "
    openjdk" } }
4 container PaymentContainer deployment technology docker
5   deploys paymentserv::org.example.PaymentService {
6     default values { basic endpoints {
7       protocols.rest, protocols.mqtt : "http://www.example.com
          :8080"; } } }
```

Line 2 imports the service model from Listing 2. In line 3, the `DeploymentTechnology` "docker" is defined together with its default `OperationEnv` "openjdk" (cf. Fig. 8). Lines 4 to 7 model a `Container` called "PaymentContainer". It exhibits a `ServiceDeploymentSpecification` for the `ImportedMicroservice` "PaymentService" (cf. Fig. 8). Additionally, lines 6 and 7 specify the `BasicEndpoints` for the "rest" and "mqtt" `Protocol` (cf. Fig. 7b) instances being imported from Listing 2. This results in the "PaymentService" to be reachable under the URI "http://www.example.com:8080". Thus, the service's "getInvoice" operation is invokable with REST via "http://www.example.com:8080/invoice/{invoiceNumber}", i.e., the logical REST `Endpoints` of the interface and operation (cf. Listing 2) are preceded by the basic endpoint URI.

5.5 *Implementation*

The viewpoint-specific modeling languages were implemented on the basis of EMF and the metamodel-first approach described in Sect. 2.1. The metamodels shown in Figs. 6, 7, and 8 were realized with Xcore (cf. Fig. 1b). Based on the Xcore metamodels, we developed the modeling languages' grammars and editors with Xtext. Therefore, each concept of the modeling languages' metamodels was expressed as an Xtext grammar rule (cf. Fig. 1c). From the Xtext grammars, Eclipse-based editors were derived. They implement syntax highlighting, model validation, and scoping. The import mechanism of the modeling languages exploits Xtext's adapter for Eclipse's *global scoping* mechanism [37] in order to define which model elements are *exported* to the global scope and can thus be *imported* into other models. For example, `DataStructure` instances are exported from domain models (cf. Sect. 5.2) to the global scope, so that service models can refer to them (cf. Sect. 5.3). The modeling languages, editors, and case study models from Sects. 5.2, 5.3, and 5.4 are available on GitHub.[12]

5.6 Discussion and Subsequent Research Questions

In the following, we discuss characteristics of the presented viewpoint-specific MSA modeling approach. Furthermore, we identify initial research questions (RQs) related to MDD of MSA, which might form a starting point for the subsequent development of a rigorous research roadmap. We align our discussion to the steps of the workflow for model-driven MSA engineering (cf. Sect. 5.1).

5.6.1 Workflow Step 1: Domain Data Modeling

The domain data modeling language enables domain experts and service developers to express the structures and relationships of domain concepts (cf. Sect. 5.2). The modeling language's concepts correspond to a subset of UML package and class diagrams. Like UML packages, versions and contexts provide basic namespace definition mechanisms, while data structures exhibit semantics of UML classes, including inheritance. We decided to integrate a UML subset in the domain data modeling language, because Evans made the experience that in DDD a reduced set of UML's static modeling concepts is sufficient for domain experts to express domain coherences [10]. Moreover, it is commonly assumed that DDD is a practicable methodology to identify and tailor microservices [23]. We are, however, not aware of a recent study that confirms the perception that DDD fosters the collaboration of domain and technical experts in the context of MSA engineering.

Furthermore, DDD-based domain models are, by intent, underspecified [29], while the domain data modeling language does not allow renouncing, e.g., data types or field names, because these information are pivotal for microservice implementation. In addition, the language is, as opposed to static DDD-based domain models [10], text-based. Given that DDD is a good fit for microservice identification and tailoring, a solution that involves graphical modeling of underspecified domain models would need to precede the Domain Data Modeling workflow step with a DDD-based modeling step. The resulting underspecified UML class diagrams could then be transformed into domain models as expected by the Domain Data Modeling Language (cf. Sect. 2.2.1). Service developers would then have to complete the models with missing technical details that were omitted in the underspecified UML diagrams. Table 4 lists RQs in the context of Domain Data Modeling for MSA that arise from the described issues.

[12] https://github.com/SeelabFhdo/ddmm.

Table 4 Research questions related to domain data modeling

#	Description
RQ.1	To what extent is DDD a good fit for collaborative microservice design by domain experts and service developers in terms of architectural correctness, consistency, and modeling efficiency?
RQ.2	What are alternative approaches for microservice design? What are their strengths and weaknesses compared to DDD?
RQ.3	On what minimal set of UML modeling concepts can domain experts and service developers agree to balance underspecification and technical rigor?

5.6.2 Workflow Steps 2 and 3: Service and Operation Modeling

These workflow steps involve the construction of service and operation models via the service and operation modeling languages (cf. Sects. 5.3 and 5.4). To this end, both languages share the same primitive type system provided by the domain data modeling language (cf. Sect. 5.2). However, the type system is aligned to Java. While Java has a comparatively mature technical ecosystem for MSA engineering and is one of the most popular languages in this field [5], alternatives like JavaScript, Python, and Go exist [35]. One of the benefits of MDD is abstraction via models and code generation (cf. Sect. 2.1). Thus, MDD could cope with MSA's programming language heterogeneity by providing code generators for different service implementation languages (cf. Sect. 2.2.2) to, e.g., increase the efficiency of service migrations. A shortcoming of this approach is that type-checking within service models is still constrained to Java.

Furthermore, the service modeling language only considers the specification of static service aspects, e.g., interfaces and operations' type signatures. The modeling of behavior of service operations or compositions is not yet possible. The operation modeling language, on the other hand, currently only allows for specifying infrastructure nodes for several microservices. However, infrastructure components exist that solely concern a single service, e.g., load balancers and circuit breakers (cf. Sect. 3). Table 5 lists RQs derived from the described issues.

Table 5 Research questions related to service and operation modeling

#	Description
RQ.4	How can conversions between different MSA programming languages be specified on the model-level to ensure correct type-checking between microservices of different languages?
RQ.5	Which existing modeling languages for behavior specification could be leveraged to express the behavior of microservice operations and compositions?
RQ.6	Which modeling concepts for service-specific infrastructure need to be integrated in the languages without introducing an extensive degree of technology dependency?

5.6.3 Workflow Steps 4 and 5: Retrieval and Execution of Model Transformations

Model transformations can be characterized by OMG's model-driven architecture (MDA) [24]. In MDA, a platform-independent model (PIM) is transformed to a platform-specific model (PSM) from which code is generated. However, the distinction between PIM and PSM is not that strict within the languages of the presented viewpoint-specific modeling approach. The Domain Data Modeling Language relies on Java's type system and can be considered platform specific to a certain degree (cf. Sect. 5.2). The service modeling language comprises concepts for the specification of protocol technologies, which may be platform specific for proprietary protocols (cf. Sect. 5.3). The operation modeling language requires to model specific operation technologies (cf. Sect. 5.4).

The degree of platform dependency hence varies across modeling languages. This makes the implementation of reusable code generators harder and code generation more opaque. First, it is not directly obvious to service developers in which primitive types of the target language the modeling languages' primitive types will result upon code generation. For instance, a code generator for Go can currently decide how to treat modeled float data fields, i.e., whether they result in `float32` or `float64` variables (cf. RQ.4 in Sect. 5.6.2). Second, it is not guaranteed that a code generator is capable of interpreting and producing protocols and data formats in service models. While REST/JSON and MQTT/JSON are quite common in MSA, proprietary or special-purpose protocols such as CoAP[13] are probably not. This is also true for container technologies and infrastructure nodes being expressed in operation models. Table 6 comprises RQs derived from the described issues.

Table 6 Research questions related to model transformations

#	Description
RQ.7	How can modelers cope with technology heterogeneity on the model level by considering different type systems, protocols, and operation technologies employed in MSA engineering?
RQ.8	How can the implementation of code generators be simplified for technical MSA experts that are not aware of the principles of MDD to encourage MSA teams to develop and share code generators for new technologies with other teams (cf. Sect. 5.1)?
RQ.9	How can code generation be integrated into *continuous delivery pipelines* [23]?

[13]http://www.coap.technology.

5.6.4 Workflow Steps 6 and 7: Propagation, Retrieval, and Application of Shared Artifacts

The workflow considers the propagation and integration of generated shared models and interface specifications between MSA teams (cf. Sect. 5.1). Interface specifications may be used by nonmodeling teams to enable their services to conformably interact with those of model-driven teams. However, the service modeling language currently only allows for importing (possibly shared) service models (cf. Sect. 5.3). Model-driven MSA teams are thus not able to import interface specifications, e.g., in the OpenAPI format (cf. Sect. 5.1), into their service models.

The propagation of shared service and operation models provides a foundation for extending the application of sophisticated MDD techniques from the intra-team to the extra-team level. Particularly, all shared models are stored in a shared repository (cf. Sect. 5.1). This allows for performing automatic model validations that concern the overall architecture, e.g., during continuous delivery (cf. RQ. 9 in Sect. 5.6.3). For example, it could be determined, prior to runtime, if all microservices being required by one team are actually deployed to a container, associated to a service discovery, and are hence discoverable at runtime (cf. Sects. 5.3 and 5.4). Furthermore, it could be checked if a microservice uses the latest version of another microservice or if a service is a candidate for investigating its possible deprecation, because it is not required by any other service. Moreover, the domain models of different teams could be compared based on similarity measures to, e.g., identify teams that probably use the same domain concepts but with different peculiarities. For example, two teams could define the domain concept of a person but with different properties. However, the validation of microservices, for which no models exist, would yet not be possible.

Additionally, we envision MSA to be a predestined area of application for Collaborative Model-Driven Software Engineering (CMDSE) [12]. CMDSE enables stakeholders to collaboratively construct and manage shared models. Moreover, it provides stakeholders with communication means to share information related to collaborative modeling activities. For example, domain models could be collaboratively constructed by domain experts that are not in the same place. Service and operation models could be stored in dedicated model repositories and imported into

Table 7 Research questions related to shared artifacts

#	Description
RQ.10	How can shared artifacts that do not represent models as expected by the viewpoint-specific modeling languages be imported into models constructed with them?
RQ.11	What model validations across team boundaries are possible and beneficial in model-driven MSA engineering?
RQ.12	How can such validations be integrated into automated continuous delivery pipelines?
RQ.13	To what extent is CMDSE a sensible area of application for MSA and what CMDSE means are beneficial to be employed for model-driven MSA engineering?

the languages' editors (cf. Sect. 5.5) without having to retrieve their files from a shared repository. Table 7 presents RQs that were inferred from the described issues.

6 Related Work

In the following, we present work related to employing specialized programming languages and MDD techniques in MSA engineering.

Jolie [21] is a programming language for the implementation of service-based software systems. A Jolie program represents a single microservice and consists of two parts. The first part specifies the behavior and business functionality of the service. It relates input data, logic, and output data. The second part focuses on the service's deployment and operation. It defines, among others, ports and interfaces. Jolie provides language primitives for, e.g., services' logic execution modalities, messaging patterns, port locations, and protocols. While Jolie represents a specific technology for microservice implementation, our modeling languages (cf. Sects. 4 and 5) are basically technology agnostic. The models can be translated via code generators to different implementation and deployment technologies like Jolie. Furthermore, our languages only provide modeling concepts for structural components of microservice architectures, e.g., data structures, service interfaces, and operation nodes. Behavioral modeling is currently not supported (cf. Sect. 5.6.2).

Bogner and Zimmermann introduce the concept of EA-mini-descriptions (EA-MDs) [4] with the aim to integrate microservices into enterprise architectures (EAs) via MDD. An EA-MD clusters service-specific information like runtime data and models of service endpoints and communication channels. Similar to our viewpoint-specific modeling approach (cf. Sect. 5), EA-MDs separate domain-specific information from service models. However, EA-MDs do not comprise models for service operation. Moreover, MDD techniques for specifying EA-MDs are not presented in [4]. One goal of EA-MDs is to derive an EA's topology from microservice compositions. In our viewpoint-specific modeling approach, an architectural model is likely to be deducible from shared service models leveraging CMDSE (cf. Sect. 5.6.4).

Düllmann and van Hoorn present a metamodel for performance and resilience benchmarking of MSA-based software systems [8]. Therefore, they generate microservice stubs, including benchmark code from models. The metamodel shares commonalities with our languages' metamodels (cf. Sects. 4 and 5). In particular, it comprises modeling concepts for operations, endpoints, and service deployment. However, it lacks concepts for interfaces, operation parameters, protocols, and data formats. Neither a workflow on how to integrate the metamodel in MSA engineering processes nor domain modeling (cf. Sects. 5.1 and 5.2) are covered.

Granchelli et al. employ MDD to recover the architecture of an MSA-based software system [15]. The recovery process comprises a static analysis of the system's source code repository in order to extract information such as service and container names, input and output ports, and the system's developers' identities.

Additionally, a dynamic analysis is conducted at system runtime to collect data like physical container addresses and network interfaces. From the results of both analysis steps, an architecture model is derived. It can be refined via a specialized modeling language, e.g., to specify dependencies between microservices. The language's metamodel shares certain commonalities with our languages' metamodels (cf. Sects. 4 and 5). For instance, it defines concepts for microservices of functional and infrastructure type, interfaces, and endpoints. However, the metamodel lacks concepts to express service operations and domain concepts. Instead, it covers the modeling of team structures and products, which could be a sensible extension to our viewpoint-specific modeling approach, possibly realized as an import relationship between our service modeling language and the language defined in [15].

MicroBuilder [39] is a tool for modeling REST-based microservice architectures. It comprises a textual modeling language and a code generator that derives microservice code based on Java and the Spring Cloud framework. MicroBuilder's modeling language allows for specifying microservices and their endpoints in the form of ports. Conversely to our modeling languages, it does not comprise modeling concepts for interfaces and operations (cf. Sects. 4 and 5.3). Instead, MicroBuilder organizes REST request methods in *entities*, which may also have domain-specific attributes. Conceptually, entities and attributes correspond to data structures and fields in the domain data modeling language (cf. Sect. 5.2). However, MicroBuilder's entity concept mixes domain and service modeling. Moreover, there exist no dedicated modeling concepts for list types, asynchronous communication, and service deployment in the MicroBuilder language. In addition, it does not consider distributed microservice modeling (cf. Sect. 5.1). Instead, each MicroBuilder model clusters all microservices of a single MSA-based software system.

Artač et al. present DICER, an Eclipse-based MDD approach for the development of Infrastructure-as-Code (IaC) solutions [1]. While being originally designed for Data-Intensive Architectures (DIA), DICER can be extended to model deployment aspects of MSA-based software systems [1]. DICER exploits UML's profile mechanism [24] to define a modeling language that abstracts from IaC-related programming languages and approaches for infrastructure creation, configuration, and management. UML deployment diagrams can be augmented with elements from DICER's UML profile and be transformed into TOSCA blueprints [26]. These blueprints specify the deployment nodes and their relationships according to the input diagram. DICER also comprises a library of predefined TOSCA types for several big data frameworks. It is utilized throughout the transformation process to generate the technology-specific parts of the modeled DIA. DICER exhibits similarities to our operation modeling language (cf. Sect. 5.4). Both modeling approaches allow for expressing different types of deployment nodes and their operation environments. While our language is more focused on modeling deployment characteristics of a microservice, i.e., the deployed artifact, DICER also covers a variety of aspects of the physical deployment infrastructure. It could therefore be beneficial to combine both approaches by transforming operation models in our operation modeling language into DICER models to derive a TOSCA-based description for service deployment.

7 Conclusion and Future Work

This chapter presented and discussed approaches and open challenges to applying model-driven development (MDD) in the engineering of software systems based on microservice architecture (MSA). To this end, we briefly introduced MDD and discussed its general applicability to MSA (cf. Sect. 2). Next, we described a case study from the electromobility domain, which was used throughout the chapter to illustrate and discuss the presented MSA modeling approaches (cf. Sect. 3). Section 4 introduced AjiL, a graphical modeling language and toolkit for model-driven MSA engineering. Due to the accessibility provided by graphical modeling approaches, we experienced AjiL to foster the understanding of basic MSA concepts. However, it is not well suited for modeling large and complex MSA-based software systems.

This insight led us to develop a textual, viewpoint-specific approach for model-driven MSA engineering (cf. Sect. 5). It provides language primitives for fundamental MSA concepts and supports a workflow for distributed, model-driven MSA engineering based on DevOps (cf. Sect. 5.1). The textual approach considers the different stakeholder roles in the workflow with dedicated modeling languages. The domain data modeling language enables domain experts and service developers to collaboratively capture relevant domain concepts (cf. Sect. 5.2). The service modeling language is used by service developers to construct microservice models (cf. Sect. 5.3). The operation modeling language is employed by service operators to specify service deployments (cf. Sect. 5.4). Models expressed with the languages are integrated on the basis of an import mechanism. Sections 5.5 and 5.6 elucidated the languages' implementation and discussed their characteristics in light of the presented workflow. From the discussion, a catalog of 13 research questions (RQs) was derived. It may provide a foundation for a rigorous research roadmap towards model-driven MSA engineering.

In our current and future works, we investigate certain RQs in the context of our viewpoint-specific MSA modeling approach. Currently, we are working on a code generation framework that eases the implementation of code generators for MSA experts who are not familiar with MDD (cf. RQ. 8 in Sect. 5.6.3). It involves a technology modeling language [31] that supports the specification and modularization of technology-related MSA information. Such information comprises, e.g., primitive types of implementation languages, protocols, and operation technologies (cf. RQs. 4 and 6 in Sect. 5.6.2, and RQ. 7 in Sect. 5.6.3). *Technology models* constructed with the technology modeling language can be imported into service and operation models to assign technology-specific aspects to microservices and operation nodes. Consequently, they determine the code generators to be employed to produce technology-specific artifacts for modeled services and nodes. With the code generation framework and technology modeling language we aim at providing an efficient solution to cope with the fast pace at which new MSA technologies arise. That is, technology-specific aspects are decoupled from technology-agnostic modeling concepts. As a result, service and operation models can largely remain stable when new technologies are to be used for their eventual realization.

However, certain assumptions were made in the design of the viewpoint-specific modeling approach, e.g., the selection of modeling concepts and the constraints for their interplay. Hence, it is possible that the modeling languages are not fully applicable yet to specific use cases of MSA. Therefore, to identify such use cases and extend the languages to cope with their specific requirements, we plan to evaluate the languages by employing them to more complex MSA-based software systems than the case study presented in Sect. 3. We are also particularly interested in the applicability of the approach when the number of services and teams, and thus the number of modeling artifacts to be maintained, increases. Moreover, we plan to explore model-driven MSA engineering on the extra-team level with holistic model validations and CMDSE (cf. RQs. 11 to 13 in Sect. 5.6.4).

References

1. M. Artač, T. Borovšak, E. Di Nitto, M. Guerriero, D. Perez-Palacin, D.A. Tamburri, Infrastructure-as-code for data-intensive architectures: A model-driven development approach, in *2018 IEEE International Conference on Software Architecture (ICSA)* (IEEE, Piscataway, 2018), pp. 156–165
2. A. Balalaie, A. Heydarnoori, P. Jamshidi, Microservices architecture enables DevOps: migration to a cloud-native architecture. IEEE Softw. **33**(3), 42–52 (2016)
3. L. Bass, P. Clements, R. Kazman, *Software Architecture in Practice*, 3 edn. (Addison-Wesley, Upper Saddle River, 2013)
4. J. Bogner, A. Zimmermann, Towards integrating microservices with adaptable enterprise architecture, in *2016 IEEE 20th International Enterprise Distributed Object Computing Workshop (EDOCW)* (IEEE, Piscataway, 2016), pp. 1–6
5. J. Bogner, J. Fritzsch, S. Wagner, A. Zimmermann, Microservices in industry: insights into technologies, characteristics, and software quality, in *2019 IEEE International Conference on Software Architecture Companion (ICSA-C)* (IEEE, Piscataway, 2019), pp. 187–195
6. B. Combemale, R.B. France, J.M. Jézéquel, B. Rumpe, J. Steel, D. Vojtisek, *Engineering Modeling Languages* (CRC Press, Boca Raton, 2017)
7. N. Dragoni, S. Giallorenzo, A.L. Lafuente, M. Mazzara, F. Montesi, R. Mustafin, L. Safina, *Microservices: Yesterday, Today, and Tomorrow* (Springer, Berlin, 2017), pp. 195–216
8. T.F. Düllmann, A. van Hoorn, Model-driven generation of microservice architectures for benchmarking performance and resilience engineering approaches, in *Proceedings of the 8th ACM/SPEC on International Conference on Performance Engineering Companion, ICPE '17 Companion* (ACM, New York, 2017), pp. 171–172
9. T. Erl, *Service-Oriented Architecture (SOA) Concepts, Technology and Design* (Prentice Hall, Upper Saddle River, 2005)
10. E. Evans, *Domain-Driven Design* (Addison-Wesley, Boston, 2004)
11. R. France, B. Rumpe, Model-driven development of complex software: a research roadmap, in *Future of Software Engineering (FOSE '07)* (IEEE, Piscataway, 2007), pp. 37–54
12. M. Franzago, D.D. Ruscio, I. Malavolta, H. Muccini, Collaborative model-driven software engineering: a classification framework and a research map. IEEE Trans. Softw. Eng. **44**(12), 1146–1175 (2018)
13. T. Goldschmidt, S. Becker, A. Uhl, Classification of concrete textual syntax mapping approaches, in *Model Driven Architecture—Foundations and Applications*, eds. by I. Schieferdecker, A. Hartman (Springer, Berlin, 2008), pp. 169–184

14. J. Gosling, B. Joy, G.L. Steele, G. Bracha, A. Buckley, *The Java Language Specification, Java SE*, 8 edn. (Addison-Wesley, Boston, 2014)
15. G. Granchelli, M. Cardarelli, P.D. Francesco, I. Malavolta, L. Iovino, A.D. Salle, Towards recovering the software architecture of microservice-based systems, in *2017 IEEE International Conference on Software Architecture Workshops (ICSAW)* (IEEE, Piscataway, 2017), pp. 46–53
16. T. Killalea, The hidden dividends of microservices. Queue **14**(3), 10:25–10:34 (2016)
17. N. Kratzke, P.C. Quint, Investigation of impacts on network performance in the advance of a microservice design, in *Cloud Computing and Services Science*, ed. by M. Helfert, D. Ferguson, V. Méndez Muñoz, J. Cardoso (Springer, Berlin, 2017), pp. 187–208
18. L. Lúcio, M. Amrani, J. Dingel, L. Lambers, R. Salay, G.M.K. Selim, E. Syriani, M. Wimmer, Model transformation intents and their properties. Softw. Syst. Model. **15**(3), 647–684 (2016)
19. J. Ludewig, Models in software engineering—an introduction. Softw. Syst. Model. **2**(1), 5–14 (2003)
20. S. Meliá, C. Cachero, J.M. Hermida, E. Aparicio, Comparison of a textual versus a graphical notation for the maintainability of MDE domain models: an empirical pilot study. Softw. Qual. J. **24**(3), 709–735 (2016)
21. F. Montesi, C. Guidi, G. Zavattaro, *Service-Oriented Programming with Jolie* (Springer, Berlin, 2014), pp. 81–107
22. I. Nadareishvili, R. Mitra, M. McLarty, M. Amundsen, *Microservice Architecture* (O'Reilly Media, Sebastopol, 2016)
23. S. Newman, *Building Microservices* (O'Reilly Media, Sebastopol, 2015)
24. Object Management Group, *Model Driven Architecture (MDA) Guide* (OMG, Needham, 2014), Version 2.0
25. Object Management Group, *Object Constraint Language (OCL)* (OMG, Needham, 2014), Version 2.4
26. D. Palma, T. Spatzier, *Topology and Orchestration Specification for Cloud Applications Version 1.0* (OASIS, Manchester, 2013)
27. M.P. Papazoglou, *Web Services and SOA: Principles and Technology*, vol. 2 (Pearson Education, Harlow, 2012)
28. M. Petre, Why looking isn't always seeing: Readership skills and graphical programming. Commun. Assoc. Comput. Mach. **38**(6), 33–44 (1995)
29. F. Rademacher, J. Sorgalla, S. Sachweh, Challenges of domain-driven microservice design: a model-driven perspective. IEEE Softw. **35**(3), 36–43 (2018)
30. F. Rademacher, J. Sorgalla, P. Wizenty, S. Sachweh, A. Zündorf, Microservice architecture and model-driven development: Yet singles, soon married (?), in *Proceedings of the 19th International Conference on Agile Software Development: Companion, XP '18* (ACM, New York, 2018), pp. 23:1–23:5
31. F. Rademacher, S. Sachweh, A. Zündorf, Aspect-oriented modeling of technology heterogeneity in microservice architecture, in *2019 IEEE International Conference on Software Architecture (ICSA)*, pp. 21–30 (IEEE, Piscataway, 2019)
32. F. Rademacher, J. Sorgalla, S. Sachweh, A. Zündorf, A model-driven workflow for distributed microservice development, in *Proceedings of the 34th ACM/SIGAPP Symposium on Applied Computing, SAC '19* (ACM, New York, 2019), pp. 1260–1262
33. F. Rademacher, J. Sorgalla, S. Sachweh, A. Zündorf, Viewpoint-specific model-driven microservice development with interlinked modeling languages, in *2019 IEEE International Conference on Service-Oriented System Engineering (SOSE)* (IEEE, Piscataway, 2019), pp. 57–66
34. M. Richards, *Microservices vs. Service-Oriented Architecture* (O'Reilly Media, Sebastopol, 2015)
35. G. Schermann, J. Cito, P. Leitner, All the services large and micro: revisiting industrial practice in services computing, in *Service-Oriented Computing—ICSOC 2015 Workshops*, eds. by A. Norta, W. Gaaloul, G.R. Gangadharan, H.K. Dam (Springer, Berlin, 2016), pp. 36–47

36. J. Sorgalla, P. Wizenty, F. Rademacher, S. Sachweh, A. Zündorf, Ajil: enabling model-driven microservice development, in *Proceedings of the 12th European Conference on Software Architecture: Companion Proceedings, ECSA '18* (ACM, New York, 2018), pp. 1:1–1:4
37. D. Steinberg, F. Budinsky, M. Paternostro, E. Merks, *EMF–Eclipse Modeling Framework*, 2 edn. (Pearson Education, Harlow, 2011)
38. D. Taibi, V. Lenarduzzi, On the definition of microservice bad smells. IEEE Softw. **35**(3), 56–62 (2018)
39. B. Terzić, V. Dimitrieski, S. Kordić, G. Milosavljević, I. Luković, *Development and Evaluation of Microbuilder: A Model-Driven Tool for the Specification of Rest Microservice Software Architectures* (Taylor and Francis, Milton Park, 2018), pp. 1034–1057
40. J. Whittle, J. Hutchinson, M. Rouncefield, The state of practice in model-driven engineering. IEEE Softw. **31**(3), 79–85 (2014)

Part IV
Development and Deployment

A Formal Approach to Microservice Architecture Deployment

Mario Bravetti, Saverio Giallorenzo, Jacopo Mauro, Iacopo Talevi, and Gianluigi Zavattaro

Abstract Following previous work on the automated deployment of component-based applications, we present a formal model specifically tailored for reasoning on the deployment of microservice architectures. The first result that we present is a formal proof of decidability of the problem of synthesizing optimal deployment plans for microservice architectures, a problem which was proved to be undecidable for generic component-based applications. Then, given that such proof translates the deployment problem into a constraint satisfaction problem, we present the implementation of a tool that, by exploiting state-of-the-art constraint solvers, can be used to actually synthesize optimal deployment plans. We evaluate the applicability of our tool on a realistic microservice architecture taken from the literature.

1 Introduction

Inspired by service-oriented computing, microservices structure software applications as highly modular and scalable compositions of fine-grained and loosely coupled services [30]. These features support modern software engineering practices, like continuous delivery/deployment [40] and application autoscaling [3]. A relevant problem in these practices consists of the automated deployment of the microservice application, i.e., the distribution of the fine-grained components over the available computing nodes, and its dynamic modification to cope, e.g., with positive or negative peaks of user requests.

In this chapter, we address the problem of planning the deployment, and redeployment, of microservice architectures in a formal manner, by presenting an approach for modeling microservice architectures that allows us to both prove

M. Bravetti (✉) · I. Talevi · G. Zavattaro
Università di Bologna, Bologna, Italy
e-mail: mario.bravetti@unibo.it; iacopo.talevi@studio.unibo.it; gianluigi.zavattaro@unibo.it

S. Giallorenzo · J. Mauro
University of Southern Denmark, Odense, Denmark
e-mail: saverio@sdu.dk; mauro@sdu.dk

A. Bucchiarone et al. (eds.), *Microservices*,
https://doi.org/10.1007/978-3-030-31646-4_8

formal properties and realize an implemented solution. We follow the approach taken by the *Aeolus component model* [24, 26, 27], which was used to formally define the problem of deploying component-based software systems and to prove that, in the general case, such problems are undecidable [24]. The basic idea of Aeolus is to enrich the specification of components with a finite state automaton that describes their deployment life cycle. Previous work identified decidable fragments of the Aeolus model: removing from Aeolus replication constraints used, e.g., to specify a minimal amount of services connected to a load balancer makes the deployment problem decidable, but nonprimitive recursive [26]; removing also conflicts used, e.g., to express the impossibility to deploy in the same system two types of components makes the problem PSpace-complete [44] or even poly-time [24], but under the assumption that every required component can be (re)deployed from scratch.

In a recent paper [17], we adapted the Aeolus model to formally reason on the deployment of microservices. To achieve our goal, we significantly revisited the formalization of the deployment problem, replacing Aeolus components with a model of microservices. The main difference between our model of microservices and Aeolus components lies in the specification of their deployment life cycle. Instead of using the full power of finite state automata, like in Aeolus and other TOSCA-compliant deployment models [19], we assume microservices to have two states: (1) creation and (2) binding/unbinding. Concerning creation, we use *strong* dependencies to express which microservices must be immediately connected to newly created ones. After creation, we use *weak* dependencies to indicate additional microservices that can be bound/unbound. The principle that guided this modification comes from state-of-the-art microservice deployment technologies like Docker [45] and Kubernetes [39]. In particular, the weak and strong dependencies have been inspired by Docker Compose [28], a language for defining multi-container Docker applications, where it is possible to specify different relationships among microservices using, e.g., the depends_on (resp. external_links) modalities that force (resp. do not force) a specific startup order similar to our strong (resp. weak) dependencies. Weak dependencies are also useful to model horizontal scaling, e.g., a load balancer that is bound to/unbound from many microservice instances during its life cycle.

In addition, w.r.t. the Aeolus model, we also consider resource/cost-aware deployments, taking inspiration from the memory and CPU resources found in Kubernetes. Microservice specifications are enriched with the amount of resources they need to run. In a deployment, a system of microservices runs within a set of computation *nodes*. Nodes represent computational units, e.g., virtual machines in an infrastructure-as-a-service cloud deployment. Each node has a cost and a set of resources available to the microservices it hosts.

In the model above, it is possible to define the *optimal deployment problem* as follows: given an initial microservice system, a set of available nodes, and a new target microservice to be deployed, find a sequence of reconfiguration actions that, once applied to the initial system, lead to a new deployment that includes the target microservice. Such a deployment is expected to be *optimal*, meaning that the total cost, i.e., the sum of the costs, of the nodes used is minimal. This problem was proved to be decidable [17] by presenting an algorithm working in three phases: (1) Generate a set of constraints whose solution indicates the microservices to be deployed and their distribution over the nodes (2) Generate another set of constraints whose solution indicates the connections to be established (3) Synthesize the corresponding deployment plan The set of constraints includes optimization metrics that minimize the overall cost of the computed deployment.

The algorithm has NEXPTIME complexity because, in the worst case, the length of the deployment plan could be exponential in the size of the input. However, since in practice the number of microservices deployable on one node is limited by the available resources, if each node can host at most a polynomial amount of microservices the deployment problem is NP-complete and the problem of deploying a system minimizing its total cost is an NP-optimization problem. Moreover, having reduced the deployment problem in terms of constraints, it is possible to exploit state-of-the-art constraint solvers [21, 35, 36], which are frequently used in practice to cope with NP-hard problems. In particular, we investigate the possibility to actually solve the deployment problem for microservices by exploiting Zephyrus2 [1], a configurator optimizer that was originally envisaged for the Aeolus model [25] but later extended and improved to support a new specification language and the possibility to have preferences on the metrics to optimize, e.g., minimize not only the cost but also the number of microservices. We have selected and customized Zephyrus2 because it can easily support the solution of the optimization problems to which we reduce the optimal deployment problem for microservices.

We have evaluated the actual exploitability of our implemented solution by computing the initial optimal deployment, and some possible reconfigurations, for a real-world microservice architecture, inspired by the reference email processing pipeline from Iron.io [34]. That architecture is modeled in the abstract behavioral specification (ABS) language, a high-level object-oriented language that supports deployment modeling [41]. Our technique is then used to compute two types of deployments: an initial one, with one instance for each microservice, and a set of deployments to horizontally scale the system depending on small, medium, or large increments in the number of emails to be processed. The experimental results are encouraging in that we were able to compute deployment plans that add more than 30 new microservice instances, assuming availability of hundreds of machines of three different types, and guaranteeing optimality.

Structure of the Chapter In Sect. 2 we formally study the microservice deployment problem. In Sect. 3 we discuss Zephyrus2, the tool used to solve such a problem, while in Sect. 4 we report the experimental results obtained by applying it to a real-world case study. Finally, Sect. 5 discusses related work and draws some concluding remarks.

Note that this chapter mainly reports and extends results published in [17] with an additional section, namely, Sect. 3, to provide more details on the Zephyrus2 tool and the extensions we implemented.

2 The Microservice Optimal Deployment Problem

In this section we present our model for representing microservice systems and their deployment. We start from an informal presentation of the model and then we move to define microservice deployment configurations, reconfiguration plans and the optimal deployment problem, providing its decidability proof and an analysis of its complexity.

2.1 Representing Microservice Systems and Their Deployment

We model microservice systems as aggregations of components with ports. Each port instantiates either a provided or a required interface. Interfaces describe offered and required functionalities. Microservices are connected by means of bindings indicating which port provides the functionality required by another port. As discussed in Sect. 1, we consider two kinds of requirements: strong required interfaces, that need to be already fulfilled when the microservice is created, and weak required interfaces, that must be fulfilled at the end of a deployment, or reconfiguration, plan. Microservices are enriched with the specification of the resources they need to properly run. Such resources are provided to the microservices by nodes. Nodes can be seen as the unit of computation executing the tasks associated with each microservice.

As an example, in Fig. 1 we report the representation of the deployment of a microservice system where a Message Receiver microservice handles inbound requests, passing them to a Message Analyzer that checks the email content and sends the attachments for inspection to an Attachment Analyzer. The Message Receiver has a port with a *weak* required interface that can be fulfilled by Message Analyzer instances. This requirement is weak, meaning that the Message Receiver can be initially deployed without any connection to instances

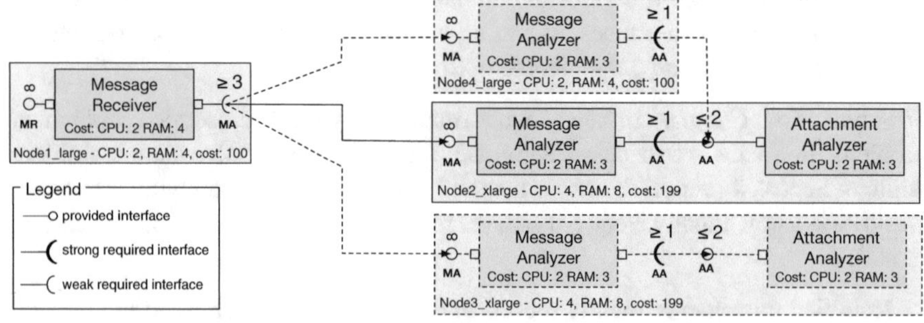

Fig. 1 Example of microservice deployment (blue boxes: nodes; green boxes: microservices; continuous lines: the initial configuration; dashed lines: full configuration)

of Message Analyzer. These connections can be established afterwards and reflect the possibility to horizontally scale the application by adding/removing instances of Message Analyzer. This last microservice has instead a port with a *strong* required interface that can be fulfilled by Attachment Analyzer instances. This requirement is strong to reflect the need to immediately connect a Message Analyzer to its Attachment Analyzer.

Figure 1 presents a reconfiguration that, starting from the initial deployment depicted in continuous lines, adds the elements depicted with dashed lines. Namely, a couple of new instances of Message Analyzer and a new instance of Attachment Analyzer are deployed. This is done in order to satisfy numerical constraints associated with both required and provided interfaces. For required interfaces, the numerical constraints indicate lower bounds to the outgoing bindings, while for provided interfaces they specify upper bounds to the incoming connections. Notice that the constraint ≥ 3 associated with the weak required interface of Message Receiver is not initially satisfied; this is not problematic because constraints on weak interfaces are relevant only at the end of a reconfiguration. In the final deployment, such a constraint is satisfied thanks to the two new instances of Message Analyzer. These two instances need to be immediately connected to an Attachment Analyzer: only one of them can use the initially available Attachment Analyzer, because of the constraint ≤ 2 associated with the corresponding provided interface. Hence, a new instance of Attachment Analyzer is added.

We also model resources: each microservice has associated resources that it consumes; see the CPU and RAM quantities associated with the microservices in Fig. 1. Resources are provided by nodes, which we represent as containers for the microservice instances, providing them the resources they require. Notice that nodes also have costs: the total cost of a deployment is the sum of the costs of the used nodes, e.g., in the example the total cost is 598 cents per hour, corresponding to the cost of 4 nodes: 2 C4 large and 2 C4 xlarge virtual machine instances of the Amazon public cloud.

2.2 Microservices, Nodes, and Deployment Configurations

We now move to formal definitions. Here we will introduce microservices (including their required/provided/conflicting interfaces and consumed resources), nodes, and deployment configurations.

We start from the definition of the types of microservices, i.e., Attachment Analyzer, Message Receiver, and Message Analyzer, in the example of Fig. 1, which can be instantiated when deploying microservice systems. In the following, we assume $\mathcal{I}$ to denote the set of all possible interfaces and $\mathcal{R}$ to be a finite set of kinds of resources. Moreover, we use $\mathbb{N}$ to denote natural numbers, $\mathbb{N}^+$ for $\mathbb{N} \setminus \{0\}$, and $\mathbb{N}^+_\infty$ for $\mathbb{N}^+ \cup \{\infty\}$.

Definition 1 (Microservice Type) The set Γ of *microservice types*, ranged over by $\mathcal{T}_1, \mathcal{T}_2, \ldots$, contains 5-ples $\langle P, D_s, D_w, C, R \rangle$ where:

- $P = (\mathcal{I} \nrightarrow \mathbb{N}^+_\infty)$ are the provided interfaces, defined as a partial function from interfaces to corresponding numerical constraints, indicating the maximum number of connected microservices.
- $D_s = (\mathcal{I} \nrightarrow \mathbb{N}^+)$ are the *strong* required interfaces, defined as a partial function from interfaces to corresponding numerical constraints, indicating the minimum number of connected microservices.
- $D_w = (\mathcal{I} \nrightarrow \mathbb{N})$ are the *weak* required interfaces, defined as the strong ones, with the difference that the constraint 0 can also be used, indicating that it is not strictly necessary to connect microservices.
- $C \subseteq \mathcal{I}$ are the conflicting interfaces.
- $R = (\mathcal{R} \rightarrow \mathbb{N})$ specifies resource consumption, defined as a total function from resources to corresponding quantities indicating the amount of required resources.

We assume sets $\mathtt{dom}(D_s)$, $\mathtt{dom}(D_w)$, and C to be pairwise disjoint.[1]

Notation In the remainder of the chapter, we denote the name of a microservice interface with the upper-case acronym of the name of its microservice, e.g., the interface of the Message Analyzer is denoted MA.

Given a microservice type $\mathcal{T} = \langle P, D_s, D_w, C, R \rangle$, we use the following postfix projections `.prov`, `.reqs`, `.reqw`, `.conf`, and `.res` to decompose it:

- `.prov` returns the partial function associating arities to provided interfaces, e.g., in Fig. 1, Message Receiver`.prov`(MR) $= \infty$.
- `.reqs` returns the partial function associating arities to strong required interfaces, e.g., in Fig. 1, Message Analyzer`.reqs`(AA) $= 1$.
- `.reqw` returns the partial function associating arities to weak required interfaces, e.g., in Fig. 1, Message Receiver`.reqw`(MA) $= 3$.
- `.conf` returns the conflicting interfaces.
- `.res` returns the total function from resources to their required quantities, e.g., in Fig. 1, Message Receiver`.res`(RAM) $= 4$.

When the numerical constraints are not explicitly indicated, we assume as default value ∞ for the provided interfaces, i.e., they can satisfy an unlimited amount of ports requiring the same interface, and 1 for required interfaces, i.e., one connection with a port providing the same interface is sufficient.

Inspired by [26], we allow a microservice to specify a conflicting interface that, intuitively, forbids the deployment of other microservices providing the same interface. Conflicting interfaces can be used to express conflicts among microservices, preventing both of them to be present at the same time, or cases in which only one

[1] Given a partial function f, we use $\mathtt{dom}(f)$ to denote the domain of f, i.e., the set $\{e \mid \exists e' : (e, e') \in f\}$.

microservice instance can be deployed, e.g., a consistent and available microservice that cannot be replicated.

Definition 2 (Nodes) The set $\mathcal{N}$ of *nodes* is ranged over by $o_1, o_2, \ldots$ We assume the following information to be associated with each node o in $\mathcal{N}$.

- A function $R = (\mathcal{R} \rightarrow \mathbb{N})$ that specifies node *resource availability*: We use $o.\texttt{res}$ to denote such a function.
- A value in $\mathbb{N}$ that specifies node *cost*: We use $o.\texttt{cost}$ to denote such a value.

As example, in Fig. 1, the node Node1_large is such that Node1_large.$\texttt{res}$(RAM) $= 4$ and Node1_large.$\texttt{cost} = 100$.

Notice that, both in Definitions 1 and 2, we use the same symbol R to denote the *resource* function: In the former case it quantifies resources consumed by microservice instances, in the latter it quantifies resources made available by nodes.

We now define configurations that describe systems composed of microservice instances and bindings that interconnect them. We use $\mathcal{Z}$ to denote the set of all possible microservice instances. A configuration, ranged over by $C_1, C_2, \ldots$, is given by a set of deployed microservice instances, with their associated type and node hosting them, and a set of bindings. Formally:

Definition 3 (Configuration) A *configuration* C is a 4-ple $\langle Z, T, N, B \rangle$ where:

- $Z \subseteq \mathcal{Z}$ is the set of the currently deployed *microservices*.
- $T = (Z \rightarrow \mathcal{T})$ are the *microservice types*, defined as a function from deployed microservices to microservice types.
- $N = (Z \rightarrow \mathcal{N})$ are the *microservice nodes*, defined as a function from deployed microservices to nodes that host them.
- $B \subseteq \mathcal{I} \times Z \times Z$ is the set of *bindings*, namely 3-ples composed of an interface, the microservice that requires that interface, and the microservice that provides it; we assume that, for $(p, z_1, z_2) \in B$, the two microservices z_1 and z_2 are distinct and $p \in (\texttt{dom}(T(z_1).\texttt{req}_\texttt{s}) \cup \texttt{dom}(T(z_1).\texttt{req}_\texttt{w})) \cap \texttt{dom}(T(z_2).\texttt{prov})$.

In our example, we have the binding (MA, inst_{mr}, inst_{ma}) where inst_{mr} and inst_{ma} are the two initial instances in continuous lines of Message Receiver and Message Analyzer type, respectively. Notice that the interface MA satisfies the inclusion constraint at the end of Definition 3 in that MA is a required interface of the Message Receiver type, while it is a provided interface of the Message Analyzer type. Moreover, concerning the microservice placement function N, we have $N(\text{inst}_{\text{mr}}) =$ Node1_large and $N(\text{inst}_{\text{ma}}) =$ Node2_xlarge.

2.3 Microservice Deployment Plans

We are now ready to formalize the notion of a microservice deployment plan, which represents a sequence of deployment configurations, with the aim of reaching a final configuration as in the example of Fig. 1, by means of *reconfiguration actions*.

The configurations traversed during a microservice deployment plan must satisfy a correctness constraint related to the intended meaning of strong and weak required interfaces and conflicts (see Definition 1). We first define *provisional correctness*, considering only constraints on strong required and provided interfaces, and then we define a general notion of configuration correctness, considering also weak required interfaces and conflicts. The former is intended for transient configurations traversed during the execution of a sequence of reconfigurations, while the latter is intended for the final configuration.

Definition 4 (Provisionally Correct Configuration) A configuration $C = \langle Z, T, N, B\rangle$ is *provisionally correct* if, for each node $o \in \mathtt{ran}(N)$, it holds[2]

$$\forall r \in \mathcal{R}.\ \ o.\mathtt{res}(r) \geq \sum_{z \in Z, N(z)=o} T(z).\mathtt{res}(r)$$

and, for each microservice $z \in Z$, both the following conditions hold:

- $(p \mapsto n) \in T(z).\mathtt{req_S}$ implies that there exist n distinct microservices $z_1, \ldots, z_n \in Z \backslash \{z\}$ such that for every $1 \leq i \leq n$, we have $\langle p, z, z_i\rangle \in B$;
- $(p \mapsto n) \in T(z).\mathtt{prov}$ implies that there exist no m distinct microservices $z_1, \ldots, z_m \in Z \backslash \{z\}$, with $m > n$, such that for every $1 \leq i \leq m$, we have $\langle p, z_i, z\rangle \in B$.

In the above definition, the initial inequality guarantees that the amount of resources provided by the nodes are sufficient to satisfy the requests of all the hosted microservices. The first item means that the strong requirements of all components are all satisfied because there are at least as many bindings on those ports as the associated lower bounds. The second item, on the other hand, guarantees that there are no extra connections on provided interfaces, because all the ports exposing a provided interface have no more bindings than the associated upper bound.

Definition 5 (Correct Configuration) A configuration $C = \langle Z, T, N, B\rangle$ is *correct* if C is provisionally correct and, for each microservice $z \in Z$, both the following conditions hold:

- $(p \mapsto n) \in T(z).\mathtt{req_W}$ implies that there exist n distinct microservices $z_1, \ldots, z_n \in Z \backslash \{z\}$ such that for every $1 \leq i \leq n$, we have $\langle p, z, z_i\rangle \in B$.
- $p \in T(z).\mathtt{conf}$ implies that for each $z' \in Z \backslash \{z\}$, we have $p \notin \mathtt{dom}(T(z').\mathtt{prov})$.

In the definition above, besides the guarantees already given by Definition 4, we have that also weak requirements are satisfied (first item), as well as conflicts (second item): i.e., if an instantiated microservice has a conflict with an interface, such an interface cannot be provided by any other microservice in the configuration.

[2]Given a (partial) function f, we use $\mathtt{ran}(f)$ to denote the range of f, i.e., the function image set $\{f(e) \mid e \in \mathtt{dom}(f)\}$.

Notice that, in the example in Fig. 1, the initial configuration in continuous lines is only provisionally correct in that the weak required interface MA, with arity 3, of the Message Receiver is not satisfied, because there is only one outgoing binding. The full configuration—including the elements in dotted lines—is instead correct: all the constraints associated with the interfaces are satisfied.

We now formalize how configurations evolve by means of atomic actions: we have *bind/unbind* actions to create/destroy bindings on ports with weak required interfaces; *new* to instantiate a new microservice instance and the necessary bindings on ports with strong required interface; and *del* to destroy a microservice and, implicitly, its bindings.

Definition 6 (Actions) The set $\mathcal{A}$ contains the following actions:

- $bind(p, z_1, z_2)$ where $z_1, z_2 \in \mathcal{Z}$, with $z_1 \neq z_2$, and $p \in \mathcal{I}$: add a binding between z_1 and z_2 on interface p, which is supposed to be a weak required interface of z_1 and a provide interface of z_2.
- $unbind(p, z_1, z_2)$ where $z_1, z_2 \in \mathcal{Z}$, with $z_1 \neq z_2$, and $p \in \mathcal{I}$: remove the specified binding on p, which is supposed to be a weak required interface of z_1 and a provide interface of z_2.
- $new(z, \mathcal{T}, o, B_s)$ where $z \in \mathcal{Z}, \mathcal{T} \in \Gamma, o \in \mathcal{N}$ and $B_s = (\mathtt{dom}(\mathcal{T}.\mathtt{reqs}) \rightarrow 2^{\mathcal{Z}-\{z\}})$; with B_s representing bindings from strong required interfaces in $\mathcal{T}$ to sets of microservices, such that for each $p \in \mathtt{dom}(\mathcal{T}.\mathtt{reqs})$, it holds $|B_s(p)| \geq \mathcal{T}.\mathtt{reqs}(p)$: add a new microservice z of type $\mathcal{T}$ hosted in o and bind each of its strong required interfaces to a set of microservices as described by B_s.[3]
- $del(z)$ where $z \in \mathcal{Z}$: remove the microservice z from the configuration and all bindings involving it.

In our example, assuming that the initially available Attachment Analyzer is named $\mathsf{inst_{aa}}$, we have that the action to create the initial instance of Message Analyzer is $new(\mathsf{inst_{ma}}$, Message Analyzer, Node2_xlarge, $(\mathsf{AA} \mapsto \{\mathsf{inst_{aa}}\}))$. Notice that it is necessary to establish the binding with the Attachment Analyzer because of the corresponding strong required interface.

The execution of actions can now be formalized using a labeled transition system on configurations, which uses actions as labels.

Definition 7 (Reconfigurations) Reconfigurations are denoted by transitions $C \xrightarrow{\alpha} C'$ meaning that the execution of $\alpha \in \mathcal{A}$ on the configuration C produces a new

[3]Given sets S and S' we use: 2^S to denote the power set of S, i.e., the set $\{S' \mid S' \subseteq S\}$; $S - S'$ to denote set difference; and $|S|$ to denote the cardinality of S.

configuration C'. The transitions from a configuration $C = \langle Z, T, N, B\rangle$ are defined as follows:

$$C \xrightarrow{bind(p,z_1,z_2)} \langle Z, T, N, B \cup \langle p, z_1, z_2\rangle\rangle$$
if $\langle p, z_1, z_2\rangle \notin B$ and
$p \in \mathtt{dom}(T(z_1).\mathtt{req_W}) \cap \mathtt{dom}(T(z_2).\mathtt{prov})$

$$C \xrightarrow{unbind(p,z_1,z_2)} \langle Z, T, N, B \backslash \langle p, z_1, z_2\rangle\rangle$$
if $\langle p, z_1, z_2\rangle \in B$ and
$p \in \mathtt{dom}(T(z_1).\mathtt{req_W}) \cap \mathtt{dom}(T(z_2).\mathtt{prov})$

$$C \xrightarrow{new(z,\mathcal{T},o,B_s)} \langle Z \cup \{z\}, T', N', B'\rangle$$
if $z \notin Z$ and
$\forall p \in \mathtt{dom}(\mathcal{T}.\mathtt{req_S}).\ \forall z' \in B_s(p).$
$p \in \mathtt{dom}(T(z').\mathtt{prov})$ and
$T' = T \cup \{(z \mapsto \mathcal{T})\}$ and
$N' = N \cup \{(z \mapsto o)\}$ and
$B' = B \cup \{\langle p, z, z'\rangle \mid z' \in B_s(p)\}$

$$C \xrightarrow{del(z)} \langle Z \backslash \{z\}, T', N', B'\rangle$$
if $T' = \{(z' \mapsto \mathcal{T}) \in T \mid z \neq z'\}$ and
$N' = \{(z' \mapsto o) \in N \mid z \neq z'\}$ and
$B' = \{\langle p, z_1, z_2\rangle \in B \mid z \notin \{z_1, z_2\}\}$

A *deployment plan* is simply a sequence of actions that transform a provisionally correct configuration without violating provisional correctness along the way and, finally, reach a correct configuration.

Definition 8 (Deployment Plan) A *deployment plan* P from a provisionally correct configuration C_0 is a sequence of actions $\alpha_1, \ldots, \alpha_m$ such that:

- There exist $C_1, \ldots, C_m$ provisionally correct configurations, with $C_{i-1} \xrightarrow{\alpha_i} C_i$ for $1 \leq i \leq m$.
- C_m is a correct configuration.

Deployment plans are also denoted with $C_0 \xrightarrow{\alpha_1} C_1 \xrightarrow{\alpha_2} \cdots \xrightarrow{\alpha_m} C_m$.

In our example, a deployment plan that reconfigures the initial provisionally correct configuration into the final correct one is as follows: a *new* action to create the new instance of Attachment Analyzer, followed by two *new* actions for the new Message Analyzers[4] and finally two *bind* actions to connect the Message Receiver to the two new instances of Message Analyzer.

Notice that since in deployment plans the requirements associated with strong interfaces must be satisfied immediately after each reconfiguration action, which must yield a provisionally correct configuration, it is possible to deploy a configuration with circular dependencies *only if at least one weak required interface is involved in the cycle*. In fact, having a cycle with only strong required interfaces would require to deploy all the microservices involved in the cycle simultaneously. We now formalize a well-formedness condition on microservice types to guarantee the absence of such configurations.

[4]Notice that the connection between the Message Analyzers and the corresponding Attachment Analyzers is part of these *new* actions.

Definition 9 (Well-Formed Universe) Given a finite set of microservice types U, that we also call *universe*, the strong dependency graph of U is as follows: $G(U) = (U, V)$ with $V = \{(\mathcal{T}, \mathcal{T}') \mid \mathcal{T}, \mathcal{T}' \in U \wedge \exists p \in \mathcal{I}.p \in \mathtt{dom}(\mathcal{T}.\mathtt{req_s}) \cap \mathtt{dom}(\mathcal{T}'.\mathtt{prov})\}$. The universe U is well-formed if $G(U)$ is acyclic.

In the following, we always assume universes to be well-formed. Well-formedness does not prevent the specification of microservice systems with circular dependencies, which are captured by cycles with at least one weak required interface.

2.4 Microservice Optimal Deployment Problem

We now have all the ingredients to define the *optimal deployment problem*, which is our main concern: given a universe of microservice types, a set of available nodes and an initial configuration, we want to know whether and how it is possible to deploy at least one microservice of a given microservice type $\mathcal{T}$ by optimizing the overall cost of nodes hosting the deployed microservices.

Definition 10 (Optimal Deployment Problem) The *optimal deployment problem* has, as input, a finite well-formed universe U of microservice types, a finite set of available nodes O, an initial provisionally correct configuration C_0, and a microservice type $\mathcal{T}_t \in U$. The output is:

- A **deployment plan** $\mathsf{P} = C_0 \xrightarrow{\alpha_1} C_1 \xrightarrow{\alpha_2} \cdots \xrightarrow{\alpha_m} C_m$ such that
  - For all $C_i = \langle Z_i, T_i, N_i, B_i \rangle$, with $1 \leq i \leq m$, it holds $\forall z \in Z_i.\ T_i(z) \in U \wedge N_i(z) \in O$.
  - $C_m = \langle Z_m, T_m, N_m, B_m \rangle$ satisfies $\exists z \in Z_m : T_i(z) = \mathcal{T}_t$.

  if there exists one. In particular, among all deployment plans satisfying the constraints above, one that minimizes $\sum_{o \in O.(\exists z.N_m(z)=o)} o.\mathtt{cost}$, i.e., the overall cost of nodes in the last configuration C_m, is outputted.
- **no** (stating that no such plan exists); otherwise.

In the remainder of this section we present an algorithm for solving the optimal deployment problem. This will allow us to complete the section by stating our main result on the decidability of such a problem.

We assume that the input to the problem to be solved is given by U (the microservice types), O (the set of available nodes), C_0 (the initial provisionally correct configuration), and $\mathcal{T}_t \in U$ (the target microservice type). We use $\mathcal{I}(U)$ to denote the set of interfaces used in the considered microservice types, namely, $\mathcal{I}(U) = \bigcup_{\mathcal{T} \in U} \mathtt{dom}(\mathcal{T}.\mathtt{req_s}) \cup \mathtt{dom}(\mathcal{T}.\mathtt{req_w}) \cup \mathtt{dom}(\mathcal{T}.\mathtt{prov}) \cup \mathcal{T}.\mathtt{conf}$.

The algorithm is based on three phases.

Phase 1 The first phase consists of the generation of a set of constraints that, once solved, indicates how many instances should be created for each microservice type $\mathcal{T}$ (denoted with $\mathtt{inst}(\mathcal{T})$), and how many of them should be deployed on node o (denoted with $\texttt{inst}(\mathcal{T}, o)$). We denote with $\texttt{bind}(p, \mathcal{T}, \mathcal{T}')$ the number of bindings that should be established for each interface p from instances of type $\mathcal{T}$—considering both weak and strong required interfaces—to instances of type $\mathcal{T}'$. We also generate an optimization function that guarantees that the generated configuration is minimal w.r.t. its total cost.

We now incrementally report the generated constraints. The first group of constraints deals with the number of bindings:

$$\bigwedge_{p \in \mathcal{I}(U)} \quad \bigwedge_{\mathcal{T} \in U,\ p \in \text{dom}(\mathcal{T}.\texttt{req}_{\texttt{S}})} \mathcal{T}.\texttt{req}_{\texttt{S}}(p) \cdot \texttt{inst}(\mathcal{T}) \le \sum_{\mathcal{T}' \in U} \texttt{bind}(p, \mathcal{T}, \mathcal{T}') \tag{1a}$$

$$\bigwedge_{p \in \mathcal{I}(U)} \quad \bigwedge_{\mathcal{T} \in U,\ p \in \text{dom}(\mathcal{T}.\texttt{req}_{\texttt{W}})} \mathcal{T}.\texttt{req}_{\texttt{W}}(p) \cdot \texttt{inst}(\mathcal{T}) \le \sum_{\mathcal{T}' \in U} \texttt{bind}(p, \mathcal{T}, \mathcal{T}') \tag{1b}$$

$$\bigwedge_{p \in \mathcal{I}(U)} \quad \bigwedge_{\mathcal{T} \in U,\ \mathcal{T}.\texttt{prov}(p) < \infty} \mathcal{T}.\texttt{prov}(p) \cdot \texttt{inst}(\mathcal{T}) \ge \sum_{\mathcal{T}' \in U} \texttt{bind}(p, \mathcal{T}', \mathcal{T}) \tag{1c}$$

$$\bigwedge_{p \in \mathcal{I}(U)} \quad \bigwedge_{\mathcal{T} \in U,\ \mathcal{T}.\texttt{prov}(p) = \infty} \texttt{inst}(\mathcal{T}) = 0 \ \Rightarrow \ \sum_{\mathcal{T}' \in U} \texttt{bind}(p, \mathcal{T}', \mathcal{T}) = 0 \tag{1d}$$

$$\bigwedge_{p \in \mathcal{I}(U)} \quad \bigwedge_{\mathcal{T} \in U,\ p \notin \text{dom}(\mathcal{T}.\texttt{prov})} \sum_{\mathcal{T}' \in U} \texttt{bind}(p, \mathcal{T}', \mathcal{T}) = 0 \tag{1e}$$

Constraints (1a) and (1b) guarantee that there are enough bindings to satisfy all the required interfaces, considering both strong and weak requirements. Symmetrically, constraint (1c) guarantees that the number of bindings is not greater than the total available capacity, computed as the sum of the single capacities of each provided interface. In case the capacity is unbounded (i.e., ∞), it is sufficient to have at least one instance that activates such a port to support any possible requirement, see Constraint (1d). Finally, constraint (1e) guarantees that no binding is established connected to provided interfaces of microservice types that are not deployed.

The second group of constraints deals with the number of instances of microservices to be deployed.

$$\texttt{inst}(\mathcal{T}_t) \ge 1 \tag{2a}$$

$$\bigwedge_{p \in \mathcal{I}(U)} \quad \bigwedge_{\substack{\mathcal{T} \in U, \\ p \in \mathcal{T}.\texttt{conf}}} \quad \bigwedge_{\substack{\mathcal{T}' \in U - \{\mathcal{T}\}, \\ p \in \text{dom}(\mathcal{T}'.\texttt{prov})}} \texttt{inst}(\mathcal{T}) > 0 \ \Rightarrow \ \texttt{inst}(\mathcal{T}') = 0 \tag{2b}$$

$$\bigwedge_{p \in \mathcal{I}(U)} \quad \bigwedge_{\substack{\mathcal{T} \in U,\ p \in \mathcal{T}.\mathtt{conf}\ \wedge \\ p \in \mathrm{dom}(\mathcal{T}.\mathtt{prov})}} \mathtt{inst}(\mathcal{T}) \leq 1 \tag{2c}$$

$$\bigwedge_{p \in \mathcal{I}(U)} \quad \bigwedge_{\mathcal{T} \in U} \quad \bigwedge_{\mathcal{T}' \in U - \{\mathcal{T}\}} \mathtt{bind}(p, \mathcal{T}, \mathcal{T}') \leq \mathtt{inst}(\mathcal{T}) \cdot \mathtt{inst}(\mathcal{T}') \tag{2d}$$

$$\bigwedge_{p \in \mathcal{I}(U)} \quad \bigwedge_{\mathcal{T} \in U} \mathtt{bind}(p, \mathcal{T}, \mathcal{T}) \leq \mathtt{inst}(\mathcal{T}) \cdot (\mathtt{inst}(\mathcal{T}) - 1) \tag{2e}$$

The first constraint (2a) guarantees the presence of at least one instance of the target microservice. Constraint (2b) guarantees that no two instances of different types will be created if one activates a conflict on an interface provided by the other one. Constraint (2c) is the other case in which a type activates the same interface both in conflicting and provided modality: in this case, at most one instance of such type can be created. Finally, constraints (2d) and (2e) guarantee that there are enough pairs of distinct instances to establish all the necessary bindings. Two distinct constraints are used: the first one deals with bindings between microservices of two different types, the second one with bindings between microservices of the same type.

The last group of constraints deals with the distribution of microservice instances over the available nodes O.

$$\mathtt{inst}(\mathcal{T}) = \sum_{o \in O} \mathtt{inst}(\mathcal{T}, o) \tag{3a}$$

$$\bigwedge_{r \in \mathcal{R}} \bigwedge_{o \in O} \sum_{\mathcal{T} \in U} \mathtt{inst}(\mathcal{T}, o) \cdot \mathcal{T}.\mathtt{res}(r) \leq o.\mathtt{res}(r) \tag{3b}$$

$$\bigwedge_{o \in O} \Big(\sum_{\mathcal{T} \in U} \mathtt{inst}(\mathcal{T}, o) > 0 \Big) \Leftrightarrow \mathtt{used}(o) \tag{3c}$$

$$\min \sum_{o \in O,\, \mathtt{used}(o)} o.\mathtt{cost} \tag{3d}$$

Constraint (3a) simply formalizes the relationship among the variables $\mathtt{inst}(\mathcal{T})$ and $\mathtt{inst}(\mathcal{T}, o)$: the total amount of all instances of a microservice type should correspond to the sum of the instances locally deployed on each node. Constraint (3b) checks that each node has enough resources to satisfy the requirements of all the hosted microservices. The last two constraints define the optimization function used to minimize the total cost: constraint (3c) introduces the Boolean variable $\mathtt{used}(o)$ which is true if and only if node o contains at least one microservice instance; constraint (3d) is the function to be minimized, i.e., the sum of the costs of the used nodes.

All the constraints of *Phase 1*, and the optimization function, are expected to be given in input to a constraint/optimization solver. If a solution is not foundit is not possible to deploy the required microservice system; otherwise, the next phases of the algorithm are executed to synthesize the optimal deployment plan.

Phase 2 The second phase consists of the generation of another set of constraints that, once solved, indicate the bindings to be established between any pair of microservices to be deployed. More precisely, for each type $\mathcal{T}$ such that $\texttt{inst}(\mathcal{T}) > 0$, we use $s_i^{\mathcal{T}}$, with $1 \le i \le \texttt{inst}(\mathcal{T})$, to identify the microservices of type $\mathcal{T}$ to be deployed. We also assume a function N that associates microservices to available nodes O, which is compliant with the values $\texttt{inst}(\mathcal{T}, o)$ already computed in *Phase 1*, i.e., given a type $\mathcal{T}$ and a node o, the number of $s_i^{\mathcal{T}}$, with $1 \le i \le \texttt{inst}(\mathcal{T})$, such that $N(s_i^{\mathcal{T}}) = o$ coincides with $\texttt{inst}(\mathcal{T}, o)$.

In the constraints below we use the variable $\texttt{b}(p, s_i^{\mathcal{T}}, s_j^{\mathcal{T}'})$, with $i \neq j$, if $\mathcal{T} = \mathcal{T}'$: its value is 1 if there is a connection between the required interface p of $s_i^{\mathcal{T}}$ and the provided interface p of $s_j^{\mathcal{T}'}$, 0 otherwise. We use n and m to denote $\texttt{inst}(\mathcal{T})$ and $\texttt{inst}(\mathcal{T}')$, respectively, and an auxiliary total function $\mathit{limProv}(\mathcal{T}', p)$ that extends $\mathcal{T}'.\texttt{prov}$ associating 0 to interfaces outside its domain.

$$\bigwedge_{\mathcal{T} \in U} \bigwedge_{p \in \mathcal{I}(U)} \bigwedge_{i \in 1 \ldots n} \sum_{j \in (1 \ldots m) \setminus \{i \mid \mathcal{T} = \mathcal{T}'\}} \texttt{b}(p, s_i^{\mathcal{T}}, s_j^{\mathcal{T}'}) \le \mathit{limProv}(\mathcal{T}', p) \tag{4a}$$

$$\bigwedge_{\mathcal{T} \in U} \bigwedge_{p \in \texttt{dom}(\mathcal{T}.\texttt{req}_{\texttt{S}})} \bigwedge_{i \in 1 \ldots n} \sum_{j \in (1 \ldots m) \setminus \{i \mid \mathcal{T} = \mathcal{T}'\}} \texttt{b}(p, s_i^{\mathcal{T}}, s_j^{\mathcal{T}'}) \ge \mathcal{T}.\texttt{req}_{\texttt{S}}(p) \tag{4b}$$

$$\bigwedge_{\mathcal{T} \in U} \bigwedge_{p \in \texttt{dom}(\mathcal{T}.\texttt{req}_{\texttt{W}})} \bigwedge_{i \in 1 \ldots n} \sum_{j \in (1 \ldots m) \setminus \{i \mid \mathcal{T} = \mathcal{T}'\}} \texttt{b}(p, s_i^{\mathcal{T}}, s_j^{\mathcal{T}'}) \ge \mathcal{T}.\texttt{req}_{\texttt{W}}(p) \tag{4c}$$

$$\bigwedge_{\mathcal{T} \in U} \bigwedge_{p \notin \texttt{dom}(\mathcal{T}.\texttt{req}_{\texttt{S}}) \cup \texttt{dom}(\mathcal{T}.\texttt{req}_{\texttt{W}})} \bigwedge_{i \in 1 \ldots n} \sum_{j \in (1 \ldots m) \setminus \{i \mid \mathcal{T} = \mathcal{T}'\}} \texttt{b}(p, s_i^{\mathcal{T}}, s_j^{\mathcal{T}'}) = 0 \tag{4d}$$

Constraint (4a) considers the provided interface capacities to fix upper bounds to the bindings to be established, while constraints (4b) and (4c) fix lower bounds based on the required interface capacities, considering both the weak (constraint (4b)) and the strong (constraint (4c)) ones. Finally, constraint (4d) indicates that it is not possible to establish connections on interfaces that are not required.

A solution for these constraints exists because, as also shown in [27], the constraints (1a)–(2e), already solved during *Phase 1*, guarantee that the configuration to be synthesized contains enough capacity on the provided interfaces to satisfy all the required interfaces.

Phase 3 In this last phase we synthesize the deployment plan that, when applied to the initial configuration C_0, reaches a new configuration C_t with nodes, microservices, and bindings as computed in the first two phases of the algorithm. Without loss of generality, in this decidability proof we show the existence of a simple plan that first removes the elements in the initial configuration and then deploys the target configuration from scratch. However, as also discussed in constraint (4), in practice it is possible to define more complex planning mechanisms that reuse microservices already deployed.

Reaching an empty configuration is a trivial task since it is always possible to perform in the initial configuration unbind actions for all the bindings connected to weak required interfaces. Then, the microservices can be safely deleted. Thanks to the well-formedness assumption (Definition 9) and using a topological sort, it is possible to order the microservices to be removed without violating any strong required interface, e.g., first remove the microservice not requiring anything and repeat until all the microservices have been deleted.

The deployment of the target configuration follows a similar pattern. Given the distribution of microservices over nodes, computed in *Phase 1*, and the corresponding bindings, computed in *Phase 2*, the microservices can be created by following a topological sort considering the microservices dependencies following from the strong required interfaces. When all the microservices are deployed on the corresponding nodes, the remaining bindings, on weak required ports, may be added in any possible order.

Given the existence of the above algorithm for solving the optimal deployment problem, we can now formally state our main result.

Theorem 1 *The optimal deployment problem is decidable.*

From the complexity point of view, it is possible to show that the decision versions of the optimization problem solved in *Phase 1* is NP-complete, in *Phase 2* it is in NP, while the planning in *Phase 3* is synthesized in polynomial time. Unfortunately, due to the fact that numeric constraints can be represented in log space, the output of *Phase 2* requiring the enumeration of all the microservices to deploy can be exponential in the size of the output of *Phase 1*, indicating only the total number of instances for each type. For this reason, the optimal deployment problem is in NEXPTIME. However, we would like to note that this applies only when an exponential number of microservices is required to be installed in a node. In practice, this does not happen since every node provides some resources that are enough to deploy only a small number of microservices. If at most a polynomial number of microservices can be deployed on each node, we have that the optimal deployment problem becomes an NP-optimization problem and its decision version is NP-complete. See the technical report [18] for the formal proofs of complexity.

3 Zephyrus

In this section we describe the Zephyrus2 tool and how it can be used to actually solve the optimal deployment problem as formalized in the previous section. Zephyrus2 is a configurator optimizer that was originally envisaged for the Aeolus model [25] but later extended and improved to support a new specification language and the possibility to have preferences on the metrics to optimize, e.g., minimize not only the cost but, for instance, also the number of microservices [1].

Zephyrus2 in particular can be used to solve the optimization problems of the first two phases described before, namely, the distribution of the microservices on the nodes, and the instantiation of the bindings between the different microservices.

3.1 Optimal Distribution of Microservices

Different from what was formally described before, for usability sake, Zephyrus2 allows a far richer way of defining what the deployment constraints of the users are. Indeed, while in the previous section the goal was to deploy at least a given microservice (see constraint (2a)),[5] Zephyrus2 natively supports a richer language powerful enough to express, e.g., the presence of a given number of microservices and their co-installation requirements or conflicts. For example, the user might require the presence of at least one `Message Receiver` and 3 `Message Analyzer` and that, for fault tolerance reasons, no two `Message Analyzer` instances should be installed on the same node.

For microservice and nodes specifications, Zephyrus2 supports the JavaScript Object Notation (JSON) format.[6] As an example, the following JSON snippet defines the `Message Receiver` microservice in Fig. 1.

```
"MessageReceiver": {
  "resources": { "CPU": 2, "RAM": 4 },
  "requires": { "MA": 3 },
  "provides": [ { "ports": [ "MR" ], "num": -1 } ]
}
```

In the first line the name of the microservice is defined. Microservice names allow for the usage of only letters, numbers, the underscore character, and they should start with a letter. For this reason, here and in the following examples, in the Zephyrus2 snippets we will rename the services removing the trailing spaces (e.g., `Message Receiver` becomes `MessageReceiver`).

In the second line, with the keyword `resources`, it is declared that `Message Receiver` consumes 2 vCPUs and 4 units of RAM. The keyword `requires` defines that the microservice has a requirement on interface `MA` with

[5]Note that despite this formal limitation, the possibility to install one microservice is enough to encode far more elaborate constraints. Indeed, by using the strong requirements, it is possible to create, e.g., a dummy target microservice that forces other microservices to be present in a certain amount.

[6]The formal JSON Schema of Zephyrus2 input is available at [43]. JSON was used since it is one of the most common data formats for information exchange, thus easing a possible support of external tools and standards.

```
b_expr : b_term (bool_binary_op b_term )* ;
b_term : ('not')? b_factor ;
b_factor : 'true' | relation ;
relation : expr (comparison_op expr)? ;
expr : term (arith_binary_op term)* ;
term : INT                                                          |
  ('exists' | 'forall') VARIABLE 'in' type ':' b_expr               |
  'sum' VARIABLE 'in' type ':' expr                                 |
  (( ID | VARIABLE | ID '[' INT ']' ) '.')? microservice            |
  arith_unary_op expr                                               |
  '(' b_expr ')'                                                    ;
microservice :  ID | VARIABLE ;
type : 'components' | 'locations' | RE ;
bool_binary_op : 'and' | 'or' | 'impl' | 'iff' ;
arith_binary_op : '+' | '-' | '*' ;
comparison_op : '<=' | '=' | '>=' | '<' | '>' | '!=' ;
preferences: ('cost' | expr ) ( ';' 'cost' | expr )*
VARIABLE : '?'[a-zA-Z_][a-zA-Z0-9_]*;
ID : [a-zA-Z_][a-zA-Z0-9_]* ;
INT : [0-9]+ ;
```

Fig. 2 User desiderata specification language grammar

a capacity constraint "$\geq$ 3". Similarly, the `provides` keyword declares that the microservice provides the interface `MR` to a possibly unbounded number of microservices, represented by -1. Note that here Zephyrus2 does not distinguish between strong and weak requirements since this notion becomes relevant only later, namely, in *Phase 2*.

The definition of nodes is also done in JSON. For instance, the JSON input to define 10 `xlarge` Amazon virtual machines is the following:

```
"xlarge": {
  "num": 10,
  "resources": { "CPU": 4, "RAM": 8 },
  "cost": 199
}
```

For specifying the target configuration, Zephyrus2 introduces a new specification language for expressing the deployment constraints to allow DevOps teams to express more complex cloud- and application-specific constraints.

As shown in Fig. 2 that reports the grammar of the specification language defined using the ANTLR tool [5], a deployment constraint is a logical combination of comparisons between arithmetic expressions. Besides integers, expressions may refer to microservice names representing the total number of deployed instances of a microservice. Location instances are identified by a location name followed by the instance index, starting at zero, in square brackets. A microservice name prefixed by a node stays for the number of microservice instances deployed on the given node.

For example, the following formula requires the presence of at least one `Message Receiver` on the second `large` node, and exactly 3 `Message Analyzer` in the entire system.

```
large[1].MessageReceiver > 0 and MessageAnalyzer = 3
```

For quantification and for building sum expressions, Zephyrus2 uses identifiers prefixed with a question mark as variables. Quantification and sum constructs can range over microservices—when the `'components'` keyword is used; nodes—when the `'locations'` keyword is used; or over microservices/nodes whose names match a given regular expression (`RE`). Using such constraints, it is possible to express more elaborate properties such as the co-location or distribution of microservices, or limit the amount of microservices deployed on a given location. For example, the constraint

```
forall ?x in locations: ( ?x.MessageReceiver > 0 impl
  ?x.MessageAnalyzer = 0)
```

states that the presence of an instance of a `Message Receiver` deployed on any node `x` implies that no `Message Analyzer` can be deployed on the same node. As another example, requiring the `Message Receiver` to be installed alone on a virtual machine can be done by requiring that if a `Message Receiver` is installed on a given node then the sum of the microservices installed on that node should be exactly 1. This can be done by stating the following constraint.

```
forall ?x in locations: ( ?x.MessageReceiver > 0 impl
  (sum ?y in components: ?x.?y) = 1 )
```

For defining the optimization metrics, Zephyrus2 extends what has been formally presented in the previous section by allowing the user to express her preferences over valid configurations in the form of a list of arithmetic expressions whose values should be minimized in the given priority order (see `preferences` in Line 17 of Fig. 2). While in the formalization in Sect. 2 the metric to optimize was only the cost, Zephyrus2 solves instead a multi optimization problem taking into account different metrics. For example, since the keyword `cost` (line 17 of Fig. 2) can be used to require the minimization of the total cost of the used nodes, the following listing specifies in the Zephyrus2 syntax the metric to minimize first the total cost of the application and then the total number of microservices.

```
cost; ( sum ?x in components: ?x )
```

This is also the default metric used if the user does not specify her own preferences.

3.2 Bindings Optimization

As described in Sect. 2, the second phase of the approach consists of the instantiation of the bindings among the microservices. In particular, the constraints (4a)–(4d)

```
1  preference: 'local' | expr ;
2  term : INT                                    |
3   'bind' '(' VARIABLE ',' VARIABLE ',' var_or_port ')'  |
4   ('exists' | 'forall') VARIABLE ('of' 'type' RE)?
5     'in' typeV ':' b_expr                      |
6   'sum' VARIABLE ('of' 'type' RE)?
7     'in' typeV ':' expr                        |
8   '(' b_expr ')'                               ;
9  microservice :  ID | ID '[' ID ']' | ID '[' RE ']' ;
10 typeV : 'ports' | 'locations' | RE ;
11 var_or_port : ID | VARIABLE ;
```

Fig. 3 Grammar to express binding preferences (missing nonterminals are as defined in Fig. 2)

enforce the satisfaction of the capacity constraints of the interfaces. However, in a real application, a user often has preferences on how microservices are connected. For instance, usually public clouds are composed of different data centers available in different regions, and load balancers deployed in a region are connected only with the backend services deployed in the same region.

To capture this kind of preferences, one can easily enrich the constraints (4a)–(4d) with new metrics to optimize. For example, to maximize the local bindings (i.e., give a preference to the connections among microservices hosted in the same node) the following metric can be added.

$$\min \sum_{\mathcal{T},\mathcal{T}' \in U, i \in 1 \ldots \mathtt{inst}(\mathcal{T}), j \in 1 \ldots \mathtt{inst}(\mathcal{T}'), p \in \mathcal{I}(U), N(s_i^{\mathcal{T}}) \neq N(s_j^{\mathcal{T}'})} \mathtt{b}(p, s_i^{\mathcal{T}}, s_j^{\mathcal{T}'})$$

Another example, used in the case study discussed in Sect. 4, is the following metric that maximizes the number of bindings[7]:

$$\max \sum_{s_i^{\mathcal{T}}, s_j^{\mathcal{T}'}, p \in \mathcal{I}(U)} \mathtt{b}(p, s_i^{\mathcal{T}}, s_j^{\mathcal{T}'})$$

Zephyrus2 supports the possibility to specify these binding preferences. The grammar to express a preference is defined in Fig. 3. A preference may be either the string `local` or an arithmetic expression (Line 1). The `local` preference is used to maximize the number of bindings among the microservices deployed in the same node. Arithmetic expressions are used instead to capture more advanced preferences. These expressions are built by using as basic atoms integers (Line

[7]We model a load balancer as a microservice having a weak required interface, with arity 0, that can be provided by its backend service. By adopting the above maximization metric, the synthesized configuration connects all possible services to such required interfaces, thus allowing the load balancer to forward requests to all of them.

2) and the predicate `bind(?x,?y,z)`, which is assumed to be evaluated to one if the microservice referenced by the variable x is connected to the microservice y using interface z, 0 otherwise. Notice that in this case z can be a concrete interface name or an interface variable. In order to instantiate the variables of the term `bind`, quantifiers (Line 4–8) and sum expressions (Line 6–7) may be used.

As an example, assume that we have two kinds of nodes: those available in region A and those available in region B. The first nodes can be distinguished from the second ones thanks to their name. Node names from region A end with `'_A'` while the other node names end with `'_B'`. If we would like a `Message Analyzer` deployed in region A to be connected with all the `Message Receivers` in the same Region, we can add the following preference:

```
sum ?x of type MessageAnalyzer in '.*_A' :
 forall ?y of type MessageReceiver in '.*_A' :
  bind(?x,?y,MA)
```

In the first line we use the `sum` expression to match to the variable `?x` all the `Message Analyzer` instances hosted by a node whose name matches the regular expression `'.*_A'`. Similarly, in the second line we use the `forall` expression to match to the variable `?y` all the `Message Receiver` deployed in a node having a name ending with `'_A'`. The `forall` expression is evaluated to 1 if, fixing the possible assignments of the variable `?y`, the predicate `bind(?x,?y,MA)` is true (`MA` is the name of the interface required by a `Message Receiver` and provided by a `Message Analyzer`, see Fig. 1). If instead there is an instance of a `Message Receiver` in region A that is not connected to the `Message Analyzer ?x` then the forall expression returns 0. Due to the fact that the first expression is a sum expression, the final behaviors of the preference is to maximize the number of instances of `Message Analyzer` deployed in region A that are connected to all the instances of `Message Analyzer` deployed in the same region. Note that, if the `Message Receiver` is seen as a kind of loadbalancer for the `Message Analyzer` instances, what we have achieved is to state the preference that all the backend services in a region should be connected with all their loadbalancers deployed in the same region.

Zephyrus2 solves the previously described multioptimization problems, by translating them into *constraint optimization problems* (*COP*) encoded in MiniZinc [46] and using state-of-the-art solvers such as Chuffed [21], Or-Tools [36], or Gecode [35]. In particular, preferences are given in a list based on user priority. The earlier the preference comes in the list, the higher is its priority. Zephyrus2 optimizes the preference with the highest priority first, and then proceeds with the other preferences sequentially based on their priority.

4 Application of the Technique to the Case Study

In this section, we evaluate the applicability of our solution by modeling several deployment configurations of a real-world microservice architecture, namely, the email processing pipeline described in [34].

The considered architecture separates and routes the components found in an email (headers, links, text, attachments) into distinct, parallel subpipelines with specific tasks, e.g., check the format of the email, tag its content, detect malicious attachments. We report in Fig. 4 a depiction of the architecture. The Message Receiver microservice is the entry-point of the architecture and acts as a proxy by receiving and triggering the analysis of incoming emails. The Message Receiver forwards an inbound email to the Message Parser, which performs some preliminary validity checks. If the message is well formatted, the Message Parser first stores a pending-analysis task under a unique identifier for the current email in a companion database (DB) service. The DB maintains the status of all pending analyses in the system and it is an element external to the architecture—this is represented by the faded part at the top in Fig. 4. After storing the pending task, the Message Parser (*i*) splits the parsed email into four components: header, links, text, and attachments; (*ii*) tags them with the unique identifier of the pending-analysis task; and (*iii*) sends the four components to their corresponding subpipelines. The first two subpipelines from the top in Fig. 4 include just one microservice, which respectively analyze the headers (Header Analyzer) and the links (Link Analyzer) contained in the mail. The third subpipeline includes a Text Analyzer that synchronously invokes a Sentiment Analyzer, to add tags to the body of the message. The last subpipeline handles attachments and it is the most complex in the system. The first microservice in the subpipeline is a Virus Scanner, which checks each attachment for the presence of malicious software. If an attachment results malicious, it is deleted and signaled as dangerous to the Message Analyzer, as described later. Safe attachments are forwarded to an Attachment Manager for further analyses. The Attachment Manager inspects

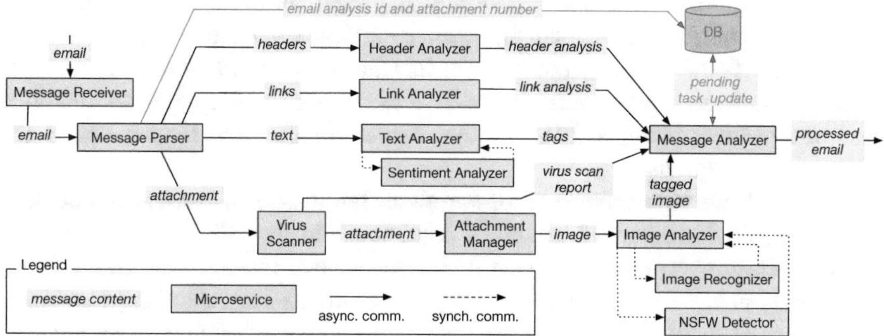

Fig. 4 Microservice architecture for email processing pipeline

each attachment to identify its content type (image, audio, archive) and route it to the appropriate part of the subpipeline. In Fig. 4 we just exemplify the concept with an Image Analyzer which synchronously calls two microservices to tag the content of each image (Image Recognizer) and whether it does not include explicit content (NSFW Detector). All subpipelines forward the result of their (asynchronous) analysis to the Message Analyzer, which collects them in the DB. After all analyses belonging to the same pending task are completed, the Message Analyzer combines them and reports the result of the processing.

To model the system above, we use the Abstract Behavioral Specification (ABS) language, a high-level object-oriented language that supports deployment modeling [41]. ABS is agnostic w.r.t. deployment platforms (Amazon AWS, Microsoft Azure) and technologies (e.g., Docker or Kubernetes) and it offers high-level deployment primitives for the creation of new *deployment components* and the instantiation of objects inside them. Here, we use ABS deployment components as computation nodes, ABS objects as microservice instances, and ABS object references as bindings. Strong required interfaces are modeled as class annotations indicating mandatory parameters for the class constructor: such parameters contain the references to the objects corresponding to the microservices providing the strongly required interfaces. Weak required interfaces are expressed as annotations concerning specific methods used to pass, to an already instantiated object, the references to the objects providing the weakly required interfaces. We define a class for each microservice type, plus one *load balancer* class for each microservice type. A load balancer distributes requests over a set of instances that can scale horizontally. Finally, we model nodes corresponding to Amazon EC2 instances: `c4_large`, `c4_xlarge`, and `c4_2xlarge`, with the corresponding provided resources and costs.

Finally, to compute deployment plans for our case study, we exploit SmartDepl [23], an extension of ABS that supports the possibility to include into ABS additional deployment annotations that, besides the other annotations describing strong and weak required interfaces and the available computing nodes, are used as input for Zephyrus2. In this way, Zephyrus2 can compute optimal deployment plans, which are then translated into corresponding ABS code.

Each microservice in the architecture has a given resource consumption, expressed in terms of CPU and memory. As expected, the processing of each email component entails a specific load. Some microservices can handle large inputs, e.g., in the range of 40 K simultaneous requests like the Header Analyzer that processes short and uniform inputs. Other microservices sustain heavier computations, like the Image Recognizer, and can handle smaller simultaneous inputs, e.g., in the range of 10 K requests.

In Table 1, we report the result of our algorithm w.r.t. four incremental deployments: the initial in column 2 and under incremental loads in 3–5. We also consider an availability of 40 nodes for each of the three node types. In the first column of Table 1, next to a microservice type, we report its corresponding maximum computational load, expressed as the maximal number of simultaneous requests that a microservice can manage. In the column, we use the standard suffix K to

Table 1 Description of different scaling scenarios

Microservice (max computational load)	Initial (10 K)	+20 K	+50 K	+80 K
MessageReceiver(∞)	1	–	–	–
MessageParser(40 K)	1	–	+1	–
HeaderAnalyzer(40 K)	1	–	+1	–
LinkAnalyzer(40 K)	1	–	+1	–
TextAnalyzer(15 K)	1	+1	+2	+2
SentimentAnalyzer(15 K)	1	+3	+4	+6
VirusScanner(13 K)	1	+3	+4	+6
AttachmentsManager(30 K)	1	+1	+2	+2
ImageAnalyzer(30 K)	1	+1	+2	+2
NSFWDetector(13 K)	1	+3	+4	+6
ImageRecognizer(13 K)	1	+3	+4	+6
MessageAnalyzer(70 K)	1	+1	+2	+2

represent numbers in thousands, e.g., 30 K corresponds to 30,000 simultaneous requests. In our example, the maximal computational load of each microservice comes from an educated guess drawn from the experience of the authors. Concretely, those estimations are straightforward to obtain through e.g., a measurement of the performance like the response times of each microservice, under increasing simulated traffic loads. As visible in columns 2–5, different maximal computational loads imply different scaling factors w.r.t. a given number of simultaneous requests. In the initial configuration we consider 10 K simultaneous requests and we have one instance of each microservice type and of the corresponding load balancer. The other deployment configurations deal with three scenarios of horizontal scaling, assuming three increasing increments of inbound messages: +20 K, +50 K, and +80 K. Concerning the deployment plan synthesis, in the three scaling scenarios, we do not implement the planning algorithm described in *Phase 3* of the proof of Theorem 1. We take advantage of the presence of the load balancers: instead of emptying the current configuration and deploying the new one from scratch, we keep the load balancers in the configuration and simply connect to them the newly deployed microservice instances. This is achieved, as described in Sect. 3, with an optimization function that maximizes the number of bindings of the load balancers.

For every scenario, we use SmartDepl to generate the ABS code for the plan that deploys an optimal configuration, setting a timeout of 30 min for the computation of every deployment scenario.[8] The ABS code modeling the system

[8]Here, 30 min is a reasonable timeout since we predict different system loads and we compute in advance a different deployment plan for each of them. An interesting future work would aim at shortening the computation to a few minutes (e.g., around the average startup time of a virtual machine in a public cloud) to obtain on-the-fly deployment plans tailored to unpredictable system loads.

and the generated code are publicly available at [16]. A graphical representation of the initial configuration is available in the technical report [18].

5 Related Work and Conclusion

In this work, we consider a fundamental building block of modern cloud systems, microservices, and prove that the generation of a deployment plan for an architecture of microservices is decidable and fully automatable; spanning from the synthesis of the optimal configuration to the generation of the deployment actions. To illustrate our technique, we model a real-world microservice architecture in the ABS [41] language and we compute a set of deployment plans.

The context of our work regards automating cloud application deployment, for which there exist many specification languages [8, 20], reconfiguration protocols [9, 31], and system management tools [37, 42, 47, 48]. Those tools support the specification of deployment plans but they do not support the automatic distribution of software instances over the available machines. The proposals closest to ours are those by Feinerer [32] and by Fischer et al. [33]. Both proposals rely on a solver to plan deployments. The first is based on the UML component model, which includes conflicts and dependencies, but lacks the modeling of nodes. The second does not support conflicts in the specification language. Neither proposals support the computation of optimal deployments. Notice that our work focuses on architectural aspects of (deployed) microservices and not on their low-level invocation flow, which regards issues of service behavioral compliance (see, e.g., [4, 13–15] where process algebra [7] related techniques are adopted) or deadlock/termination analysis (see, e.g., [11, 22]) that are not a concern of this chapter.

Three projects inspire our proposal: Aeolus [26, 27], Zephyrus [1], and ConfSolve [38]. The Aeolus model paved the way to reason on deployment and reconfiguration, proving some decidability results. Zephyrus is a configuration tool based on Aeolus and it constitutes the first phase of our approach. ConfSolve is a tool for the optimal allocation of virtual machines to servers and of applications to virtual machines. Both tools do not synthesize deployment plans.

Regarding autoscaling, existing solutions [2, 6, 29, 39] support the automatic increase or decrease of the number of instances of a service/container, when some conditions, e.g., CPU average load greater than 80, are met. Our work is an example of how we can go beyond single-component horizontal scaling policies, as analyzed, e.g.,, in [12] by using Markovian process algebras [10].

As future work, we want to investigate local search approaches to speed up the solution of the optimization problems behind the computation of a deployment plan. Shorter computation times would open our approach to contexts where it is unfeasible to compute plans ahead of time, e.g., due to unpredictable loads.

Acknowledgement The research was partly supported by the H2020-MSCA-RISE project ID 778233 "Behavioural Application Program Interfaces (BEHAPI)."

References

1. E. Ábrahám, F. Corzilius, E.B. Johnsen, G. Kremer, J. Mauro, Zephyrus2: on the fly deployment optimization using SMT and CP technologies, in *SETTA*. *LNCS*, vol. 9984, pp. 229–245 (2016)
2. Amazon: Amazon Cloudwatch. https://aws.amazon.com/cloudwatch/. Accessed January 2019
3. Amazon: AWS Auto Scaling. https://aws.amazon.com/autoscaling/. Accessed January 2019
4. D. Ancona, V. Bono, M. Bravetti, J. Campos, G. Castagna, P. Deniélou, S.J. Gay, N. Gesbert, E. Giachino, R. Hu, E.B. Johnsen, F. Martins, V. Mascardi, F. Montesi, R. Neykova, N. Ng, L. Padovani, V.T. Vasconcelos, N. Yoshida, Behavioral types in programming languages. Found. Trends Program. Lang. **3**(2–3), 95–230 (2016)
5. ANTLR (ANother Tool for Language Recognition). http://www.antlr.org/. Accessed January 2019
6. Apache: Apache MESOS. http://mesos.apache.org/. Accessed January 2019
7. J.C.M. Baeten, M. Bravetti, A ground-complete axiomatisation of finite-state processes in a generic process algebra. Math. Struct. Comput. Sci. **18**(6), 1057–1089 (2008)
8. A. Bergmayr, U. Breitenbücher, N. Ferry, A. Rossini, A. Solberg, M. Wimmer, G. Kappel, F. Leymann, A systematic review of cloud modeling languages. Assoc. Comput. Mach. Comput. Surv. **51**(1), 22:1–22:38 (2018)
9. F. Boyer, O. Gruber, D. Pous, Robust reconfigurations of component assemblies, in *ICSE* (IEEE Computer Society, Piscataway, 2013), pp. 13–22
10. M. Bravetti, Reduction semantics in Markovian process algebra. J. Log. Algebr. Meth. Program. **96**, 41–64 (2018)
11. M. Bravetti, G. Zavattaro, On the expressive power of process interruption and compensation. Math. Struct. Comput. Sci. **19**(3), 565–599 (2009)
12. M. Bravetti, S. Gilmore, C. Guidi, M. Tribastone, Replicating web services for scalability, in *TGC*. *LNCS*, vol. 4912 (Springer, Berlin, 2008), pp. 204–221
13. M. Bravetti, I. Lanese, G. Zavattaro, Contract-driven implementation of choreographies, in *Trustworthy Global Computing, 4th International Symposium, TGC 2008, Barcelona, Spain, November 3–4, 2008, Revised Selected Papers. Lecture Notes in Computer Science*, eds. by Kaklamanis, C., Nielson, F., vol. 5474 (Springer, Berlin, 2009), pp. 1–18
14. M. Bravetti, M. Carbone, G. Zavattaro, Undecidability of asynchronous session subtyping. Inf. Comput. **256**, 300–320 (2017)
15. M. Bravetti, M. Carbone, G. Zavattaro, On the boundary between decidability and undecidability of asynchronous session subtyping. Theor. Comput. Sci. **722**, 19–51 (2018)
16. M. Bravetti, S. Giallorenzo, J. Mauro, I. Talevi, G. Zavattaro, *Code repository for the email processing example*. https://github.com/IacopoTalevi/SmartDeploy-ABS-ExampleCode. Accessed January 2019
17. M. Bravetti, S. Giallorenzo, J. Mauro, I. Talevi, G. Zavattaro, Optimal and Automated Deployment for Microservices, in *FASE* (2019)
18. M. Bravetti, S. Giallorenzo, J. Mauro, I. Talevi, G. Zavattaro, Optimal and automated deployment for microservices (2019). https://arxiv.org/abs/1901.09782. Technical Report
19. A. Brogi, A. Canciani, J. Soldani, Modelling and analysing cloud application management, in *ESOCC*. *LNCS*, vol. 9306 (Springer, Berlin, 2015), pp. 19–33
20. M. Chardet, H. Coullon, D. Pertin, C. Pérez, Madeus: a formal deployment model, in *HPCS* (IEEE, Piscataway, 2018), pp. 724–731
21. Chuffed Team: The CP Solver. https://github.com/geoffchu/chuffed. Accessed January 2019
22. F.S. de Boer, M. Bravetti, M.D. Lee, G. Zavattaro, A petri net based modeling of active objects and futures. Fund. Inform. **159**(3), 197–256 (2018)
23. S. de Gouw, J. Mauro, B. Nobakht, G. Zavattaro, Declarative elasticity in ABS, in *ESOCC*. *LNCS*, vol. 9846 (Springer, Berlin, 2016), pp. 118–134
24. R. Di Cosmo, S. Zacchiroli, G. Zavattaro, Towards a formal component model for the cloud, in *SEFM 2012*. *LNCS*, vol. 7504 (2012)

25. R. Di Cosmo, M. Lienhardt, R. Treinen, S. Zacchiroli, J. Zwolakowski, A. Eiche, A. Agahi, Automated synthesis and deployment of cloud applications, in *ASE* (2014)
26. R. Di Cosmo, J. Mauro, S. Zacchiroli, G. Zavattaro, Aeolus: a component model for the cloud. Inf. Comput. **239**, 100–121 (2014)
27. R. Di Cosmo, M. Lienhardt, J. Mauro, S. Zacchiroli, G. Zavattaro, J. Zwolakowski, Automatic application deployment in the cloud: from practice to theory and back (invited paper), in *CONCUR*. *LIPIcs*, vol. 42, (Schloss Dagstuhl-Leibniz-Zentrum fuer Informatik, 2015), pp. 1–16
28. Docker: Docker Compose Documentation. https://docs.docker.com/compose/. Accessed January 2019
29. Docker: Docker Swarm. https://docs.docker.com/engine/swarm/. Accessed January 2019
30. N. Dragoni, S. Giallorenzo, A. Lluch-Lafuente, M. Mazzara, F. Montesi, R. Mustafin, L. Safina, Microservices: yesterday, today, and tomorrow, in *PAUSE* (Springer, Berlin, 2017), pp. 195–216
31. F. Durán, G. Salaün, Robust and reliable reconfiguration of cloud applications. J. Syst. Softw. **122**, 524–537 (2016)
32. I. Feinerer, Efficient large-scale configuration via integer linear programming. AI EDAM **27**(1), 37–49 (2013)
33. J. Fischer, R. Majumdar, S. Esmaeilsabzali, Engage: a deployment management system, in: *PLDI* (2012)
34. K. Fromm, *Thinking Serverless! How New Approaches Address Modern Data Processing Needs*. https://read.acloud.guru/thinking-serverless-how-new-approaches-address-modern-data-processing-needs-part-1-af6a158a3af1. Accessed January 2019
35. GECODE: An Open, Free, Efficient Constraint Solving Toolkit. http://www.gecode.org. Accessed January 2019
36. Google: Optimization Tools. https://developers.google.com/optimization/. Accessed January 2019
37. R. Hat, *Ansible*. https://www.ansible.com/. Accessed January 2019
38. J.A. Hewson, P. Anderson, A.D. Gordon, A declarative approach to automated configuration, in *LISA* (2012)
39. K. Hightower, B.Burns, J. Beda, *Kubernetes: Up and Running Dive into the Future of Infrastructure*, 1st edn. (O'Reilly Media, Inc., Sebastopol, 2017)
40. J. Humble, D. Farley, *Continuous Delivery: Reliable Software Releases Through Build, Test, and Deployment Automation* (Addison-Wesley Professional, Upper Saddle River, 2010)
41. E.B. Johnsen, R. Hähnle, J. Schäfer, R. Schlatte, M. Steffen, ABS: a core language for abstract behavioral specification, in *FMCO* (2010)
42. L. Kanies, Puppet: Next-generation configuration management. `;login:` the USENIX Magazine **31**(1) (2006)
43. J. Mauro, *Zephyrus2 code repository*. https://bitbucket.org/jacopomauro/zephyrus2
44. J. Mauro, G. Zavattaro, On the complexity of reconfiguration in systems with legacy components, in *MFCS*. *LNCS*, vol. 9234 (Springer, Berlin, 2015), pp. 382–393
45. D. Merkel, Docker: lightweight Linux containers for consistent development and deployment. Linux J. **2014**(239), 2 (2014)
46. N. Nethercote, P.J. Stuckey, R. Becket, S. Brand, G.J. Duck, G. Tack, MiniZinc: towards a standard CP modelling language, in *CP* (2007), pp. 529–543. http://dl.acm.org/citation.cfm?id=1771668.1771709
47. Opscode: Chef. https://www.chef.io/chef/. Accessed January 2019
48. Puppet Labs: Marionette Collective. http://docs.puppetlabs.com/mcollective/. Accessed January 2019

Autonomic Decentralized Microservices: The *Gru* Approach and Its Evaluation

Elisabetta Di Nitto, Luca Florio, and Damian A. Tamburri

Abstract Cloud applications are more and more featuring microservices as a design pattern, using related technologies (containerization, orchestration, continuous deployment, integration, and more) to speed up design, development, and operation. However, microservices are not bullet-proof: they increase design and management issues in the cloud adding to the mix all the intrinsic complexities of highly distributed systems. This addition can render ineffective all centralized management technologies like Docker or clustering systems like Swarm and Kubernetes. Conversely, autonomic and decentralized microservices management is still largely unexplored. We address this problem with *Gru*, an approach based on multiagent systems that adds an autonomic adaptation layer for microservice applications focusing on Docker, the de facto market leader in container technology. *Gru* is designed to support fully decentralized microservices management, and can be integrated with ease in dockerized applications, managing them with autonomic actions to satisfy application quality requirements. We evaluate *Gru* with a concrete case study showing autoscaling dockerized microservices matching variating and bursty workloads. Evaluation shows encouraging results for *Gru* autonomic management.

1 Introduction

The adoption of microservices to design, develop, and operate cloud applications enables an improved exploitation of cloud computing [25, 30], structuring applications into a flexible design of small, independent, intercommunicating architecture

E. Di Nitto · L. Florio
Politecnico di Milano, Milan, Italy
e-mail: elisabetta.dinitto@polimi.it; luca.florio@polimi.it

D. A. Tamburri (✉)
Technical University of Eindhoven, Eindhoven, Netherlands

The Jheronimus Academy of Data Science, 's-Hertogenbosch, Netherlands
e-mail: d.a.tamburri@tue.nl

A. Bucchiarone et al. (eds.), *Microservices*,
https://doi.org/10.1007/978-3-030-31646-4_9

elements. In the resulting architecture, every element is a *microservice*, i.e., a self-contained service which is totally independent from the others and is available in its own architectural building block (i.e., a microservice container such as Docker and managed by technologies such as Docker-Swarm[1] or Kubernetes[2]). On the one hand, the resulting architecture pattern presents several advantages, making it more and more popular (e.g., immediate support for continuous integration, continuous architecting, continuous testing, etc.). For example, most of the leading IT companies have adopted microservices as the basis for their applications (e.g., Netflix is completely based on microservices [27] but so are Groupon, SoundCloud, and more [15, 28]). On the other hand, microservices are not a "free lunch" [26]: they make the application more difficult to design and develop. Hundreds, often thousands, of pieces need to be run and coordinated, thus making management and service governance even more difficult [2, 29]. To address this gap, we introduce *Gru*, an approach that allows autonomic, decentralized, and collaborative (self-)management of microservice applications. In comparison to technologies such as Swarm or Kubernetes, *Gru* reasons locally from within the microservice and using the sole assumptions that can be made upon containerization technology (e.g., the APIs existing between container managers and containers). *Gru* introduces automations that help handling microservices autonomously, actuating the proper adaptation or autoscaling actions according to the status of the system. The goal of autonomic actions is to meet pre-specified requirements such as a specific level of availability or quality of service [22]. *Gru* features a totally decentralized approach based on agents organized according to a peer-to-peer multiagent system (MAS) [33]; each agent actuates management actions on the basis of partial knowledge acquired through the interaction with its direct peers; this feature makes *Gru* well suited for the management of a large-scale, highly distributed cloud applications, since no centralized authority of governance is needed. What is more, *Gru* is designed to be noninvasive and can be easily integrated into preexisting microservice solutions. In this chapter we present and evaluate the architecture of *Gru*, outlining the main algorithms that govern its behavior. We evaluate the approach using case study research: we considered the video-on-demand domain and prepared a video-stream processing microservice application running on an OpenStack cloud computing infrastructure. The current chapter extends our previous work [18], where a preliminary definition of the *Gru* framework was presented from an architectural and conceptual perspective. The extensions we offer in this manuscript are detailed as follows:

- A working implementation of the *Gru* approach
- An outline of the operational details and algorithms behind this implementation

[1] https://docs.docker.com/engine/swarm/.

[2] https://platform9.com/blog/kubernetes-docker-swarm-compared/.

- A validated set of metrics that *Gru* uses for autonomic decentralized management—these stand out as a contribution on their own and could be used in technologies similar to *Gru*
- An experimental evaluation of *Gru*, its operational details, and metrics, using a realistic cloud infrastructure and sample case study application.

We conclude that *Gru* successfully supports autonomic adaptation dynamics in the complex and costly context of microservices applications.

Chapter Structure The rest of the chapter is organized as follows. Section 2 provides a short overview of background information on autonomic systems and Docker. Section 3 gives a global view of *Gru*, describing architecture and main features. Then, we show the evaluation of *Gru* in Sect. 4, while in Sect. 5 we compare it to relevant works from the state of the art. The chapter concludes with Sect. 6 where we outline future evolution of our work.

2 Background and Design Motivations

2.1 Microservices Background

Quoting from "microservices.io", microservices are an architectural style structuring an application as a collection of services that are: (1) sufficiently decoupled to be highly maintainable and testable; (2) loosely coupled from the application glue logic (e.g., orchestration, monitoring, etc.); (3) independently deployable; and (4) organized around single business capabilities.

Since the key enabler for microservices is the containerization technology, the microservice architecture style enables the continuous delivery/deployment of large, complex applications at a large scale. With the term containerization, we indicate the practice of operating system (OS) virtualization as opposed to the adoption of virtual machines (VMs), which is, conversely, hardware virtualization. In the scope of this work, we focus on Docker as a containerization technology; the choice is sound since Docker is practically the de facto standard in containerization but this is merely one of many (up to 40+) possible choices for containerization technology in practice.

From an organizational perspective, combining microservices and containerization enables the microservice architecture style to allow an organization to evolve its technology and organizational stack in conjunction with its architectural structures.

2.2 *Autonomic Microservices*

In a highly distributed context such as the one introduced by microservices, understanding if the application is running properly is not trivial, and, if a problem arises, it is even more difficult to cope with it tempestively. Autonomic and self-adaptive infrastructures are being developed to address such situations and the literature shows a number of different approaches [23]. The limitation of most approaches is that either they perform simple operations (e.g., drive the autoscaling offered by many clouds such as AWS) or they require a reimplementation of the system to be adapted using specifically proposed frameworks and paradigms (see, for instance, the work by Chen et al. or Rajagopalan et al. [12, 32]). Conversely, *Gru* aims at reducing to zero the assumptions made on the contributions by both operators and developers in the process of driving large-scale microservice solutions.

Gru was designed to be less invasive as possible relying exclusively on the microservice architectural style and on containerization features offered by infrastructure management technologies and languages such as Docker [6, 16, 35]. Docker containers can share resources and are lightweight: it is possible to run multiple containers on the same machine starting them in seconds. Services deployed in a Docker container can be scaled or replaced just starting or stopping the container running that specific service. This is accomplished through the REST API or the Command Line Interface (CLI) offered by Docker itself. Thanks to these interfaces, an external observer can also inspect the state of the container and of the resources it is using.

Gru tries to offer intelligent adaptation mechanisms that take into account various aspects of the system to be kept under control. This key design principle makes the design and development of cloud applications substantially easier: developers can focus on application microservices behavior, later exploiting *Gru* to employ and configure the desired adaptation features.

From the point of view of its users, *Gru* is an adaptation enabler. It associates with each Docker Daemon a *Gru*-Agent that controls it and exploits it to operate on microservice instances. In the following section we present an overview of the approach and of its architecture.

3 *Gru*: Architecture and Behavior

Gru operates in a noninvasive fashion on enhancing microservice-based systems with autonomic capabilities. *Gru* focuses on Docker as the de facto market leader in microservices implementation. The full *Gru* codebase is freely available on GitHub[3] with read-me and installation notes.

[3]https://github.com/elleFlorio/gru.

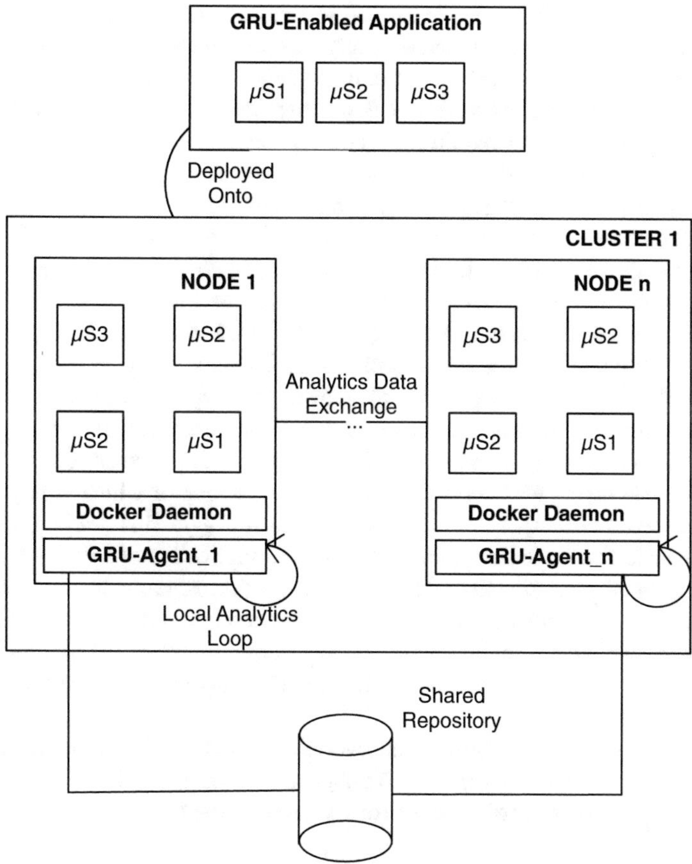

Fig. 1 *Gru*, General overview. Cluster 1 with 'n' nodes featuring GRU-agents that: (**a**) self-register, self-discover, and share through joint repos; (**b**) gather local analytics; (**c**) enact local adaptation actions

The *Gru* operational framework (i.e., its operational architecture, policies, and procedures) features a set of Gru-*Agents* deployed in *clusters* of *nodes*. As an example, Fig. 1 outlines a simple cloud application controlled by *Gru*. This simple application is composed of three microservices running in multiple instances, each encapsulated in a Docker container, in a cluster of n nodes; each node is running its own Docker Daemon as well as the corresponding *Gru*-Agent.

Nodes are the hosts where *Gru*-Agents and microservices are running. Each node has a unique name and ID and it is characterized by a *base-services* property, which represents the set of microservices that should be running in that specific node—*Gru* ensures that at least one instance of these microservices will be running on that node. At the same time, clusters are set of nodes, with each cluster presenting a unique name and ID. Each *Gru*-Agent should register the node where it is running into a cluster in order to be visible to other agents and to exchange information with them. Nodes can belong to one cluster only. Clusters are initially defined randomly and self-arranged following the autonomic behavior of each *Gru*-agent.

Figure 1 also highlights a *Shared Repository* that has a dual role: (1) it stores configuration information required by *Gru*-Agents to interact with the others and with Docker Daemons and (2) it acts as an agent registry.

Gru-Agents are in charge of controlling the execution of microservices under their direct responsibility, i.e., those that are running on the same node of the agent. In doing so, they can decide to enact *adaptation policies*. For instance, in the case a node features two instances of microservice μS1 and two of microservice μS2, and μS1 receives significantly less requests than μS2, then the *Gru*-Agent for the node may decide to apply a *switch* policy to replace one of the two μS1 instances with one of type μS2. The decisions taken by agents can also depend on the state of other nodes acquired through their peer agents. In the example above, the agent may even decide not to apply the switch policy if it knows that another node is available to get requests for its μS2 service instance. The decision of which policy to apply is taken by each *Gru*-Agent based on a specified *strategy*. This last one essentially establishes the criteria to be applied to choose the application of a policy rather than the others. In all cases, the final decision of every *Gru*-Agent is made according to two insights: (1) the internal status of the agent node, i.e., the data gathered from the Docker containers running the microservices of the application in the same host of the *Gru*-Agent; (2) the data coming from a randomly selected subset of the total number of peers.

In the next sections we provide an overview of the way the framework can be configured, on the internals of the *Gru*-Agents and on the policies and strategies that have been implemented in the current version of the *Gru* framework.

3.1 Gru *Configuration*

The *agent configuration* defines all important parameters that govern the way all *Gru*-Agents work. It includes the following information: (a) parameters needed to connect to Docker Daemons—these are laid out once and are general for all agents at work; (b) *Gru*-Agent-specific parameters that influence agents internal behavior, such as the strategy to use for selecting adaptation policies; and (c) communication parameters that influence the frequency of interaction between peer agents and the number of agents that interact with each other. It should be noted that the *Gru*-Agents configuration is defined by *Gru* users and is the only feature that necessitates specific user input. On the one hand, there is no single centralized controller as an architecture element of the *Gru* approach. On the other hand, *Gru* users need only specify how to arrange nodes in a cluster and how each such cluster should behave with the specified *Gru* configuration.

This configuration is loaded by *Gru*-Agents as soon as they register to the Repository, together with μService-Descriptors. These are models for the microservices of the application; these are needed by *Gru*-Agents to understand how to properly manage each microservice. μService-Descriptors convey the following information:

- **Service Meta-data**. The general meta-data about the service, such as its name, its type and the associated *Docker Image*. This last one is a description of what a Docker container should run and is used to create multiple instances of the same container. Despite the information about the type of the microservice is not used at this stage of development, it could be exploited to reason about the composition of the application, applying specific actions for specific microservice types.
- **Docker configuration**. This contains all the parameters needed to properly create a Docker container running the microservice, such as the resources needed (number of CPUs, amount of memory), any environmental variables, and the parameters that should be passed to the microservice when it is started.
- **Microservice Adaptation Constraints**. The set of application-specific constraints to impose on the microservice (e.g., the maximum response time of the service) along with any analytics that should be computed to instrument adaptation, e.g., CPU usage to be used for adaptation for the purpose of lossless CPU usage.

More in particular, *Gru*-Agents interact with the Docker containers in their home node through the **Docker Daemon** running in background. *Gru*-Agents exploit the API provided by Docker to query the Docker Daemon about the status of the containers: it is possible to retrieve low-level information about the consumption of resources (CPU and memory usage, storage, I/O operations, etc.), as well as the specific properties of each container, such as the number of CPU assigned, the memory limit, the network interface, etc. *Gru*-Agents can also read the logs of the microservices that are exposed by the container, accessing higher-level information. This information is used to understand the status of a container and the total consumption of resources of the node, as well as the status of the microservices inside the container.

3.2 Gru-*Agents*

Gru-Agents are deployed in each node of the cluster and interact with the Docker Daemon to manage the containers running the microservices of the application. In the following we describe how they work.

3.2.1 *Gru*-Agent Lifecycle

The lifecycle of *Gru*-Agents is outlined in Fig. 2. Essentially, when a *Gru*-Agent starts, it automatically discovers and registers itself to the shared repository with its ID and address. The record of each agent has a predefined Time-to-Live (TTL),

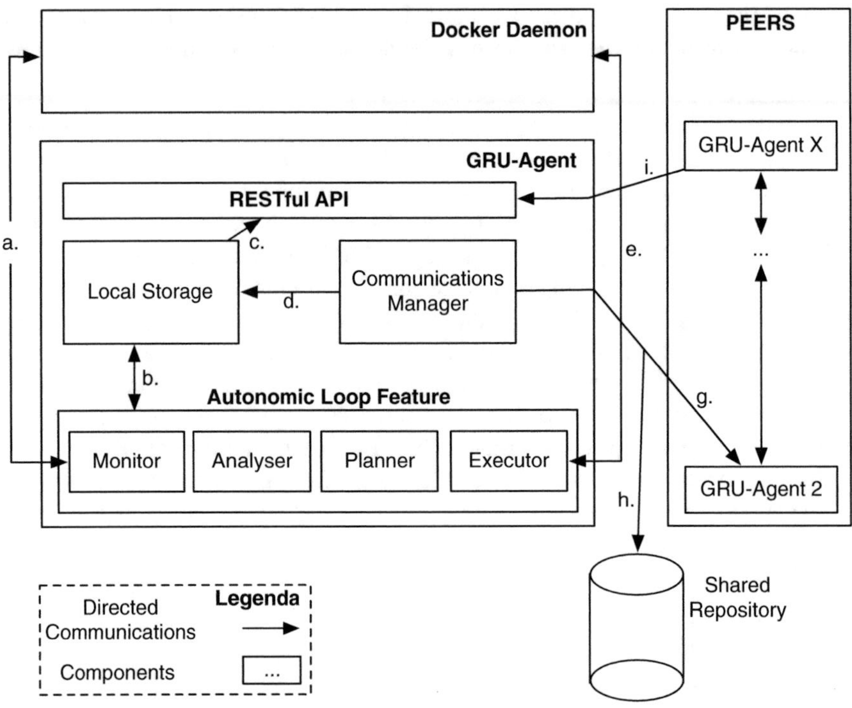

Fig. 2 Internal schematics of a *Gru*-Agent: (**a**) docker-daemon to GRU-agent communication for gathering local monitoring data and executing adaptations (**e**); (**b**) a local storage provides for data retention and forwarding upon REST requests (**c** and **i**); (**d**) an intercom manager retrieves and forwards data to peers (**g**) intercommunicating with a shared repo as needed (**h**)

so if an agent fails and cannot confirm that it is active at every regular poll[4] by the shared repository, it is removed from the repository itself. *Gru*-Agents are organized according to the classical **MAPE-K** feedback-loop design pattern [14], i.e., they are composed of four main architecture elements: a *monitor*, an *analyzer*, a *planner*, and an *executor*, along with an Internal Storage that represents the *knowledge base* of each *Gru*-Agent (see Fig. 2). Other components that complement the agents architecture are the RESTful API that is used to offer services to other agents, and the communication manager. This last component is in charge of ensuring that each agent communicates with the shared repository and the other agents in order to acquire information useful to support the adaptation process. More specifically, the communication manager queries the shared repository to get the references to a number of active peers. Such a number is a configuration parameter of *Gru*. In the case it is as large as the size of the system, all agents will acquire a global knowledge exchanging their information; in the case it is equal to zero, each agent

[4]Poll intervals are specifically hardcoded in the repository service by can be configured at will.

will be isolated and will have to take decisions without any knowledge of the surroundings. Usually, this value is set to 3; that is a reasonable one considering that microservices triads are emerging as a best practice for human-based management of microservices according to the 12-factor app development guide for practitioners [37]. The specific peers a *Gru*-Agent enters in contact with are determined randomly by the Shared Repository. Such a randomness guarantees that each agent is aware of a different subset of the whole system. Once the subset of peers is chosen, the Communication Manager periodically polls the peers getting the necessary data through the REST APIs, storing it in the Internal Storage. Such data includes: (a) the information on the CPU and memory usage—these are used by *Gru* for standard adaptation and control; (b) the value of any user-specific metric defined when the framework is configured; (c) last chosen *policy*, i.e., the action that *Gru* undertook to control and adapt microservice. *Gru* currently supports four policies, namely, *"scale-in"*, *"scale-out"*, *"switch*, and *"no-action"*; these are all computed locally to each microservice (more details on policies in Sect. 3.3). These data are stored in the Internal Storage as *cluster data*. Cluster data represents a partial view, i.e., as previously explained, limited by the number of active peers selected for neighborhood size, where 3 is the default number. This partial view is less computationally expensive and equally effective, according to our experimentation. Consequently, this feature reflects a powerful benefit behind our research solution.

In summary, the use of customizable partial views over the entire microservice application allows *Gru* and *Gru*-agents to make locally informed decisions which are still effective.

3.2.2 *Gru*: MAPE-K Autonomic Adaptation

Gru-Agents come with built-in monitoring facilities that gather and report the necessary low-level analytics needed to compute the necessary adaptation metrics and, ultimately, adopt opportunistic adaptation policies based on measured data. The **Monitor** component interacts with the local Docker Daemon through its standard API to get information about the status of the controlled containers: it is possible to retrieve low-level information about the consumption of resources (CPU and memory usage, storage, I/O operations, etc.), as well as the specific properties of each container, such as the number of CPU assigned, the memory limit, the network interface, etc. *Gru*-agents can also read the logs of the microservices that are exposed by the container, accessing higher-level information. This information is used to understand the status of a container and the total consumption of resources of the node, as well as the status of the microservices inside the container

The monitor presents two major components: (1) a "live" component that is constantly running and monitoring the containers—this component is entrusted with eliciting the necessary metrics to evaluate adaptation policies; (2) a "passive" component, activated at every iteration of the feedback loop—this component formats, packages, and sends the data to the analyzer component for further processing.

In turn, the **analyzer** component receives the data coming from the monitors' passive components of neighboring peers and elaborates them to obtain percentage-scores that dictate to the planner component the actions to be taken. The analytics currently supported by *Gru* focus on all CPU- and memory-specific metrics (e.g., usage, saturation, leftover quantity, etc.), as well as additional user-defined analytics—more details on analytics and how they are used to decide how to adapt microservices are available in Sect. 3.3.

The **planner** component actuates adaptation policies based on the results of the analysis and on the strategy it is currently configured to address—for further details on strategies and their relation to strategies in the context of *Gru*, see Sects. 3.3 and 3.4.

Finally, the **executor** component actuates the appropriate actions on the target microservices. Before executing an action, the executor chooses the resources to allocate, automatically creating the resource's configuration file if needed, e.g., a Docker config for a container to be mounted up by the Docker Daemon. It is critical to remember that *all actions are executed locally*, on the node that runs the *Gru*-Agent.

On one hand, the executor listens to its peers, receiving their current adaptation information and, based on that input, the executor can trigger adaptation actions in a reactive way, without waiting for its typical feedback loop iteration to be executed. On the other hand, this feature is experimental, and is currently used only to start and stop specific microservices on the node manually from remote. Further research could address the investigation, design, and implementation of fault tolerance mechanisms specific to the above, more advanced and reactive container management strategy. This approach could be valuable in cases where a high-availability is needed—in those instances, managers may require that, at the precise instant in which a container running a specific microservice fails, an autonomic management instrument such as *Gru* start a new microservice immediately, rather than wait for the feedback-loop latency time.

3.3 Policies

Policies are rules that trigger some actions that are actuated on the containers, while strategies are algorithms that choose a policy from among a set of weighted ones.

Policies have a name that identifies the policy, a list of actions that need to be actuated to satisfy the policy, a target service for the actions and a weight. The weight is a value between 0 and 1 that is computed according to an equation that is different for each policy. Policies can be enabled or disabled in the policy configuration. The planner creates a weighted policy for every microservice to manage, resulting in a list of PxM weighted policies, where P is the number of enabled policies and M is the number of microservices to manage. Currently there are four implemented policies to be enacted by *Gru*-Agents: the *scale-in* policy, the *scale-out* policy, the *switch* policy, and the *no-action* policy. Beyond this set of policies, *Gru* was also designed to welcome the usage of user-defined policies and connected analytics but this facility is made available as is and was never tested nor evaluated. Here follows an outline of the policies currently implemented in *Gru*.

3.3.1 *Gru*: Scale-In

The **scale-in** policy triggers the *stop* and *remove* actions that stop a container running the target microservice and remove it from the node freeing the resources, respectively. The weight of the policy is an average defined according to Eq. (1):

$$w_{policy,ms} = \frac{\sum_{i=0}^{n_{analytic}} w_{analytic,i}}{n_{analytic}} \tag{1}$$

where $n_{analytic}$ is the number of the analytics the policy should consider in the computation of its weight, and $w_{analytic,i}$ is the weight of every analytic that is computed according to Eq. (2):

$$w_{analytic} = 1 - \frac{\min(v_{analytic}, thr_{scale-in})}{thr_{scale-in}} \tag{2}$$

where $v_{analytic}$ is the value of the analytic, and $thr_{scale-in}$ is the threshold for scale-in defined in the policy configuration. To savor the resulting average, imagine that a *Gru* is set to weigh the scale-in policy using two metrics only, “microservice-lifetime-in-s” and “average-CPU-usage.” For both metrics, *Gru* first evaluates Eq. (2): *Gru* elaborates the minimum value between the current measure and compares that measurement to a predefined threshold (which depends on the specific microservice’s service-level agreement), returning that minimum, dividing it by the specified threshold (i.e., a ratio), and evaluating the complement to 1 of this number. The sum of both results divided by 2 (i.e., the number of metrics currently considered) constitutes the *Gru* policy weight. For example, in the same example, imagine that the exact values in a certain moment X are as follows: $[microservice_{LifetimeInSec} = 41, average_{CpcuUsage} = 67, threshold_{CPU} = 75, threshold_{Lifetime} = 35]$; *Gru* performs two applications of Eq. (2) to obtain min (67.75) and min (41.35). Subsequently, *Gru* divides and complements these minimums, 1-67/75 and 1-35/35, obtaining “0,107” for metrics 1 and “0” for the second metric, which exceeded the threshold in this loop. At this point *Gru* will average the resulting values for a total weight of the scale-in policy of “0,053.”

In the case that a microservice has only one running instance and is in the base-services set of the node, the scale-in policy is not evaluated and its weight is set to 0.

Using Eqs. (1) and (2), we see the weight of the policy is proportional to how much load of the microservice is below a user-defined threshold: The analytics used to compute the weight of this policy are related to the load that the microservice is facing (e.g., the response time of the service, the resource consumption, etc.).

3.3.2 *Gru*: Scale-Out

The **scale-out** policy triggers the *start* action, which starts a new instance of a container running the target microservice. The start action starts a container if it is in a stop status, or creates and starts a new one otherwise. The weight of the scale-out policy in computed according to the same equation of the scale-in (see Eq. (1)). However, the $w_{analytic,i}$ value is computed as follows:

Equation (3)

$$w_{analytic} = 1 - \frac{\max(v_{analytic}, thr_{scale-out}) - thr_{analytic}}{1 - thr_{scale-out}} \tag{3}$$

where $thr_{scale-out}$ is the threshold for scale-out defined in the policy configuration. In case there are not enough resources (CPU and memory-space, defined as part of *Gru* configuration) to start a new instance of a microservice, the scale-out policy is not evaluated and its weight is set to 0.

This policy is the dual equivalent of the scale-in one, so Eqs. (1) and (3) have been chosen to compute a weight that is proportional to how much a service is overloaded, taking as a reference a threshold defined by the user. For this reason, the analytics involved in the computation of the weight of this policy should be related to the load that the microservice is facing, as in the scale-in policy.

3.3.3 *Gru*: Switch

The **switch** policy allows to switch a running microservice with another one that is not running in a single iteration. This policy triggers first the stop and remove actions on a running container of a microservice, then triggers the Start action on a container of a different microservice. This policy is actuated only if the node does not have the resources needed to start a new microservice, but needs to stop another one in order to obtain such resources. The switch policy is computed on pairs of microservices, in order to understand if one service should be replaced by another.

The equations used to compute the weight of the switch policy have been studied to express the difference on the load that two microservices are facing: the weight of this policy computed between two microservices is proportional to a maximum distance that the user imposes between the load of the two microservices.

First, microservices are divided into running ones and inactive ones, then a switch policy is created for each pair running-inactive, assigning a weight. The weight of this policy is computed according to the following equation:

$$w_{policy,pair} = Max(0, \frac{\sum_{i=0}^{n_{analytic}} w_{analytic,i}}{n_{analytic}}) \tag{4}$$

where $w_{analytic,i}$ is computed according to Eq. (5)

$$w_{analytic} = Min(1, \frac{ratio_{analytic}}{ratio_{max}}) \tag{5}$$

The value $ratio_{max}$ is the maximum ratio that can occur between the value of two analytics and it is defined in the policy configuration. Equation (6) is used to compute the ratio between two metrics, i.e., $ratio_{analytic}$:

$$ratio_{analytic} = v_{analytic,inactive} - v_{analytic,running} \tag{6}$$

where $v_{analytic,inactive}$ and $v_{analytic,running}$ are the values of the same analytic for the inactive and the running microservices, respectively. Obviously, the computation of the switch policy is evaluated only between microservices that share the same analytics.

3.3.4 *Gru*: No-Action

The **no-action** policy simply does not trigger any action. It is weighted according to Eq. (7).

$$w_{noaction} = 1 - \max(policiesWeights) \tag{7}$$

The value $policiesWeights$ is the set of weights of all the other computed policies, so the weight $w_{noaction}$ is computed as the difference between one and the maximum value computed for the other policies.

The no-action policy should be actuated as an alternative to other policies when they are not required. Using Eq. (7) we can assign to this policy a weight that depends on the ones computed for the other policies, and that expresses that the system does not require any adaptation action.

3.4 Gru*: Operational Strategies*

Once a weight is assigned to each policy for each service, policies are analyzed according to a specific strategy. **Strategies** are algorithms used to choose the right policy to actuate among the list of the available ones taking into account their weight. The relation between strategies and policies is analogous to the relation between strategic decisions at the high level and tactical decisions at the lower level of abstraction. *Gru* allows the customization of both levels, but in the scope of this chapter, we concentrate on the single strategy we implemented in the current version, namely, a *probabilistic strategy*, which relies on a probabilistic computation

Algorithm 1 Probabilistic strategy algorithm

$policies \longleftarrow Shuffle(policies)$
$totalWeight \longleftarrow \sum_{p \in policies} p.weight$
$threshold \longleftarrow rand(0, 1)$
$delta \longleftarrow 1$
$index \longleftarrow 0$
for $p \in policies$ **do**
    if $\frac{p.weight}{totalWeight} > threshold$ **then**
        return p
    else
        if $(threshold - \frac{p.weight}{totalWeight}) < delta$ **then**
            $delta \longleftarrow threshold - \frac{p.weight}{totalWeight}$
            $index \longleftarrow index_p$
        end if
    end if
end for
return $policies[index]$

to choose the policy to be actuated, based on local and peer knowledge over the currently active context and constraints.

Using a probabilistic approach, the Planner can avoid local optima in the selection of the policy to actuate, and concentrate on generating an optimal configuration which is valid in the currently observable circumstances. Algorithm 1 implements the probabilistic strategy in *Gru*.

The strategy acquires as input an array of weighted policies $policies$ and shuffles it. It computes the $totalWeight$ as the sum of the weights of all the policies and uses this in the next steps to normalize all policy weights. Moreover, it chooses randomly a $threshold$. It then checks for each policy in $policies$ if its normalized weight is greater than the $threshold$. If this is the case, it then selects that specific policy for execution. Otherwise it looks for the remaining policies in the array. In the search, to address the case in which none of the policy normalized weights passes the threshold, it keeps track of the difference between such weights and the threshold, storing the index of the policy that is closest to the threshold in $index$. Thus structured, the adaptation strategy is always eventually able to select the policy with a weight closest to the threshold. The probabilistic approach was tested in previous work, proving its effectiveness in a scenario with a high (>25) number of nodes [7].

The policies and the strategies discussed previously are currently the only ones available to *Gru* and hard-coded inside the prototype. This is a limitation of our research solution. We plan to expand the available policies and strategies allowing the user to define its own equations and algorithms using specific configuration files that will be read by *Gru*-Agents.

Once the policy has been chosen, the Planner component creates a *plan* that contains the policy to execute and the target service. The plan is then sent to the Executor component.

4 Experimental Evaluation

The objectives of our evaluation are as follows:

- **OBJ1**: Show that the system provides the requested services limiting the violations of the maximum response time defined by the user
- **OBJ2**: Show that the system self-adapts according to the workload while limiting under- or over-provisioning of resources
- **OBJ3**: Evaluate the use of a dynamically computed adaptation loop times
- **OBJ4**: Evaluate the probabilistic strategy used for the decision-making process

We evaluated *Gru* by controlling the adaptation of an application featuring video streaming and manipulation. We performed two experiments: (experimentation I—**resilience**) evaluate the capability of *Gru* to adapt the application to a sudden increase in the workload with either a fixed or dynamic adaptation loop time interval; (experimentation II—**reality-check**) evaluate if *Gru* is able to manage the application facing a realistic workload.

Table 1 provides a summary of the objectives of the evaluation with the contributions we describe in this section.

4.1 Case Study Application: Online Video-on-Demand

Video-on-demand cloud applications account for over 70% of the total internet traffic in 2016, with Netflix traffic accounting for more than 1/3 of that traffic. Cisco Systems predict that by 2020 82% of the world's internet traffic will be video streaming [13]. Starting from these considerations, we developed a case study demonstrator that simulates a **video-on-demand cloud application**. Its usage is

Table 1 Evaluation objectives and analyses

Objective	Description	Evaluation analysis
OBJ1	Show that the system provides the requested services limiting the violations of the maximum response time defined by the user	Analysis of the response time of the application with two different workloads
OBJ2	Show that the system self-adapts according to the workload and limiting under- or over-provisioning of resources	Analysis of the active instances of the microservices with two different workloads
OBJ3	Validate the use of a dynamically computed adaptation loop time	Comparison between the fixed time adaptation loop and the dynamic computed one
OBJ4	Validate the probabilistic strategy used for the decision-making process	Comparison between the probabilistic selection strategy and a random selection strategy used as baseline

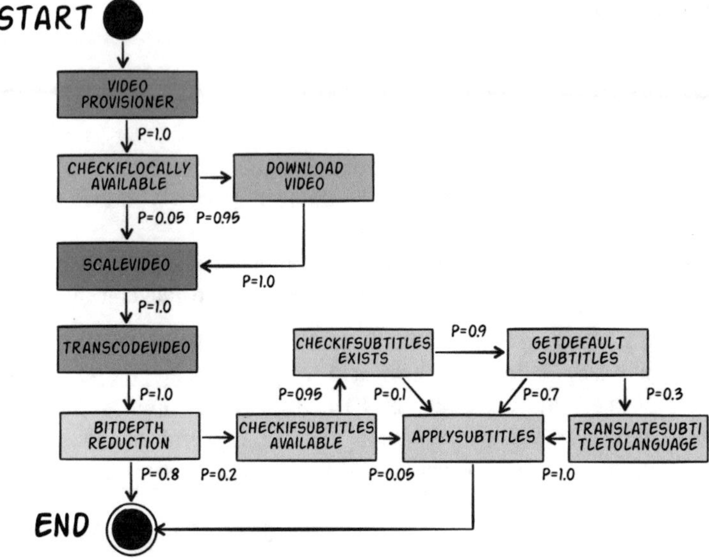

Fig. 3 Execution flow of video provisioner case study: all probabilities in the figure are conditional probabilities subject to the execution flow of the algorithm

simple: users request a video and can operate modifications on it (e.g., scaling the video) or add subtitles. The application is composed of 11 microservices, each of them executing a specific task part of the above scenario. (e.g., video request, video trimming, etc.)

The application starts with the `videoprovisioner` microservice, which receives the requests and manages the session for the user. The application first checks if the video is available locally, otherwise downloads it (`checkiflocallyavailable`, `downloadvideo`). Once the video is available, the application can operate modifications on it according to the user's choices (from `scalevideo` to `bitdepthreduction`). The last step are the operations on subtitles (from `checkifsubtitlesavailable` to `applysubtitle`), that are executed if requested by the user. Once the video is ready, the user is notified and can download it from the application.

The execution flow of the application is depicted in Fig. 3. In order to simulate the possible choices of the user, each microservice has a specific probability (P) to send a message to another one, represented as the value next to each arrow.

From a technical perspective, all microservices in our sample application are implemented using the *Go* programming language and deployed in a Docker container. The execution of a request is simulated keeping busy the CPU for an amount of time (*job-time*) that is computed according to an exponential distribution with λ representing the *expected demand* (D) of the microservice (see Table 2). The value of the λ has been chosen taking into account the type of microservice to simulate

Table 2 Microservices parameters

Service name	D	P	MRT	MRPM
applySubtitles	600	0.2	1200	110
bitDepthReduction	1300	1.0	3900	50
checkIfAvailable	1200	1.0	2400	55
checkIfSubtitlesAvailable	700	0.2	2100	95
checkIfSubtitlesExists	1500	0.95	3000	45
downloadVideo	1500	0.95	4500	45
getDefaultSubtitle	1200	0.9	2400	55
scaleVideo	28,500	1.0	85,500	3
transcodeVideo	900	1.0	1800	75
translateSubtitleToLanguage	500	0.3	1500	135
videoProvisioner	500	1.0	1000	135
Application	34,100	–	102,302	–

D is the demand of a microservice, while P is the probability to be executed; MRPM stands for the mean requests per minute that the service receives while MRT stands for the mean response time accounted for the service

and referencing similar online video manipulation applications such as YouTube.[5] The only exception is the *scalevideo* microservice, whose demand is derived from statistical data on video scaling is inherited from previous research [31]. All requests are processed in series to keep the application relatively simple but realistic.

Following the above design principle, each microservice has a **destination**, that is, the next microservice in the execution flow, along with a probability to send a message to that destination. With this technical device we can randomly simulate the possible choices made by the user about the operations to actuate on the requested video. In case more than one instance of the destination is available, the microservice balances the load among the available instances using a round-robin policy.

The requests coming to the system are registered with a unique ID in an **external key-value store**. This enables a microservice B to respond to any active instances of any microservice A who may have sent a request to B, bringing more flexibility to the application where instances are turned on and off dynamically.

The microservices of the application log the job time of every request and the number of requests that they received every minute (RPM). This information is exploited by *Gru* to manage the application. The microservices communicate with an external monitoring service sending statistical data about their job time, the RPM. The microservice *videoprovisioner* also sends the response time corresponding to every request to the monitoring service. The monitoring system is used only for debugging purposes and to check the status of the system during the experiments.

[5]http://youtube.com/.

4.2 Cluster Configuration and Experimental Setup

The cluster we used for our experiments was set up on *PoliCloud*,[6] a private cloud infrastructure at Politecnico di Milano. The cluster in question consists of *29 nodes*, each of which is to be considered a *Gru*-node, in the scope of this evaluation and all of which are therefore running *Gru*-Agents along with their respective microservice targets. Concluding the aforementioned set, one additional node (*main-node*) is used for the deployment of the external repository and our own experimental monitoring and observation infrastructure.

Every *Gru*-node has 2 CPUs and 1 GB of memory, while the main-node is powered by 4 CPUs and 8 GB of memory. Despite this experimental configuration, it should be noted that *Gru* is able to handle the dynamic creation of nodes that may join or leave the cluster; for the sake of simplicity all the nodes are preallocated here, for evaluation purposes. We deployed one active instance of every microservice belonging to the application in one different server, except for the `scalevideo` microservice that has five active instances by default, following guidelines from previous research and practice [31]. *Gru*-Agents run inside a Docker container with limited resource access—i.e., CPU-shares set to 256 and maximum memory set to 512 Mb—this reduces their impact on the available resources for the microservices.

The main-node features an instance of the etcd server[7] as the external repository used by *Gru*, along with Apache Jmeter[8] for traffic generation and InfluxDB[9] (a time-series data storage) to store the statistical data about the status of the system. Finally, the Grafana web service was used for real-time visualization of the InfluxDB data.

4.3 Gru *Experimental Configuration*

Agent Configuration To account for best, worst, and average usage scenarios, the time interval for the feedback loop of every agent was set to 120 and 90 s for experimentations with a fixed adaptation time interval, while the interval was computed dynamically for the experimentation with the dynamic adaptation time interval.

The maximum number of peers to communicate with has been set to 5. This value has been chosen according to the number of nodes in the cluster to avoid the communication with all the peers and to create a useful partial view of the system.

The strategy used in the cluster is *probabilistic*, as described in Sect. 3.3.

---

[6]http://policloud.polimi.it.

[7]https://github.com/coreos/etcd.

[8]http://jmeter.apache.org.

[9]https://influxdata.com/time-series-platform/influxdb/.

μService-Descriptors μService-Descriptors are created for every microservice composing the application. Every μService-Descriptor has the information about the microservice and the parameters needed to create a new instance of the specific microservice.

The analytics to compute for every service are the *response-time-ratio* and the *utilization* (described in the following paragraph).

The constraints imposed on every service are the *maximum response time* (MRT) and the *maximum number of requests per minute* (MRPM) the microservice can handle. The MRT has been defined as two to three times the demand of the microservice, while the MRPM value has been chosen according to the number of requests the service can satisfy in a minute considering the demand plus 10% of that value. The MRT and MRPM values for every microservices can be seen in Table 2 The demand of the entire application is obtained as the sum of the demand of each microservice multiplied by its probability of execution (Eq. (8)), while the MRT of the application is computed as three times its demand:

$$D_{app} = \sum D_{ms} * P \tag{8}$$

Analytics The analytics we defined are the response-time ratio and the utilization. The **response-time ratio** is defined as the ratio between the average job time of a microservice and its MRT defined in the μService-Descriptor, so it is computed with Eq. (9), where $jobtime_{avg}$ is the average job time monitored for all the known instances of the microservice.

$$value_{rtr} = \frac{jobtime_{avg}}{MRT} \tag{9}$$

The *utilization* is computed as the ratio between the average number of requests arrived at the microservice in a minute and the MRPM defined in the μService-Descriptor. Equation (10) is used for the computation of the value of the utilization, where rpm_{avg} is the average requests per minute for all the known instances of the microservice.

$$value_{util} = \frac{rpm_{avg}}{MRPM} \tag{10}$$

Policies The three available policies, i.e., *scale-in*, *scale-out*, and *switch*, are all enabled. The *scale-in policy* has a threshold of 0.35 and takes into consideration only utilization for the computation of the weight. This choice is based on the consideration that the demand of the microservices has been manually set and the MRT is imposed according to this value as two to three times the demand. This would keep the response-time ratio over the scale-in threshold, reducing the probability of scale-in even if the microservices is underused.

The *scale-out policy* has a threshold of 1 and the analytics used for the computation of the weight are both the utilization and the response-time ratio.

The *switch policy* has a delta of 0.6 and uses both utilization and response-time ratio analytics for weight computation.

The values chosen for the above adaptation loops and thresholds are consistent with industrial standards [1].

4.3.1 Experimentation I: Reactive *Gru*

Our objective is to verify whether *Gru* is able to adapt the application to a sudden increase in the workload. The traffic sent to the application is depicted in Fig. 4a. We start sending to the application 0.1 requests per second (RPS), then, after a time interval, the RPS are doubled; this happens thrice, reaching a maximum of 0.8 RPS. After every step, the RPS are kept stable for a time interval in order to let the system stabilize, the load last for 3 h and 45 min.

4.3.2 Experimentation II: Bimodal *Gru*

The second experimentation is based on a workload extracted from the data obtained monitoring the traffic of a real website for several days. The original workload was shrunk from 48 to 6 h and the number of requests was scaled to peak at 0.8 RPS. The scaling in the number of RPS has been done to adapt the workload to the resources available for the experimentation. The resulting workload presents a bimodal shape and is depicted in Fig. 4b. Our objective is to understand whether *Gru* is able to scale the number of active instances of the microservices in order to follow the traffic shape and, at the same time, to keep the response time of the application under its intended MRP.

4.4 Fixed Adaptation Time Interval Tests

The **time interval** for the feedback loop of every agent is set to 120 s and then any substantial variations are controlled with a setting of 90 s. These values were chosen taking into account the job-time and the constraints about the Maximum Response Time of the microservices composing the application. To elicit experimental data, we collected the results of 10 runs, representing and evaluating their statistical average.

First, we present the results obtained with *experimentation I* (see Fig. 5). The response time of the application (averaged every 5 min) is depicted in Fig. 5a. When there is a step in the RPS, the response time goes over the MRP but quickly returns in the desired range of values. This is the effect of the adaptation that scales the number of instances to handle RPS changes (**OBJ1**).

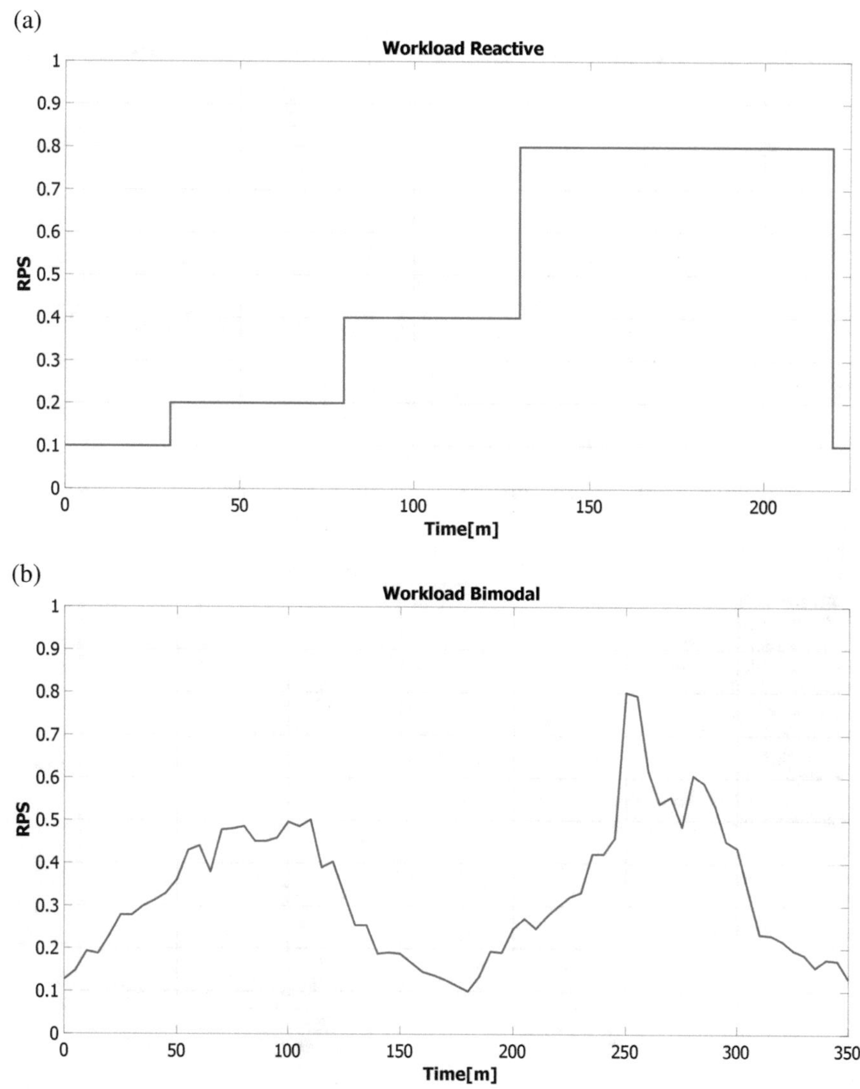

Fig. 4 Requests sent to the application. (**a**) Workload reactive. (**b**) Workload bimodal

The number of active instances of the microservices is depicted in Fig. 5b. After every step in the RPS, the number of active instances of the microservices is incremented to handle the new workload. There is an initial overscaling after every step that is due to the fact that the requests in the queue should be completed, so the response time of the microservice is over the threshold for an adaptation period. Once the adaptation is finished, the number of instances are decreased and it is stabilized in order to keep the utilization in the correct range. The

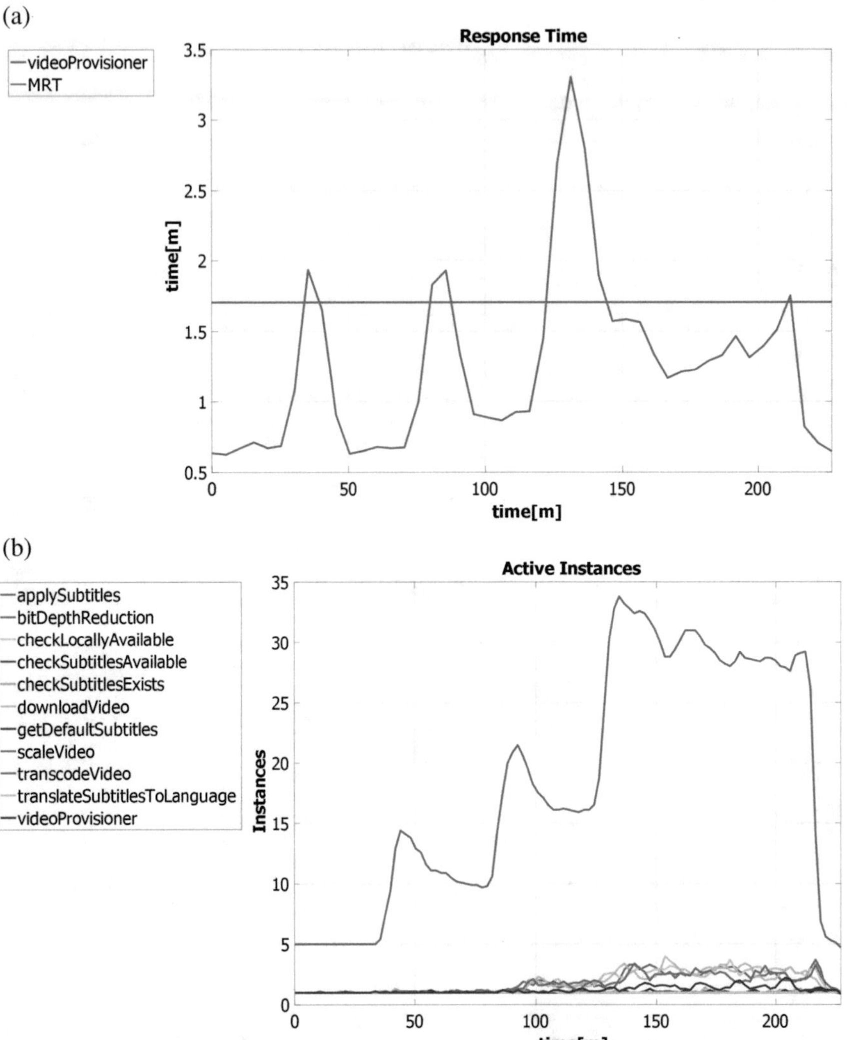

Fig. 5 Experimentation I: results using a 120 s adaptation time interval. (**a**) Response time of the application. (**b**) Active instances over time

scalevideo microservice is the main target of scaling out, being the most demanding microservice of the application. Other services are scaled only for few periods to handle a sudden increase in their response time (**OBJ2**).

The results obtained with *experimentation II* are depicted in Fig. 6 The response time of the application, depicted in Fig. 6a, show that ***Gru* can adapt effectively the application to the workload**, ensuring only a few violations in the MRT (**OBJ1**).

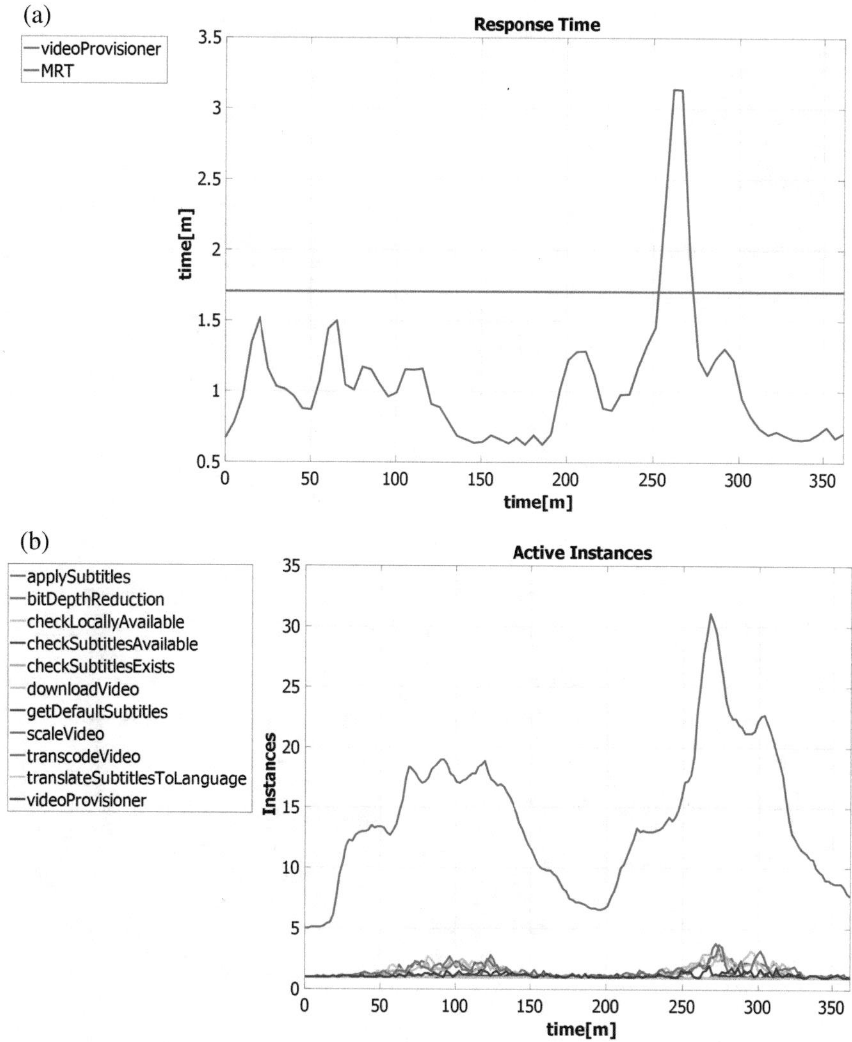

Fig. 6 Experimentation II: results using a 120 s adaptation time interval. (**a**) Response time of the application. (**b**) Active instances over time

The number of active instances for every microservice is depicted in Fig. 6b. The application is adapted by *Gru* scaling the microservices to follow the traffic shape (**OBJ2**). Since the system is reactive, there is an adaptation time needed by *Gru* to understand the change in the workload and to actuate the needed adaptation actions.

Resource Consumption The CPU usage of the microservices and the cluster is depicted in Fig. 7 for both our experimentations. The charts clearly show that CPU usage of the microservices remains constant for the entire duration of the

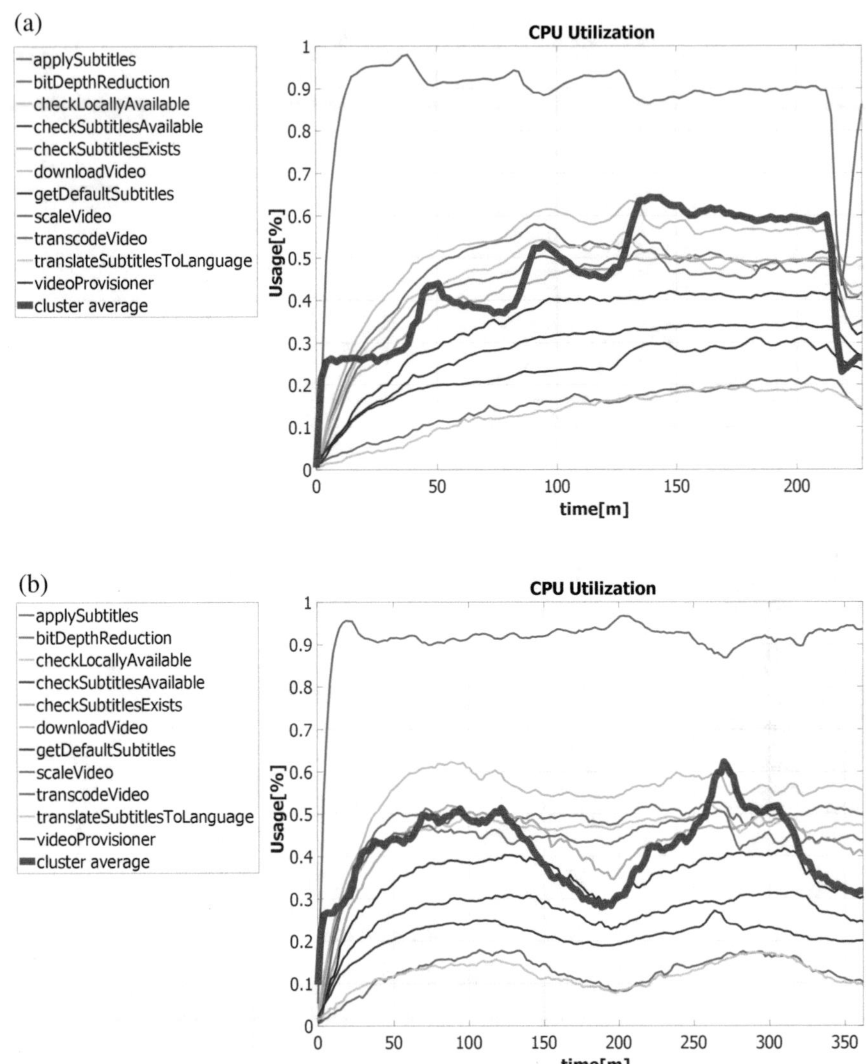

Fig. 7 CPU usage of the microservices. (**a**) Reactive CPU usage. (**b**) Bimodal CPU usage

experimentations, without it being affected by the increase or decrease in the number of active instances (**OBJ2**) managed by *Gru*.

However, the charts show that the cluster is underused in some time slots. This is due to the design of the application itself: the *scalevideo* microservice has a demand that is several times higher than the other services. The consequence of this higher demand is that the workload is created taking into consideration mainly that microservice, while the others result underused. The use of a system based on affinity between microservices may lead to a better usage of the resources of a node, favoring the scaling out of microservices on the same Node that can better use all of its resources. This can be implemented as a future *Gru* extension, exploiting the information about the type of the microservices contained in the μService-Descriptors.

Design of Analytics The design of the analytics of the system is fundamental to obtain an effective adaptation. The values of the analytics used during the evaluation—i.e., *Response Time Ratio* and *Utilization*—are depicted in Figs. 8 and 9.

The response-time ratio follows the variation in the performance of the application and can trigger the scaling of the system to adapt to an increase in the workload for every microservice. We conclude that this analytic represents a good choice for the adaptation of the application under study. The Utilization analytic is effective with the `scaleVideo` microservice, but other microservices presents very low values for the entire duration of both the experimentations. This is again due to the considerable difference between the demand of the *scaleVideo* and one of the other microservices composing the application.

Controlling Adaptation-Loop Times: An Alternative 90 s Setting Our objective is to understand how the variation of the time interval for the adaptation loop can influence the behavior of the system. Figures 10 and 11 show the results with a time interval for the adaptation loop set to 90 s instead of 120 s. The charts represent the mean of five runs.

We can see that the system can respond quickly to the changes in the workload, scaling the instances faster to follow the traffic coming to the application. This generally also improves the response time of the application. The drawback is the introduction of system instability, which does not ensure to keep the response time under the defined threshold when the traffic stabilizes after an adaptation step.

This result highlights the importance of the time interval for the adaptation loop. To evaluate this importance in action and understand its evolution we studied sets whereby adaptation time interval values are generated dynamically.

4.5 Dynamic Adaptation Time Interval Tests

To test for time-interval dynamicity and its efficiency, we implemented an algorithm to set dynamically the time interval of the autonomic loop, based on information available to the microservices running in the *Gru*-Agent node (see Algorithm 2).

The algorithm iterates over all the running microservices on the node ($services_{run}$), and stores in the variable t_{loop} the maximum response time MRT of the current service s, only if it is bigger than the previous one. In this way, at the end of the iteration, t_{loop} is set to the maximum MRT value among the microservices

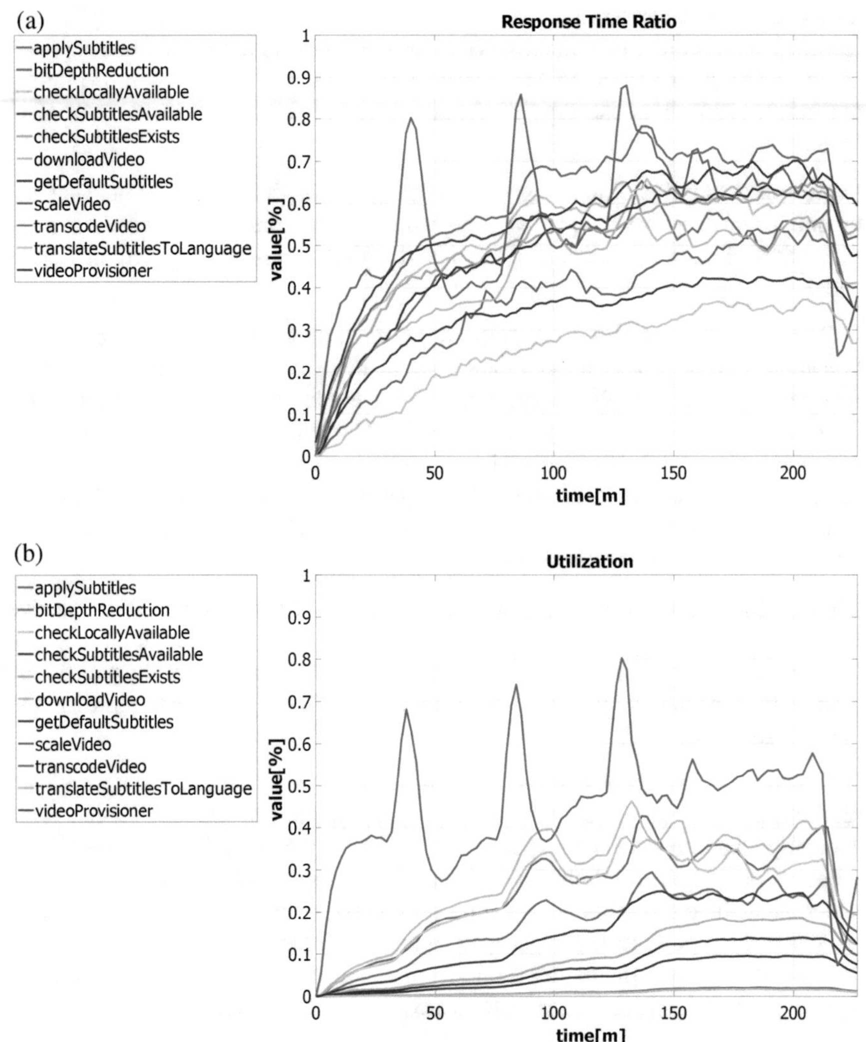

Fig. 8 Experimentation I: analytics values. (**a**) Response-time ratio. (**b**) Utilization

running in the node. The algorithm is triggered every time a running microservice is stopped, or a new one is started.

As a result, each *Gru*-agent has its own adaptation loop time interval, according to the microservices currently running in its node—this value is inherent to that node and independent from the other agents in all ways. We chose to set it dynamically to the highest MRT to create a time window suitable to collect the data needed to understand the state of the slowest microservice running in the node.

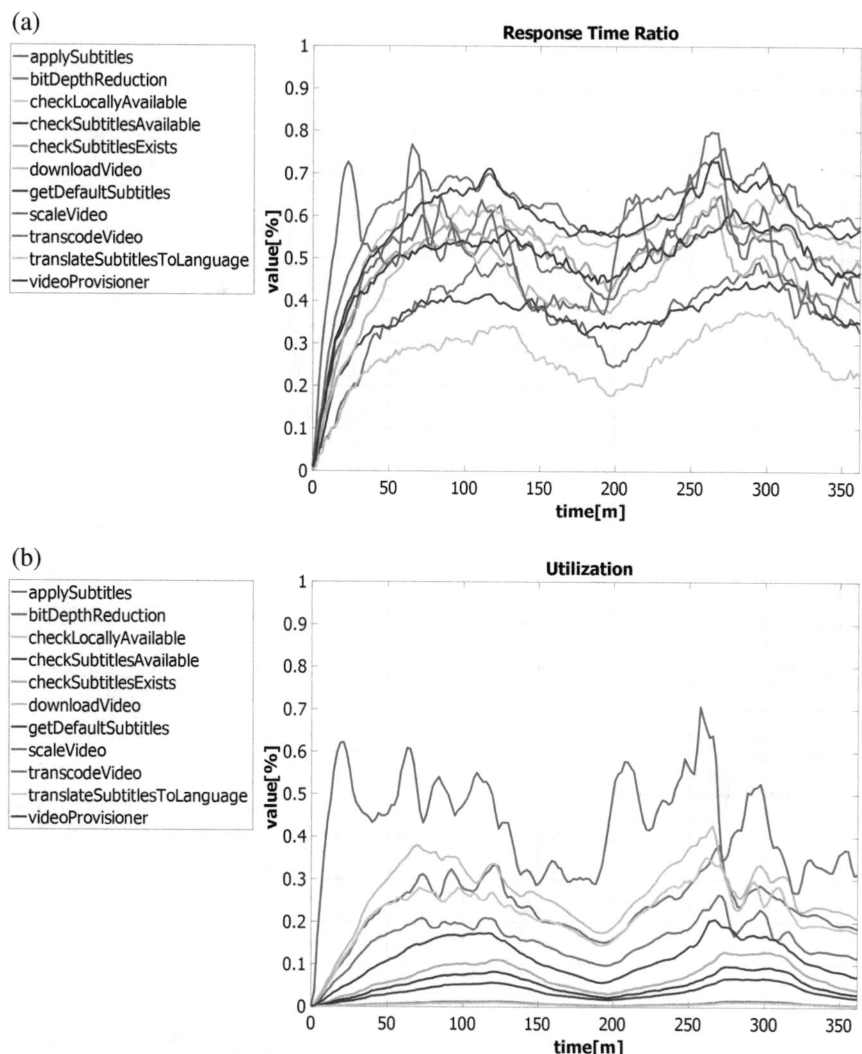

Fig. 9 Experimentation II: analytics values. (**a**) Response-time ratio. (**b**) Utilization

We executed five experimentations for each workload, presenting the mean of the results (**OBJ3**). The response time of the application is greatly improved compared to the system using a fixed time autonomic loop (both 120 and 90 s), as shown in Figs. 12a and 13a. The system can respond quickly to the spikes in the workload, both in the reactive (Fig. 12a) and bimodal (Fig. 13a) experimentations, and is able to keep it under the MRT of the application when the workload is stable. The use of a dynamic time interval lets the system avoid the over-provisioning of resources, starting the amount of microservices best suited to handle the current workload (see

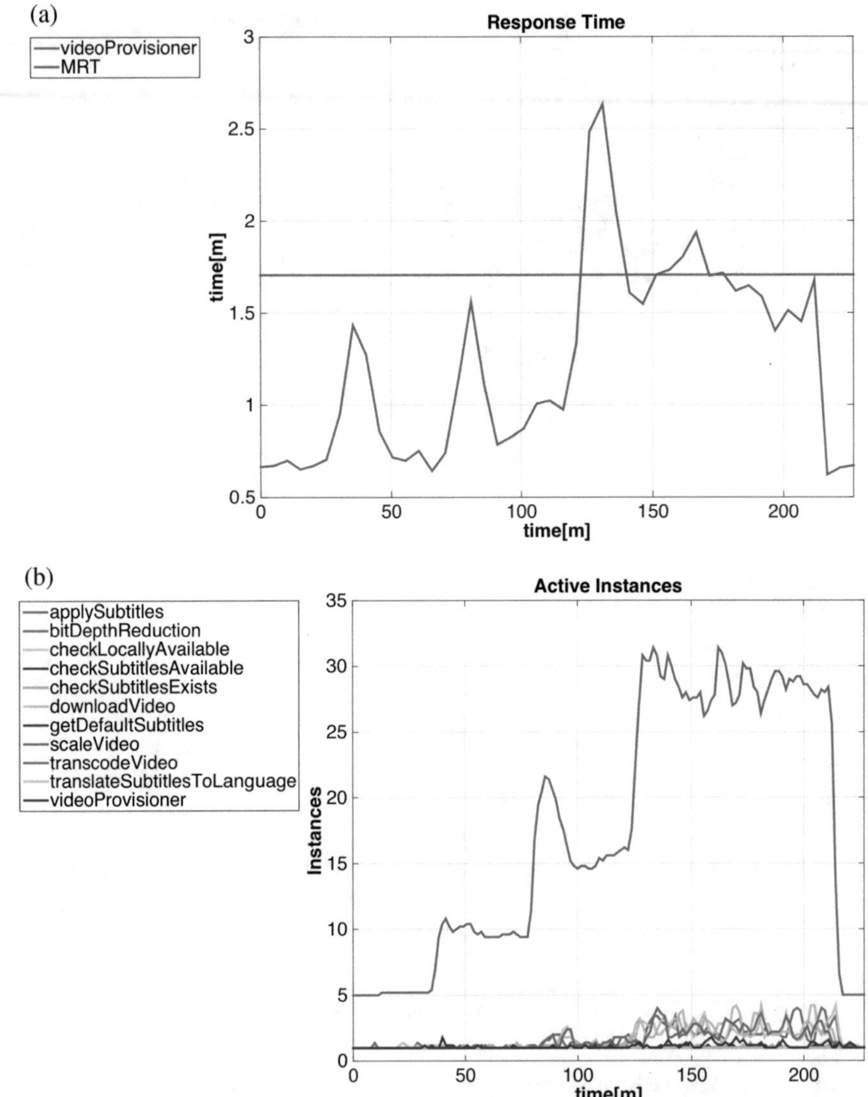

Fig. 10 Experimentation I: results using a 90 s adaptation time interval. (**a**) Response time of the application. (**b**) Active instances over time

Figs. 12b and 13b). This is evident especially with the reactive workload, as depicted in Fig. 12b, where the over-provisioning is avoided even when there are spikes in the workload. The dynamic approach to the autonomic loop time interval proved to bring advantages compared to the fixed one. The response time is improved, as well as the usage of resources. This emphasizes the importance of the algorithm used to set it, so it will require a deeper study and new techniques to tune it the best way.

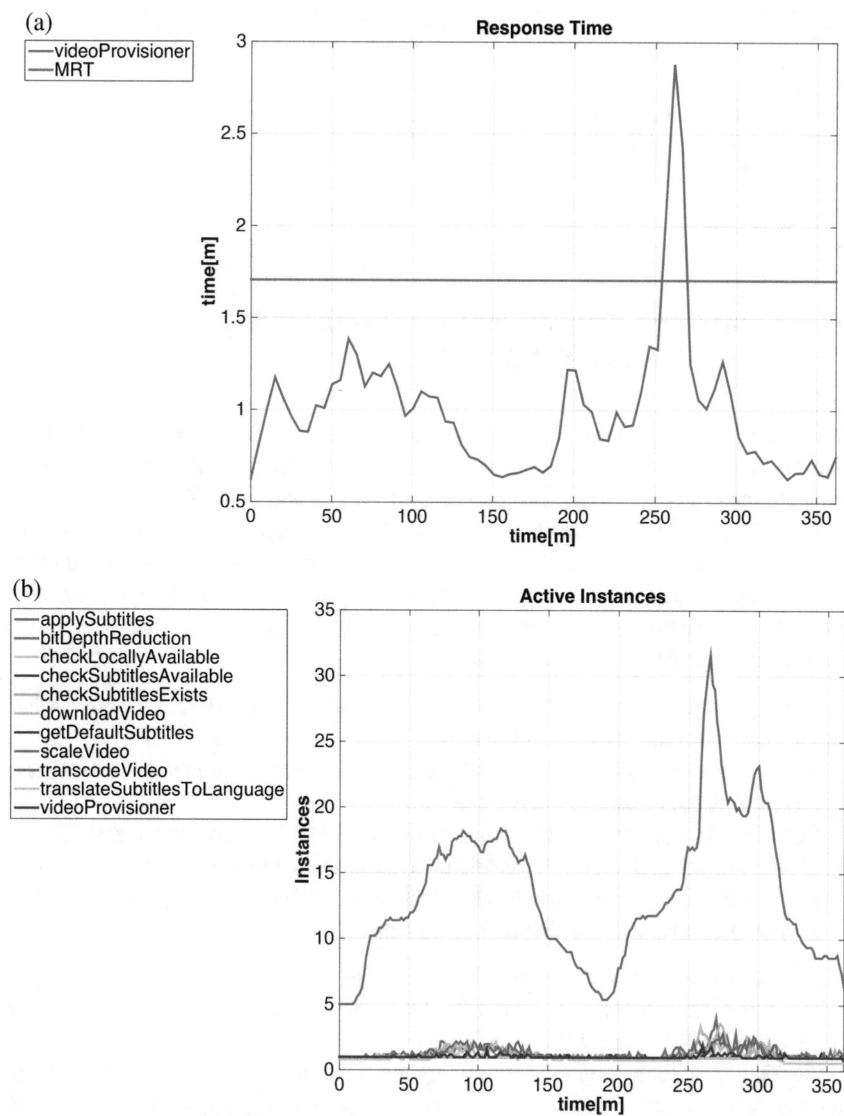

Fig. 11 Experimentation II: results using a 90 s adaptation time interval. (**a**) Response time of the application. (**b**) Active instances over time

Algorithm 2 Dynamic time loop algorithm

```
t_loop ⟵ 0
for s ∈ services_run do
    if s.MRT > t_loop then
        t_loop ⟵ s.MRT
    end if
end for
return t_loop
```

4.6 Controlling Policy Selection: Experimenting with a Random Null Model

Up to this point, we reported on our experimentation of *Gru* using a probabilistic policy selection. We now use these reported experimental results as a baseline to evaluate the effectiveness against random null-model approach (**OBJ4**).

Gru settings are the same we illustrated in Sect. 4.3, and the adaptation loop time interval is again set to 120 s. However, the selection of the policy to execute at every iteration of the adaptation loop is done randomly, that is, without taking into account the weight of the policies and considering only policies that are applicable given the context information available. In particular:

- For the scale-in policy, we discard the adaptation actions that would violate constraints on the services of the node.
- For the scale-out policy, we discard the adaptation actions related to services that have not enough resources to be started.
- For the swap policy, we discard actions that would violate constraints on the services of the node, the actions related to services that have not enough resources to be started, and the actions related to services that are not idempotent (i.e., mutually equivalent) and cannot be substituted.

The response time of the application using the policy selection schema outlined above is depicted in Figs. 14a and 15a, while the active instances during time are depicted in Figs. 14b and 15b.

Services are scaled without following the changes in the workload, and the system cannot reach a stable state. As a consequence, the response time quickly goes over the maximum one imposed as a constraint. We can conclude that the random selection of a valid policy cannot guarantee the constraints imposed on the application, and the probabilistic approach with which we originally experimented outperforms a random null-model counterpart.

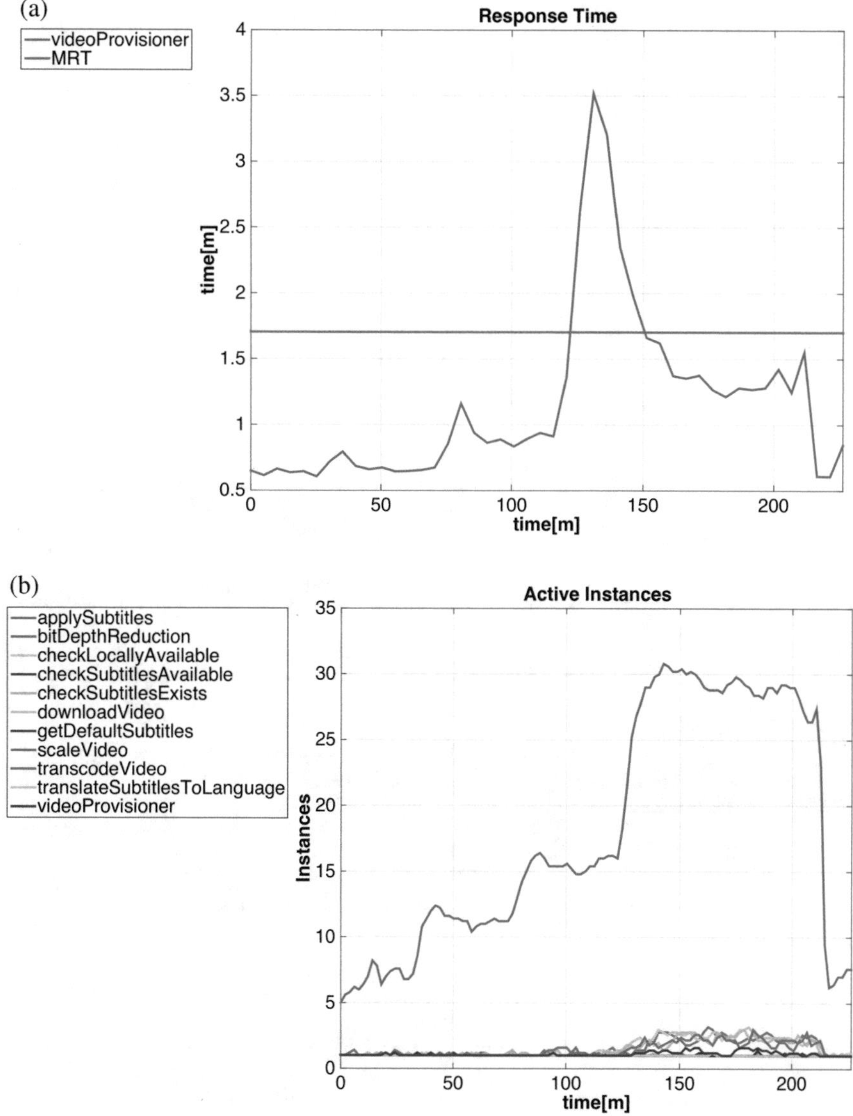

Fig. 12 Experimentation I: results using a dynamic adaptation time interval. (**a**) Response time of the application. (**b**) Active instances over time

4.7 *Discussion and Experimental Limitations*

The results of the experimentations show that *Gru* can successfully manage autonomically and in a fully distributed fashion any application developed using microservices and deployed in Docker containers. *Gru* can make that application

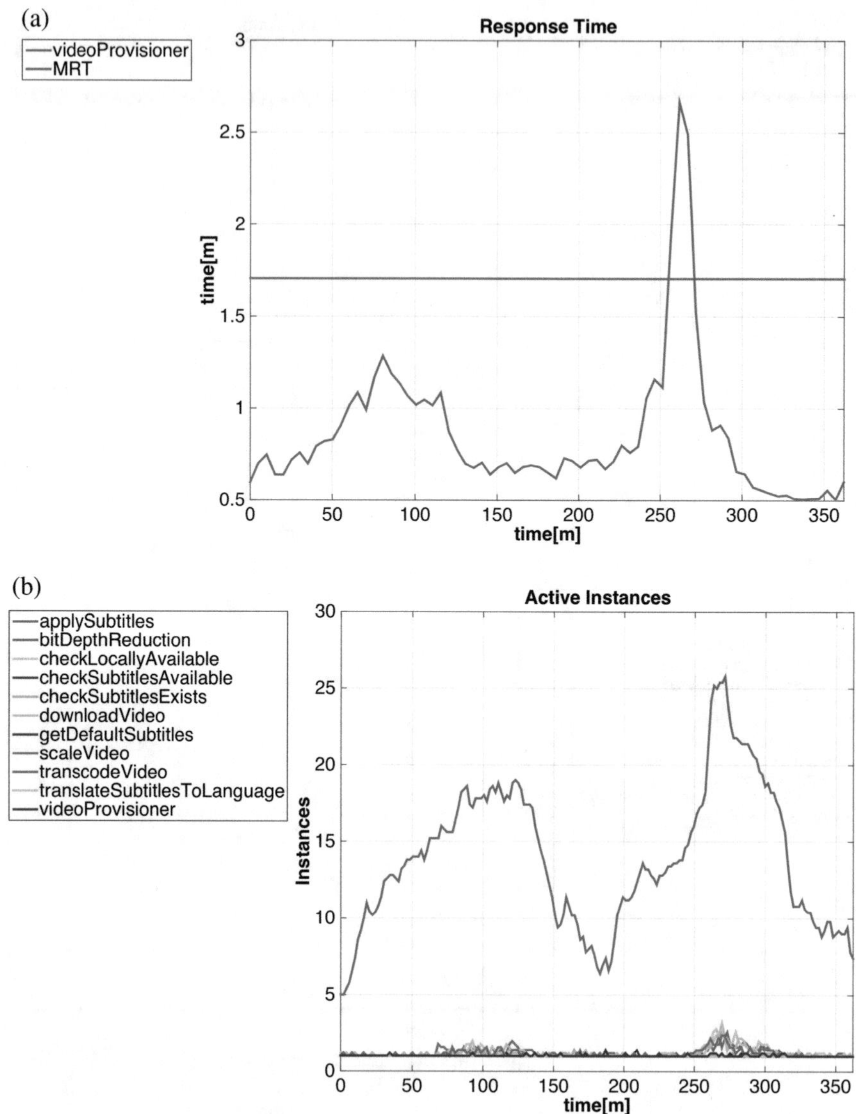

Fig. 13 Experimentation II: results using a dynamic adaptation time interval. (**a**) Response time of the application. (**b**) Active instances over time

autonomic though the interaction with the containers, actuating autonomic actions on the basis of a partial knowledge to adapt the application to the variation of the environment where it is running. The autonomic actions are still limited to the scaling of the microservices; however, this is enough to ensure that the application is adapted to the changing workload in order to respect the constraints imposed by

(a)

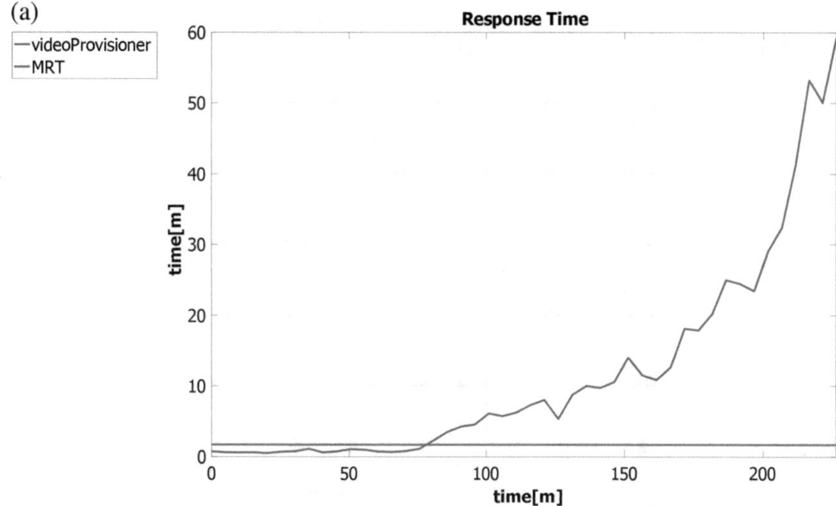

(b)

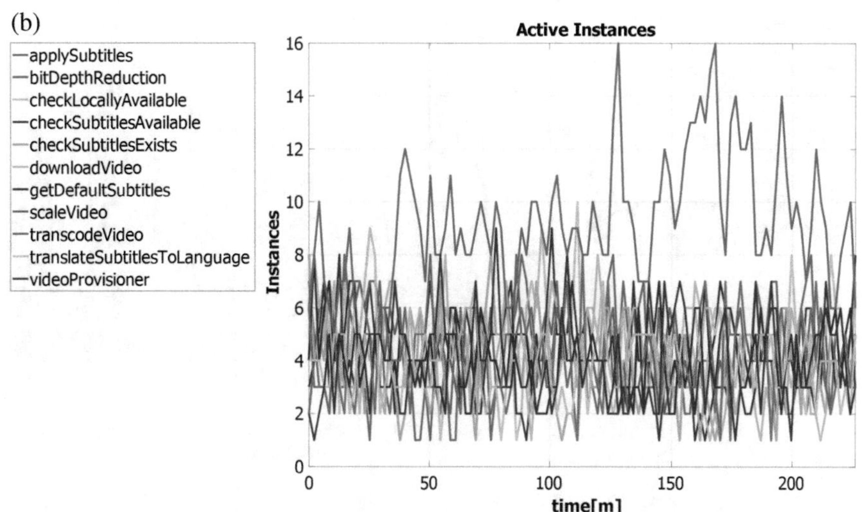

Fig. 14 Experimentation I: results using random policy selection. (**a**) Response time of the application. (**b**) Active instances over time

the user (i.e., the MRT). The results show also that even if the application is not monitored by *Gru* in its totality, it is sufficient to monitor and respect the constraints imposed on the single microservices to obtain the effective adaptation of the entire application.

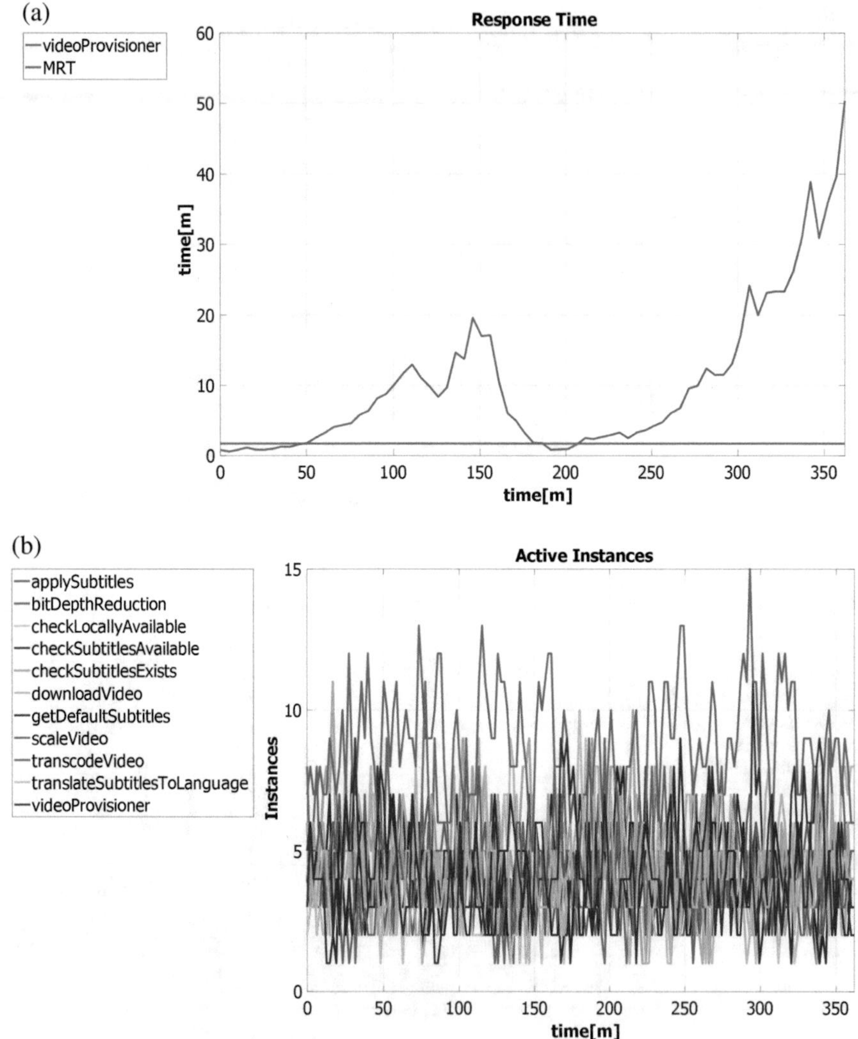

Fig. 15 Experimentation II: results using random policy selection. (**a**) Response time of the application. (**b**) Active instances over time

Despite the good results obtained in the experimentations, we discuss threats to validity for solution and its current evaluation—these can be improved in future work.

Adaptation Reactiveness *Gru* is by design a reactive system that actuates autonomic adaptation actions when certain conditions are met. The results of our experimentations show that this can be enough to adapt the application; however, the use of a proactive system could lead to even better results. This could be implemented as a component between the analyzer and the planner, that exploits a *Machine Learning* algorithm based on the partial view of the system build by the Analyzer to predict the adaptation needed.

Autonomic Capability *Gru* implements only policies that involve the scaling of the containers running the microservices. This is enough to adapt the application to variations in the workload. However, the implementation of new policies based on different actions can lead to more interesting and sophisticated autonomic capabilities, such as the migration or reconfiguration of microservices. The policies and strategies creation could be left to the user, who can customize the autonomic actions and the decision-making process according to their needs. The purpose of our experimentations was to show the exercise of *Gru* in action using an application which is not explicitly designed to be autonomic, so the interaction between *Gru* and the application is transparent and happens exploiting the containers. The elaboration of a design pattern consistent with *Gru* or the experimentation of an application that is designed to be integrated with *Gru*, maybe exposing in every microservice an endpoint to receive some commands by *Gru* itself, can further improve the autonomic capabilities of our research solution.

5 Related Work

The idea to use a multiagent systemic approach like *Gru* for self-adaptation is not novel per se, and has been already described thoroughly in the literature [36] with limited experimentation.

On the one hand, the concept of autoscaling for web applications deployed in containers was previously addressed by Baresi et al. [3]. Here, the traditional MAPE loop is enriched with a new planner that consists of a discrete-time feedback controller. The proposed self-adaptive framework is applied to multitier cloud-based web applications, managing virtual machines and containers to provide a better granularity in the resource management of the application. This lets the system enable a coordinated infrastructure and platform adaptation. The self-adaptive framework has been evaluated with two different applications deployed in the Amazon Web Services cloud infrastructure, showing the improvement in the usage of resources using containers and in comparison with the autoscaling mechanism provided by Amazon itself. However, the evaluation has been done using a very limited resource pool, i.e., 10 VMs with 1 core in one case and 1 VM with 8 cores in the other one, so it does not represent a realistic setting for large-scale microservices applications. More advanced results along the same path concern the extensibility of the approach to TOSCA-based applications and workflows [5] or following a control-theoretical and container-based approach [4].

On the other hand, architectures for self-managing microservices have been proposed previously in order to enable the scalable and resilient self-management of microservices [34]. The authors propose a distributed architecture based on self-managing atomic services and on the election of a cluster leader that takes the decisions and actuates the actions. The management logic is present in each service, so if the leader fails, another one can be elected to manage the other nodes. The system is composed of two layers: the *local cluster* that contains the microservices and one leader, and a *composition cluster* composed of all the leaders for endpoint discovery across microservices and for leader election. This solution is totally different from the one we propose: the management logic is inside the microservices (internal approach), while we propose a totally external approach, and the system presents a hierarchical structure, while we adopt a fully decentralized one. Moreover, in [34] there is no experimental evaluation of the proposed approach, which is defined purely theoretically.

Similar critiques arise for application frameworks such as App-Bisect. This latter option defines a self-healing mechanism and policy of cloud applications based on the typical microservices architecture pattern adopted in large-scale production environments [32]. App-Bisect operates like a versioning system for deployed microservices. If there is a loss in performance of the application after an update, App-Bisect is able to revert a specific microservice to a version that originally ensured the desired performance specifics.

Beyond the aforementioned limitations, technologies such as DoCloud [21] offer an elastic cloud platform that exploits Docker to adapt the web application to the changing workload scaling the Docker containers composing the app [21]. DoCloud integrates a load balancer (HAProxy) and a private Docker registry to store the containers images. The platform uses a hybrid elastic controller that incorporates a proactive and reactive model for the scaling of the containers. Subsequently, proactive and reactive models are used for scale-out policy enactment, while for the scale-in only proactive models are used. Despite the good adaptability results of the proposed solution, the experimental evaluation is limited to a few number of active containers (i.e., up to nine containers). The experimental evaluation that we propose is far more complex and reflecting the realistic scenarios behind online large-scale video streaming applications.

From an open-source infrastructure quality of service perspective, the state of the art offers technologies such as Swarm and Kubernetes intended as solutions for the clustering of containers [6, 17, 24].

First, Swarm is the native solution for the clustering of Docker containers. Once a Swarm agent is installed in every node of the cluster, the user can control them through the manager. The user can start and stop containers letting Swarm decide where to place them according to different strategies (random, bin-packing, spread) that take into account the resources available in the nodes. The user can also specify some affinities between containers, so Swarm can try to place together containers that have an affinity. The implementation of *Gru* has been inspired by that of Swarm but based on Docker. Docker containers themselves have already been exploited to obtain the elastic scaling of the application [20]. Using a multiobjective optimization model to allocate containers on top of Virtual Machines, the application can be scaled elastically, reducing the consumption of resources. The optimization model works both at the level of virtual machines and Docker containers, actuating vertical and horizontal scaling. The evaluation has been done using only three different types of containers in a simple experimental setting.

The advantage of having *Gru* with respect to both the above solutions (i.e., Docker swarming and refinements by Hoenisch et al. [20]) is that *Gru* offers no single point of failure configuration and is not only focused on elasticity; rather, elasticity is the property that we focus upon in the scope of this work but the autonomic and local-knowledge approach featured in *Gru* could be extended to any operational property featured in large-scale infrastructures.

On the other side, Kubernetes is a solution provided by Google for containers orchestration and clustering. Kubernetes handles scheduling of containers on the nodes and managing workloads to ensure that the system meets some user constraints. Containers are grouped into *pods* and using *labels* to create logical units for easy management and discovery. Kubernetes offers also a system for failure recovery: using a *replication controller* a container or machine that fails can be restarted automatically. These are commercial solutions used in production systems and greatly simplify the management of the application. However, they do not provide autonomic capabilities and the management of the application still depends on a user's manual intervention. *Gru* aims to make the application autonomic and as independent as possible from user intervention, and therefore makes no assumption with respect to the ability to centrally control every microservice and its operational parameters; rather, *Gru* offers a distributed swarming mechanism which acts locally to achieve global stability.

Furthermore, an external but centralized approach is the one adopted by Rainbow [19]. Rainbow exploits the Architecture-Based Self-Adaptation and implements an autonomic manager composed of the system layer infrastructure, the architecture layer, the translation infrastructure, and a system-specific adaptation knowledge. Through a distributed set of *probes* and *gauges* data are gathered from the application. The centralized *architecture evaluator* analyze the data to detect problems and the *adaptation manager* decides the best action to actuate, which is then executed by the *effectors*. Rainbow has been applied to an industrial system to improve its self-adaptive capabilities [8, 9]. The industrial system, a middleware used to monitor and manage networks of devices, had already self-adaptive capabilities but has been improved making it more flexible and maintainable. Despite a centralized approach being easier to implement and manage, it can be a bottleneck in very large distributed systems like the ones we are considering, so we decided to study and apply a fully decentralized approach. Moreover, the integration of Rainbow requires an upfront effort in terms of specifications and development, while *Gru* is designed to be integrated in a very straightforward way.

Finally, GoPRIME is a middleware for the autonomic service assembly based on PRIME, a previous work of the same author [10, 11]. GoPRIME is fully decentralized and is designed for the adaptive self-assembly of distributed pervasive systems. In general, GoPRIME operates on distributed systems composed of set of peers that cooperate between them to accomplish a task. Services are able to perform a specific task, but each service could depend on services provided by another one. GoPRIME is able to manage the system in order to select the correct assembly that fulfills global nonfunctional requirements. The core of GoPRIME is a gossip protocol for information dissemination and decentralized decision-making. This system is based on a fully decentralized approach like *Gru*; however, it is a middleware and it is designed specifically for adaptive self-assembly of distributed services. *Gru* aims to be a more complete autonomic solution that operates dynamically on the application it has to manage.

6 Conclusion and Future Work

In this chapter we presented *Gru*, an approach that brings autonomic capabilities to cloud applications developed as microservices featuring Docker containers. *Gru* can be applied with ease to any microservices application already deployed, simplifying its management in a decentralized fashion. In fact, *Gru* is based on a decentralized multiagent approach where every agent is able to decide the best action to actuate according to a partial knowledge of the status of the entire application. The results we obtained in our experiments show that *Gru* is able to actuate autonomic actions on the managed application to uphold constraints imposed by the user, thus showing the effectiveness of our approach. As such, we can conclude that *Gru* represents a promising approach that applies autonomic and decentralized computing to industrial-grade, highly distributed, microservice-based cloud applications.

Gru is still subject to a number of extensions and improvements that we hope to develop in the future. These concern: the creation of new adaptation policies that go beyond the current scaling capabilities, the possibility to integrate in the framework a proactive adaptation process able to predict the need for an adaptation, and an improvement in the way resources are used for allocating the application microservices.

Acknowledgements The research reported in this chapter is partially supported by the European Commission grant no. FP7-ICT-2011-8-318484 (MODAClouds). Also, Damian and Elisabetta's work is partially supported by the European Commission grant no. 644869 (H2020 - Call 1), DICE, and grant no. 779656 (H2020), SODALITE.

References

1. Auto Scaling in the Amazon Cloud, http://techblog.netflix.com/2012/01/auto-scaling-in-amazon-cloud.html. Accessed 18 Jan 2017
2. A. Balalaie, A. Heydarnoori, P. Jamshidi, Microservices architecture enables DevOps: migration to a cloud-native architecture. IEEE Softw. **33**(3), 42–52 (2016)
3. L. Baresi, S. Guinea, A. Leva, G. Quattrocchi, A discrete-time feedback controller for containerized cloud applications, in *Proceedings of the 2016 24th ACM SIGSOFT International Symposium on Foundations of Software Engineering* (ACM, New York, 2016), pp. 217–228

4. L. Baresi, S. Guinea, A. Leva, G. Quattrocchi, A discrete-time feedback controller for containerized cloud applications, in ed. by T. Zimmermann, J. Cleland-Huang, Z. Su. *Proceedings of the 2016 24th ACM SIGSOFT International Symposium on Foundations of Software Engineering* (ACM, New York, 2016), pp. 217–228. http://dblp.uni-trier.de/db/conf/sigsoft/fse2016.html#BaresiGLQ16
5. L. Baresi, S. Guinea, G. Quattrocchi, D.A. Tamburri, Microcloud: a container-based solution for efficient resource management in the cloud, in *SmartCloud* (IEEE Computer Society, Washington, 2016), pp. 218–223. http://dblp.uni-trier.de/db/conf/smartcloud/smartcloud2016.html#BaresiGQT16
6. D. Bernstein, Containers and cloud: from LXC to docker to kubernetes. IEEE Cloud Comput. **1**(3), 81–84 (2014)
7. N. Calcavecchia, B. Caprarescu, E. Di Nitto, D. Dubois, D. Petcu, DEPAS: a decentralized probabilistic algorithm for auto-scaling. Computing **94**, 701–730 (2012). http://dx.doi.org/10.1007/s00607-012-0198-8
8. J. Cámara, P. Correia, R. De Lemos, D. Garlan, P. Gomes, B. Schmerl, R. Ventura, Evolving an adaptive industrial software system to use architecture-based self-adaptation, in *2013 ICSE Workshop on Software Engineering for Adaptive and Self-Managing Systems (SEAMS)* (IEEE, Piscataway, 2013), pp. 13–22
9. J. Cámara, P. Correia, R. de Lemos, D. Garlan, P. Gomes, B. Schmerl, R. Ventura, Incorporating architecture-based self-adaptation into an adaptive industrial software system. J. Syst. Softw. **122**, 507–523 (2016)
10. M. Caporuscio, C. Ghezzi, Engineering future internet applications: the prime approach. J. Syst. Softw. **106**, 9–27 (2015). http://dx.doi.org/10.1016/j.jss.2015.03.102. http://www.sciencedirect.com/science/article/pii/S0164121215000783
11. M. Caporuscio, V. Grassi, M. Marzolla, R. Mirandola, GoPrime: a fully decentralized middleware for utility-aware service assembly. IEEE Trans. Softw. Eng. **42**(2), 136–152 (2016). https://doi.org/10.1109/TSE.2015.2476797
12. Y. Chen, Y. Kakuda, Autonomous decentralised systems in web computing environment. Int. J. Crit. Comput.-Based Syst. **2**(1), 1–5 (2011). http://dblp.uni-trier.de/db/journals/ijccbs/ijccbs2.html#ChenK11
13. Cisco: Cisco visual networking index: forecast and methodology, 2015–2020 (2016), http://www.cisco.com/c/en/us/solutions/collateral/service-provider/visual-networking-index-vni/complete-white-paper-c11-481360.html
14. Dar, MAPE-k adaptation p control loop p (2012), https://www.bibsonomy.org/bibtex/2d3cd41f1bc9f09286bc73b1a3456827b/olemeyer
15. Dismantling the monoliths, https://engineering.groupon.com/2013/misc/i-tier-dismantling-the-monoliths/. Accessed 26 Aug 2016
16. Docker, https://www.docker.com/. Accessed 26 Aug 2016
17. Docker Swarm, https://docs.docker.com/swarm/. Accessed 26 Aug 2016
18. L. Florio, E. Di Nitto, Gru: an approach to introduce decentralized autonomic behavior in microservices architectures, in *2016 IEEE International Conference on Autonomic Computing (ICAC)* (2016), pp. 357–362. https://doi.org/10.1109/ICAC.2016.25
19. D. Garlan, S.W. Cheng, A.C. Huang, B. Schmerl, P. Steenkiste, Rainbow: architecture-based self-adaptation with reusable infrastructure. Computer **37**(10), 46–54 (2004)
20. P. Hoenisch, I. Weber, S. Schulte, L. Zhu, A. Fekete, Four-fold auto-scaling on a contemporary deployment platform using docker containers, in *International Conference on Service-Oriented Computing* (Springer, Berlin, 2015)
21. C. Kan, Docloud: an elastic cloud platform for web applications based on docker, in *2016 18th International Conference on Advanced Communication Technology (ICACT)* (IEEE, Piscataway, 2016), pp. 478–483
22. J.O. Kephart, D.M. Chess, The vision of autonomic computing. Computer **36**(1), 41–50 (2003)
23. C. Klein, R. Schmid, C. Leuxner, W. Sitou, B. Spanfelner, A survey of context adaptation in autonomic computing, in Fourth *International Conference on Autonomic and Autonomous Systems* (2008)

24. Kubernetes, http://kubernetes.io/. Accessed 26 Aug 2016
25. Microservices, http://martinfowler.com/articles/microservices.html. Accessed 26 Aug 2016
26. Microservices Are not a Free Lunch!, http://highscalability.com/blog/2014/4/8/microservices-not-a-free-lunch.html. Accessed 14 June 2017
27. Microservices at Netflix, http://www.slideshare.net/stonse/microservices-at-netflix. Accessed 26 Aug 2016
28. Microservices Evolution at SoundCloud, https://www.infoq.com/articles/microservices-evolution-soundcloud. Accessed 26 Aug 2016
29. Microservices Trade-Offs, http://martinfowler.com/articles/microservice-trade-offs.html. Accessed 27 July 2016
30. S. Newman, *Building Microservices* (O'Reilly Media, Newton, 2015)
31. M. Premoli, C.F. Riva, Analisi delle prestazioni per la conversione di video distribuita con mapreduce. Master's Thesis, Politecnico di Milano (2013)
32. S. Rajagopalan, H. Jamjoom, App–bisect: autonomous healing for microservice-based apps, in *7th USENIX Workshop on Hot Topics in Cloud Computing (HotCloud'15)* (2015)
33. L. Steels, The origins of ontologies and communication conventions in multi-agent systems. J. Agents Multi-Agent Syst. **1**(2), 169–194 (1998)
34. G. Toffetti, S. Brunner, M. Blöchlinger, F. Dudouet, F. Edmonds, An architecture for self-managing microservices, in *Proceedings of the 1st International Workshop on Automated Incident Management in Cloud, AIMC'15* (ACM, New York, 2015), pp. 19–24. https://doi.org/10.1145/2747470.2747474
35. J. Turnbull, *The Docker Book: Containerization Is the New Virtualization* (2014), https://dockerbook.com/
36. D. Weyns, M. Georgeff, Self-adaptation using multiagent systems. IEEE Softw. **27**(1), 86–91 (2010)
37. A. Wiggins, The twelve-factor app (2012), http://12factor.net/. Accessed 29 June 2016

A Hybrid Approach to Microservices Load Balancing

Marco Autili, Alexander Perucci, and Lorenzo De Lauretis

Abstract During the past few years, microservices have been becoming a common architectural pattern increasingly used to realize flexible and scalable service-based applications. Microservices have grown in popularity as a mainstay in the business environment, allowing companies to increase development and maintenance speed, predict performance and scale, with scalability being one of the most important nonfunctional requirements to be fulfilled. Load balancing is the most prominent approach in support of scalability. In the realm of microservices, one usually distinguishes between two types of load balancers, namely, client-side and server-side load balancers. This work proposes a novel hybrid approach to microservices load balancing that combines the benefits of client-side and server-side load balancing.

1 Introduction

Microservices can be seen as a technique for developing software applications that, inheriting all the principles and concepts from the service-oriented architecture (SOA) style, permit to structure a service-based application as a collection of very small, loosely coupled software services. *Services are very small (micro) as for their contribution to the application, not because of their lines of code* [10]. In [18], James Lewis and Martin Fowler introduce microservices as:

> an approach to developing a single application as a suite of small services, each running in its own process and communicating with lightweight mechanisms, often an HTTP resource API. These services are built around business capabilities and independently deployable by fully automated deployment machinery. There is a bare minimum of centralized

M. Autili (✉) · A. Perucci · L. De Lauretis
Department of Information Engineering, Computer Science and Mathematics,
University of L'Aquila, L'Aquila, Italy
e-mail: marco.autili@univaq.it; alexander.perucci@univaq.it;
lorenzo.delauretis@graduate.univaq.it

A. Bucchiarone et al. (eds.), *Microservices*,
https://doi.org/10.1007/978-3-030-31646-4_10

management of these services, which may be written in different programming languages and use different data storage technologies.

For what concerns the relationship between SOA and microservices, we can say that microservices are an architectural style competing with SOA in that they can be seen as (1) a synonym for "*SOA done right*" [29] and (2) an implementation approach to SOA [25]. In this sense, microservices can be seen as a substyle refining SOA with additional constraints [27].[1] Thus, as any SOA-based design technique, microservices describe a particular way of designing software applications as suites of independently deployable (micro)services, yet with stronger attention to isolation and autonomy. Microservices are independently scalable and can be replaced and upgraded independently, with the objective to support scalability. For this reason, microservices are becoming a common architectural pattern being increasingly used to realize flexible and scalable applications [1, 8, 27, 31, 34]. In particular, in the business environment, microservices have grown in popularity as a mainstay, allowing companies to increase their development and maintenance speed, predict performance and scale, with *scalability* being one of the most important nonfunctional requirements to be fulfilled.

Load balancing is the most prominent approach in support of scalability in a microservices architecture (MSA) [1, 4, 22]. The concept of load balancing spans many different application fields. Broadly speaking, in computing, a load balancer permits to distribute workloads across multiple computing resources, spanning from different server computers, through different network layers down to network links, from different processing units to disk drives. In a service-oriented setting, load balancing is the act of distributing service requests from clients to multiple servers that offer services, e.g., running in different containers distributed among physical or virtual machines. Containers allow the explicit specification of resource requirements, which makes it easy to distribute containers across different hosts so as to improve resource usage.

In the realm of microservices, load balancing concerns the arrival rates or concurrent number of requests [3]. The load balancer then attempts at distributing the workload of requests across multiple microservice instances with the aim to, e.g., optimize resource use, maximize throughput, minimize response time, and avoid bottlenecks (i.e., overload of any single instance). Moreover, characterizing and managing the workload of microservices is also beneficial in terms of cost for both cloud vendors and developers [33].

In the literature, there are many valuable works that, in different forms and for different purposes, concern load balancing. As also reported in [12, 30], a number of architectural patterns based on load balancing have also been proposed [7, 22, 23, 28, 35] (just to mention a few). Strictly focusing on microservices, state-of-the-art approaches, which are more closely related to our approach (Sect. 6), principally distinguish between two types of load balancing, namely, server-side and client-side

[1] A detailed analysis and comparison of microservices characteristics and principles can be found in [36].

load balancing. However, despite this interest and the fact that from an architectural point of view the two approaches can be easily understood and recognized as different, it is not always easy to make a clear distinction of the pros and cons of the two approaches at runtime, nor is it easy to grasp trade-offs between the two when considering the many factors that may influence the load balancing efficacy and efficiency during system execution. In both types, the load balancer distributes the workload of requests among available microservice instances, proxyfing the incoming requests and forwarding them to the correct instance. In the server-side approach, load balancing is centralized, in a way that a load balancer is interposed among available instances or each type of microservice has its own central load balancer. In the client-side approach, instead, the load balancer is fully distributed, in a way that each client is assigned a local load balancer. Both approaches have pros and cons.

This work makes an effort to understand and build upon architectural and runtime trade-offs between client-side and server-side load balancing, and proposes a hybrid approach to microservices load balancing that combines the benefits of the two approaches. A microservice-based application is then used to describe the hybrid load balancer at work on it. The application, called Sock Shop, is the user-facing part of an online shop that sells socks. It is intended to aid the demonstration and testing of microservice.[2]

The chapter is structured as follows. Section 2 compares the server-side and client-side load balancing approaches. Section 3 draws interesting conclusions from previous sections and forms the basis for our hybrid approach, which will be then presented in Sect. 4. Section 5 describes the Sock Shop application, highlights the scalability issues it may have, and describes our hybrid load balancer at work on it. Section 6 discusses related work, and Sect. 7 concludes the chapter and plans future work.

2 Server-Side Versus Client-Side Load Balancing

As already introduced, the concept of load balancing spans different areas. In computing, a load balancer permits distribution of workloads across multiple computing resources, spanning from different server computers to network links, from different processing units to disk drives. As far as we are concerned, this section compares server-side load balancing (Sect. 2.1) with client-side load balancing (Sect. 2.2) for microservice-based applications. The comparison will create the case for a hybrid approach to microservice load balancing, which will be discussed in Sect. 3. Our hybrid approach will be then presented in Sect. 4.

[2]https://github.com/microservices-demo/microservices-demo.

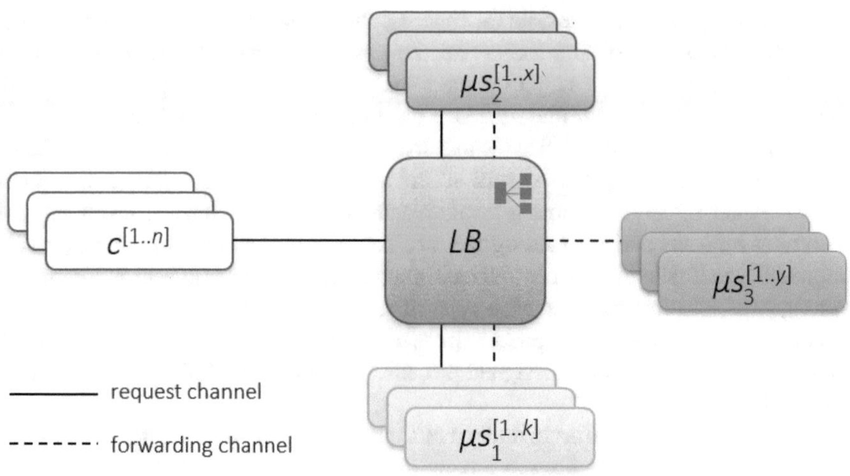

Fig. 1 Single server-side load balancing

2.1 Server-Side Load Balancing

Server-side load balancing is a centralized approach for distributing requests among available microservice instances. In its basic form, a single load balancer is interposed among all the microservices and listens on the port(s) where external clients connect to access the available instances.

Figure 1 depicts a sample microservices-based system with a central load balancer *LB* for the microservices μs_1, μs_2, and μs_3. In the figure, the labels $\mu s_1^{[1..k]}$, $\mu s_2^{[1..x]}$, and $\mu s_3^{[1..y]}$ indicate that the examples considers k, x, and y instances for the microservice types μs_1, μs_2, and μs_3, respectively.

The load balancer LB receives requests through the request channels (solid lines) from both the n client instances $c^{[1..n]}$ and the $k + x$ microservice instances for μs_1 and μs_2. It distributes the corresponding workload towards the forwarding channels (dashed lines) to the $k + x + y$ microservice instances for μs_1, μs_2, and μs_3. Note that the microservices μs_1 and μs_2 are *prosumer* microservices meaning that, beyond receiving requests, they also make requests to other microservices (i.e., they are both *providers* through provided interfaces, and *consumers* through required interfaces). Also note that the microservice μs_3 is provider only, since it does not perform requests to any other microservices and, as such, it does not have a request channel associated.

Since all traffic to every microservice has to pass through the load balancer, the two main drawbacks of this kind of *fully centralized* load balancing approach are: (1) it introduces a single point of failure in the entire system; (2) it can slowdown or it may even fail to handle the traffic due to a large number of simultaneous requests, thus becoming a bottleneck for the whole system [15, 19].

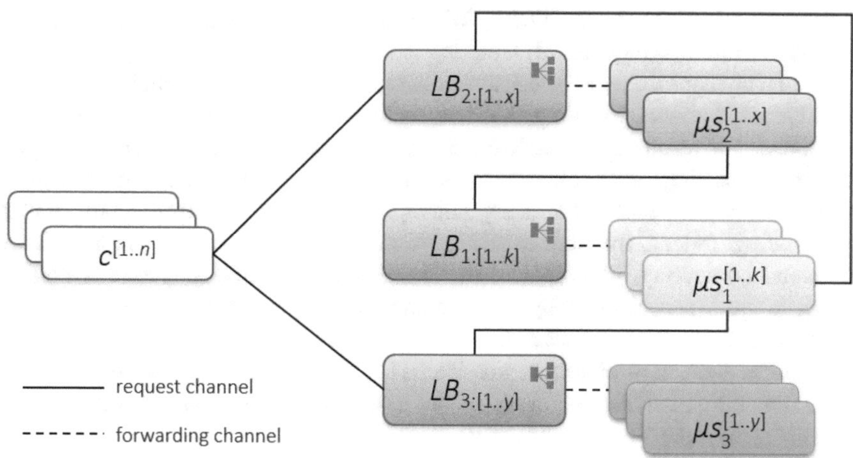

Fig. 2 Separate server-side load balancers per microservice type

A possible improvement for the fully centralized architecture style adopted in Fig. 1 is to have more than one central load balancer, one for each microservice type. In Fig. 2, the notation $LB_{i:[1..j]}$ indicates that the load balancer LB is in charge of balancing the requests for the microservice μs_i by distributing the corresponding workload to the j instances $\mu s_i^1,\ldots,\mu s_i^j$. Accordingly, the microservice instances $\mu s_1^{[1..k]}$, $\mu s_2^{[1..x]}$, and $\mu s_3^{[1..y]}$ are "proxified" by the three load balancers $LB_{1:[1..k]}$, $LB_{2:[1..x]}$, and $LB_{3:[1..y]}$, respectively. Thus, the sample system in Fig. 2 adopts a *partially centralized* solution to load balancing, where each load balancer handles only the requests of a specific type of microservice.

When compared with the fully centralized solution in Fig. 1, in this solution the distribution of requests is certainly more balanced among the (per-type) load balancers. However, similar to the fully centralized case, the load balancers still introduce multiple points of failure for the entire system, i.e., a point of failure for each load balancer. That is, if one of the load balancers fails in some way, all the instances of the controlled type of microservice becomes entirely unavailable which may, in fact, render the whole system unusable if the affected microservice is vital and, as such, it is indispensable to the continuance of the system's functioning. Moreover, on the basis of similar considerations, each load balancer can still become a bottleneck for the whole system.

Another issue of considerable concern is scalability. In general terms, scalability is the capability of a system, network, or process to handle a growing amount of work, or its potential to be enlarged to accommodate that growth [1, 5, 6, 13, 26]. Microservice scalability covers many aspects, including understanding the qualitative and quantitative growth scales, hardware efficiency, identification of resource requirements, capacity awareness and planning, scalable handling of traffic, the scaling of dependencies, task handling and processing, and scalable data storage [8, 11, 17, 21, 23, 24, 27, 32]. When concerned with load balancing, the term scalability refers to the *scalable handling of traffic*.

Two main approaches can be distinguished when dealing with scalability: vertical scaling and horizontal scaling. Vertical scaling concerns increasing/reducing the computational resources available for the load balancer(s) or microservice instances. Horizontal scaling, on the other hand, is about augmenting/diminishing the number of microservice instances, hence augmenting/diminishing concurrency and possible partitioning. Indeed, the term elasticity would also be somehow appropriate here. In cloud computing, it is defined as "the degree to which a system is able to adapt to workload changes by provisioning and de-provisioning resources in an autonomic manner, such that at each point in time the available resources match the current demand as closely as possible" [14]. Hereafter, we will make use of the term scalability, leaving the usage of the term elasticity in contexts where cloud computing is more strictly concerned.

The server-side load balancing approach permits to naturally support horizontal scaling. In fact, since all traffic passes through the load balancer(s), it is basically effortless to be constantly aware of the workload of each microservice instance. As a direct consequence, it is also easy to understand when to add or remove microservice instances according to the traffic going up or down, respectively, in a transparent way to clients. Then, depending on the scaling requirements of the system, any of the scaling mechanisms/algorithms proposed in literature can in principle be used to perform the actual scaling decision.

Horizontal scaling alone does not solve, nor mitigate, possible bottlenecks caused by server-side load balancers. Indeed, vertical scaling can be performed on the load balancer machine(s) to mitigate the problem, not to solve it however, due to physical limitations in terms of available computational resources. Further considerations on scalability will be discussed in Sect. 4.

On the positive side, the server-side load balancing approach may have security benefits. It prevents clients from directly contacting the microservice instances, without them ever knowing about the internal structure of the application. It also permits to hide the structure of the internal network, by preventing clients from contacting backend servers directly, hence also preventing attacks on other unrelated services listening on other ports.

2.2 Client-Side Load Balancing

Client-side load balancing is a fully distributed approach according to which each client instance (and each prosumer microservice instance) is assigned a local load balancer.

Figure 3 shows a sample microservice-based system that makes use of client-side load balancers, each one of them directly responsible for routing only the requests coming from either the client application or the prosumer microservice it is assigned to. Note that, following the examples for the server-side case in Sect. 2.1,

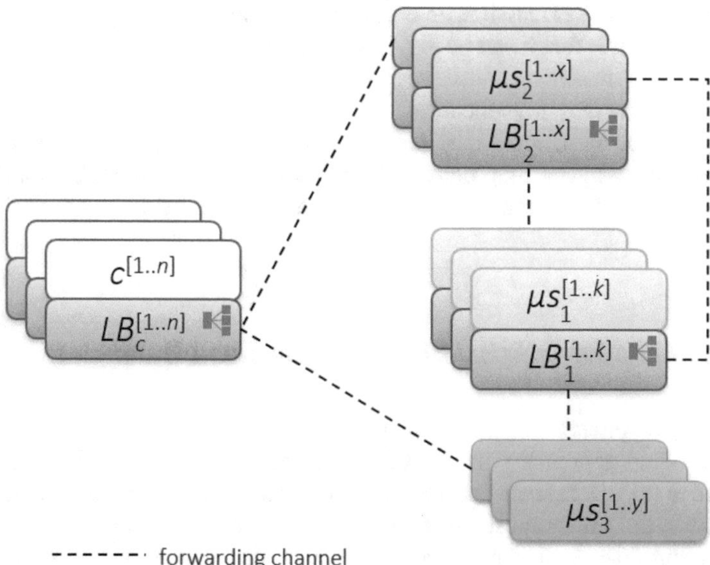

Fig. 3 Client-side load balancing

the y instances $\mu s_3^{[1..y]}$ do not need any load balancer, since the microservice μs_3 is provider only.

Thanks to its fully distributed nature the client-side load balancing approach does not introduce single points of failure in the system. Each local load balancer, in fact, handles all traffic for its local (client or prosumer) instance regardless of which or how many other microservices it communicates with. This differs significantly from central load balancing where all the requests go to the load balancer, which in turn sends them to the target (type of) microservice.

Moreover, by using a client-side load balancing approach, the balanced system is bottleneck free. Using a series of fully distributed client-side load balancers working in concert with each other enables, in fact, automatic scaling in accordance with the growing or diminishing traffic. That is, client-side load balancing supports horizontal scaling by naturally adding new load balancing capacity to the system each time a new instance comes into play, hence exhibiting linear scalability. Basically, the client side obtains a list of possible microservice instances it may use, and it implements the logic to decide how to distribute its own requests among the list of available instances. A simple round-robin logic is such an example. According to a round-robin algorithm, clients are given availability and workload information following a circular pattern. Thus, by storing availability and workload information locally to each load balancer instance, the client-side approach ensures that all active microservice instances can still route traffic, even if some instances of the same microservice have gone down.

As per the above discussion, an overall point in favor of the client-side load balancing approach is that it can be employed with very little additional infrastructure in favor of cost benefits. Contrariwise, server-side load balancing usually requires heavier infrastructure investment.

Last but not least, local load balancers permit clients to directly contact the microservice instances they communicate with. Thus, the security benefits that naturally come with server-side load balancing are set aside in client-side load balancing.

3 The Case for a Hybrid Approach to Load Balancing

Our hybrid approach to load balancing results from a suitable combination of the server-side approach with the client-side approach. The hybrid approach is designed to find the balance between pros and cons of the server-side and client-side approaches. For this purpose, in this section, we leverage trade-offs from previous sections and draw some interesting conclusions that will form the bases for our hybrid approach, which will be then presented in Sect. 4.

As well as can be expected, both server-side and client-side load balancers introduce latency, although for different reasons. The client-side load balancer introduces latency because it does not have direct and ready-to-use global visibility on the availability of servers and the load of the microservice instances running on them. If a client-side load balancer is attempting to forward a client request when the receiving server is offline or the target microservice is overloaded, then the client-side load balancer may have to wait for a timeout before trying with other microservice instances running on another server.

Propagating the load status among all the client-side load balancers does not even improve latency because the propagation delay itself (especially during a pending request) would only contribute to increase the overall overhead.

The availability degree of servers is also a highly dynamic dimension that measures the proportion of time the system is in a functioning condition. As such, the client-side load balancers cannot reuse this information for an extended period of time; rather, frequents updates should be propagated to all the load balancers, once again increasing the overall overhead.

On the other hand, as already said in Sect. 2.1, for a server-side load balancer, it is basically effortless to be constantly aware of the workload of each microservice instances, and the cost for querying server availability can also be amortized over many requests.

Summing up, during normal traffic conditions, with server availability up and in the absence of microservice instances overload, client-side load balancing exploits direct connection with backend servers (no proxy extra hops), and no latency is experienced by clients. Under high traffic conditions, with no availability or overload, client-side load balancing tends to suffer worse latency with respect to server-side load balancing. Server-side load balancing, therefore, incurs no latency penalty to the clients due to workload or availability propagation, although it always suffers the unavoidable latency due to the load-balancer proxy extra hop.

For what concerns throughput, a server-side load balancer always becomes a unique destination for many clients, and its uplink can be easily saturated. As already said in Sect. 2.1, employing a separate load balancer for each different microservice type can only mitigate the problem. Still, in the case of requests smaller than responses (which is often the case, not always however), direct routing could further alleviate the problem of load-balancer throughput bottleneck(s). Direct routing [20] would, in fact, permit the backend microservices to return responses directly to clients. In any case, this solution would not scale as naturally as client-side load balancing, which usually tends to offer higher throughput than server-side load balancing. The reason is that there can possibly be different network paths to be taken for each client-server communication, potentially one different path for each client or prosumer instance distributed over the network. Although this can easily lead to a saturation of the affected backend microservice instances, more microservice instances can be easily added. Clearly, if a client application (or a prosumer microservice) attempts to communicate with many other microservices in the system, it would saturate its own uplink first.

Table 1 summarizes pros and cons of the server-side and client-side approaches.

From the comparison in Sect. 2 and the considerations above, it emerges that the differences between the two approaches are quite large, although the boundaries of the balancing effects on the system in term of pros and cons are not always easily and clearly discernible. The reason is that, most often, load balancing requirements can be fulfilled only by employing trade-offs, and the best approach lies somewhere in the middle.

An intuitive consideration that inspired our hybrid approach to load balancing is as follows: a cluster of server-side load balancers can make a specific type of microservice highly available, which naturally guarantees no latency penalty, as well as less setup time and service consumption time with respect to the varying number of clients. In turn, client-side load balancing can be used to direct clients towards such multiple clusters for higher throughput. Clearly, that makes matters a bit more complicated, but having gotten this far, a little price must be paid.

Table 1 Pros and cons of server-side and client-side load balancing

	Server-side load balancing	Client-side load balancing
Security benefits	✓	✗
No point(s) of failure	✗	✓
No bottleneck(s)	✗	✓
Automatic scaling	✗	✓
Lighter infrastructure investment	✗	✓
Lower status propagation latency	✓	✗
Higher throughput	✗	✓

4 Hybrid Load Balancing

In this section, we present our hybrid approach to load balancing. Figure 4 shows a snapshot of a sample microservice-based system that adopts the hybrid approach.

One thing that leaps to the eye when looking at the hybrid approach is that a client-side load balancer can also be connected to more than one instance of the same server-side load balancer, e.g., the client-side load balancers $LB_2^{[1..x]}$ are all connected to both the server-side load balancer instances $LB^1_{1:[1..k]}$ and $LB^2_{1:[k+1..z]}$. In turn, a server-side load balancer, for a given microservice type, can even proxify only a subset of instances, and not all as in the case of separate server-side load balancers per microservice type in Fig. 2. In Fig. 4, this is in fact the case of the server-side load balancer $LB^1_{1:[1..k]}$, which is in charge of balancing the requests for the microservice instances μs_1^1 to μs_1^k, only. Instead, a second instance of the same load balancer $LB^2_{1:[k+1..z]}$ is in charge of balancing the microservice instances μs_1^{k+1} to μs_1^z, only.

A profitable consequence here is that additional server-side load balancer instances (and hence additional instances of the proxyfied microservice types) can be more flexibly activated when the instances already in place are close to saturation, and are no more able to properly handle the incoming traffic. For instance, in the sample system in Fig. 4, this happened because the load balancer instance $LB^1_{1:[1..k]}$ (before the activation of the second instance $LB^2_{1:[k+1..z]}$) was a unique destination

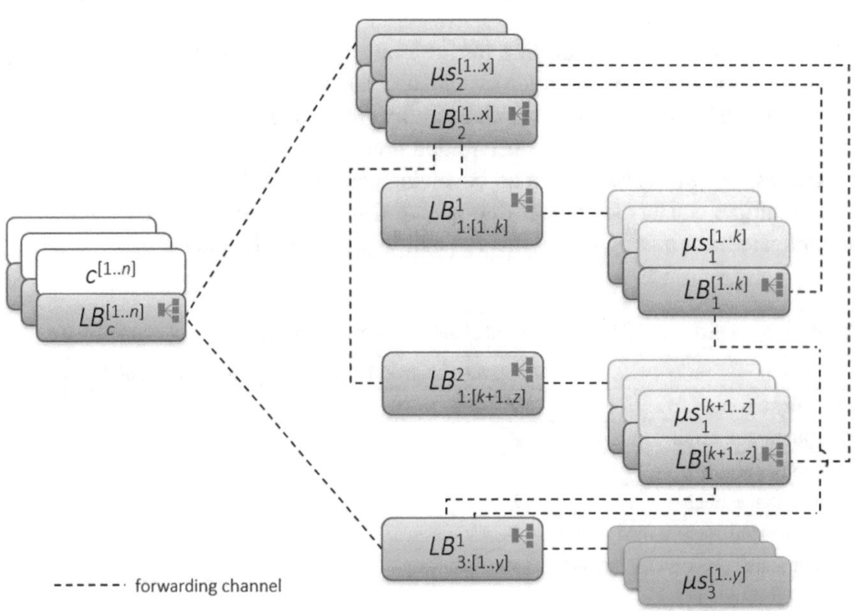

Fig. 4 Hybrid load balancing

for all the instances of the microservice type μs_1, hence acting as a bottleneck for the system. As it is evident, a significant difference with the server-side load balancing approach is that, while the server-side approach permits to support a limited form of horizontal scaling by adding or removing microservice instances only, the hybrid approach permits to support a more flexible and more powerful form of horizontal scaling by adding or removing both microservice instances and load balancer instances. As a result, the hybrid approach offers higher throughput compared to the pure server-side load balancing.

The considerations above lead to another dimension of scaling, named z-axis scaling. The notion of z-axis scaling is commonly used to scale databases where, based on specific attributes, data can be partitioned across a set of servers [1]. In our setting, this translates into profitably partitioning microservice instances in a way that each server-side load balancers only deals with a subset of them, suitably dimensioned according to available resources, costs or service-level agreements (SLAs). For example, in the snapshot of the microservice-based system in Fig. 4, operating the appropriate partitioning at a given time during execution might account for suitably choosing the numbers k and z for the microservice μs_1, as well as the number y for the microservice μs_3. This flexibility enables dedicated "routing" criteria based on, e.g., the customer type. In a pay-per-use setting, the hybrid approach might naturally provide paying clients with a higher SLA than free customers by redirecting their requests to a dedicated set of microservice instances through dedicated server-side load balancer instances, e.g., running on servers with more capacity.

Dedicated premium access policies, where certain clients are afforded higher performance guarantees, can also be supported without any particular effort. Selected microservice instances might be prioritized and scaled out faster to improve performance. Then, only premium clients are allowed to access this sort of "gold" microservice instances.

Another point in favor of the hybrid approach is that it also improves fault isolation. If one server-side load balancer fails in some way (e.g., $LB^1_{1:[1..k]}$), only the controlled subset of μs_1 instances becomes unavailable and, even if these instances were indispensable to the continuance of the system life, z-axis scaling avoids rendering the whole system unusable.

Concerning latency, the hybrid approach can reduce the time delay experienced by clients during high traffic conditions, when compared with the client-side approach. In fact, as anticipated in Sect. 3, when routing requests to a server that is offline or to microservice instances that are overloaded, the client-side load balancer may have to wait for a timeout before trying with other microservice instances running on other servers. In the hybrid approach, client-side load balancers can reroute requests directly to the available server-side load balancers, which in turn have direct global visibility on the availability of the (up-to-date at all times) proxyfied servers and the load of the microservice instances running on them. Basically, the client-side load balancers ask the server-side load-balancers for which servers, and hence which microservice instances, they should connect to. Thus, although the hybrid approach still suffers latency due to the presence of server-side load balancer(s) proxy extra hop(s), the overhead due to server availability and overload propagation is reduced if the system resources are correctly dimensioned and the number of microservices instances per server-side load balancer instance is properly calculated (again, k, z and y in Fig. 4).

The hybrid approach does not want to be a substitutive alternative to the client-side or server-side approaches; rather, it must be considered as a complementary (more flexible, although more complex) alternative that, when the benefits outweigh the price to be paid, can be put in place to reduce the cons of the client-side and server-side approaches, if employed in isolation. That is, the hybrid nature of our approach, beyond the mixed arrangement, permits to architect the system so as to include either pure client-side or server-side load balancers for specific subsets of microservices or microservice clusters. According to system requirements, and in favor of simplicity and costs, this is surely the case when the cons of the client-side or server-side approaches do not negatively impact the user experience related to the affected subsets of microservices.

5 Hybrid Load Balancing at Work

In this section, we introduce a microservice-based application and then describe the hybrid load balancer approach at work on it.

We use Sock Shop, a microservice-based application which is open source and freely available on GitHub.[3] Sock Shop simulates the user-facing part of an e-commerce website that sells socks. It is intended to aid the demonstration and testing of microservice and cloud-native technologies. The application is maintained by WeaveWorks[4] and Container Solutions.[5] The Sock Shop microservices are designed to have minimal expectations, using DNS to find other services. This means that it is possible to insert load-balancers as required or desired. There are pre-built configuration scripts for various platforms that aim to make running the whole application simple. The application also includes a load test, which can be used to measure the load of each computational resources for each microservice instance by benchmarking a live demo.[6] Moreover, Sock Shop has been found to be a representative microservice application regarding several aspects [2]. For our purpose, the main criteria for selecting the Sock Shop were: the usage of well-known microservice architectural patterns to support the creation of scalable and robust microservices applications; the support of automated load test tools; and the use of container orchestration tools to address some key challenges of deploying microservices applications, such as service discovery and load balancing.

[3]https://github.com/microservices-demo/microservices-demo.

[4]https://www.weave.works/.

[5]https://container-solutions.com/.

[6]https://cloud.weave.works/demo/.

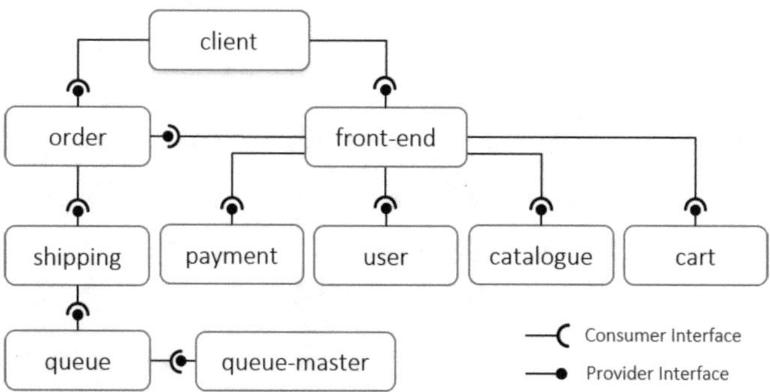

Fig. 5 Sock Shop architecture

As depicted in Fig. 5, the Sock Shop application involves five prosumer[7] microservices (*order*, *front-end*, *shipping*, *queue*, and *queue-master*), and four provider microservices (*payment*, *user*, *catalogue*, and *cart*). *Clients* can interact with the system through a web application or a dedicated mobile app; only the *front-end* and *order* microservices are contacted directly.

By featuring a graphical user interface for clients performing their orders, the *front-end* forwards orders from clients to the *order* microservice, which in turn communicates with *shipping* to get specific shipping information. In order to simulate the actual shipping of orders, the shipping requests are consumed by the *queue* and then by the *queue-master* microservices. The *user* and *payment* microservices manage user-related information and payment transaction, respectively. Finally, the catalog of socks is managed by the *catalog* microservice, and socks can be added to the cart through the *cart* microservice.

We consider an extension of the Sock Shop that allows clients to make requests also to the *order* microservice directly. As it is the case for many existing e-commerce applications, this extension allows clients (e.g., by using dedicated applications or by accessing a URL generated after the payment) for checking the status of their orders and shipping information directly, without passing through the front end.

It is worth anticipating that the hybrid solution to load balancing that we propose hereafter for the Sock Shop system represents only one configuration (among the all possible ones) that we devised in order to fulfill the hypothetical requirements we supposed. Depending on the most varied requirements that may apply just as well to a system such as the Sock Shop system, many other solutions could have been proposed.

[7]With reference to Sect. 2.1, we recall that *prosumer* microservices are both *providers* and *consumers*.

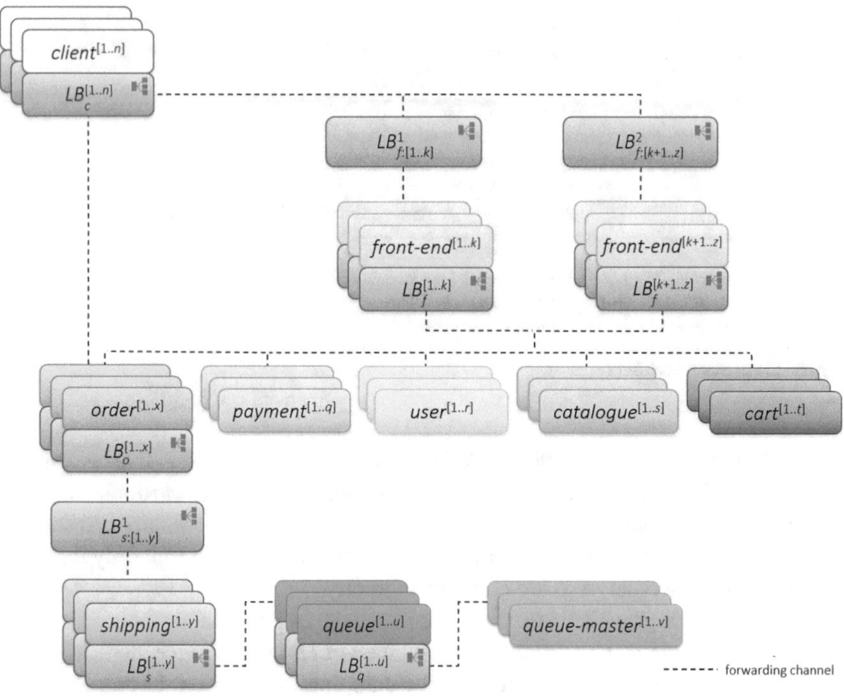

Fig. 6 Hybrid load balancer for Sock Shop (a possible configuration)

Figure 6 shows a snapshot of a generic instance of the Sock Shop application in which each client instance and each prosumer microservice instance is assigned a local (client-side) load balancer. The instances of the *front-end* prosumer are further proxified by two instances of the same server-side load balancer LB_f, in a way that $LB^1_{f:[1..k]}$ proxifies the provider side of the instances *front-end*^{1} to *front-end*^{k}, and $LB^2_{f:[k+1..z]}$ proxifies the provider side of the instances *front-end*$^{k+1}$ to *front-end*^{z}. Instead, the provider side of all the instances of the *shipping* prosumer are proxified by $LB^1_{s:[1..y]}$, only.

Rather frequently, Sock Shop reduces the price of socks for a short period of time, and it is subject to a large number of requests. According to the incoming traffic, the number of instances for the involved microservices should be scaled up and down. This would permit to avoid rejections without wasting resources.

Two kinds of clients can be distinguished: occasional buyers and frequent buyers. The former spend most of the time browsing catalogs and rarely buy something. The latter, instead, know what they want and frequently access the Sock Shop for buying products at the best price. Different client behavior patterns can generate different workloads across the available microservices: occasional buyers mainly make requests to the instances of the front end and the catalog; frequent buyers make requests also to the other instances for adding products into the cart, for paying the selected products, and for checking the status of their orders.

Sock Shop also offers clients the possibility of choosing the right plan for them. For example, frequent buyers can choose to pay for a monthly or annual subscription plan; whereas, occasional buyers might opt for a free subscription plan. Paying clients are afforded a higher SLA than free customers, as well as unlimited, free and fast delivery, with no restrictions on the minimum order threshold.

The considerations above led us to introduce two instances of the server-side load balancer, i.e., $LB^1_{f:[1..k]}$ and $LB^2_{f:[k+1..z]}$, in the initial deployment configuration of the system. The former instance is in charge of routing the requests of occasional buyers, the latter those of frequent buyers. It is then reasonable to offer the instances *front-end*$^{[k+1..z]}$ from servers with more capacity. As described in Sect. 4, this diversification permits to activate additional server-side load balancer instances, e.g., $LB^3_{f:[z+1..z+i]}$ (together with additional instances of the front-end microservice *front-end*$^{[z+1..z+i]}$) when the instances already in place $LB^2_{f:[k+1..z]}$ are close to saturation and are no more able to properly handle the increased traffic generated by a large numbers of frequent buyers purchasing socks at a reduced price.

Another interesting consideration is that the *front-end* microservice is the main, yet most sensible, access point to the Sock Shop application and would benefit from insulation and security. In this respect, the server-side load balancers $LB^1_{f:[1..k]}$ and $LB^2_{f:[k+1..z]}$ (and the additional instances that are activated during discounts) are also beneficial in that they hide the structure of both the application and the internal network, by preventing clients from directly contacting the front-end instances. This helps preventing malicious clients from getting sensitive information, such as user-related information, payment transaction, and shipping information.

Another advantage for both occasional and frequent buyers is that fault isolation is also ensured for the *front-end* microservice, which is indeed a vital microservice for the entire system.

Concerning the connection between the *clients* and the *order* microservice, no server-side load balancer is introduced. One reason is that, according to our hypothetical requirements, this connection is less sensible in terms of security since clients can access information strictly related to the order only. That is, the configuration in Fig. 6 is enough to guarantee a high throughput to clients that want to simply visualize the tag associated with their order, such as "under process," "processed," "under delivery," "delivered." In fact, for the *order* microservice to reply, it is enough to perform a rapid task by accessing its own database, without the need for accessing shipping information (hence, consuming very few computational resources). Instead, if clients want to also access shipping information, the *order* microservice forwards the incoming requests to the server-side load balancer $LB^1_{s:[1..y]}$, which in turn contacts the *shipping* microservice. This means that security benefits are reintroduced at the price of a slightly more latency during normal traffic condition due to the introduction of an extra hop. However, still concerning latency, this is beneficial during high traffic conditions when routing requests to instances of the *shipping* microservice that are overloaded or to servers running them that are offline.

6 Related Work

In this section, we limit the focus on and compare with those state-of-the-art approaches that are more closely related to our work by either proposing an approach to microservices load balancing or treating some dimensions that somehow relate to our load balancing approach or by providing useful insights into the issues we have worked out.

As already introduced, load balancing spans many different application fields. It is a relatively simple concept that can easily be grasped. However, in practice, it requires a broad spectrum of technologies and procedures which, at different layers, may differ greatly from one another depending on the specific application purpose. For example, with reference to the OSI model, layer 4 load balancing is in charge of directing traffic based on data from network and transport layer protocols, such as IP address and TCP port; layer 7 load balancing, together with content switching, makes routing decisions based on application layer data and attributes, such as HTTP header, uniform resource identifier, SSL session ID, and HTML form data; global server load balancing extends the core layer 4 and layer 7 capabilities and applies them across geographically distributed server farms. That said, it can be argued that there might be *different-purpose* approaches to load balancing that we are not considering here and that could perform/work better when applied to microservices. A full-coverage assessment in this direction would require a dedicated systematic study to deeply review the whole literature. Such a study is out of the scope of this work, and it is left for future work.

In [19], Richard Li describes a client-side approach to avoid bottlenecks in microservice-based systems. After arguing against server-side approach, the work focuses on client-side load balancing. Each local load balancer handles all traffic for its local microservice instance, regardless of which or how many other microservices it communicates with. The approach needs to track the availability and location of all instances of the involved microservices, and this is done using (1) a routing system running locally with each microservice instance so as to determine where requests from that instance should go, (2) a health checker with each local instance to register when it goes live and sends a notification message, (3) a lightweight, global service discovery mechanism that receives availability information from each checker instance, and propagates changes in availability to local router instances as needed. As stated by the author, one possible argument against using the proposed client-side load balancer is the effectiveness of actually balancing the usage of a service across the entire global network of instances. The odds of this happening are low, especially in large distributed systems. It is, however, enough to design the service discovery used by the local load balancers so that the load balancers give a slight bias to nearby instances. As described in Sect. 4, during high traffic conditions, our hybrid approach offers a reduced latency when propagating the system status, i.e., server availability changes and microservice workloads.

In [7], Butzin et al. describe patterns and best practices that are used in MSA-oriented approaches and how they can be used in the Internet of Things (IoT). The work discusses self-containment of services, monitoring and prevention of fault cascading, choreography and orchestration, container technologies, and handling different service versions. Although the focus is on IoT applications and on design decisions that might be adopted to improve the ability to create value-added applications from a multitude of services, the authors also describe how a circuit breaker pattern can be used in conjunction with a load balancer to enable the routing of traffic only to services with good health status. The circuit breaker can be used to check the health status of microservice instances by monitoring for failures, evaluating failures threshold, and remembering the number of unsuccessful calls. A circuit breaker pattern could be employed in the server side of our hybrid approach to "protect" those non-healthy (subset of) microservice instances from being called so as to avoid wasting critical resources and cascading failures.

In their preliminary work [21], Malavalli et al. propose a microservices-based architecture to implement dual tone multi-frequency (DTMF) management profiles in the middle tier of commercial management consoles. A specific web layer provides an HTTP interface that also acts as a load balancer for the business layer, which in turn implements the domain logic of the management consoles. Depending on the request, the console sends requests to the target microservice types. On the positive side, the web layer insulates clients from how the application works internally and from how it is partitioned, hence gaining security benefits. On the other hand, the proposed web layer is a fully centralized server-side stratum and, as such, it inherits all the advantages and disadvantages of server-side load balancing (in the case a single central load balancer is employed). Indeed, since the proposed approach distinguishes three types of microservices, the adoption of three separated load balancers would have mitigated the suffered disadvantages. These aspects are described in Sect. 2.1.

In [22], Antonio Messina et al. describe some of the patterns related to microservices architecture, used to solve the drawbacks related to maintenance, upgrade, and scale of monolith systems. Two important patterns related to load balancing are considered: the client-side discovery and the server-side one. In the client-side discovery pattern the clients obtain the location of a service instance querying a service registry; in the server-side one, the client makes requests using a router (that basically works as a load balancer). The router queries a service registry and forwards the requests to an available service instance. This work helped us understand some interesting issues related to discovery and routing. It would have been interesting if the authors had discussed possible intermixes of the client-side with the server-side discovery pattern.

In [32], Toffetti et al. propose a novel architecture that helps to enable scalable and resilient self-management microservices-based applications. A load balancer is used to balance the load between the servers. The load balancer uses internal metrics in combination with a tool called LogStash[8] to provide statistics and health data, such as the average request rate, response time, and queue length (for the last seconds and minutes). These metrics are enough for an autoscaling logic to take decisions on the number of the needed servers. The same kind of metrics could be used in our hybrid approach to perform autoscaling logic.

In the remainder of this section, we briefly discuss other works that, although not closely related to our work, provided us with useful insights and contributed to complete the overall picture.

In [34], Villamizar et al. evaluate the monolithic and the microservices architecture pattern, and describe how cloud computing aids the deployment of web applications capable of scaling the requested resources on demand. The authors developed and experimented with a case study that allowed them to identify some of the benefits and challenges that microservice architectures provide to businesses that want to offer applications to thousands or millions of users. In order to scale the system, the authors used a separated server-side load balancer for each microservice type and several web servers (with some of them using a database to store information).

In [16], Kookarinrat et al. propose a decentralized message bus that facilitates communication among microservices and increases decoupling. The message bus is distributed among different nodes, with each node comprising four main components: public API, messaging, load balancer, and service discovery. In particular, each load balancer uses a round-robin logic to circularly distribute the load among available service instances, grouped through namespaces. The approach basically uses a client-side approach to load balancing, in that each load balancer stays along with the service (namespace) it controls.

In [5], Baresi et al. present a serverless edge computing architecture that enables the offloading of computation in favor of low latency and high throughput. In the mobile and IoT domain, the purpose is to enable low-latency mobile applications by minimizing the impact on resource-constrained devices. As a refinement of the cloud computing model, serverless architecture allows one to write and deploy code without the need for considering the execution environment, resource allocation, load balancing and scalability issues, all these aspects being handled by the provider. Amazon Lambda[9] is a concrete example of a serverless architecture, also known as Function as a Service (FaaS). Developers just need to upload code using dedicated services and Lambda will take care of everything else, from resource allocation to scalability. As clearly stated in [5], these advantages allow companies to drastically reduce the cost of their infrastructures with regard to typical monolithic architectures or even microservice architectures. At the granularity of functions, serverless architectures naturally offer a form of load balancing having as a pro its simplicity of use, efficiency, and automatism.

[8]https://www.elastic.co/products/logstash.

[9]https://aws.amazon.com/lambda/.

In [9], the author briefly discusses different load balancing strategies. Beyond discussing the server-side and the client-side strategies, the author proposes an "external" load balancing strategy. According to the proposed strategy, clients communicate with the external load balancer in order to request the URLs of the servers to be contacted (in this sense, the load balancer basically acts as a discovery service). Once the URls are received, the clients communicate with the servers directly, without being proxyfied by the load balancer itself. There are two main advantages of this strategy: absence of proxy extra hops and no bottlenecks, with scalability depending on the number of available servers. On the cons side: some complexity must be handled by the clients, complex maintenance (libraries update, etc.) as the implementation is language specific, and the clients must be trusted.

7 Conclusions and Future Work

The notion of load balancing concerns many aspects of scalability, it covers many different areas and spans a wide range of application fields. In the realm of microservices, load balancing concerns the arrival rates or the concurrent number of requests. In the literature, two main approaches to load balancing can be distinguished, namely, server-side and client-side load balancing. Although from an architectural point of view the two approaches can be easily understood and differences can be easily recognized, it is not always easy to clearly distinguish the pros and cons at runtime and grasp trade-offs between the two.

This chapter proposed a hybrid approach to microservices load balancing that combines the benefits of client-side and server-side load balancing. More than a substitutive alternative to the client-side or server-side approaches, the hybrid approach proposed in this chapter must be considered as a complementary alternative that can be put in place to reduce the cons of the client-side and server-side approaches.

As future work, we plan to perform a dedicated systematic study to deeply review the whole literature also on multi-purpose approaches to load balancing (not specifically targeted to microservices) that we did not consider in this work and that could perform/work better when applied to microservices. Then, we plan to formally characterize our hybrid load balancer in order to enable a rigorous assessment of the stated advantages against a broader range of approaches in the literature. In particular, a formal reasoning will help us precisely determine and weigh up the negative consequences of possible conflicting situations that may tamper with the claimed efficiency of the approach in the most general application scenarios.

We also plan to fully implement the approach and validate it against the set of microservice-based applications identified in [2] as good candidates for benchmarking requirements for microservices architecture, namely, *Sock Shop* (i.e., the one we already used in Sect. 5), *Acme Air*, *Spring Cloud Demo Apps*, and *MusicStore*.

References

1. M.L. Abbott, M.T. Fisher, *The Art of Scalability: Scalable Web Architecture, Processes, and Organizations for the Modern Enterprise* (Addison-Wesley, Boston, 2015)
2. C.M. Aderaldo, N.C. Mendonça, C. Pahl, P. Jamshidi, Benchmark requirements for microservices architecture research, in *Proceedings of the 1st International Workshop on Establishing the Community-Wide Infrastructure for Architecture-Based Software (ECASE)* (IEEE, Piscataway, 2017), pp. 8–13
3. A. Avritzer, V. Ferme, A. Janes, B. Russo, H. Schulz, A. van Hoorn, A quantitative approach for the assessment of microservice architecture deployment alternatives by automated performance testing, in *Software Architecture*, ed. by C.E. Cuesta, D. Garlan, J. Pérez (Springer, Cham, 2018), pp. 159–174
4. A. Balalaie, A. Heydarnoori, P. Jamshidi, Migrating to cloud-native architectures using microservices: an experience report, in *Advances in Service-Oriented and Cloud Computing*, ed. by A. Celesti, P. Leitner (Springer, Cham, 2016)
5. L. Baresi, D.F. Mendonça, M. Garriga, Empowering low-latency applications through a serverless edge computing architecture, in *Service-Oriented and Cloud Computing*, F. De Paoli, S. Schulte, E.B. Johnsen (Springer, Berlin, 2017), pp. 196–210
6. A.B. Bondi, Characteristics of scalability and their impact on performance, in *Proceedings of the 2nd International Workshop on Software and Performance* (ACM, New York, 2000), pp. 195–203
7. B. Butzin, F. Golatowski, D. Timmermann, Microservices approach for the internet of things, in *2016 IEEE 21st International Conference on Emerging Technologies and Factory Automation (ETFA)* (2016), pp. 1–6
8. A. Christoforou, M. Garriga, A.S. Andreou, L. Baresi, Supporting the decision of migrating to microservices through multi-layer fuzzy cognitive maps, in *Service-Oriented Computing*, ed. by M. Maximilien, A. Vallecillo, J. Wang, M. Oriol (Springer, Berlin, 2017), pp. 471–480
9. Damien, Load balancing strategies, in *Beyond the Lines* (2018). http://www.beyondthelines.net/computing/load-balancing-strategies/. Accessed Feb 2019
10. N. Dragoni, S. Giallorenzo, A.L. Lafuente, M. Mazzara, F. Montesi, R. Mustafin, L. Safina, *Microservices: Yesterday, Today, and Tomorrow* (Springer, Cham, 2017), pp. 195–216
11. S.J. Fowler, *Production-Ready Microservices: Building Standardized Systems Across an Engineering Organization*, 1st edn. (O'Reilly Media, Newton 2016)
12. P.D. Francesco, I. Malavolta, P. Lago, Research on architecting microservices: trends, focus, and potential for industrial adoption, in *2017 IEEE International Conference on Software Architecture (ICSA)* (2017), pp. 21–30
13. A. Gandhi, M. Harchol-Balter, R. Raghunathan, M.A. Kozuch, Autoscale: dynamic, robust capacity management for multi-tier data centers. ACM Trans. Comput. Syst. **30**(4), 14:1–14:26 (2012)
14. N.R. Herbst, S. Kounev, R. Reussner, Elasticity in cloud computing: what it is, and what it is not, in *Proceedings of the 10th International Conference on Autonomic Computing (ICAC13)* (USENIX, Berkeley, 2013), pp. 23–27
15. N. Jackson, *Building Microservices with Go: Develop Seamless, Efficient, and Robust Microservices with Go* (Packt Publishing, Birmingham, 2017)
16. P. Kookarinrat, Y. Temtanapat, Design and implementation of a decentralized message bus for microservices, in *2016 13th International Joint Conference on Computer Science and Software Engineering (JCSSE)* (2016), pp. 1–6
17. A. Krylovskiy, M. Jahn, E. Patti, Designing a smart city internet of things platform with microservice architecture, in *2015 3rd International Conference on Future Internet of Things and Cloud* (2015), pp. 25–30
18. J. Lewis, M. Fowler, Microservices: a definition of this new architectural term (2014), https://martinfowler.com/articles/microservices.html. Accessed May 2019

19. R. Li, Baker street: avoiding bottlenecks with a client-side load balancer for microservices (2015), https://thenewstack.io/baker-street-avoiding-bottlenecks-with-a-client-side-load-balancer-for-microservices/. Accessed Feb 2019
20. H. Liu, R. Zhang-Shen, On direct routing in the valiant load-balancing architecture, in *Proceedings of the Global Telecommunications Conference (GLOBECOM)*, vol. 2 (2005), p. 6
21. D. Malavalli, S. Sathappan, Scalable microservice based architecture for enabling DMTF profiles, in *2015 11th International Conference on Network and Service Management (CNSM)* (2015), pp. 428–432
22. A. Messina, R. Rizzo, P. Storniolo, M. Tripiciano, A. Urso, The database-is-the-service pattern for microservice architectures, in *International Conference on Information Technology in Bio- and Medical Informatics*, vol. 9832 (2016), pp. 223–233
23. A. Messina, R. Rizzo, P. Storniolo, A. Urso, A simplified database pattern for the microservice architecture, in *DBKDA 2016: The Eighth International Conference on Advances in Databases, Knowledge, and Data Applications* (2016)
24. D. Namiot, M. Sneps-Sneppe, On micro-services architecture. Int. J. Open Inf. Technol. **2**(9), 24–27 (2014)
25. S. Newman, *Building Microservices: Designing Fine-Grained Systems*, 1st edn. (O'Reilly Media, Newton, 2015)
26. H. Nguyen, Z. Shen, X. Gu, S. Subbiah, J. Wilkes, AGILE: elastic distributed resource scaling for infrastructure-as-a-service, in *Proceedings of the 10th International Conference on Autonomic Computing (ICAC13)*, San Jose (USENIX, Berkeley, 2013), pp. 69–82
27. C. Pautasso, O. Zimmermann, M. Amundsen, J. Lewis, N. Josuttis, Microservices in practice, part 1: reality check and service design. IEEE Softw. **34**(1), 91–98 (2017)
28. P. Potvin, M. Nabaee, F. Labeau, K.K. Nguyen, M. Cheriet, Micro service cloud computing pattern for next generation networks. CoRR, abs/1507.06858 (2015)
29. M. Stiefel, What is so special about microservices? An interview with Mark Little (2015), https://www.infoq.com/news/2015/02/special-microservices-mark-litle/. Accessed June 2019
30. D. Taibi, V. Lenarduzzi, C. Pahl, Architectural patterns for microservices: a systematic mapping study, in *Proceedings of the 8th International Conference on Cloud Computing and Services Science, CLOSER 2018, Funchal, Madeira, Portugal, March 19–21, 2018* (2018), pp. 221–232
31. J. Thönes, Microservices. IEEE Softw. **32**(1), 116–116 (2015)
32. G. Toffetti, S. Brunner, M. Blöchlinger, F. Dudouet, A. Edmonds, An architecture for self-managing microservices, in *Proceedings of the 1st International Workshop on Automated Incident Management in Cloud*, AIMC'15 (ACM, New York, 2015), pp. 19–24
33. T. Ueda, T. Nakaike, M. Ohara, Workload characterization for microservices, in *2016 IEEE International Symposium on Workload Characterization IISWC* (2016), pp. 85–94
34. M. Villamizar, O. Garcés, H. Castro, M. Verano, L. Salamanca, R. Casallas, S. Gil, Evaluating the monolithic and the microservice architecture pattern to deploy web applications in the cloud, in *2015 10th Computing Colombian Conference (10CCC)* (2015), pp. 583–590
35. H. Zeiner, M. Goller, V.J.E. Jiménez, F. Salmhofer, W. Haas, SeCoS: Web of things platform based on a microservices architecture and support of time-awareness. e & i Elektrotechnik und Informationstechnik **133**(3), 158–162 (2016)
36. O. Zimmermann, Microservices tenets. Comput. Sci. Res. Dev. **32**(3), 301–310 (2017)

Part V
Applications

Towards the Digital Factory: A Microservices-Based Middleware for Real-to-Digital Synchronization

Michele Ciavotta, Giovanni Dal Maso, Diego Rovere, Radostin Tsvetanov, and Silvia Menato

Abstract In the last few years, research and industrial communities have spent a considerable effort in the designing and early commissioning of digitalized manufacturing environments with the primary objective of achieving a new automation paradigm, more flexible, responsive to changes, and safe. This work presents the architecture and discusses the applications through a real-life case study, of a microservices-based middleware supporting the next generation of smart-factory applications with particular attention paid to simulation tools. The proposed platform aims at being among the first solutions capable of empowering industrial cyber-physical systems (CPSs), providing an environment that streamlines the management of digital twins along the whole plant life cycle. The platform features a distributed architecture based on microservices and big data best practices; it supports the definition of CPS digital representations and the handling of data conveyed from the shop floor for real-to-digital synchronization.

1 Introduction

Manufacturing has always been an extremely competitive field wherein the players strive to build increasingly more efficient and flexible solutions in order to take on challenges dictated by a global economy. In particular, the worldwide competition carries on the necessity for mass-customization to meet volatile customers' trends and consequent unpredictable workloads. Such a scenario calls for scalable and

M. Ciavotta (✉)
University of Milano-Bicocca, Milano, Italy
e-mail: michele.ciavotta@unimib.it

G. D. Maso · D. Rovere
Technology Transfer System S.r.l., Milano, Italy
e-mail: dalmaso@ttsnetwork.com; rovere@ttsnetwork.com

R. Tsvetanov · S. Menato
University of Applied Sciences of Southern Switzerland, Manno, Switzerland
e-mail: radostin.tsvetanov@supsi.ch; silvia.menato@supsi.ch

A. Bucchiarone et al. (eds.), *Microservices*,
https://doi.org/10.1007/978-3-030-31646-4_11

fast reconfigurable automation platforms, as much as possible integrated into the enterprise information systems (EIS).

The industrial internet, that is, the convergence of industrial manufacturing and information and communication technologies (ICT), is generally considered the core of the fourth industrial revolution (Industrie 4.0) [22]. ICT trends as machine learning, cloud computing, big data, Internet of Things (IoT) [3, 38, 39], and cyber-physical systems (CPSs) [18] are the innovation drivers towards this paradigm shift, aka the Smart Factory [15, 20], that merges at various levels of automation and computation. In recent years, an ever-growing number of industrial devices came with embedded computational capacity; they are usually referred to as cyber-physical systems. Gartner reports that in 2016 around 1.2 billion CPSs were active, estimating a steady growth up to 2.9 billion devices by 2020. It is noteworthy that those numbers, accounting for an annual turnover of $991 billion, do not include consumer (tablets, smartphone, and computers) or cross-industry devices (such as light bulbs or sensors). In the mass-production context, CPSs are increasingly replacing classical programmable logic controllers (PLCs) since atop their flexible and ubiquitous paradigm, more intelligent and automated manufacturing processes can be built. Furthermore, CPSs are able to communicate (via closed industrial networks and protocols but often also over the Internet) with other CPSs and with enterprise software (like ERP, SCADA, MES, and simulators). In this way, they can implement that modularity, service orientation, and decentralized automation, theorized by Industrie 4.0 and predicted to flatten the automation pyramid and lead to large scale distributed and decentralized automation solutions.

The integration between automation and information systems entails the creation of a heterogeneous ecosystem where industrial CPSs, software middleware, and enterprise applications seamlessly interact using the protocols of the Internet of Things (IoT). In this context, CPSs assume a digital (virtual) nature in addition to the cyber-physical one. Specifically, if on the one hand a CPS is equipped with computational onboard capabilities (cyber nature), able to sense, control, and react to changes in the shop floor (physical nature), on the other it also provides a digital interface to allow the integration within the EIS (Virtual nature).

In the manufacturing domain, the term digital twin has gained importance in the last decade as a comprehensive physical and functional description of a real asset. A digital twin consists of a computerized description of the physical asset (through, for instance, rigid body dynamics and electric consumption models), its virtual counterpart, the data that tie these two parts together, and the algorithms that describe the real counterpart behavior and decide on actions to be taken in the production environment based on the processed data [14, 30]. This concept has been primarily associated with simulation in the industry 4.0 manufacturing systems, since the digital twin can reproduce the status of (up to) a whole factory and its interactions in a virtual environment [14]: it is a digital avatar encompassing CPS data and intelligence, and representing structure, semantics, and behavior of the associated CPS, providing services to mesh the virtual and physical worlds. In order to exploit the digital twin in simulation practices, supporting manufacturing and production processes, continuous synchronization with the physical world is essential. This is achieved using existing data in highly automated equipment or taking advantage of the widespread usage of IoT sensing. Moreover, to guarantee semantic-preserving information exchange among heterogeneous platforms, a high level of interoperability is also required. In this sense, communication middleware technology can provide a flat communication environment for exchanging information between independent environments in a real-time manner, such as DDS, HLA/RTI, MQTT, RT-CORBA [41].

This work significantly extends [6] presenting, evaluating, and discussing the lessons learned from the implementation of a distributed middleware developed within the frame of MAYA,[1] an H2020 European project, tailored to enable scalable interoperability between enterprise applications, especially simulators, and CPSs. The proposed platform aims at being the solution that joins microservices [9, 10, 29], digital twin [27], and big data [23] paradigms to empower shop floor CPSs along the whole plant life cycle, and realize the real-digital synchronization, ensuring at the same time security and confidentiality of sensible factory data.

The remainder of this chapter is organized as follows. In Sect. 2 the literature on microservices platform implementations for digital twins management is reviewed. The real-to-digital synchronization challenge is presented in Sect. 3 whereas the overall MAYA ecosystem is introduced and discussed in Sect. 4. Then, in Sect. 5 the architecture of our solution is detailed and the design choices discussed. A case study in which our middleware has been deployed is reported in Sect. 6 while Sect. 7 presents and discusses the lessons learned. Finally, conclusions and future steps are drawn in Sect. 8.

2 Microservices for Digital Twins Management: Overview

In the last decade, different industry demands and production paradigms have influenced the way software is created and operated. In particular, the service-oriented architecture (SOA) [29] appeared to be the answer to multiple requirements of large enterprises. SOA is a design approach where multiple services collaborate to provide separate operating system processes, promoting the reusability, maintenance, and rewriting of software, as long as the semantics of the service don't change too much. According to [29], SOA suffers from problems in the communication protocols, vendor middleware, weak guidance about service granularity, and on picking places to split the system, and requires significant upfront commitment from the entire company IT. A few years ago, the microservices architecture gained greater interest in this context [9], as opposite to monolithic (and coarse-grained SOA) systems. Both SOA and microservices rely on the decomposition of systems into services accessible over a network to be integrated and shared across heterogeneous platforms. Differently from SOA, however, microservices manage smart services in

[1] www.maya-euproject.com.

a more decentralized way, bringing higher autonomy and decoupling, and involve light and heterogeneous protocols for service interaction [5]. Such an approach has been adopted by various large companies recently and has already attracted the interest of the research community in the domain of manufacturing systems [37].

The manufacturing domain is in turmoil under the influence of the Industry 4.0 revolution and IoT technologies, cloud computing, data analytics and CPSs [3, 38, 39]. Modern production ecosystems should be able to scale and evolve over time to satisfy the changing requirements of the market adopting innovative technologies and designs [2]. The microservices architecture has been recently adopted by various large companies and is becoming popular, appearing in some cases as the only feasible solution for reducing the growing complexity of systems [35]. Microservices enable, to a certain extent, easiness of components management, reduce development and maintenance costs, and support distributed deployments [19]. These characteristics make this approach a promising technology for manufacturing systems. Benefits include increase in agility, developer productivity, resilience, scalability, reliability, maintainability, separation of concerns, and ease of deployment [1]. In this context, we are thus proposing a microservices-big data architecture providing a simulation-oriented environment for digital twins along the plant life cycle, supporting the management of data streams coming from the shop floor for real-digital synchronization and the publication of multidisciplinary simulation models.

In [17], a collaborative Industry 4.0 platform has been proposed, which enables IoT-based real-time monitoring, optimization, and negotiation in manufacturing supply chains, integrating microservices. Similar to our proposal, as a service communication channel, the HTTP or the Apache Kafka messaging service have been adopted. An IoT component has also been introduced to support communication among IoT devices and the microservices of the proposed platform using MQTT [36]. An infrastructure for automated deployment of microservices collaborating for monitoring purposes is presented in [8], based on the open cloud computing interface and relying on long-exploited classical communication patterns (pipes, TCP Sockets, RMI). Thramboulidis et al. [37] proposes a framework for the exploitation of both IoT technologies and microservices architecture in the manufacturing domain, using LwM2M IoT protocol implemented over CoAP [36]: traditional technologies can be used for the implementation of smart machinery in the form of cyber-physical microservices and expose its functionality through IoT. In [27], the authors propose a design framework for synchronizing the digital twin and the microservices architecture. The use of digital twins can be considered as one of the enablers of decentralization of production systems control and, therefore, key to achieving a new level of flexibility in automation systems, leading also to large-scale distributed automation solutions. However, to the best of our knowledge the support infrastructure proposed in Sect. 4 is the first microservices infrastructure ever built that manages digital twins and real-to-digital synchronization. Thanks to decentralized management insisting on microservices architecture this software development technique can be adopted in the development of digital twins. Moreover, irrespective of whether the digital twin has been designed in a modular way, products parts can be directly available to the production units, enabling the latter to orchestrate the part flow autonomously [33].

3 Melding Real and Digital in the Factory of the Future

In the vision fostered by Industrie 4.0, the shop floor ceases to be a rigid environment, firmly regulated by clock-based automation systems; the approach to manufacturing has to be entirely redesigned to be composed of intelligent elements (from simple sensors to production machines and robots) that are often identified with the acronym CPS [18]. These elements are capable of interacting with each other, with the environment, and with products by sharing information on their state, making the entire production environment highly flexible. In order for this vision to be achievable, the elements of the digital factory need to be *smart* [15, 20], that is, programmable and with sufficient computational capacity to react to events in the appropriate time frame; moreover, they must also be connected through communication channels that guarantee a reduced latency.

The role of communication in smart manufacturing environments is twofold. On the one hand, it guarantees that the actors at the shop floor level can interact, by exchanging valuable information, and orchestrate production in a distributed way. On the other hand, it enables the almost real-time monitoring, paving the way for the creation of digital twins, which are the CPS digital doppelgangers meant as live faithful digital copies of environments and processes. The information collected in large quantities from CPSs can serve both to refine/learn their behavior to obtain always-accurate simulation models (*Real-to-Digital Synchronization*) and to feed the simulation with events and data coming from the factory in real time (*Mirroring*). Both features prelude the integration of simulation in the heart of the production process to exploit its potential not only in the factory design and planning phase but also in the operative one with a multitude of possible applications (*Simulation-in-the-loop*).

Achieving such an ambitious objective confronts us with a plethora of challenges, including the creation of a flexible, modular, and extensible middleware that is a bridge between the elements of the shop floor, their digital twins, and the control and simulation software of the digital factory. Figure 1 displays at a high level the pivot elements of the digital twin management middleware, which is the subject of this work. In our view, the digital twins are created and managed via an API/UI, which can be used both by modelers to create the digital representation of the factory at issue and by the simulator (and by the MES and the ERP as well). The digital twins are saved in a repository and continuously updated through a module in charge of implementing real-to-digital synchronization. As regards the API for virtualization, it is structured in two levels. The lower level allows the management of core meta-model elements [7] while the upper level features higher endpoints, specific for each factory software. This second level maps the particular concepts of the domain using

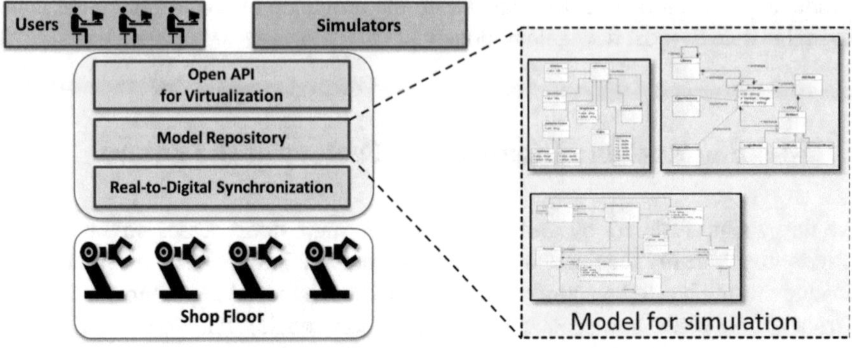

Fig. 1 Real-to-digital synchronization: overview

the underlying API. In this level all the logic that enforces a semantic coherence of the domain (e.g., integrity check, validation) is implemented.

The real-to-digital synchronization can be defined as the process of continuously updating CPS models stored in the repository, tracking the evolution of the shop floor. Having up-to-date models is especially important in simulation since CPSs along their life cycle are subject to aging, straining, and reconfiguration processes, which can change their behavior and performance; in this situation the simulation outcomes may be substantially different from reality and, therefore, of very limited utility. In order to be able to make decisions based on reliable simulation models, it is of paramount importance to detect changes in the CPSs automatically and continuously, and to adapt parameters and scenarios accordingly.

4 A Vision of the Future of Manufacturing

In order to fully understand the objectives and the role played by the middleware targeted by this study in the framework of the factory of the future, it is necessary to provide a brief introduction to the overall simulation-oriented workflow envisioned by the project MAYA.

4.1 MAYA

MAYA is an H2020 EU funded project aiming at flattening the traditional hierarchical view of automation by developing simulation-oriented methodologies and tools for the design, engineering, and management of CPS-based factories along all the phases of the factory life cycle. The concurrence and the cross-combination of the cyber and the physical dimensions with the Simulation domain are considered

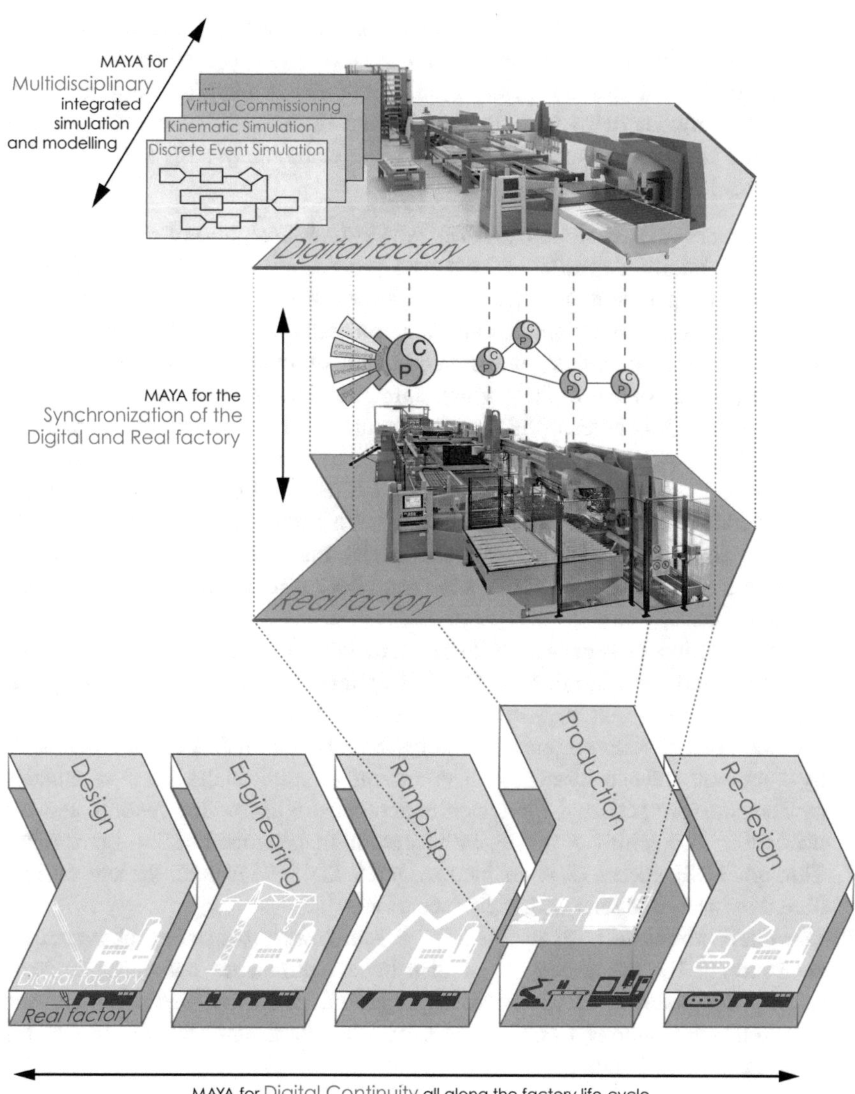

Fig. 2 Infographic on MAYA's principal objectives

a cornerstone in MAYA innovations, to successfully address a new generation of smart factories for future industry responsiveness.

In order to realize such a vision, the following three main objectives are addressed (see Fig. 2): (1) **digital continuity**, that is, the ability to maintain digital information availability throughout the factory life cycle, despite changes in purpose and tools; (2) **real-to-digital synchronization**, that is, the convergence of physical and virtual worlds, where the latter must closely mirror the first to achieve an ever-updated digital representation of the factory (3) **multidisciplinary integrated simulation and modeling**, that is, the virtual validation of manufacturing equipment and systems prior to/during the actual manufacturing, thanks to integration of digital twins and simulators from different domains. To this end, a distributed platform is proposed wherein three main subsystems are involved in various capacities. They are:

MAYA Support Infrastructure (MSI), the system this piece of research hinges on; it is a microservices/large-scale data processing middleware in charge of managing digital twins throughout the factory life cycle, enabling definition, synchronization, and enrichment via data processing and dismissal. Importantly, it provides functionalities for the publication of multidisciplinary simulation models (as part of the digital twins), enforcing security and confidentiality of sensitive data. It is noteworthy that, to support multidisciplinary simulation and real-to-digital synchronization of CPSs, digital twins features two types of assets, namely, simulation and functional models (FMs). Whereas the former are a host of files representing the CPS behavior in a certain domain (e.g., electricity consumption and rigid body dynamics models), the latter are microservices used to process data streams collected at the shop floor level to update the state of the digital twins.

MAYA Simulation Framework (MSF), a dedicated run-time for the concurrent execution and orchestration of multidisciplinary simulators. Supporting this approach requires that any suitable simulation tools be able to use in process the outcomes of other engines, activating in real-time models already published by other tools and synchronizing the execution. To fulfill such objectives, suitable mechanisms are required for concurrent orchestration of the models and the publishing/dispatching of results with a careful management of time constraints. Through MSF, each tool is enabled to query the MSI to look up and retrieve digital twins to integrate with their execution [4].

MAYA Communication Layer (MCL), a middleware consisting of a runtime environment for the execution of distributed automation software. Its main role in the platform is to enable aggregation, discovery, orchestration, and communication among CPSs, at the shop floor level and with the rest of the smart factory appliances.

A graphical representation of platform macrocomponents and their relationships is presented in Fig. 3. The image shows a direct link between MSI and MSF meaning that the former provides a set of services to the latter. Examples of those services are: services that store, retrieve, and return digital twins, simulation models, endpoints to save the results of the simulation along with the related configuration files, and services for authentication and privacy enforcement.

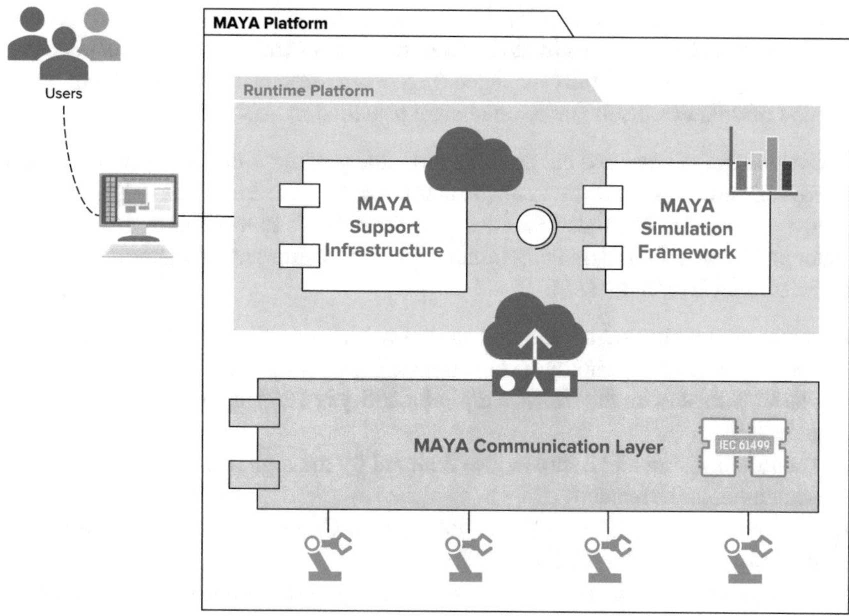

Fig. 3 Overview of the MAYA platform

4.2 MAYA Support Infrastructure

As discussed above, the main objectives of the MSI are: managing the life cycle of digital twins to support simulation and provide suitable mechanisms for the CPS-to-DT synchronization. Essentially, the MSI implements the following functionalities:

Digital twin management. The platform provides an API and a UI enabling the definition of new digital twins and the management of their life cycles. In particular, a RESTful API for manipulating the set of digital twins is provided, which has been designed to allow trusted actors the execution of CRUD (Create, Read, Update, Delete) operations to search, filter, and manipulate digital-twin-related information.

Interaction with shop floor CPSs. The MSI implements a machine-to-machine (M2M) protocol for CPS authentication and authorization employing modern encryption mechanisms. Once the CPS is set up and logged in (authenticated and authorized) it may require to push data to the platform for online/offline processing in a secure way; consequently, a suitable mechanism to create a secured WebSocket channel [13] is provided.

Real-to-digital synchronization. In order to support simulation in all phases of the factory life cycle, it is critical to ensure that digital twins mirror steadily and faithfully the state of CPSs. For this reason, as introduced earlier, digital twins may come with one (or more) functional models, which are microservices that analyze the data sent by the CPSs. Such routines can regularly update CPS reference values, estimate indirect metrics, or train predictive maintenance models [26]. FMs are fully managed (registered, executed, and monitored) by the MSI middleware itself (more details are provided in Sect. 4.3).

Several usage scenarios are possible; nonetheless, the following is proposed as a reference use case, as it involves all the components of the overall platform, touching a large part of the MSI functionalities. The objective is to use it as a reading key to better understand the relationships among the subsystems and how they are reflected in the architecture of the MSI.

1. A human operator registers a new digital twin. This action can be performed via the graphical UI or employing convenient REST endpoints.
2. The CPS logs in on the MSI, its digital identity is verified, and the digital twin is activated.
3. The functional model microservice featured by the digital twin (if any) is set up, scheduled, and executed.
4. WebSocket channel is established between the CPS and the MSI. The CPS starts streaming data to the platform.
5. The functional model periodically generates updates for a subset of attributes of the corresponding digital twin.
6. The MSF accesses CPS digital twin and the related simulation models and performs the simulation.

4.3 Real-to-Digital Synchronization with Functional Models

The core of the digital-to-real synchronization grounds in the processing of large amounts of data collected at the shop floor level. Such a general approach, based on data analysis, enables not only the tracking of CPS parameters but it also unlocks scenarios in which, for instance, digital twins can be enriched with information that cannot be directly measured from the field. This can be even the case of predictive maintenance information. The other side of the coin is that, with this approach, the definition of the synchronization procedure must be implemented as part of the digital twin data model. This is because each digital twin might require a different data processing procedure (i.e., functional model) to be synchronized with its real counterpart, which has to be managed by the MSI.

Functional models (presented in detail in [25] and here recalled for the sake of completeness) describe the logic for processing shop data to update the digital twins attributes or to estimate indirect values and create new attributes. Specific components will be in charge of managing the life cycle of functional models, which include:

1. **Checking the execution schedule**: Depending on the synchronization scenario the functional model can be continuously executed against streams of raw data,

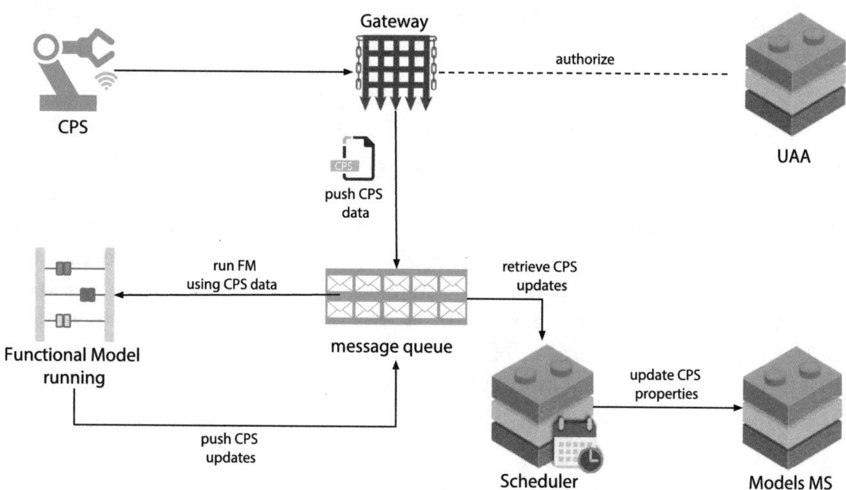

Fig. 4 Graphical representation of the digital twin synchronization process

or it is scheduled to run periodically, say, for instance, once a day over historical data.

2. **Fetching the model**: The functional model, persisted in a suitable repository, is looked up and retrieved.
3. **Running the model**: The functional model is executed exploiting the large-scale processing subarchitecture of the MSI (see Sect. 5).
4. **Generation and application of the updates**: The functional model generates values that are used to update the attributes of the digital twin to which the model refers.
5. **Dismissing the model**: Once the dismissal condition is met (e.g., the CPS disconnects or the synchronization process ends) the functional model is released.

Figure 4 describes graphically a typical scenario where a CPS, registered and connected to the platform, is activated. The platform checks the CPS account and permissions via a user account and authentication (UAA) server. A data flow is spawned via the communication layer. The MSI is notified and, if a functional model is associated with the digital twin in the repository, it will be retrieved and executed. In such a scenario, the functional model will process the input data flow and generate in output a new stream containing for each time interval the updates to be applied to the digital twin. A specific service of the MSI is in charge of carrying out the model update process.

5 Under the Hood of the MSI

We have seen how the functionalities of the MSI primarily refer to the management of digital twins, to the interaction with CPSs and, thirdly, to the realization of real-digital synchronization. Within the middleware presented in this work, two groups of services can be identified, and this should be apparent from Fig. 5: a relevant part of the platform consists of a microservices-based infrastructure devoted mainly to the management of digital twins' life cycle and the interaction with CPSs, as described in Sect. 4.2. The remainder is a large-scale data processing ecosystem accountable for managing the functional models (another embodiment of the microservices pattern) to treat shop floor data. Since these two subsystems have different requirements, thus grounded on different technological solutions, in what follows they are discussed separately.

5.1 The Digital Twins and CPS Management Ecosystem

In a nutshell, the core features a microservices-based architecturein which the application is seen as a suite of small services devoted to as single activity [29]. Within the MSI, each service, following the *single responsibility principle* (SRP), exposes a small set of functionalities and runs in its own process, communicating with other services mainly via HTTP resource API or messages [5, 10]. The MSI features five groups of microservices, which are discussed below.

Front-end services: they are designed to provide the MSI with a single and secure interface to the outer world. Therefore, any other service can be accessed only

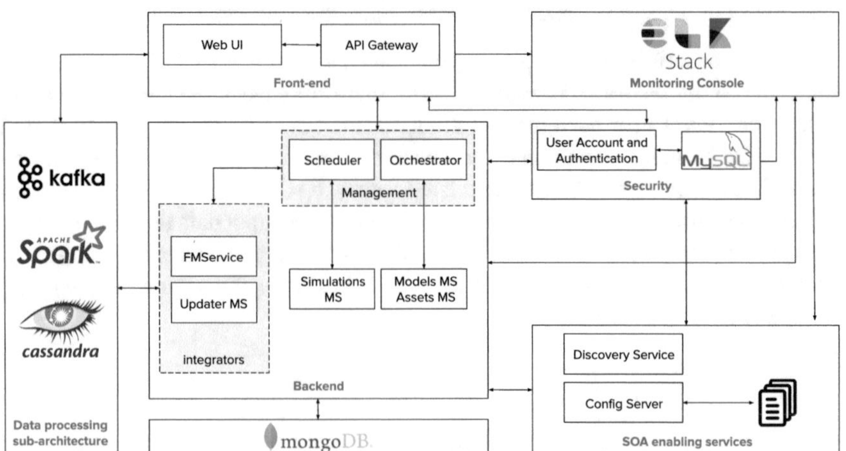

Fig. 5 MSI service diagram

through the front-end and only by trusted entities. The main services in this group are the UI (that is a single page web application) and the API gateway [28]. The former is a web application for the human-machine interaction; it provides a graphical user interface to register new DTs or to execute manipulation queries over them. Administration functionalities such as security management and platform monitoring are available as well via the web application. The API Gateway, instead, is a service designed to provide dynamically configurable and secure API routing, acting as a front door for the requests coming from authorized players, namely, users via the web UI and devices/CPSs executing REST/WebSocket calls. The gateway service is based on Netflix Ribbon,[2] a multiprotocol interprocess communication library that, in collaboration with service registry (see the SOA enabling services), dispatches incoming requests applying a customizable load-balance policy. The API gateway, finally, offers an implementation of the Circuit Breaker [28] pattern impeding the system to get stuck in case the target backend service fails to answer within a certain time.

Security services: Two services belong to this group, the user account and authentication (UAA) service, which are in charge of the authenticating and authorization operations; they check users' (human operators, CPSs or microservices) credentials to verify the identity and issue a time-limited token to authorize a subset of possible permitted actions that depends on the particular role to which the user has been assigned. Security assumes paramount importance in Industrial IoT [31, 34]; in the MSI those aspects are taken care and enforced since the earliest stages of design, focusing on suitable privacy-enhancing technologies (PETs) that encompass authentication, authorization, and encryption mechanisms. Specifically, seeking for more flexibility we adopted an extension of SecureUML [21] role-based access control model that permits the authentication process to depend on the actor's role. Suitable authentication/authorization mechanisms (based on the Oauth2[3] protocol) have been developed. Securing communication is the third piece of this security and privacy puzzle, as no trustworthy authentication and authorization mechanism can be built without the previous establishment of a secure channel. For this reason, the platform committed to employ trusted encryption mechanisms (SSL and TLS) for the communication and data storage.

SOA enabling services: This group of services represents the backbone of the platform facilitating the correct implementation of the microservices paradigm; it features (1) the service registry [28], which provides the functionality of service discovering. This service is meant to allow transparent and agnostic service communication and load balancing. Based on Netflix Eureka,[4] it exposes APIs for service registration and querying, allowing the services to communicate

[2]https://github.com/Netflix/ribbon.

[3]https://oauth.net/2/.

[4]https://github.com/Netflix/eureka.

without referring to their specific IPs. Streamlining the platform management in the scenario in which services are replicated to handle a high workload. (2) Configuration server [32], the main task of which is to store properties files in a centralized way for all the microservices involved in the MSI. Among the benefits of having a configuration server we mention here the ability to change the service runtime behavior in order to, for example, perform debugging and monitoring.

Monitoring console: This macrocomponent with three services is in charge of log gathering and ingesting, analyzing and indexing, and monitoring services. In other words, logs from every microservices are continuously collected, stored, processed, and presented in graphical form to users with administrator rights. A query language is also provided to enable the administrator to interactively analyze the information coming from the platform. The monitoring console is implemented via the ElasticSearch-Logstash-kibana (ELK[5]) service stack, which is an extremely common battle-tested cloud-ready solution.

Back-end services: To this group belong those services that expose the functional endpoints for the creation, update, deletion, storage, retrieval, and query of the digital twins. In particular, the orchestrator and scheduler microservices coordinate and organize the other services to create high-level composite business processes. On the other hand, models and assets services handle the persistence of digital-twins-related information (their internal representation and assets, respectively) providing CRUD operations. Finally, the FM server and the updater service interact with the data processing environment to submit, monitor the execution, apply the updates generated, and release the functional models.

5.2 *Data Processing Environment*

One of the principal innovation drivers of the fourth industrial revolution is the capability of processing massive volumes of data generated by the physical factory empowered by the CPS technology [40]. Since one of the objectives of the MSI is to track the state of the real factory in order to update responsively the digital one to achieve simulation reliable over time, a distributed platform for data processing featuring the Lambda architecture [24] has been designed and put in place. In layman's terms, the Lambda architecture encompasses a batch and a speed layer. The batch layer is appointed to the analysis of large volumes of data whereas the speed layer is in charge of timely processing of infinite streams of information. In our implementation, both layers have been implemented using a single distributed data processing engine (namely, Apache Spark[6]). This engine is responsible for

[5]https://www.elastic.co/elk-stack.

[6]https://spark.apache.org/.

running functional models on a cluster of resources. A fast, scalable, and persistent queue solution (namely, Apache Kafka[7]) has been used to canalize the streams of data produced by CPSs (towards the functional models to be processed) and by the functional models alike (which can generate streams of updates for the digital twins). Finally, in case the CPS data do not come in the form of a continuous stream (i.e., they can be accessed periodically and downloaded in bulk) or in the case the functional model for a specific CPS does not operate on information flows, it is necessary to include a storage area where the information will be stashed and then analyzed in batches. To do this we used a columnar NoSQL database, Apache Cassandra,[8] which is decentralized, scalable, and particularly suitable for fast updates.

It is worth to be noticed that the data processing platform employs a reduced number of tools; all of them are considered state of the art, are reliable, used in production by hundreds of companies worldwide, and are backed by large communities and big ICT players. Furthermore, it is a multi-paradigm and general-purpose platform; that is, batch and stream processing as well as ad hoc queries are supported and can run concurrently. Moreover, the unified execution model, coupled with a large set of libraries, permits the execution of complex and heterogeneous tasks (as machine learning, data cleaning, ETL, etc.). Lastly, several functional models can run in parallel sharing computational resources (multitenancy and scalability).

6 Use Case: Plant Design

The MSI middleware, together with the other systems of the MAYA platform, has been deployed and validated in a real scenario against the needs of a small and medium enterprise (SME) company that manufactures punching and bending machines. Particularly, the case study presented in this section focuses on the division that designs, produces, and sells a fully integrated turn-key solution based on such machines together with additional devices (such as automatic storage, transfer conveyors, and buffers) and the related software.

It is worth noting that the introduction of a microservices architecture in the manufacturing software stack and the adaptation of the current hardware and software to exploit the new functionalities provided by such a new deployment is a disruptive action in a mostly conservative environment like the industrial automation one. Unexpected downtimes or failed safety policies for the operators can have very damaging consequences for the company. Moreover, even if the new architecture does not introduce new failure points, there are supplementary costs due to the re-training needed for engineers and operators.

[7]https://kafka.apache.org/.

[8]http://cassandra.apache.org/.

For those reasons, the return on investment must be substantial to justify such an effort. Under these circumstances, although the ultimate goal is to demonstrate the feasibility of a new manufacturing paradigm that integrates CPS, digital twins, and microservices along the whole factory life cycle, the case study is limited to the early design stage. In this phase, sales agents and engineers must promptly and reliably formulate a proposal for the buyer (namely, product design based on digital twins and commissioning of the assembly line and the software platform). Nevertheless, the steps of the workflow for this scenario can cover many of the aspects of the factory life cycle.

In these contexts, there are the three areas of interest that represent different aspects of the same early design scenario, in which a computation and analysis of data on the system performance and the process cost are achieved. In order to obtain a faithful model, those three areas are explored as they constitute connected elements of the same simulation scenario:

1. Demonstration and visualization of machines and systems to customers
2. Production system performance analysis and optimization
3. Time studies for punching, cutting, and bending

6.1 Plant and Software Setup

The use case factory line is capable of machining metal sheets executing operations of punching, shearing, forming, and bending. For the scenario, a physical device (CPS) and the related digital twin have been created for each machine in the line, as shown in Fig. 6. In the upper part of the figure, the material flow of the line is depicted, which represents a nontrivial emblematic configuration of the plants built by the considered SME, as it features multiple input and output bays and buffers.

In the scenario under consideration, many software applications have to interact, some of them have been created ad hoc or modified to communicate directly with the MSI through its API. Others (such as Matlab, for example) require the user to interact with the web interface to upload the assets of the digital twins. To summarize, as shown in Fig. 7, it is possible to identify three types of interactions:

Client-server connection (red): These connections are initiated by the client connecting to the server (as shown by the arrow direction) and are based on a client-server protocol (i.e., REST, WebSocket [13]).

Direct invocation (blue): The client (master) directly starts the server (slave) process executable and communicated through the gRPC[9] protocol.

[9]https://www.grpc.io/.

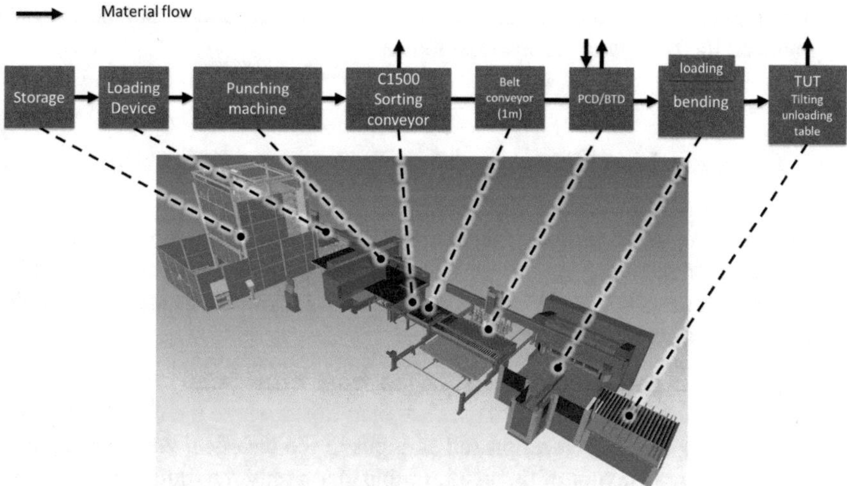

Fig. 6 The material flow, machines, and devices of the factory line

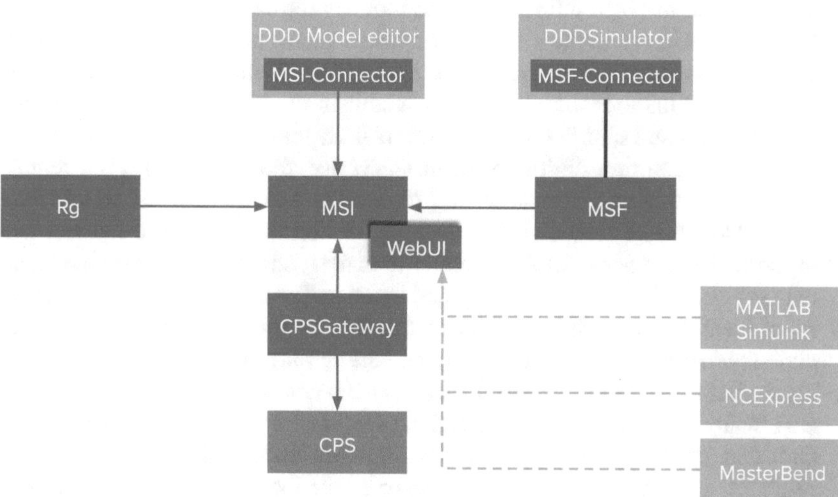

Fig. 7 The software components and their connections

Manual (green): The end user utilizes the web user interface to upload the data produced by third party commercial tools.

6.2 Use Case Workflow

As stated before, the case study focuses on the early design phase where the sales agent and the engineering team must collaborate to prepare a proposal (backed by simulation) for the customer. Within this process, it is possible to identify multiple phases that are discussed below:

1. **Requirements gathering.** The first step to define a new factory line is the meeting between the sales agents and the customer; this is where the requirements are elicited. They are, therefore, passed as input to the technical engineering team to prepare a draft layout of the plant. In this phase only the digital model of the plant exists: exploiting the MSI, the digital entities are created together with all the needed assets. A typical production plan is modeled as well. To this purpose, a custom-built tool called *requirements gathering tool* (Rg) has been developed to connect to the MSI REST API. The tool can retrieve digital twin prototypes and use them to create the actual digital twins and the production plan. The sales agent can directly operate the tool at the customer premises. On the SME side, since all information is immediately available in the MSI, the engineering team can retrieve it and start building the draft plant layout.
2. **Creation of the line digital twin.** In this phase, the digital twins are refined. To carry out this task, it is necessary to develop a plug-in for the *DDD Model Editor* [12], the commercial modeling application that is used to interact with the MSI. The plug-in extends the editor to make it connect and create the digital twin prototype for the CPSs and upload functional models and simulation assets. In an ideal scenario, the producer of the CPS would also provide the related digital twins (for instance, via a URI), and the editor would have an ever-updated library featuring a broad set of devices; however, new devices, or those that do not already have a corresponding digital twin, can be modeled using the editor.
3. **Creation of the plant layout and simulation model.** Based on the list of machines and the production plan prepared in the first step, the simulation engineering team creates the digital version of the factory layout, which is composed of two parts: the first is the simulation model containing the instances of the digital twins corresponding to the chosen machines (Fig. 8), whereas the second is the 3D representation in a graphical environment that can be animated based on the real behavior of the machines (Fig. 9). The output of this phase is a complete simulation model with a 3D environment, representing the digital twin of the whole factory line.
4. **Time studies with CAM systems.** Before a simulation can be performed, it is needed to convert the production plan into executable tasks for the machines and to estimate the time required to complete those tasks. For most of the operations,

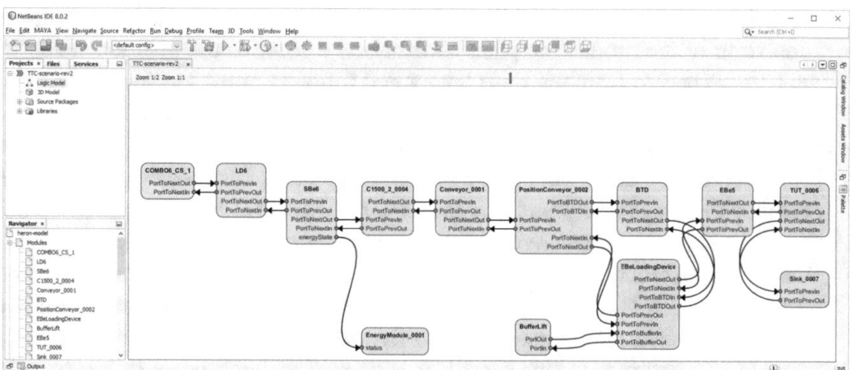

Fig. 8 Simulation model of the factory line containing the CPS instances inside the *DDD Model Editor* logic view

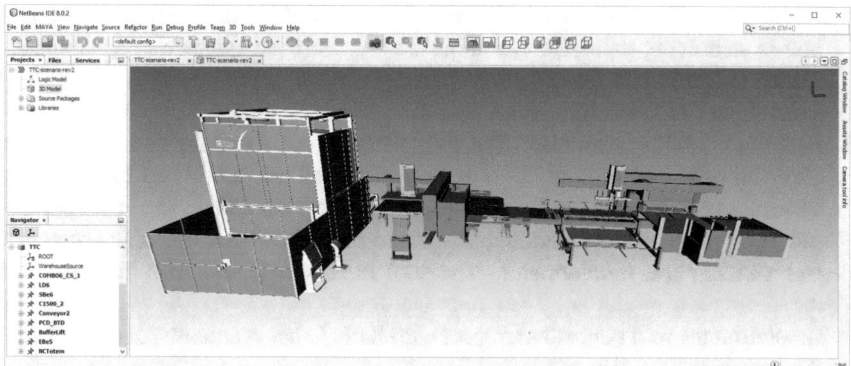

Fig. 9 3D representation of the factory line inside the *DDD Model Editor* environment viewer

this time study can be performed with a computer-aided manufacturing (CAM) tool that converts the CAD design of the product into instruction code for the machine PLCs.

5. **Time studies with physical line.** Sometimes it is required to execute some sample production on the real machines in order to collect timings and other parameters, and to compare them with the simulated ones. For this step, the connection between the real machine and the MSI is exploited so that a CPS interacts directly with its digital twin and updates it with the values generated by the PLC. The parameters can be updated from values read directly from the PLC but most commonly by values processed by the CPS monitoring and data analysis algorithms that are able to process the data and provide higher value outputs.
6. **Layout simulation and optimization.** The previous three phases deal with the preparation of the actual layout simulation, where all the digital twins are

created and updated to reflect the real behavior of the corresponding devices. A simulation of the production plant assesses the timings and, hopefully, achieves the KPIs expected from the draft layout and following time studies. Notice that the simulation models is often simplified with respect to the actual factory; however, it is beneficial for commercial purposes as it is possible to visualize to the customer how the factory line will ultimately work. The most important value added by this step is the possibility to simulate different production plans in order to validate that the expected performances are met under various conditions. While it is essential to design a factory line that meets the minimum expected performances, it is also important not to sell a line that is oversized for the purpose as this would probably make the offer less competitive than that of possible competitors. In this regard, it is of utmost importance to better scale the different layout characteristics, such as machine performance, input storage capacity, number and size of buffers, for the possibility of optimizing the virtual plant. The plant layout can be shared with the sales personnel by uploading the simulation on the MSI directly from the *DDD Model Editor*. Lastly, the proposed line is iteratively validated and adjusted against the customer's requirements. Notice that it is possible that some changes in the requirements would require a new time study and simulation model.

7. **Feedback to the customer.** The last phase is the feedback to the customer after the proposed factory line has been modeled and simulated based on the customer requirements gathered during the first phase. The sales manager can run the *requirements gathering tool* again to show the simulation to the customer and validate the requirements. The tool connects to the MSI to download the simulation model and then runs the simulation viewer. At the end of the simulation the tool generates a report with KPIs to be, eventually, discussed with the customer (Fig. 10).

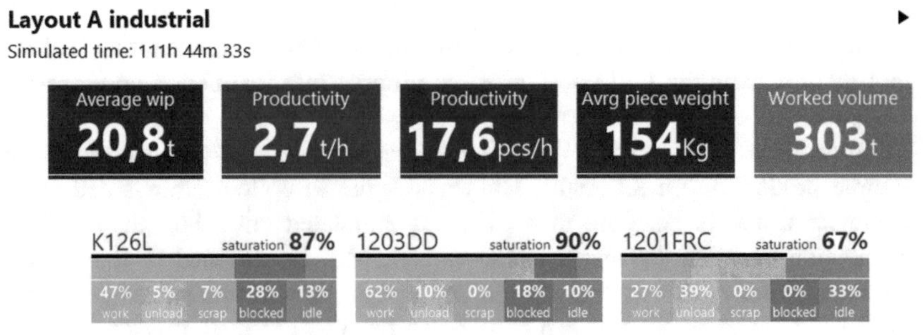

Fig. 10 Simulation report showing some KPIs and machine saturation

6.3 *Achievements and Benefits*

The microservices architecture has enabled the development of a complex software platform needed to satisfy the main project goals. In the architecture design phase it was determined that the best way to implement a solution for the three main objectives (described below) was to use different architectural solutions as needed.

Digital Continuity. To ensure that all the tools interacting together share and understand the data in the same way, the data is accessed through a common middleware (MSI) using a service that exploits a REST API to manage the entities. The typical REST pattern of POST/PUT/GET was the best fit for this type of service an ensured an easy integration with tools a the web frontend.

Synchronization of the Digital and Real Factory. The synchronization of the digital and real factory is achieved by processing the data stream produced by the CPSs, which are fed to the digital twin of the plant. In this case the service is exposed through a websocket protocol for efficiently streaming input and output values. It is still a solution that allowed easy integration in industrial PLC/IoT devices. Furthermore the stream data can be processed in the data processing environment to transform raw signal into meaningful information or to aggregate multiple data sources into higher-level output.

Multidisciplinary Integrated Simulation and Modeling. The integration of multidisciplinary simulation, like the energy consumption model of the factory digital twin, exploits the MSI service to store and retrieve the behavioral model associated with the digital twin and the gRPC protocol to control the simulation execution.

7 Discussion and Lessons Learned

This section reviews briefly and discusses the lessons learned on applying the microservices paradigm in the smart manufacturing industry. Doubtless, the adoption of such a paradigm has provided several benefits but also has presented inconveniences and challenges. The principal benefits and challenges are discussed below:

Agility. The microservices paradigm is fully implemented and yields its soundest results within an Agile/DevOps framework [16] wherein it should enable businesses to start small and innovate fast by iterating on a core solution without affording substantial downtimes and upfront investment costs. A minimal version of our middleware, in fact, has been developed in a short time (about 2 months); this has meant for us to be able to experiment faster and provide our partners with an initial solution atop of which implement the MAYA platform. The subsequent versions of the MSI have been realized by (almost) seamlessly adding new microservices. However, since with every blessing comes a burden, we experienced how the management of a large number of services can be really cumbersome as it requires a disciplined team and an automated infrastructure to streamline the development-testing-deployment pipeline. Although such requirements are relatively common in the commodity software world with a broad audience of customers, as for SaaS available through the web, the manufacturing industry is substantially different and requires a distinct approach, often in contrast to the dictates of DevOps. First, users, that is, manufacturing companies, are considerably less and are more interested in usability and integration (software they use is somehow tailored if not custom-made) than in the continuous inclusion of features; moreover, having to comply with strict timelines, they are reluctant to accept incremental software evolution with short release cycles that could potentially require them to halt production. For such companies, downtime means enormous economic and credibility losses. Ultimately, we must mention that, while in a web environment it is now standard practice to have a pipeline of continuous delivery, in an industrial environment where the software is almost exclusively installed on premises for issues of privacy, competitive advantage, and integration with the shop floor, the deployment and management of releasing tools often appears as a fancy and unnecessarily, if not deleterious, superstructure.

Isolation and Resilience. A failure in a monolithic software can be a catastrophic event, as the platform must recover as a whole. In a microservices solution, instead, each service can fail and heal independently with a possibly reduced impact on the exposed functionalities. Resilience strongly dependents on compartmentalization and containment of failure (isolation). Microservices can be easily containerized and deployed as single processes, reducing the probability of cascade-fail of the overall application. Isolation is a trait that is particularly appreciated by industrial customers as it enables unbundling of the most critical processes, such as those that control the production plant and can, therefore, be deployed in high availability, from nonessential services. The main lesson we have learned in this area is as follows: to achieve resilience, it is also imperative to put in place proper monitoring and testing environments, together with mechanisms to respond in case of failure. Containerization, for its part, in an enterprise environment involves the setting up and operation of complex orchestration infrastructures such as Kubernetes.[10] It also makes the development and debugging processes more complex. Needless to add that, although resource virtualization, in the form of private cloud, is increasingly found also in manufacturers, this is fundamentally still taking its first steps. Thus, in most cases, it is not possible to encounter, even in large businesses, the necessary competencies not only to manage but often also to understand the potential of these technologies.

Elasticity. A platform can be subject to variable workloads especially on seasonal basis. This is usually mitigated via the scaling up and down of services. This

[10] https://kubernetes.io/.

process can be particularly painful and costly in case of on-premise software, and easier and automated in case of cloud-based applications. Nonetheless, microservices allows for a finer grained approach in which services in distress (e.g., those not meeting their quality of service) can be identified and singularly scaled with provisioning of just the right amount of resources. In order to obtain elasticity, it is necessary to have a pervasive and precise monitoring system, also to avoid the long queues of response times should be able to predict the variations of the load rather than react to them. Moreover, the services involved need to be stateless and the mechanisms for distributed transitions carefully designed. Notice, however, that the environment of a plant is usually confined, so it is quite unlikely that the workload varies enough to put some processes under pressure and consequently to require scaling out. Elasticity is arguably the least appealing feature of microservices in this context. Notwithstanding, together with statelessness and the insulation, it indeed enables to cope with possible shifting requirements throughout the factory life cycle. An example of this evolution is the expansion of the shop floor with the addition of new machines and new CPS, which would necessitate the software to manage an increased load of data and requests.

8 Conclusions and Future Work

In this work, the MAYA support infrastructure has been presented and discussed; it is a microservices-based middleware designed to support simulation in smart factories, providing a centralized environment where other industrial software tools can share information in the form of the factory digital twin. The MSI, moreover, also provides a sound mechanism to implement the real-to-digital synchronization between shop floor level CPS and their digital counterparts. To the best of our knowledge, it represents the first example of a microservices platform for manufacturing to manage digital twins. The proposed platform has been described in detail in connection to CPSs and simulators, discussing as well the lessons learned in terms of benefits and challenges. Finally, the platform has been deployed and tested in a real-world scenario involving the definition, simulation, and synchronization of a complex digital twin representing a full-fledged manufacturing line.

Future work will include the deployment of the middleware on an existing plant (brown field) in order to validate the scalability of the platform under different workload conditions. Furthermore, we plan to refine and formalize the interaction protocol with CPSs, including other protocols like XMPP and MQTT. The reason behind this choice is facilitating the integration with third-party solutions. Finally, we intend to support enterprise applications other than simulation. To ease the process, we are studying the possibility of basing the interapplication communications on a standard data exchange format, such as AutomationML [11].

Acknowledgement This work has received funding from the European Union's Horizon 2020 research and innovation program under grant agreements Nos 678556 and 723094.

References

1. N. Alshuqayran, N. Ali, R. Evans, A systematic mapping study in microservice architecture, in *2016 IEEE 9th International Conference on Service-Oriented Computing and Applications (SOCA)* (2016), pp. 44–51
2. A. Barni, A. Fontana, S. Menato, M. Sorlini, L. Canetta, Exploiting the digital twin in the assessment and optimization of sustainability performances, in *2018 International Conference on Intelligent Systems (IS)* (2018), pp. 706–713
3. Z. Bi, L.D. Xu, C. Wang, Internet of things for enterprise systems of modern manufacturing. IEEE Trans. Ind. Inf. **10**(2), 1537–1546 (2014)
4. V. Brandstetter, J.C. Wehrstedt, A framework for multidisciplinary simulation of cyber-physical production systems. IFAC-PapersOnLine **51**(11), 809–814 (2018)
5. T. Cerny, M.J. Donahoo, M. Trnka, Contextual understanding of microservice architecture: current and future directions. ACM SIGAPP Appl. Comput. Rev. **17**(4), 29–45 (2018)
6. M. Ciavotta, M. Alge, S. Menato, D. Rovere, P. Pedrazzoli, A microservice-based middleware for the digital factory. Proc. Manuf. **11**, 931–938 (2017)
7. M. Ciavotta, A. Bettoni, G. Izzo, Interoperable meta model for simulation-in-the-loop, in *2018 IEEE Industrial Cyber-Physical Systems (ICPS)* (2018), pp. 702–707
8. A. Ciuffoletti, Automated deployment of a microservice-based monitoring infrastructure. Proc. Comput. Sci. **68**, 163–172 (2015)
9. N. Dragoni, S. Giallorenzo, A.L. Lafuente, M. Mazzara, F. Montesi, R. Mustafin, L. Safina, Microservices: yesterday, today, and tomorrow, in *Present and Ulterior Software Engineering* (Springer, Berlin, 2017), pp. 195–216
10. N. Dragoni, I. Lanese, S.T. Larsen, M. Mazzara, R. Mustafin, L. Safina, Microservices: how to make your application scale, in *Perspectives of System Informatics - 11th International Andrei P. Ershov Informatics Conference, PSI 2017, Moscow, Russia, June 27–29, 2017, Revised Selected Papers* (2017), pp. 95–104
11. R. Drath, A. Luder, J. Peschke, L. Hundt, AutomationML-the glue for seamless automation engineering, in *IEEE International Conference on Emerging Technologies and Factory Automation, 2008. ETFA 2008* (2008), pp. 616–623
12. L. Ferrarini, C. Veber, 3d graphic simulation of flexible manufacturing systems with day dream daemon and 3dcreate, in *2008 6th IEEE International Conference on Industrial Informatics* (2008), pp. 1401–1406
13. I. Fette, A. Melnikov, The websocket protocol. Technical Report (2011)
14. M. Grieves, J. Vickers, Digital twin: mitigating unpredictable, undesirable emergent behavior in complex systems, in *Transdisciplinary Perspectives on Complex Systems* (Springer, Berlin, 2017), pp. 85–113
15. E. Hozdić, Smart factory for industry 4.0: a review. Int. J. Mod. Manuf. Technol. **7**(1), 28–35 (2015)
16. M. Httermann, *DevOps for Developers* (Apress, New York, 2012)
17. J. Innerbichler, S. Gonul, V. Damjanovic-Behrendt, B. Mandler, F. Strohmeier, Nimble collaborative platform: microservice architectural approach to federated IoT, in *2017 Global Internet of Things Summit (GIoTS)* (2017), pp. 1–6
18. N. Jazdi, Cyber physical systems in the context of Industry 4.0. *2014 IEEE Automation, Quality and Testing, Robotics* (2014), pp. 2–4
19. K. Khanda, D. Salikhov, K. Gusmanov, M. Mazzara, N. Mavridis, Microservice-based IoT for smart buildings, in *2017 31st International Conference on Advanced Information Networking and Applications Workshops (WAINA)* (2017), pp. 302–308

20. J. Lee, Smart factory systems. Informatik-Spektrum **38**(3), 230–235 (2015)
21. T. Lodderstedt, D. Basin, J. Doser, SecureUML: a UML-based modeling language for model-driven security, in *International Conference on the Unified Modeling Language* (Springer, Berlin, 2002), pp. 426–441
22. Y. Lu, Industry 4.0: a survey on technologies, applications and open research issues. J. Ind. Inf. Integr. **6**, 1–10 (2017)
23. J. Manyika, M. Chui, B. Brown, J. Bughin, R. Dobbs, C. Roxburgh, A.H. Byers, *Big Data: The Next Frontier for Innovation, Competition, and Productivity* (McKinsey Global Institute, New York, 2011)
24. N. Marz, J. Warren, *Big Data: Principles and Best Practices of Scalable Realtime Data Systems* (Manning Publications, Shelter Island, 2015)
25. G.D. Maso, D. Rovere, M. Ciavotta, M. Alge, D2.2 MAYA functional models framework. H2020 MAYA Project Deliverable (2018). https://ec.europa.eu/research/participants/documents/downloadPublic?documentIds=080166e5b573e49c&appId=PPGMS
26. R.K. Mobley, *An introduction to Predictive Maintenance* (Elsevier, Amsterdam, 2002)
27. G.E. Modoni, E.G. Caldarola, M. Sacco, W. Terkaj, Synchronizing physical and digital factory: benefits and technical challenges. Proc. CIRP **79**, 472–477 (2019)
28. F. Montesi, J. Weber, Circuit breakers, discovery, and API gateways in microservices. arXiv preprint arXiv:1609.05830 (2016)
29. S. Newman, *Building Microservices: Designing Fine-Grained Systems* (O'Reilly Media, Newton, 2015)
30. A. Parrott, L. Warshaw, *Industry 4.0 and the Digital Twin* (Deloitte University Press, New York, 2017), pp. 1–17
31. A. Razzaq, A. Hur, H.F. Ahmad, M. Masood, Cyber security: threats, reasons, challenges, methodologies and state of the art solutions for industrial applications. *2013 IEEE Eleventh International Symposium on Autonomous Decentralized Systems (ISADS)* (2013), pp. 1–6
32. C. Richardson, *Microservices Patterns* (Manning Publications, Shelter Island, 2018)
33. R. Rosen, G. Von Wichert, G. Lo, K.D. Bettenhausen, About the importance of autonomy and digital twins for the future of manufacturing. IFAC-PapersOnLine **48**(3), 567–572 (2015)
34. A.-R. Sadeghi, C. Wachsmann, M. Waidner, Security and privacy challenges in industrial internet of things. *Proceedings of the 52nd Annual Design Automation Conference - DAC 15*, vol. 17 (2015), 1–6
35. D. Taibi, V. Lenarduzzi, C. Pahl, Processes, motivations, and issues for migrating to microservices architectures: an empirical investigation. IEEE Cloud Comput. **4**(5), 22–32 (2017)
36. D. Thangavel, X. Ma, A. Valera, H.-X. Tan, C. Keng-Yan Tan, Performance evaluation of MQTT and CoAP via a common middleware, in *2014 IEEE Ninth International Conference on Intelligent Sensors, Sensor Networks and Information Processing (ISSNIP)* (2014), pp. 1–6
37. K. Thramboulidis, D.C. Vachtsevanou, A. Solanos, Cyber-physical microservices: an IoT-based framework for manufacturing systems, in *2018 IEEE Industrial Cyber-Physical Systems (ICPS)* (2018), pp. 232–239
38. K. Witkowski, Internet of Things, big data, industry 4.0 - innovative solutions in logistics and supply chains management. Proc. Eng. **182**, 763–769 (2017)
39. L.D. Xu, W. He, S. Li, Internet of Things in industries: a survey. IEEE Trans. Ind. Inf. **10**(4), 2233–2243 (2014)
40. C. Yang, W. Shen, X. Wang, Applications of Internet of Things in manufacturing, in *Proceedings of the 2016 IEEE 20th International Conference on Computer Supported Cooperative Work in Design, CSCWD 2016* (2016), pp. 670–675
41. S. Yun, J.-H. Park, W.-T. Kim, Data-centric middleware based digital twin platform for dependable cyber-physical systems, in *2017 Ninth International Conference on Ubiquitous and Future Networks (ICUFN)* (2017), pp. 922–926

Using Microservices to Customize Multi-tenant Software-as-a-Service

Hui Song, Franck Chauvel, and Phu H. Nguyen

Abstract Enterprise resource planning (ERP), customer relationship management (CRM), and other enterprise solutions are not used out of the box: Companies hire consultants to customize these software solutions that are deployed "on premises" to fit their specific business processes. When software vendors move to multitenant software-as-a-service (SaaS), they cannot onboard their customers who heavily customized their "on-premises" installation. In SaaS, all customers share the same source code and computing resources to ensure economies of scale. We present here a novel approach to support SaaS customization using microservices architectures: Each customization is encapsulated as a microservice that replaces the standard functionality. We evaluated the feasibility of our approach on two industrial studies of ERP and CRM service vendors and discussed different design choices. The results of our experiments show that our approach can achieve both the *isolation* required by multitenancy and the *assimilation* required by deep customization.

1 Introduction

All businesses rely on enterprise resource planning (ERP), customer relationship management (CRM), or other enterprise systems to support their day-to-day activities, such as sales, human resources, financial, etc. Since every company has its unique organization, processes, and culture, no off-the-shelf software directly fits. Companies eventually *customize* these software to meet their specific requirements. For simple scenarios, software vendors predict where and how their applications may be customized, and provide their customers with application programming interfaces (API), extension points, or configuration choices. Customization is then performed either by the customer's developers or by third-party consultants. However, there are always customers whose requirements overstep the embedded

H. Song · F. Chauvel (✉) · P. H. Nguyen
SINTEF, Oslo, Norway
e-mail: hui.song@sintef.no; franck.chauvel@sintef.no; phu.nguyen@sintef.no

A. Bucchiarone et al. (eds.), *Microservices*,
https://doi.org/10.1007/978-3-030-31646-4_12

customization capacity. These customers need the vendors to provide mechanisms for performing *deep customization*, which goes beyond the vendor's prediction.

Traditionally, software vendors support deep customization by allowing the customers to directly modify the source code of their software products. The customers acquire a special license, directly modify the original source code, and then deploy the customized product on their own premises. In an empirical study on eight companies deploying ERP systems [20], most ERP adopters ended up implementing heavy customizations involving code modifications. The two software vendors that commissioned our research also have customers who made deep customizations to their products [22]. In addition to the flexibility, "on-premises" deep customization also has benefited from retaining the customized product as an integral piece. Moreover, vendors do not need to invest a lot of resources to design and implement the sophisticated API or extension points.

However, as the industry moves from single-tenant, on-premises applications to cloud-based, multitenant software as a service (SaaS), "on-premises" deep customization is no longer feasible. In a multitenant SaaS, all customers, so-called "tenants," share the same code base of the software application. No customer can thus modify its source code without directly impacting all other tenants. This motivates the mainstream multitenant SaaS vendors such as Salesforce and Oracle NetSuite to only support limited customizations.

In this chapter, we first discuss different strategies for customizing multitenant SaaS. Then, we present a novel approach to implement deep customization on multitenant SaaS, using *intrusive custom microservices*. Customers have the "read-only" access to the source code of the main service, and can choose fine-grained pieces in the code base, such as a C# method, to customize. Instead of directly modifying the code, they redevelop the code and wrap it as a self-contained microservice, called "custom microservice." The execution to the original pieces will be redirected to this custom microservice at runtime. These custom microservices are intrusive to the main service, because they return callback code, which the main service executes to provide any necessary data. In this way, the custom code is theoretically capable of doing anything the original code can do. This approach achieves both the *isolation* required by multitenancy and the *assimilation* required by deep customization. On the one hand, the custom code is running separately from the main service, and can be deployed dynamically without rebooting the main service. On the other hand, the custom code has the same expression power as the original source code. Therefore, customers can implement the customization in the same way as if they are the vendor's developers.

In the remainder of this chapter, Sect. 2 gives a sample online shopping system to explain the requirements for deep customization and summarizes these requirements. We present in Sect. 3 the strategies for deep customization that we know of, including an overview of the microservices-based approach, and Sect. 4 elaborates it with key techniques. Section 5 evaluates the microservices-based approach by applying it on the sample open-source shopping application. We discuss the different aspects of the microservices-based approach in Sect. 6. After that, we give in Sect. 7

a direction for using microservices for customization in a nonintrusive way. Finally, Sect. 8 discusses related approaches and Sect. 9 concludes the chapter.

2 Motivations and Requirements for Deep Customization

We describe below the customization scenarios, which illustrate on an open-source shopping application named MusicStore [11]. We use this application as a running example to demonstrate the challenges that obstruct the support of deep customization on multitenant SaaS. Then, we summarize the generic requirements of deep customization for multitenant SaaS.

2.1 *The Customization Process*

As shown in Fig. 1, the customization of an enterprise solution involves three main actors (or roles): the software vendor, a third-party consultant, and a customer. The software vendor builds a generic solution, say a CRM product, hereafter called "the product." The vendor anticipates the most common features in the initial design—to the extent it is possible. As every business is unique, this product necessarily misses some of the customer's requirements, and the customer thus hires third-party consultants (in most cases) to develop an ad hoc customization.

Until the advent of cloud computing, customized products were deployed on the customer's premises. Each customer runs a fully isolated customized version.

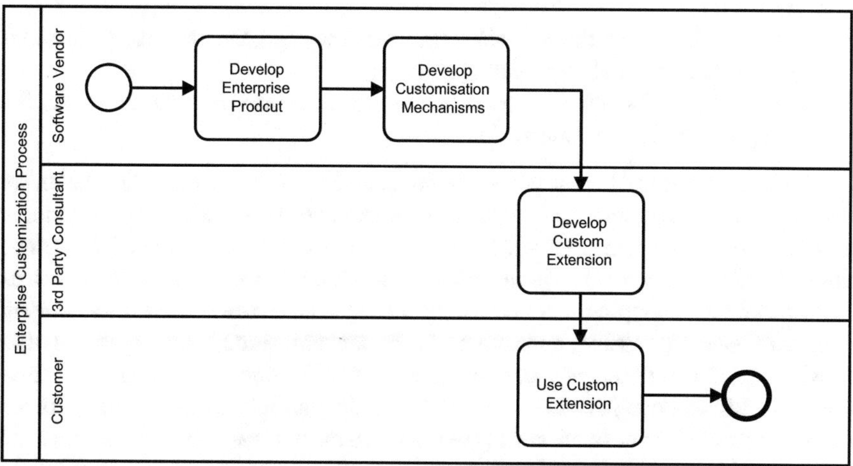

Fig. 1 Interaction between the software vendor, the third-party consultant, and the customer during the customization of the enterprise software, shown as a BPMN process

Because the software vendors now offer their product as SaaS, customization is no longer straightforward.

2.2 *The MusicStore, a Running Example*

The Microsoft MusicStore [11] is an official test application for ASP.NET Core, the next-generation web development framework of Microsoft. MusicStore provides many of the essential features of an online shopping system, such as user management, catalogue, shopping cart, and checkout, using music albums as a commodity. We use MusicStore to build a multitenant SaaS: The owner of a small music shop can then become a tenant and start selling its albums without deploying and maintaining a separate MusicStore instance on its own premises. There could be many shops (i.e., many tenants) using the same MusicStore SaaS. Shops could have different needs that would require different customizations. This accurately portrays the transition that the two companies that commissioned this research are undertaking.

A major challenge is to ensure tenant-isolation while enabling tenant-specific customization, which means that no customization specific to a tenant shall ever affect any other tenants. Consider a tenant *A* who partners with a charity organization and wants to introduce a donation feature into her own shop. When an end user buys an album, the system must now ask what fraction of the album's price she would like to donate. The final price shall automatically account for her donation. This scenario comprises three use cases:

1. *Add donation.* When the user adds an item to the shopping cart, a new page should pop up to let her choose what percentage of the album's price she would like to donate.
2. *Display donations.* In the shopping cart overview page, the amount of donations should be shown for each shopping cart item.
3. *Get total price.* When the system calculates the total price of a shopping cart, the donations should be accounted for.

These use cases imply changes across three layers. In the user interface layer, we need to create a new page and change the component in an existing page (adding a "donation" column in a table). In the business logic layer, we need to change the logic of total price calculation. In the data layer, we need to store the donation amount for each shopping cart item. These changes are beyond what the Microsoft engineers have anticipated, and require "deep customization." As we are offering MusicStore as a multitenant SaaS, direct code modification is not feasible because the same MusicStore instance will be shared by multiple tenants. The software vendors of multitenant SaaS must provide mechanisms that enable each tenant to customize the main product without directly modifying the source code of the main product that is shared by multiple tenants. Moreover, no customization specific to a tenant shall ever affect any other tenant. In case of the MusicStore multitenant SaaS, the three use cases described above will only apply for the end users of tenant A. The end users of the other tenants will only have the main functions of the main product MusicStore, and their own customized features, if any, applied for them.

We detail in the remainder of this section what the main requirements are for enabling deep customization of multitenant SaaS.

2.3 Deep Customization Requirements for Multitenant SaaS

We discuss below the main requirements for customization of multitenant SaaS. We distinguish between first functional requirements (Sect. 2.3.1) and then extrafunctional requirements (Sect. 2.3.2).

2.3.1 Functional Requirements

The main functional requirement is that consultants should be able to customize anything in the SaaS, just as they were able to do with on-premises customization. They can customize user interface (UI), database (DB)schema, and business logic (BL) as needed.

- As for the UI, consultants should be able to modify existing screens, that is, reorder UI elements (labels, text fields, etc.), but also add new UI elements (or remove existing), as well as modify the related validation code. They should also be able to add new screens or remove existing ones.
- As for the BL, consultants should be able to override existing logic (i.e., code) but also remove or add new logic. In addition, they should be able to trigger events and create new types of events (or delete existing ones). Finally, they should be able to call external services for integration purposes.
- As for the DB, consultants should be able to add new columns to tables (or delete existing ones), or create new tables including foreign keys (or delete existing ones). In addition, they should also be able to override the whole data source, with a new dedicated one.

The key point here is that in a multitenant environment (as opposed to previous on-premises deployments) all the above customizations of a specific tenant shall only affect that single tenant. We shall return to these functional requirements in the Evaluation sections (see Table 2).

2.3.2 Isolation/Security, Assimilation, Multitenancy

During the development of a new customization, the main extrafunctional requirement is *assimilation*, that is, the degree to which the development of the customization's code is integrated with the code of the product—as it would have been if we had modified the product's code directly. During the deployment of new customizations, the multitenant system should be able to deploy new versions of customizations and to decommission older ones.

During execution, the main extrafunctional requirement is to maintain a proper multitenant environment despite the existence of multiple customizations, which unfolds into performance and security concerns. As for performance, each tenant should have enough computing resources (CPU, memory, storage, and network) to carry out its custom processes, but should not however consume additional resources that may affect its neighbor tenants (e.g., from erroneous CPU-consuming customizations). As for security, each tenant must only be able to access its own data space.

3 Deep Customization Approaches

We define "deep-customization" as any customization of the product code that goes beyond what preferences, settings, and integration standard API can realize. A deep customization goes beyond the natural "seams" [2] of the product, be they instructions, functions, or classes (Sect. 3.1); components (Sect. 3.2); services (Sect. 3.3); or languages (Sect. 3.4). Therefore, deep customization here involves an extra software development process on top of the main software product. This extra software development process is to develop custom code to customize the main software product. Ideally, deep customization for multitenant SaaS should be as powerful as "on-premises" deep customization, i.e., the main product can be customized in UI, BL, and DB.

The need for customization as deep as possible conflicts with the need to protect the vendor's product from malicious changes. Customization at the instruction level thus seems irrelevant as there is no direct relationship between programs' instructions and business concepts. Customization is eventually about deciding which business concepts vendors must open for changes, and making these changes possible in the technology. In that sense, all other seams are viable customization approaches for enterprise systems. Regardless of the approach chosen, the system must be multitenant in the first place, and this leads to the development of dedicated function, class, component, or service that manages tenants, the so-called *tenant manager*.

3.1 At the Functions/Classes Level

One approach is to offer the tenants a dedicated source-code-level extension points they can use to implement customizations. This implies that the vendors have anticipated "customization points" (i.e., those function, class, components, or services that match relevant business concepts) and designed relevant mechanisms to integrate tenants' code fragment.

Design patterns [3] such as *strategy*, *decorator*, and *factory* can address some customization requirements at function or class levels. We briefly summarize these patterns below, but we refer the reader to [3] for a comprehensive treatment.

- The strategy pattern helps dynamically change the implementation of a given method. We encapsulate the foreseen variations, so-called "strategies," into separate classes that adhere to a common interface. The client object can now switch strategy dynamically, by delegating to another strategy object. This strategy pattern facilitates, for instance, the use of alternative compression algorithms such as LZ or LZW [8].
- The decorator pattern helps extend the behavior of a given function or group of functions. To do so, we first create a "decorator" class that offers the same interface as the original object. Within this decorator, we are then free to perform additional actions before and after to delegate the execution to the original object. We can, for instance, log invocations without modifying the original method's code. The decorator pattern works on the class level. To extend a particular method, the decorator class will reimplement this method, and invoke the original method in the middle.
- The factory pattern helps control what classes we instantiate. Factories are methods that we call instead of using the "new" keyword (in C++, C#, Java, and the like) to create class instances. In these factory methods, we are free to dynamically select the class we want to instantiate. Factory methods enable loading a user-defined class to perform a predefined activity.

3.2 At the Component Level

The above code-level approach falls short because custom classes and objects cannot be loaded directly. Classes and objects are not units of deployment, but rather units of abstraction and execution. Classes capture domain concepts and specify how their instances (i.e., the objects) will interact during execution. Classes and objects are oblivious to their deployment, which requires dedicated and platform-specific mechanisms, such as deployment bundles, class loaders, etc. These limitations have led to the development of component-based software engineering [23], where a component is a unit of both composition and deployment that often contains class definitions. Applications thus connect together so-called "components," whose life cycle is managed by a dedicated execution platform. The platform controls this "architecture" and enables replacing and rewiring the component assembly, dynamically. Various technologies have flourished throughout the 1990s, such as CORBA promoted by the OMG, DCOM/ActiveX on Microsoft technologies, or JavaBeans from Sun Microsystems. While these technologies have already faded away in favor of service-oriented architectures, the concepts and ideas they promoted are now embodied in various frameworks such as the Open Service Gateway (OSGi), which the Glassfish[1] application server and the Eclipse IDE[2] use.

3.3 *At the Service Level*

Beyond the object level, other design patterns exist at the architecture level such as microkernels, layered architectures, service-oriented architectures, and microservices, to name a few. We will focus here on service-oriented architecture and microservices and explain how they help support the customization of multitenant SaaS.

3.3.1 Service Orchestrations

A service-oriented architecture is made of independent units of functionality, so-called "services," which have well-defined interface communication protocols. In principle, services interact following the publish-discover-invoke principle: A service provider first publishes in a public repository its service interface, together with the endpoint of its implementation. The client later obtains this endpoint when it searches the repository for a compatible interface. A client can now invoke any of the endpoints it knows, as all adhere to the same known interface. While the use of such repositories may have fallen out of favor, it yet offers some interesting advantages to support multitenant customization. One may dynamically register new end points in the repository that will be picked up at runtime.

Service orchestrations are one means to aggregate multiple services in order to support business processes. Languages such as the business process execution languages (BPEL) capture the workflow underlying a business process: each activity maps to a service, and an orchestration engine coordinates these services, discovering endpoints, sending requests, and collecting responses. A business process is a program that the orchestration engine executes every time someone invokes this process. In a multitenant setting, each tenant may register a different orchestration and therefore run its own business process on the same orchestration engine.

3.3.2 Microservices Architectures

While the idea of centralization surfaces in service-oriented architectures, the trend is now opposite: decentralization towards many smaller services, so-called "microservices." The core idea of microservices [13] is independence: "less depen-

[1] See https://javaee.github.io/glassfish/.

[2] https://www.eclipse.org/ide/.

dency, more isolation." A microservice realizes only one small and autonomous unit of business functionality, often following a bounded context or the context map advocated by domain-driven design (DDD) [1]. Each service thus has a very limited set of responsibilities and must be deployable independently of any other services. Such independent services are indeed designed, developed, deployed, and scaled independently. To foster independence, each service gets its own private data store. From an organization standpoint, microservices therefore advocates smaller autonomous teams responsible for the whole life cycle of a single service, ideally fed on only "two pizza."

Figure 2 illustrates such an architecture. Our example includes three bounded contexts, projects, sales, and notifications. A separate service realizes each of these bounded contexts. Mobile or desktop client applications access these services through a single API gateway. Behind this gateway, microservices interact asynchronously, using a message queue. Using microservices is a promising way to customize multitenant cloud software because microservices architectures offer several benefits. First, a microservice encapsulates a customization, it can be packaged and deployed in isolation from the main product, which is an important requirement in the multitenant context. Moreover, independent development and deployment ease the adoption of continuous integration and delivery, and reduce, in turn, the time to market for each service. Independence also allows engineers to choose the technology that best suits the service, while other services may use different programming languages, database, etc. Each service can be operated independently, including upgrades, scaling, etc.

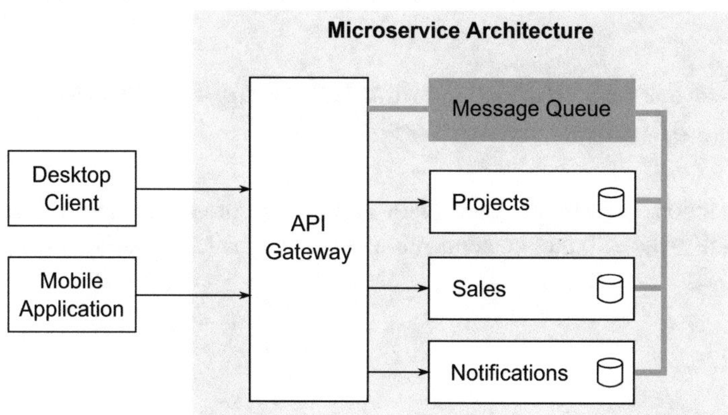

Fig. 2 Blueprint of a microservice architecture

3.4 DSL/Script-Based Approaches

Finally, all the above approaches deal with the implementation of the business logic in the application. This way hence requires dedicated developers familiar with the underlying technologies. Domain-specific languages (DSL) alleviate this: They hide technical details (e.g., API, ad hoc datastructure) behind a syntax that focuses on business-level concepts.

SalesForce[3] and its APEX language[4] is one prominent example of DSL used to support multitenant customization. APEX is a strongly typed, object-oriented language whose syntax is very similar to Java. The language has direct access to the Salesforce database through the Salesforce API, and can be used to develop controllers or triggers. Controllers define new business logic, and are attached to various UI elements such as button click, or Visualforce pages. Triggers define new actions to database events, such as the validation of new data before they are inserted into the database. Beyond classical conditional and loops constructs, APEX also permits in-lining other DSL, namely, querying databases using the Salesforce Object Query Language (SOQL) and manipulating data using the data manipulation language (DML).

Another example of a DSL is CRMScript[5] for in-product customization. Customers use CRMScript to write database queries, event handlers, etc. The script code is executed by a dedicated engine within the product. Isolation is achieved on a language level, where only white-listed methods and operations are allowed. The execution is governed by a basic monitoring and throttling algorithm, preventing the script to do too much harm.

3.5 Comparison of Deep Customization Approaches and the Use of Intrusive Microservices

In this section, we compare the main approaches presented above (Sect. 3.5.1) and initially present our customization approach using intrusive microservices (Sect. 3.5.2).

[3] https://www.salesforce.com/eu/.

[4] https://developer.salesforce.com/docs/atlas.en-us.apexcode.meta/apexcode/apex_intro_what_is_apex.htm.

[5] https://github.com/SuperOffice/CRMScripts.

Table 1 Possible approaches to deep customization and how they address assimilation, isolation, and multitenancy

Granularity	Approach	Isolation	Assimilation	Multi-tenancy
Class/Function	Factory pattern	Thread	Language	No
	Decorator pattern	Thread	Language	No
	Strategy pattern	Thread	Language	No
Components	Bundles	Process	Language	No
Services	Orchestrations	Network	Architecture	Yes
	Microservices	Network	Architecture	Yes
Languages	DSL	Process	Language	Yes

3.5.1 A Comparison of the Main Approaches

Table 1 summarizes how the main deep customization approaches tackle the requirements of isolation, assimilation, and multitenancy described in Sect. 2.3.2. Isolation increases as we move from thread-based isolation, to process-based isolation and then to network-based isolation. Assimilation decreases when customizations are not written in the same language than the main product. Multitenancy is always possible but we marked "No" when any approach requires ad hoc mechanisms that are not provided by programming languages out of the box. Aspect-oriented programming (AoP) may be a means to carry out customizations. AoP [7] injects cross-cutting concerns such as logging by weaving new behavior (advice) at specific places (specified by a *point-cut*). As opposed to AoP, which addresses cross-cutting concerns, in our experience, customizations are not cross-cutting concerns. They are large-scale developments that heavily affect the main product in multiple places (UI, BL, and database). Besides, AoP does not provide any direct support for either multitenancy or isolation.

Among the approaches that are marked "Yes" for multitenancy, service orchestrations offer means to aggregate multiple services to support business processes. Therefore, the customization by service orchestrations is not really "deep," which is at a high-level modification and relies on the vendors to provide the adequate "atomic services" as the building blocks for customized composite services (as discussed later in Sect. 8). The big vendors such as Salesforce[6] and Oracle NetSuite,[7] choose a heavyweight direction, transforming themselves from a product into a development platform for customers to implement their own applications using provided DSLs.[8] In this way, such solutions require huge investment from the vendors and strong solution-specific expertise from the customization developers. Table 1 shows how isolation and assimilation conflicts with each other. As we move customization on separate nodes, we gain in isolation but we lose in assimilation

[6]https://www.salesforce.com.

[7]https://netsuite.com.

[8]https://developer.salesforce.com.

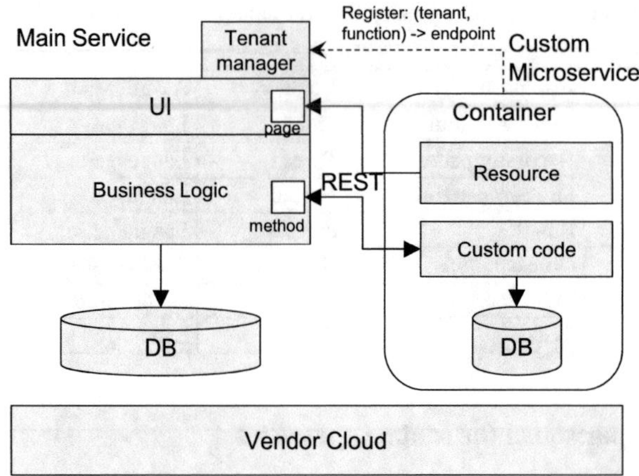

Fig. 3 The structural overview of intrusive custom microservices

because the customization and the main product become completely separate software systems. The microservices-based approach with its benefits as discussed in Sect. 3.3.2 is promising because it does not require huge investment from the vendors or strong solution-specific expertise from the customization developers like in the DSL approaches. Moreover, it can enable customization at a lower level of granularity than in the service orchestrations approach.

The authors of this chapter propose to leverage microservices to enable deep customization of multitenant SaaS. In the remainder we propose an architecture to reconcile isolation, assimilation, and customization.

3.5.2 Deep Customization Using Intrusive Microservices

We combined the function/class level and microservices level presented above into an architectural pattern we called *intrusive microservices*. In a nutshell, we override local class methods with separate microservices. Figure 3 illustrates its basic structure. We will fully elaborate on this architecture in Sect. 4.

The main service is a running instance of the standard product, provided by the service vendor. This service is hosted in a public or private cloud, managed by the service vendor.

A customization by each tenant is running as one or more microservices. Each custom microservice reimplements a small number of fine-grained structures within the main service source code, such as class methods in the business logic, or HTML templates in the UI level. The custom microservice may maintain a separate database if it needs to. Following the microservice ideas, the main service and the custom microservices do not share databases or storage directly.

A *tenant manager* registers which microservice supersedes which part of the main product and for which tenant, so that when a tenant request arrives, the product will forward it to the registered microservice, instead of executing the original standard code.

These custom microservices are intrusive to the main product through callback code, which are small code snippets sent by the custom microservice that are executed by the latter under the same execution context as the to-be-replaced standard code. The microservices use callback code to query data from the main service and to possibly modify the behavior of the service.

4 Supporting Intrusive Custom Microservices

We detail here our intrusive microservices approach according to the .NET Core stack, but the challenges and solutions are generic to other stacks.

Following the common practice of microservices, we made the following high-level design decisions.

1. The main service and the custom code unit communicate with each other only via REST invocations.
2. The data exchanged between the product and custom code unit are JSON documents, and should be small in size.
3. The main service does not make any assumption on what the custom code will need and what it will do.

Deep customization must provide ultimate flexibility to custom code developers, which means that if a custom code unit is to replace a standard method, then the custom code should be able to query or manipulate any data that the original method body can query or manipulate. In other words, the custom code is exposed to the same context as the standard source code. However, the design decisions we identified above determine that the custom code cannot directly query or manipulate the context, as it is not practical to transfer the entire C# objects in the context through JSON. We address this issue by employing a callback code mechanism and a multistep communication that transfers data on demand.

In this section, we first give an overview of the interactions between the product and custom code in Sect. 4.1. After that, we detail in Sect. 4.2 the syntax and execution of callback code and how it works on the context. Then, we define the concrete REST API of a custom code unit in Sect. 4.3. The UI customization is presented in Sect. 4.4. Finally, we describe the deployment and life cycle of microservices in Sect. 4.5.

4.1 Communication Between Main Service and Custom Code

The original behavior of a method is overridden by a custom code unit through a sequence of REST communications between the main product and the custom microservice.

The communications are initiated and driven by the interceptor, which is injected into every method in the main product. Whenever a method is invoked, the interceptor will pause the execution of the original method body, and first check with the tenant manager if the current tenant has registered a customization for this method. If so, the tenant manager will return the associated endpoint. The interceptor then starts the communication with the customization by invoking this endpoint with a POST request. This first request carries no payload, because the product does not know what data the customization needs. When the customization receives this request, it executes and replies with changes to apply onto the context of the original method, the next steps,[9] and what data the customization service will need in the next step. The interceptor then operates the context as indicated, prepares the required data, and uses them as parameters to invoke the given next step. The communication terminates when the custom code responds without a subsequent step. Moreover, as the response of the last step, the customization can provide a preemptive return value. If so, the interceptor will return this value without executing the original method body. On the other hand, if the last response does not have a return value, the interceptor will continue to execute the original method body, under the manipulated context.

We present the customization mechanism based on a sample customization, i.e., Step 3 in Sect. 2.2, to compute the total price of the shopping cart. Figure 4 illustrates the communication based on the "get total price" use case. When an end user checks out, the vendor's product processes the request and finally invokes the `GetTotal` method defined in the product to calculate the total price. This method invocation is intercepted, and by consulting the `TenantManager` it receives an endpoint to the `Donation ShoppingCart` microservice. The interceptor invokes this endpoint with an empty POST request. In the first step, the custom code does nothing but directly sends back a response with callback code to ask the main product what items are in the current shopping cart. It also provides the endpoint to the second step. The interceptor executes the callback code to query the items, and sends them as JSON objects to the customization microservice by invoking the endpoint for the second step.

In the second step, the customization microservice receives the request and obtains the current items and their prices. Then it queries its own database to get the donation amount recorded for each item, and sums them up into a total price for the shopping cart. As the second response, the custom microservice instructs the

[9]This is a "continuation" in functional programming parlance.

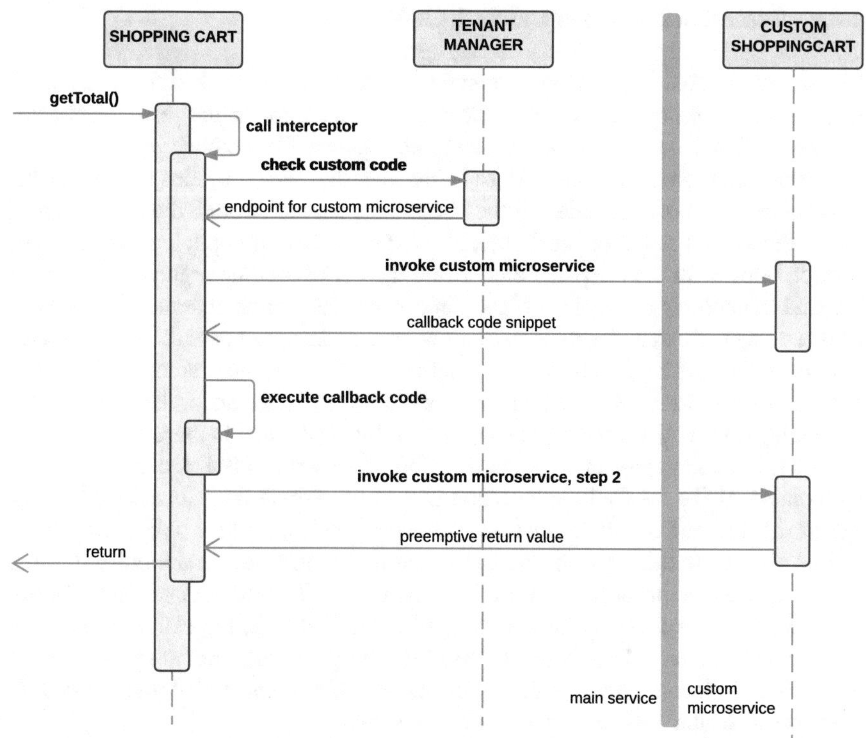

Fig. 4 Communication between main service and custom code

interceptor to use the new total price as the return value. The interceptor returns this value to its caller without executing the original method body.

4.2 Intrusive Callback Code

This section explains the callback code mechanism which enables a remote customization service to query and manipulate the data and state of the main product. In summary, a callback code is an instruction that is created by the custom code and executed by the interceptor in the main product under the same context of the original method body. The fact that the callback code and the original method body are exposed to the same context is essential to the requirement of deep customization. In the rest of this section, we first define the execution context of the callback code, and then introduce the language to write callback code and how they are executed by the interceptor.

4.2.1 Execution Context of Callback Code

The execution context is the environment in which the callback code is executed, i.e., a set of objects that the callback code can refer to. In the .NET stack, this context is identical to the context of the to-be-replaced C# method.

When a method in the main service is invoked, the context needed to evaluate the original method body includes all the parameters passed through the invocation. If the method is not static, the host object is also passed as an implicit parameter. The method body refers to the parameters using the corresponding argument names, or the `this` identifier for the host object, in order to read or change the internal state of these objects. After the method body is executed, it may extend the context by a return value, which is passed to the caller. In addition, the method body is also exposed to a global context which consists of all the classes under the current class loader, together with all the static methods and fields defined in these classes.

When the interceptor of a standard method receives a callback code, it inherits the context of the original method, and uses it to execute the callback code. This means that the callback code can refer to the parameters, the host object, and all the visible classes. In this way, the callback code is able to obtain and modify the data and state of the main service, just in the same way as the original method body. For example, in the get total price use case, after the first step, the callback code can query out the current shopping cart items by calling the `GetItems` method on the host object. In the second step, the callback code adds the new total price value into the context, which will be used as the return value.

4.2.2 Callback Code Language

A callback code snippet is sent from the custom service to the main product as plain text, and then in the product it is compiled into an executable code and evaluated at runtime. We design and implement a simple language to write callback code, based on the DynamicLinq library [6]. DynamicLinq is a .NET library that dynamically compiles a piece of C# query from plain text into an executable function (a Delegate in .NET). The C# query supported by DynamicLinq is essentially a reference to an object or a chain of method invocations from an object. We make simple extension to DynamicLinq to extend its expression power, and Fig. 5 summarizes the syntax.

Query is a piece of code that returns a value. A query can be simply a reference to a context variable, starting with a $ symbol and followed by the variable name. From a query, we can invoke a method that is defined on the type of its returned object. As long as the method has a return value, the invocation is still a query. Similarly, we can access the field of an object or do operations of two objects. A conditional branch returns one of the alternative queries, and list comprehension iterates a collection and uses its items to make a new collection.

A query must always return a value, and if we invoke Void-typed methods, DynamicLinq will raise an exception. To address this issue, we introduce a new concept called "Instructions." We can use a CALL keyword to invoke a Void-typed

```
Query ::= '$'ContextVar | Query'.'Method Params
    | Query'.'Field | Query (+|-|==|>|...) Query
    | 'IF' Query 'THEN' Query 'ELSE' Query
    | [Query FOR '$'Id OF Query]
Params ::= '()' | '(' Query (, Query)* ')'
Instr ::= 'CALL' Query'.'Method Params
    | 'SET' Query.Field '=' Query
```

Fig. 5 Syntax

```
context_op1 = {
  "rawItems": "$this.GetCartItems().Result",
  "items": "$rawItems.Select(i => \
     new{id=i.CartItemId, price=i.Album.Price})" }
context_op2 ={ "total": "_VAL_number 25.99",
  "msg": "_VAL_string New total price is 25.99",
  "void": "CALL System.Console.WriteLine($msg)",
  "returnx": "$total" }
```

Fig. 6 Sample context operations

method on the returned object of a query, or use a SET keyword to assign value to a field of this object.

4.2.3 Context Operation

The callback code language can be used to write a single instruction. After each step, the custom code sends back a group of instructions, which we call the *context operation*. A context operation is a dictionary, and each of its items comprises a *key* in the form of a string and a *value* which is either an instruction or a text. We support the following types of items. When the key is the name of a context variable, the value could be either a query or a string starting with `_VAL_` followed by a type (string, number, date, boolean) and a value of this type. The query result or the direct value will be assigned to the key variable. If the specified variable does not exist in the current context, we create the variable first. The value can be an instruction; then we will only evaluate the instruction (which has an effect on the context) without assigning a value to any context variable. When the key is a keyword "returnx," we will use the resulted value of the query as the return value of the original method.

Figure 6 shows two sample context operations, returned by the two steps of the GetTotal example, respectively. We present the two dictionaries in JSON format, as it is in the actual REST communication.

The first context operation is to query the items in the current shopping cart. In the first line, we query all the items and assign the list of items to a temporary context variable named `rawItems`. The query uses an existing context variable, `this`, which represents the current Shopping Cart, and invokes the `GetCartItems` method on the object. In the second line, we extract only the identifier and the price from each item, because these are the only information useful to the custom code.

The second context operation prints a log about the new total price, and modifies the original return value. The first two lines transfer the total price and the log message from the custom code to the main product. The two values are in types of number and string, respectively. The third line invokes a static method to print the message to the console. It utilizes both a context variable (`$msg`) and a static class (`System.Console`). Finally, the last line instructs the main service to use the value in the `total` variable as the new return value.

4.3 Customization Protocol

Each custom code unit replaces one method in the main product, using several steps. Each step is triggered by the POST request to a unique URL. The customization protocol defines the input and output of these steps.

The input to each custom code step is a POST request, with an optional JSON document as the request body. The JSON document is a key-value map that contains data obtained from the main product. What data is carried by a request body is defined by the output of the previous step.

The output of each step is also a JSON document, in a predefined format. The whole JSON document is called a "Manual" (which means that the main service needs to work accordingly), and it contains three optional properties. The `context` property contains a context operation, as defined in the previous section. The `nextcall` property defines the next step, where `function` is the URL of the subsequent step, and `body` provides an additional context operation, where the variables and their values will be passed to the POST request for the subsequent step. The data type of the output is extensible. We will add new properties later on to introduce more functionalities into the customization.

Figure 7 shows a sample custom code unit developed in TypeScript under this protocol, which implements the GetTotal customization. The custom code unit is implemented as a TypeScript object called `gettotalcc`. In the object, the `endpoint` and `mainhandler` defines the first step. In this step, the custom code asks the main product to query out the current shopping cart items (see `context_op1` in Fig. 6). After that, it sets up the next step as `compute`, and the request body contains one parameter, that is, the queried items. In this example, we only have one subsequent step. In this step, we first get the items from the request body, which has been automatically decoded into an array of objects in JavaScript. For each object (a shoppingcart item) in the array, we get the item identifier and price, query the custom database to get the donation amount, and add it into the total value. When all the items have been counted, we return a new manual, whose context operator is the one defined as `context_op2` in Fig. 6.

```
var gettotalcc = new cirrusapi.CustomCode()
gettotalcc.endpoint = "/shoppingcartx/gettotal";
gettotalcc.mainhandler = (req, res) => {
  res.json({
    context: ... //context_op1
    nextcall: {
      body: {items: '$items'},
      function: 'compute',
    }}); }
gettotalcc.steps["compute"] = (req, res) =>{
  var items = req.body.items;
  var total = 0;
  items.forEach(item => {
    var id = item.id
    ... //query own db and compute total
    if (/*all items handled*/)
      res.json({
        context: ...#context_op2
      }); }
```

Fig. 7 Sample custom code unit for GetTotal price

4.4 UI Customization

Our customization mechanism is focused on the business logic, i.e., how to replace a method in the main product. The customization of UI is driven by the business logic, based on the MVC structure in ASP.NET.

In ASP.NET, every browser request is received and handled by a specific method in a controller class (within the Business Logic layer). If the request leads to a UI, i.e., an HTML page, the method will call the `View` method of the controller class with an identifier to an HTML template that is preloaded from a local file. The controller will then interpret the embedded C# code in the template to generate the HTML file, and return it to the browser.

We extend the ASP.NET Core behavior to allow the load of HTML templates from a remote file, which can be obtained from the custom microservice through an HTTP GET request. After a remote custom template is loaded, it can be used in the same way as the original templates. After that, we can use the normal business logic customization mechanism to make a controller method use the custom template.

The custom view templates are evaluated by the same generation engine as the standard template. Therefore, the custom view template shares all the resources with the standard templates, such as the reusable view components, the CSS styles, and the scripts. This saves customers from reimplementing the common parts and also guarantees that the custom views have the consistent style with the standard ones. With our customization approach at the UI level, a tenant can override any UI component from the main product by the UI component provided by the custom microservice, for example, HTML code, CSS styles, or scripts. Note that for assimilation, the tenant should follow the same UI styles as the main product even though it is up to the tenant to decide. Moreover, the custom templates are also interpreted under the same context as the standard views, and have access to the controller object. This allows the view to exchange data with the business logic using the standard way in ASP.NET, i.e., through the model and the view data carried by the controller.

4.5 Custom Microservice Life Cycle and Development Support

One side effect of building customizations as separate microservices is that it opens the architecture for variations of the life cycle and its development. We describe below the life cycle of the microservices for customization and some microservices development support, including some we experimented with.

4.5.1 Custom Microservice Life Cycle

The first variation is to decide who hosts and operates the customization microservices. Whereas during the "on-premises" era, software vendors did not take any responsibility for hosting and operating customized products, it now becomes an alternative business model (see Sect. 6.5). Microservices can be hosted either by the customer, by the vendor, or even possibly by the third-party consultancy company.

In our experiments, the customization microservices were hosted and managed by the same cloud vendor as the main product is hosted for the sake of performance and manageability.

The deployment of custom code relies on container technologies (Docker in our case) and follows a "serverless" style. Customers or their consultants deliver to the vendor the source code and the deployment descriptors (e.g., Docker file, Kubernetes pods). These descriptors specify the underlying software stacks such as Node.js, Python, Java, and the auxiliary components (such as databases), as well as the libraries used by the custom code. Then the vendor's container engine provisions and manages containers enclosing the customization services, and possibly additional containers for the related storages.

Once a custom microservice is up and running, the vendor registers it in the running SaaS product as an alternative customization endpoint for the customized methods.

Choosing where to host the customization microservices also drives their monitoring and maintenance, because monitoring, reporting, and issues fixing depends on one another. In our experiment, the product vendor is in charge of the entire operation of customization microservices (as opposed to their development). The vendor monitors and controls the resource consumption of each container, pausing or scaling out the containers when necessary to meet the service-level agreement. It also restarts the failed containers and reports the errors to the customers. Within the main service, the callback code engine monitors the execution of each context operator and terminates the ones that spend too much resources, or those that raise unexpected exceptions.

4.5.2 Development Support for Writing Microservices for Customization

On top of Visual Studio Code,[10] we developed some specific support for the development of microservices for customization, such as the source code editor, code generator, and the deployment facility. These are some extensions in the IDE to support the development and deployment of microservices for customization. Our IDE eases the development of custom code by providing the "create custom code" command for generating custom code snippets and templates. The IDE also provides a set of simple commands to achieve the one-key deployment of the custom code. For example, the developers only need to launch a VS Code command (selected from the Command Palette) to deploy the custom code as a docker container and register it as a customization into the main product. We implement this through the configuration feature of VS Code together with predefined Docker specifications.

5 Evaluation

To evaluate our approach, we implemented the generic mechanisms of Sect. 4 on the MusicStore, transforming it into a deeply customizable SaaS. We then tested its customization capability by developing a custom microservice, implementing the three customization use cases from Sect. 2.2. The results confirm the feasibility of our approach, but also show that it supports most customization types without dedicated APIs or extension points.

5.1 Implementation of the Customizable SaaS

We adapted the source code of MusicStore in two steps: we first added a generic library and then went through a simple and automated code rewriting.

The generic library implements the mechanisms in Sect. 4, and includes the following components. A simple *tenant manager* maps the standard MusicStore's methods to specific customization endpoints. A generic *interceptor* drives the communication between the main product and the customizations. An *callback code interpreter* executes the callback code on the local context. Finally, a *remote RAZOR*

[10]https://code.visualstudio.com/.

file provider loads custom HTML templates that can be obtained through REST requests. The entire library is implemented in 800 lines of C# code.

We perform an automatic code rewriting on MusicStore, adding three lines of code in the beginning of each method. The first line initializes a local context as a Dictionary object and fills it with the method parameters. The second line invokes the generic interceptor with the context and the method name. The third line checks if a return value is available in order to decide whether to skip the original method body. We choose source code rewriting rather than binary instrumentation for the sake of simplicity.

All the effort is focused on generic mechanisms, without specific consideration of the actual customization requirements or features.

5.2 *Sample Custom Code*

On top of the customizable MusicStore, we performed three customization use cases.

- **UC1: Donation** is the one described in Sect. 2.2, with three sub-use cases: choosing donations, listing the donations, and computing the total price.
- **UC2: Visit Counting** records how many times each album has been visited. It has two sub-use cases: recording a visit and showing global statistics.
- **UC3: Real Cover** uses the album title to search the cover picture from Bing Image and replaces the original place-holder picture.

We design these use cases deliberately, in order to achieve a good coverage of the general requirements of customization on web-based enterprise services.

The two companies that commissioned this research have summarized the changes that their customers require when customizing their web-based ERP and CRM systems. We list these general requirements in the first column of Table 2, in three different tiers, namely, the user interface, the business logic and the database. The requirements are in a high abstraction level, and each item represents a category of required changes.

The rest of Table 2 shows how the three use cases cover the general requirement items. The effect of the customized MusicStore can be seen by a screenshot video.[11] In the video, we are using a MusicStore service through a fictional tenant named foo@bar.com. We first see the standard way to buy a music album through the MusicStore, i.e., browsing the album detail, add it to the shopping cart, and check the overview of the shopping cart items. After that, we deploy the custom code as a microservice and register it into the MusicStore via the REST API. The effect of the customization is immediate: When we repeat the same shopping process, we will first see a new cover image of the album (UC3) obtained from Bing.com. The

[11]https://www.youtube.com/watch?v=IIuCeTHbcxc.

Table 2 Coverage of general requirements for customization

Requirements	UC1	UC2	UC3	#
User interface				
Move original control			✓	✓
Remove original control			✓	✓
Add control	✓			✓
Add new page		✓		✓
Replace page	✓			✓
Add scripts			✓	✓
Override scripts				
Business logic				
Override logic	✓			✓
Add new logic		✓		✓
React to events		✓		✓
Trigger events				
Link control to data	✓			✓
Execute external service			✓	✓
Database				
Override datasource				
Add field to table	✓			✓
Add new table		✓		✓
Update database	✓	✓		✓
Query database	✓			✓

layout is altered to fit the big image, and a remark pops on when the cursor is on the image, which is driven by a new JavaScript code snippet added to the page. When we add the album to shopping cart, we are led to a new page to select the donation amount, and then shown a shopping cart overview with additional columns showing donations and a different total price (UC1). Finally, we open a new page to check the statistics about the album visits (UC2). Such visits are recorded in a table with album ID and visit time stamp, and counted afterwards by a new function in the business logic layer. At the end of the video, we log off the tenant foo@bar.com, and the service immediately goes back to the standard behavior, which shows that the customization only affects one tenant.

The custom code is deployed and registered to the MusicStore dynamically, without rebooting the main service. The customized behavior is seamlessly integrated into the main service: The new pages and the modified ones all keep the same UI style as the original MusicStore, and are accessed through the standard MusicStore address.

We implemented the three customization scenarios in TypeScript, using the Node.js HTTP server to host the custom microservice. The first two scenarios request data storage, and we used MongoDB as the customer database. The entire custom code includes 384 LoC in 5 TypeScript files (one file for each scenario, plus two common files to configure and launch the HTTP server) and 175 LoC in

4 Razor HTML templates (of which, two templates are new and the other two are copy-pasted from MusicStore, with 176 LoC that are not changed).

5.3 *Performance*

The intrusive customization microservices does not cause significant performance penalty to the main service.

We carried out a set of experiments to compare the latency of the user requests for the original service and the customized ones. The latency, measured by the browser, captures the time spent between the emission of an HTTP request (such as clicking on a link) and the rendering of a new page. The latency comprises roughly two parts: loading the page source from the server and rendering the page in the browser. Customization only affects the first part. The loading time of original services ranges from 5 to 100 ms, and the longest ones happen when a page is first requested. The additional latency caused by customization ranges from 10 to 300 ms. Customization without UI (the "get total price" example) causes in average 11 ms latency. The ones that need a new page can cause up to 300 ms of additional latency when the page is first accessed, after that the additional latency is normally between 50 and 90 ms. We believe the additional latency is hardly noticeable to end users, as the time to render the page is in average 2 s, be it customized or not.

The memory consumption of this sample microservice remains stable around 50 MB. A further experiment reveals that a 16 GB RAM laptop can easily host 100 instances of the same microservice.

While such overhead remains reasonable, we certainly need additional experiments to make this claim general, and especially to understand how performances scale with customization complexity. We believe, however, that more complicated interactions must be carefully designed (by the third party consultant). Customization should adhere to the well-known best practices [18] such as avoiding chatty communications and restricting data exchange to the minimum to name a few.

As for reliability, calling a remote service requires more work than calling local methods. To maintain the same level of reliability, each remote calls to a customization must therefore as well as adhere to performance best practices [16] such as using appropriate timeout and retry policies, circuit breakers, default answers, etc.

6 Discussion

We discuss below additional aspects of microservices-based customization, that is, database customization (Sect. 6.1), triggering customization (Sect. 6.2), security (Sect. 6.3), and implications for business models (Sect. 6.5).

6.1 *Database Customization*

Customization often requires extending the standard data schema. Two types of extension on the data schema must be supported: adding a new entity and adding a field to an existing entity. Removing an entity or a field is not necessary for customization, since the customization service can simply ignore them. Changing the type of a field can be achieved by adding a new field and ignoring the original one. Since the customization service is not allowed to change the data schema of the product database, all data under the extended entity of field have to be stored in a separate custom database. A new data entity can be implemented as a table in the custom database. A new field can also be implemented as a table in the custom database, as a mapping from the primary key of the original table to the extended field. In our example, we extend the shopping cart items with a new field to record the amount of donation. This is achieved by a table with two fields, the shopping cart item ID and the amount of donation.

The customization service registers to the tenant manager how it extends the standard data schema. In this way, the product service knows how each tenant extends its database, so that it can utilize the extended data. For example, MusicStore has a page listing all the shopping cart items, originally with price and quantity. When rendering this page, MusicStore checks the tenant manager and gets the information that the customization extends shopping cart items with a new field of donation amount. Therefore, it adds a new column in the shopping cart information table for this field and queries the customization service to fill in this column.

Custom databases usually have simple schema and relatively small amount of data. Therefore, it is reasonable to use lightweight technologies such as PostgreSQL or MySQL. NoSQL database is also a good choice.

6.2 *Triggering of Microservices*

The customization service registers itself to one of the predefined extension points in the product service. When the control flow reaches this extension point, the product service picks the registered customization service, and *invokes* it. There are two types of invocations, i.e., *synchronous triggering*, when the product service awaits the customization service to finish the triggered logic, and *asynchronous triggering* when it does not.

Synchronous triggering can be implemented as a direct REST invocation from the product service to the customization service. In the product service, the implementation of an extension point can be simplified as a *if-then-else* structure: *if* the product service finds a customization service registered for this point, *then* it invokes this service and continues with the returned value, *else* it executes the standard logic. The more extension points the product service has, the more customization it supports. As an extreme case, the vendor can inject an extension point before each method in the product, using the Aspect-Oriented Programming (AOP) technology. Synchronous triggering applies to the customization scenarios when the behavior of the product service has to be influenced by the customization immediately.

Asynchronous triggering can be implemented by the event technology. At an extension point, the product service ejects an event indicating that it has reached this point, together with some context information. The event is published to a message queue. If a customization service subscribes this message queue at the right topic, it will be notified by the message queue and triggered to handle this event. The product usually has its internal event mechanism, and therefore to support asynchronous triggering of customization service, the vendor just needs to publish a part of these internal events to the public message queue. Although asynchronous triggering is easier to implement, the customization cannot immediately influence the behavior of the product service, because the control flow of the product service is not blocked by the customization service.

A customization service usually needs both synchronous and asynchronous triggering. Consider the visit counting scenario, for instance: Each time an album is visited, the customization service needs to be triggered asynchronously to increase the number of visits in its database. Later on, in the overview page, the product service needs to synchronously trigger the customization service to get the numbers of visits for all the albums. This time it needs to wait for those numbers to be returned from the customization service in order to show them on the overview page.

6.3 Security

The main SaaS and customization microservices are executed on the servers inside the public cloud hosting environment, which is a multitenant environment. Security is a critical requirement for customization in a multitenant environment, e.g., how to prevent a custom code from accessing data and resource that the tenant has authority over. We must ensure that the custom code that one tenant provides does not access or damage—accidentally or intentionally—the custom code and the data of other tenants. There can be different ways of performing tenant separation, but the tenant manager is responsible for isolation of tenant isolation. The tenant manager facilitates access to custom code that replaces standard functionality or inject custom functionality. It is responsible for isolation of customization, i.e., ensuring the correct customizations are applied to the correct tenants, and only those. The runtime environment executes customization and depends on the tenant manager to get hold of custom codes. The custom code repository ensures isolation between custom code provided by different partners. The tenant manager owns the access and authentication requirements to be able to access the custom code repository.

In intrusive customization, the dynamic loading is not a problem as the services are always running and are not maintained by the main product. However, the product still needs a way to switch between services to serve different tenants, even if the switch is as simple as changing the endpoint to call services. Resource sharing will be handled outside the main product, by the environment provider, such as Docker, virtual machine, or cloud providers. For security, we need to guarantee that the API between the main product and the external services are safe. For multitenant SaaS, the drawbacks of deep customization are tight coupling and security issues. On the one hand, the custom code is tightly coupled with the main service, and therefore updates of the main service will eventually break some customization. On the other hand, deep (intrusive) customization in theory allows customers to make any change to the services shared among tenants, which may cause severe security issues. Our approach at this stage does not solve these two problems. Vendors that allow deep customization have to introduce supporting facilities, such as sandbox, continuous automatic testing, vendor-involved code review, customer certification, etc. As a future plan, we will also investigate potential automatic support to mitigate these two problems, e.g., the generation of test cases to check the compatibility of custom code after main service updates, the static code analysis across main service and custom code for security purpose, etc.

6.4 Migration from On-Premises to SaaS

The migration of a legacy system to the microservice architecture style we advocate remains difficult, both for the product vendor and for the customer. Migration procedures form one of our ongoing research topic but we highlight below what could be the main steps.

From the vendor's standpoint, the minimal change (provided the product is a so-called "monolith") is to develop a means to intercept any method call. This depends on the underlying technology and some application servers have appropriate features, such as Glassfish, for instance. Next, the vendor must expose the tenants' information to the interceptor, so that it can retrieve the target endpoint based on the activated tenant and the intercepted method.

Provided the vendor's product is a customizable multitenant SaaS, the customer (or a third-party consultant) must then collect every change they have implemented on their on-premises version and reformulate them into meaningful microservices. This is a critical and yet manual process that requires an in-depth knowledge of both the vendor's product internals as well as the custom code already deployed on premises.

Finally, once the customization microservices are tested and operational, they must be integrated to the vendor product. This requires the collaboration of the vendors and the customer to run integration tests and become confident that the new changes remain concealed to other tenants. We envision that sandbox mechanisms are one possible solution to these integrations.

6.5 Implications for Business Models

To open a multitenant service for customization implies a change in the Business model. The more software vendors allow their clients to customize, the more they transfer ownership to their clients. A highly customizable multitenant SaaS therefore falls somewhere between a SaaS and a platform-as-a-service (PaaS). Regular SaaS does not run custom code whereas PaaS is a dedicated solution for that.

This change of business model surfaces in the responsibilities that vendors accept regarding deployment, monitoring, and maintenance of customizations. Our intrusive microservice approach remains open to both approaches. Excluding the code that is dynamically interpreted within the vendors' product, the rest lies outside, in separate microservices. On the one hand vendors may decide to take as little responsibilities as possible and hence will demand that their clients run their customized microservices on their own. On the other hand, the vendors may accept to run the custom microservices on their clients' behalf. As the vendors take on the responsibility of operating custom code, they must set up a development process to help integrate the life cycles of both their products and their users' customization.

We believe a transition from SaaS to PaaS is a big leap that has to be carefully considered. In this transition, our approach allows vendors to gradually open their system to customization. One of the partners that commissioned this research has only made customization available for two important partners that they trusted. Only one "big partner" really needed many deep customizations. The rest of their clients did not need that many deep customizations.

7 Towards Nonintrusive Customization

We discuss here the need for nonintrusive customization strategy and provide an outline of a nonintrusive customization solution. While intrusive microservices are technically sound, its practical adoption by industry may be hindered by the intrusive way of custom code, which would be developed by "third parties" that cannot be trusted by software vendors to be dynamically compiled and executed within the execution context of the main service.

We are working towards a microservice-based nonintrusive customization framework for multitenant Cloud applications, called MiSC-Cloud [15]. Figure 8 shows an overview of the MiSC-Cloud framework. In this architecture, the nonintrusive MiSC-Cloud solution avoids using call-back code for customization and rather orchestrates customization using the API gateway(s) to which the API of the main software product (developed by vendor) and the APIs of the microservices (owned by tenants) implementing the customizations for different tenants are exposed. The WebApp UI service provides support for traditional MVC web application, which has business logic implemented in the main product application accessible via the API Gateway. The microservices of each tenant, the main product application,

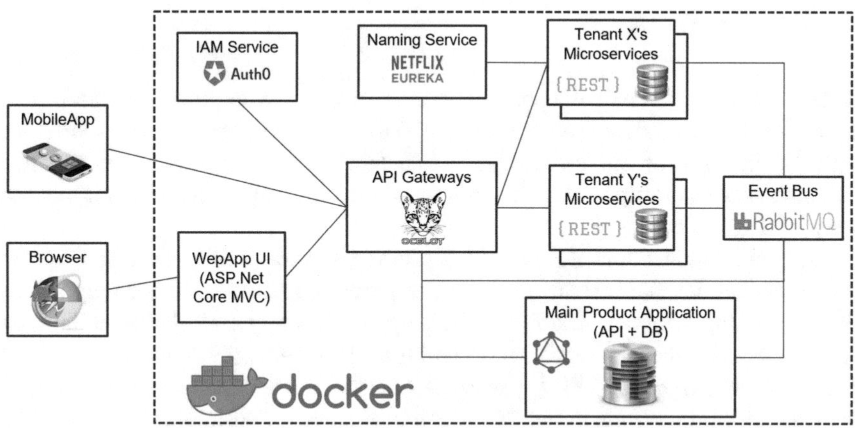

Fig. 8 An overview of the MiSC-Cloud framework

WepApp UI, API gateways, and other supporting services are deployed in separate Docker containers.

After being tested and approved, the microservices of "tenants" are deployed and controlled by the software vendors for customizing the main product. Figure 8 shows microservices specific for tenant X and tenant Y to customize the main product according to the tenants' needs. Only the end users of tenant X after having logged in the system will have access to the customized features specific for tenant X. Via web browsers (or mobile apps), end users can interact with the main product and the corresponding microservices for customization via the API Gateways (e.g., Ocelot[12]). If end user has not logged in, the API Gateway(s) redirects them to the Identity and Access Management (IAM) service (e.g., Auth0). After the end user has logged in successfully via the IAM service, their identity, tenant ID, and access tokens to the main product and the related customization codes will be used by the API Gateway(s) to orchestrate the interactions of the end user with the main product and the specific microservices available to them. The API gateway leverages a naming service (e.g., Netflix Eureka[13]) to get the instances of the provided microservices. The API gateway also leverages a message queue server such as RabbitMQ[14] to support for its orchestration tasks among the main product and the microservices.

[12]http://threemammals.com/ocelot.

[13]https://github.com/Netflix/eureka.

[14]https://www.rabbitmq.com.

8 Related Work

There are many technical approaches to customize enterprise software, such as design patterns, dependency injection (DI), software product lines (SPL), or API. To the best of our knowledge, while these approaches help to predefined customizations at design time, they fail to address the requirements of unforeseen deep customization.

Software product line (SPL) [19] captures the variety of usages in a global variability model, and actual products are generated based on the configuration of the variability model. Traditional SPL approaches target all the potential user requirements by the software vendor, and thus does not apply to our definition of customization. Dynamic SPL [5] is closer to customization, and some approaches, such as [10], propose the usage of variability models for customization. However, such model-based configuration is in a much higher abstraction level than programming [20], and does not fit the deep customization definition, as the customization points have to be predefined by the vendors.

There are many approaches to SaaS customization in the context of service-oriented computing. However, most approaches focus on a high-level modification of the service composition. Mietzner and Leymann [12] present a customization approach based on the automatic transformation from a variability model to BPEL process. Here customization is a recomposition of services provided by vendors. Tsai and Sun [24] follow the same assumption, but propose multiple layers of compositions. All the composite services (defined by processes) are customizable until reaching atomic services, which are, again, assumed to be provided by the vendors. Nguyen et al. [14] develop the same idea, and introduce a service container to manage the life cycle of composite services and reduce the time to switch between tenants at runtime. These service composition approaches all support customization in a coarse-grained way, and rely on the vendors to provide the adequate "atomic services" as the building blocks for customized composite services.

As market leading SaaS for CRM and ERP, the Salesforce platform and Oracle NetSuite provide built-in scripting languages [9, 17, 21] for fine-grained, code-level customization. Since these scripting languages are not exposed to the same execution context as the main service, the customization capability is defined by the underlying APIs of the main service. In order to maximize the customization capability, both vendors provide very extensive and sophisticated APIs, which is costly and not affordable by smaller vendors. In contrary, intrusive microservices does not require the vendors to spend much time on designing and implementing such APIs.

Middleware techniques can also support the customization of SaaS. Guo et al. [4] discuss, in a high abstraction level, a middleware-based framework for the development and operation of customization, and highlight the key challenges. Walraven et al. [25] implemented such a customization enabling middleware. In particular, they allow customers to develop custom code using the same language as the main product, and use Dependency Injection to dynamically inject these custom Java class into the main service, depending on the current tenant. Later work from the same group [26] develop this idea and focus on the challenges of performance isolation and latency of custom code switching. The dependency injection way for customization is close to our work, in terms of the assimilation between custom code and the main service. However, operating the custom code as an external microservice eases performance isolation, a misbehavior of the custom code only fails the underlying container, and the main product only perceives a network error, which will not affect other tenants. Besides, external microservices ease management: scaling independently resource-consuming customization and eventually billing tenants accordingly.

9 Conclusion

This chapter described an approach to use microservices for deep customizations of multitenant SaaS. We presented the key techniques to implement this architecture style based on the .NET platform, and evaluated it by enabling deep customization in an open-source shopping application. The results of our experiments showed that deep customization using intrusive microservices is indeed feasible for multitenant SaaS. This approach achieves both the *isolation* required by multitenancy and the *assimilation* required by deep customization. Even though it is technically sound, using intrusive microservices is not the silver bullet to solve all customization requirements. Its practical adoption by industry suffers from its lack of security as it executes code developed by "third parties" that cannot be trusted by the software vendor. But, it still provides a feasible option when customization beyond the vendor's prediction is a must, and only for a few trusted partners of the vendor. We are working on a nonintrusive approach and will also investigate potential automatic support to mitigate this security issue, e.g., the generation of test cases to check the compatibility of custom code after main service updates, the static code analysis across main service, and custom code for security purposes.

Acknowledgements The research leading to these results has received funding from the Research Council of Norway under the grant agreement number 256594 (the Cirrus project). We want to thank our colleagues at Supper Office and Visma for the fruitful collaboration in the Cirrus project. This chapter is an extension of [1] presented at the 11th International Conference on the Quality of Information and Communications Technology (QUATIC 2018).

References

1. E. Evans, M. Fowler, *Domain-driven Design: Tackling Complexity in the Heart of Software* (Addison-Wesley, Boston, 2004). https://books.google.no/books?id=xColAAPGubgC
2. M. Feathers, *Working Effectively with Legacy Code*. (Martin, Robert C. Prentice Hall PTR, New Delhi, 2004). https://books.google.no/books?id=CQlRAAAAMAAJ

3. E. Gamma, R. Helm, R. Johnson, J. Vlissides, *Design Patterns: Elements of Reusable Object-Oriented Software*. Addison-Wesley Professional Computing Series (Pearson Education, New Delhi, 1994). https://books.google.no/books?id=6oHuKQe3TjQC
4. C.J. Guo, W. Sun, Y. Huang, Z.H. Wang, B. Gao, A framework for native multi-tenancy application development and management, in *The 9th IEEE International Conference on E-commerce Technology and the 4th IEEE International Conference on Enterprise Computing, E-commerce, and E-Services, 2007. CEC/EEE 2007* (IEEE, Piscataway, 2007), pp. 551–558
5. S. Hallsteinsen, M. Hinchey, S. Park, K. Schmid, Dynamic software product lines. Computer **41**(4), 93–95 (2008)
6. S. Heyenrath, The .NET Standard/.NET Core version from the System Linq Dynamic functionality (2018). https://github.com/StefH/System.Linq.Dynamic.Core
7. G. Kiczales, J. Lamping, A. Mendhekar, C. Maeda, C. Lopes, J.M. Loingtier, J. Irwin, Aspect-oriented programming, in *European Conference on Object-oriented Programming* (Springer, Berlin, 1997), pp. 220–242
8. T. Kida, M. Takeda, A. Shinohara, M. Miyazaki, S. Arikawa, Multiple pattern matching in LZW compressed text, in *Proceedings DCC'98 Data Compression Conference* (IEEE, Piscataway, 1998), pp. 103–112
9. T. Kwok, A. Mohindra, Resource calculations with constraints, and placement of tenants and instances for multi-tenant SaaS applications, in *International Conference on Service-Oriented Computing* (Springer, Berlin, 2008), pp. 633–648
10. J. Lee, G. Kotonya, Combining service-orientation with product line engineering. IEEE Softw. **27**(3), 35–41 (2010)
11. Microsoft: MusicStore test application that uses ASP.NET/EF Core (2018). https://github.com/aspnet/MusicStore
12. R. Mietzner, F. Leymann, Generation of BPEL customization processes for SaaS applications from variability descriptors, in *IEEE International Conference on Services Computing, SCC'08*, vol. 2 (IEEE, Piscataway, 2008), pp. 359–366
13. S. Newman, Building microservices: designing fine-grained systems. O'Reilly Media (2015). https://books.google.no/books?id=jjl4BgAAQBAJ
14. T. Nguyen, A. Colman, J. Han, Enabling the delivery of customizable web services, in *2012 IEEE 19th International Conference on Web Services (ICWS)* (IEEE, Piscataway, 2012), pp. 138–145
15. P.H. Nguyen, Nguyen, H. Song, F. Chauvel, E. Levin, Towards customizing multi-tenant Cloud applications using non-intrusive microservices, in *The 2nd International Conference on Microservices, Dortmund* (2019)
16. M.T. Nygard, *Release it!: Design and Deploy Production-Ready Software*, 2nd edn. (Pragmatic Bookshelf, Raleigh, 2018)
17. Oracle, Application Development SuiteScript (2018). http://www.netsuite.com/portal/platform/developer/suitescript.shtml
18. T. Parsons, J. Murphy et al., Detecting performance antipatterns in component based enterprise systems. J. Object Technol. **7**(3), 55–91 (2008)
19. K. Pohl, G. Böckle, F.J. van Der Linden, *Software Product Line Engineering: Foundations, Principles and Techniques* (Springer Science & Business Media, Berlin, 2005)
20. M.A. Rothenberger, M. Srite, An investigation of customization in ERP system implementations. IEEE Trans. Eng. Manag. **56**(4), 663–676 (2009)
21. Salesforce, Apex Developer Guide (2018). https://developer.salesforce.com/docs/atlas.en-us.apexcode.meta/apexcode/
22. H. Song, F. Chauvel, A. Solberg, B. Foyn, T. Yates, How to support customisation on SaaS: a grounded theory from customisation consultants, in *Proceedings of the 39th International Conference on Software Engineering Companion* (IEEE, Piscataway, 2017), pp. 247–249
23. C. Szyperski, D. Gruntz, S. Murer, *Component Software: Beyond Object-oriented Programming*. ACM Press Series. (ACM, New York, 2002). https://books.google.no/books?id=U896iwmtiagC

24. W.T. Tsai, X. Sun, SaaS multi-tenant application customization, in *2013 IEEE 7th International Symposium on Service Oriented System Engineering (SOSE)* (2013), pp. 1–12
25. S. Walraven, E. Truyen, W. Joosen, A middleware layer for flexible and cost-efficient multi-tenant applications, in *Proceedings of the 12th International Middleware Conference* (International Federation for Information Processing, Amsterdam, 2011), pp. 360–379
26. S. Walraven, D. Van Landuyt, E. Truyen, K. Handekyn, W. Joosen, Efficient customization of multi-tenant software-as-a-service applications with service lines. J. Syst. Softw. **91**, 48–62 (2014)

You Are Not Netflix

Jakša Vučković

Abstract Microservices promise to solve scalability problems, streamline deployment, reduce time to market, and improve the reliability of enterprise systems. While for certain projects and corporations switching to microservices was a major success factor, the harsh reality that many projects which went down this road needed to face is often very different. In this chapter we will explore what are the costs and pitfalls of a microservice-based architecture and how to avoid them.

1 Introduction

This chapter provides some guidance on when to adopt a microservice-based architecture [7] and how to gain the most benefits out of it while avoiding pitfalls and keeping the costs under control. The approach taken starts with a skeptical point of view challenging some of the notions brought up by the microservices hype, then afterwards it refines the positive and negative implications of this architectural style in order to present a better understanding on how to mitigate common problems of distributed systems introduced by the use of microservices.

More specifically in Sect. 2 the case is made for not using microservices by analyzing the peculiar nonfunctional requirements that lead to the rise of the microservice-based architecture in order to understand what makes a system suitable for a microservice-based architecture. In Sect. 3 some common assumptions are examined in more detail in order to better define the extent of the benefits gained by the adoption of microservices. Furthermore this section analyses the less obvious costs introduced by microservices. Subsequently in Sect. 4 criteria are defined on how to decompose a system into microservices taking into consideration all the aspects analyzed in the previous sections combined with common approaches used

J. Vučković (✉)
Zühlke Engineering, Belgrade, Serbia
e-mail: jaksa.vuckovic@zuhlke.com

A. Bucchiarone et al. (eds.), *Microservices*,
https://doi.org/10.1007/978-3-030-31646-4_13

by the distributed systems research community in the past decades. Finally in Sect. 5 all of the conclusions are summarized from a less skeptical point of view.

2 Suitability for a Microservice Architecture

One of the factors that mostly contributed to the widespread adoption [7] of microservices was the series of blog posts from Netflix about how they achieved a breakthrough by dividing their monolith application into microservices. Their backend system reached a size and complexity that required subdivision into more manageable chunks. For Netflix this resulted in immediate benefits when it came to providing scalability and deployment.

In the following years many medium and large projects transitioned towards a microservices-based architecture [3, 12, 20] with the hope of achieving scalability, simplifying development, and reducing time-to-market. However, in many cases the results were mixed at best [6].

A false assumption is that if a project is as big as the Netflix backend, or has as many users, it will indubitably benefit from microservices. The subtle difference lies, not in the size, but in the type of application that may benefit most from microservices.

2.1 Types of Operations

For the most part the operations executed on the Netflix servers are read only. Read only operations pose much less of a problem when it comes to scalability. Replicating data that does not change often and does not need to be up to date, does not require any complex replication algorithms like distributed locks [22] or consensus [18]. The only significant cost is storage space.

In terms of scalability, read operations are followed by write operations that involve user private data. For these kinds of operations partitioning techniques like database sharding work very well. Since each data instance is updated only by one user, conflicts are rare and tend not to be a problem.

The most difficult kind of operations to scale are write operations on same shared data (e.g., seat reservations). These operations require coordination of the different replicas and are the most complex to scale [17] especially when multiple entities are involved in the updates.

The type of operations does not itself affect the suitability of a system for a microservice architecture directly, it is rather the uneven scalability requirements for each type of operation. In the case of Netflix, video streaming heavily exceeds all the other types of operations in terms of server load. By separating video streaming into its own microservice, Netflix managed to guarantee an independent level of service for the other operations that were previously being starved of system resources.

The usage profile was comprised of many read operations, which required a lot of scalability, and few write operations, which required less scalability. That was an ideal scenario for separating the system into two parts with different scalability requirements using different solutions. From one point of view, it could be argued that microservices were a generalization of that decision.

2.2 Complexity of Updates

Systems that have a lot of independent operations that do updates to a small part of the data tend to be much easier to subdivide into microservices. On the contrary, operations that involve many updates in several parts of the system tend to have major costs once split into microservices. A particularly difficult category of problems arise when these update operations need to preserve consistency criteria. There are many solutions [4, 11] that address maintaining distributed data to various levels of consistency, however they all come with significant costs in terms of performance and especially maintenance, which make the benefits of a microservice architecture less appealing.

2.3 Separation of Concerns

Another important prerequisite that had been fulfilled by Netflix is the rather clean separation of data according to functionality. Systems that have a lot of functionality that pertains the same data tend to be much more difficult to split into microservices particularly if the data is subject to frequent changes. On the other hand, systems that have a lot of functionality involving separate, even if correlated, data, such as "video content," "thumbnails," "watch history," "rating," "payment information," etc., tend to be much easier subdividing the system into microservices.

All these factors combined made the Netflix backend a perfect candidate for breaking down into microservices. Understanding whether and why a system fits this profile is the first step for deciding whether and how to make the transition to a microservice-based architecture.

3 Myths and Misconceptions

As every popular technology, microservices are followed by a vast amount of articles, blog posts, videos, and marketing material. Some of that content comes from experimental research and direct experience, but for highly popular trends such as microservices, a lot of it is repetition with a slight amount of distortion based on assumptions. We will try to demystify some common misconceptions around microservices.

3.1 Freedom of Choice

One of the selling points of microservices especially appreciated by developers is that microservice-based systems allow individual microservices to be built using different languages and platforms. While this can solve some particular requirements where part of the application needs to be highly specialized it comes at a significant cost.

A *heterogeneous microservice*-based system is one where all the microservices are developed using different languages, and a *homogeneous* one is developed using just a few languages. In reality there is no precise boundary between these two categories because there always tends to be a technology for frontend development (JavaScript/Typescript) [9, 25], one for the middle tier (Java/C#) [13, 23], and a database query language (SQL/JPQL/LINQ) [1, 5, 21].

The most important factor driving up the cost is knowledge management. For each programming language in the project, there have to be several developers that are experienced in that language. Having only one expert per language causes problems with absences, code reviews, and introduces bottlenecks in the software development process. Despite being undesirable, it is a common situation that a change to the software behavior requires modifications to several microservices. In a heterogeneous system, we can either have different developers coordinating the changes across microservices, which requires additional management overhead, or a single developer having to work with various programming languages, which requires more experienced developers. Keeping the developers up to date with technology is more expensive in a heterogeneous system. On the other hand, a homogeneous system provides more flexibility in assigning developers to microservices, better continuity in the software development process, allows for shared code ownership and introduces synergy in the knowledge management of adopted techniques for the various microservices.

Another factor that inflates the cost of heterogeneous microservices is the complexity of writing multiple clients in different languages. It is common practice for the developers of a microservice to provide client libraries for that microservice. The more heterogeneous the system, the more client libraries need to be written each with a certain degree of impedance mismatch. This cost is often mitigated by defining service APIs in some interface definition language [24] and automatically generating various clients from this specification. This approach is less expensive but limits the control developers have over the client interface.

For all these reasons, in microservices-based projects, the balance between freedom of choice and standardization often begins closer to the former but then converges towards the latter, up to the point that significant effort has been made to develop languages specifically for microservices [15].

3.2 *Scalability*

A term often associated with microservices is scalability [8]. It is a common misconception that microservices provide scalability out of the box or at least that microservices are more scalable than a monolith. Scalability is something that needs to be implemented by every microservice. Architectural solutions to scaling a microservice are exactly the same solutions to scaling a monolith and provide the same level of scalability. These solutions can range from a combination of a stateless middle tier backed by a distributed database across application level sharding to high degrees of replication for read-mostly systems. Even a monolith system can use several of these solutions for the various parts of the application. N instances of a monolith will be able to handle as much load as N instances of various microservices; the only difference will be the memory footprint of the application running on those instances, which compared to the data tends to be negligible.

The real benefit microservices provide when it comes to scalability is the ability to independently scale each microservice. As seen in the Netflix example, if some functionality is used very often and can generate significant load on the hardware resources it can be separated from the functionality which is not used that often but which is nonetheless important and requires reasonable response times. So we could have hundreds of active instances of a microservice providing functionality A, but only a few instances of a microservice providing functionality B. In this way, microservices prevent load in one part of the application from affecting performance of another part and allow allocation of hardware resources selectively for each bit of functionality.

4 Dividing a System into Microservices

A careful analysis and understanding of the costs and benefits of microservices is a good starting point for deciding how to partition the functionality of a system in microservices. After that initial analysis, there are many other aspects that need to be taken into considerations that will drive the architecture, sometimes even in opposite directions.

4.1 *The Right Size of a Microservice*

In the early days of microservices one of the most common questions and a common topic of debate, was the right size of a microservice. The spectrum of answers ranged wildly from a single table in the database to the entire domain of a company department.

Domain-driven design [10] proved to be a popular methodology on how to reason about these decisions. Translated to DDD terms, the answer for the microservice size problem varied from having a microservice per entity to a microservice per bounded context. Most often a microservice would contain an aggregate.

With time architects converged on the idea that there is no single "right" size of a microservice, but rather a number of aspects that need to be considered to decide whether to keep functions together, separate them, or even replicate them in different microservices.

4.2 Subdivision According to Update Operations

While domain-driven design encourages a data-oriented approach, it is primarily focused on software design and less on architectural decisions in a distributed system setting. Another way to look at the subdivision problem would be by analyzing the consistency requirements of operations that update data in the system.

Some systems have operations that require updating a lot of data as a consequence of a single user action (or external invocation). For example placing an order in an online shop requires emptying the shopping cart, updating the inventory, starting an order fulfillment business process, updating the data that suggest products to customers, updating the business intelligence data used for internal reports, performing the money transfer, sending the financial data to the accounting department, etc. In a microservice scenario this data might be distributed over several services. An operation can be broken down into multiple updates on the system and each of these updates can be categorized in the following levels:

Atomic core contains all updates that can fail and the whole operation should be aborted if the update cannot be performed. From the previous example, updating the inventory and making the money transfer are part of the atomic core, i.e., if any of those updates cannot be performed, the whole operation should be aborted.

Consistency support layer contains the updates that cannot fail, or can be retried until they succeed, but are required in order to make a part of the system appear consistent to external clients [16]. An example of this would be emptying the shopping cart and updating the list of pending orders after the placing of the order. These updates are required for a consistent customer experience, but cannot cause the whole operation to be aborted.

Eventual consequences layer contains all the updates that, like in the consistency support layer, cannot fail, and affect parts of the system that do not need to appear consistent to external clients (e.g., sending financial data to the accounting department, updating the business intelligence data, etc.).

Many systems will not have all three types of updates and this is perfectly normal. The important thing to keep in mind is that the level of consistency is not just an implementation technicality. It is a business decision because it directly impacts user experience [2].

Distributing the data affected by updates belonging to the *atomic core* of operations across several microservices poses significant problems. In those cases some mechanism must be introduced to ensure atomicity in a distributed scenario. In simple scenarios this mechanism can be a relatively straightforward, two-phase commit [14, 19], but in an evolving system this can easily turn into full distributed transactions. One of the pitfalls of this natural evolution is that iterations of custom solutions are implemented and distributed transactions systems are written from scratch instead of reusing existing ones. Other times, systems remain in a limbo where the business logic is not separated from the mechanism ensuring the atomicity and a business process is created that mimics a two-phase commit.

If the data belonging to the *atomic core* is hosted by a single microservice, it is possible to use local transactions which are much cheaper in terms of performance than any distributed atomic commit algorithm.

The updates in the *consistency support layer* need to be performed in a synchronous way. Due to the noncritical nature of the operations, mechanisms like a two-phase commit are not needed. However, transactions can still be required to maintain isolation in case there is a lot of contention for updates over the same data. Like for the *atomic core* of a system, keeping the data belonging to the consistency support layer in a single microservice avoids a lot of problems. In the case the data is split across several microservices, due to the unreliable nature of distributed systems, additional measures must be taken to ensure exactly-once semantics.

Finally the data that belongs to the eventual consequences layer can be hosted by separate microservices and updated asynchronously. Among various asynchronous solutions, the publish/subscribe mechanisms guarantees loose coupling and tends to be the most future proof for evolving complex systems.

4.3 Serial vs. Parallel Arrangement

Another important aspect to consider when subdividing a system into microservices is managing the dependencies and arrangement of microservices. Architectural patterns can vary a lot, from having a client directly accessing a number of independent microservices to orchestration microservices providing a layer of indirection to chains of microservices invoking each other. All these choices have several implications that are often realized after the system has been in production for months.

One of the fundamental laws from reliability theory is that serially arranged components are less reliable than parallel components. Furthermore a system of serially arranged components is less reliable than a single component.

When several microservices invoke each other in a chain, several servers can be involved that can have hardware failures, there are more configurations to maintain in order to ensure that the right downstream service is invoked and there are network connections to cross which could potentially fail and require some complex distributed algorithms in order to maintain consistency of the system. While distributed systems have the potential to make an application more reliable through techniques such as replication, if implemented naively they tend to be less reliable than a monolithic system.

If services are arranged in a parallel fashion, a viable fault tolerance technique is to separate functionality that can be allowed to fail independently. For example, in the previous online shop scenario, separating the order placement from the seller rating and product comments can make the system usable even if not all of the functionality is available.

Another downside of chains of microservices invoking each other is the increased latency. Instead of a single remote invocation from the frontend to the backend and potentially a database, chains of microservices perform multiple remote invocations, each with its own marshalling, unmarshalling, network latency, and security and/or transactional context propagation. The impact of this is especially evident when using web standards like HTTP+XML or JSON to do interservice communication which can introduce delays of tens of milliseconds. This inefficiency can be compensated to some degree by switching to more efficient protocols like gRPC and Thrift, but is still not comparable to a local invocation.

In a microservice scenario, latency can be either *extrinsic*—caused by the current load of the system, or *intrinsic*—caused by the architectural choices. Extrinsic latency is affected by intrinsic latency and with long chains of invocations becomes very difficult to understand, model, and manage. Intrinsic latency cannot be mitigated by adding more nodes to the system, thus it is of utmost importance take it into account when arranging microservices.

Perhaps the most important impact of microservices is the time required to develop features. In an ideal scenario, implementing a feature would involve changing one microservice and performing a release of just that microservice. Chains of microservices invoking each other often come with a poor separation of concerns. As a consequence, developing features requires changing several microservices and several APIs. The longer the chain, the more overhead work there is. Sometimes this can be further aggravated by independent release cycles. If each microservice is released according to its own schedule, all changes in microservices involved in the feature will need to be released starting from the bottom to the top.

Mitigations include setting up a release train process which means releasing all microservices together in reverse order of dependency. One advantage of this approach is that backward compatibility between intermicroservice APIs is not needed.

Another option is to have *continuous deployment* on all microservices. In this way, microservices can be released on demand as soon as a new feature is implemented. This approach requires careful planning of the API changes in order to preserve backward compatibility. Continuous deployment is sometimes difficult to achieve without introducing the risk of releasing buggy software. Certain categories of software require various stages of lengthy testing before release regardless of the level of test automation.

4.4 Microservice Interaction Styles

Historically, the term API (application programming interface) has been used to describe the set of functions offered by an operating system that provided some handy abstractions to application developers. With time this became the interface of any library or framework, and in recent years it has been predominantly used to refer to remote APIs (typically REST) that are invoked remotely.

A common scenario in projects where a monolith is being broken down into microservices is that microservice interaction keeps being treated as local invocations without too much consideration about introduced latency and possible message losses and crashes. As a consequence, the interfaces of microservices resemble APIs of libraries. A better approach is to treat interaction between microservices for what it is: a protocol. Designing a protocol is somewhat different from designing the API of a library. Additional aspects have to be taken into consideration and some design driving factors are fundamentally different.

First of all, when designing a protocol we have to take into consideration the statefulness of that protocol. A stateful protocol is one where the semantics of every operation (or message) depend on the previous messages exchanged by the parties. A stateless protocol instead has independent invocations which will produce the same result regardless of any previous operations. Stateful protocols are more difficult to implement on the client and server side, they require more complex fault tolerance mechanisms and additional synchronization in case of replication.

An example of a *stateful protocol* is a shopping cart whose state is managed by the server. Whenever a user adds an item to the shopping cart, the client must make a remote invocation to the server. Once the user is ready to pay, the client just sends a request to the server saying that whatever is in the shopping cart should be purchased.

On the other hand, with a *stateless protocol* the state of the shopping cart would be kept entirely on the client and the server would not even have the notion of the shopping cart. As the user adds items to the cart, there are no invocations towards the server. Only when the user is ready to pay, the entire order with the contents of the shopping cart are sent to the server.

While the solution with the stateful protocol would allow users to see the same contents of the shopping cart across different devices, implementing this solution would require many more interactions with the server, which means a more complex API and more load. Server restarts need to be handled appropriately to avoid purchasing an empty shopping cart. In case that the server is replicated, the replicas would need to share the state either through a shared database or through some shared data structure.

In practice, most protocols are stateful to varying degrees, at least for the simple reason that they rely on TCP. More often than not, the best that can be done is to minimize the state shared between the client and the server.

Statefulness is a design aspect that is very important when designing a protocol, but is close to insignificant when designing a local API.

There are many communication paradigms used in distributed systems. One way of categorizing them is according to whether the client awaits for the server to process the request. This is called *synchronous communication*. The simplest form of synchronous communication is the remote invocation. The client sends a request and the server responds. Many internet protocols follow this paradigm.

More complex forms of synchronous communication can be two-phase commits, consensus, or full blown distributed transactions. For all these protocols, a client will send one or more requests to a group of servers and will wait till all or at least a quorum of the servers have processed the request.

In *asynchronous communication* the client sends a message and continues with the computation without waiting for any response. The request will eventually be processed by the server. This interaction can be direct, like in actor-based systems or it can go through a message queue for additional resilience. For the highest decoupling, an event-based approach can be achieved through a publish subscribe mechanism.

Synchronous communication has the advantage that operations can return results thus making it easier to combine several operations. This will also make it easier to write end-to-end tests and preserve consistency. Synchronous invocations will also block the calling thread. Blocking significantly impacts latency and while it does not actively consume hardware resources it may still reduce the throughput of a service by exhausting software resources such as thread pools, connection pools, or simply keeping locks longer than necessary.

Asynchronous communication allows for significantly lower latency and easier identification of performance bottlenecks in the distributed system. Chains of operations that are dependent on each other can be implemented using asynchronous invocations, but the resulting code will be very difficult to understand and maintain. Asynchronous operations are also more difficult to test, and ensuring consistency across a system requires developers skilled in distributed algorithms. While asynchronous communication can be simulated using synchronous primitives and threads, asynchronous primitives are more low level, efficient, and flexible, but require more know-how in the area of distributed algorithms in order to be used correctly.

The decision on which form of interaction to use should be done on a case-by-case basis. According to what we said in the "Subdivision According to Update Operations" paragraph, we provide some guidelines on how to choose the appropriate interaction paradigm.

For updates that belong to the *atomic core* (i.e., updates that need to be performed all or none) the preferred option is to use synchronous communication from the frontend to the backend, have all the corresponding data in the same microservice, and use a cheap consistency mechanism such as database transactions. If it is not possible to keep all data required for the *atomic core* updates in the same microservice, an atomic commit protocol can be used. There are several libraries that provide some help in implementing a two-phase commit protocol, but the participants have to be adapted.

Notice that there is a subtle difference between a consensus and an atomic commit. For a consensus, any participant must be able to accept the chosen outcome. On the other side in an atomic commit any participant can abort the entire operation.

If the individual updates are independent, a two-phase commit should be enough, but if there are dependencies between the individual updates, such as one update requiring the outputs of another update, distributed transactions may be necessary. There are several implementations of distributed transactions that make it very easy to connect several microservices in a single transaction. Distributed transactions are more than just an implementation of the atomic commit. They propagate the transactional context, which is also used to provide isolation at the database level and typically involves an external transaction manager. A two-phase commit is typically used just at the end of a distributed transaction. Distributed transactions have performance implications and pose restrictions on the underlying technologies.

For updates belonging to the *consistency* support layer, remote invocations can be performed synchronously after the atomic core has been performed. Given that the client needs to observe a consistent system for this subset of updates, asynchronous communication is not an option.

Updates that need to be performed as a consequence of the user-triggered operation (or some other external event) but are not required for keeping any form of strong consistency can be invoked using some asynchronous communication mechanism. Using a publish-subscribe mechanism decouples the downstream microservices. A good practice is to publish events using the data model of the producer including all possible data about the event and let each consumer transform the data according to its needs. This way it is easy to add consumers without having to modify the producers. Legacy consumers may need a bridge to transform the events. Sometimes it is a sensible choice even to publish events for which there are no consumers yet.

When publishing events, it is important to take into consideration the granularity of the events. Fine-grained events may be missing context and some aggregator may be needed to correlate different types of events together. On the other hand, coarse-grained events may simply not be detailed enough for some use cases.

Regardless of the synchronicity of communication, and even with eventual consistency requirements, it is necessary to ensure that operations are performed exactly once. Guaranteeing delivery semantics is one of the fundamental challenges of distributed systems. There are three common delivery guarantees in the order of increasing difficulty: At most once—this is the default, the operation will be invoked if everything goes smoothly, but there are no guarantees. This is the typical delivery semantics for asynchronous communication. At least once—this usually involves a retry mechanism if no response is received from the server. It may end up invoking the server multiple times in case the response gets lost. Exactly once—this is usually achieved with the combination of a retry mechanism along with some idempotence mechanism. Sometimes operations are idempotent by business logic, at other times, request ids and response caching can be used in the communication layer to achieve the same effect.

Delivery semantics may apply to both, synchronous and asynchronous communication. In the synchronous case by the time the remote invocation or another protocol is finished, it is guaranteed that the invoked services has been invoked exactly once. In the asynchronous case, it is guaranteed that the recipient of the message will eventually consume the message exactly once, regardless of process crashes and network partitions. One mechanism that ensures asynchronous exactly once delivery are transactional message queues.

Just like the subdivision of a system into microservices, interaction styles are crucial for determining whether a microservice architecture becomes a solution or a burden. There is no single correct answer when it comes to communication paradigms and the appropriate paradigm has to be chosen and regularly revised in any distributed system.

5 Summary

The important lesson to learn here is that microservices, while being an effective answer to the growing complexity problem, are a not a silver bullet and are a costly solution. They require more sophisticated tools, a mature development process, and a sound understanding of distributed system problems. Microservices have the potential to either drastically improve or degrade the time to market, reliability, and maintainability of a system depending on the context where they are being applied and the way they are being used. In this chapter a number of factors have been presented that have to be carefully taken into consideration before deciding whether to switch to a microservice-based architecture. These factors are far from being exhaustive and provide just a starting point, but are enough to identify certain categories of systems that will particularly benefit from microservices and certain ones that will not.

Going beyond the hype and marketing is fundamental for a thorough understanding of the problems solved and problems introduced by microservices. They do not improve the scalability of a system but rather allow applying independent scalability solutions for different parts of the system. They also do not guarantee a higher reliability out of the box, but rather need to be carefully planned in order to allow system functionality to be unavailable independently. The time to market is reduced only if certain prerequisites are fulfilled by the project development process. A microservice-based architecture does not simplify a system, but rather makes individual microservices easier to manage by shifting the cognitive load from developers to architects.

Finally dividing a system into microservices is far from straightforward and introduces all the problems typical for distributed systems, such as keeping consistency in case of failures and managing reliability. Splitting functionality across different microservices makes it more difficult to maintain consistency. This problem can be mitigated by meticulously analyzing the consistency requirements of the system operations and adopting appropriate communication paradigms between microservices. Layering microservices can hide implementation complexity, but also negatively affects reliability if overused. Distributed systems have been a research area for several decades and combining the knowledge and techniques from it with the latest trends in software engineering allow us to take full advantage of microservice-based architectures.

References

1. ANSI: Information technology – database languages – SQL multimedia and application packages. Technical report, ANSI (2003). http://webstore.ansi.org/RecordDetail.aspx?sku=ISO%2fIEC+13249-2%3a2003
2. J. Bogart, Busting some CQRS myths. https://lostechies.com/jimmybogard/2012/08/22/busting-some-cqrs-myths/
3. A. Bucchiarone, N. Dragoni, S. Dustdar, S.T. Larsen, M. Mazzara, From monolithic to microservices: an experience report from the banking domain. IEEE Softw. **35**, 50–55 (2018)
4. A. Buchman, M.T. Ozsu, M. Hornick, D. Georgakopulos, F.A. Manola. A transaction model for active distributed object systems, in *Database Transaction Models for Advanced Applications*, ed. by A.K. Elmagarmid (Morgan Kaufmann, San Mateo, 1992)
5. L. DeMichiel, M. Keith, JSR 220: Enterprise JavaBeansTM, Version 3.0 - Java Persistence API (2006)
6. Dimensional Research, Global microservices trends: a survey of development professionals (2018), https://cdn2.hubspot.net/hubfs/2720296/White%20Papers/GlobalMicroservicesTrends-April2018.pdf?submissionGuid=6e8151d1-6ff7-4ce9-940b-997e1cfb10d4
7. N. Dragoni, S. Giallorenzo, A. Lluch-Lafuente, M. Mazzara, F. Montesi, R. Mustafin, L. Safina, Microservices: yesterday, today, and tomorrow, in *Present and Ulterior Software Engineering* (2017), pp. 195–216
8. N. Dragoni, I. Lanese, S.T. Larsen, M. Mazzara, R. Mustafin, L. Safina, Microservices: how to make your application scale perspectives of system informatics, in *11th International Andrei P. Ershov Informatics Conference, PSI 2017*, Moscow, Russia, June 27–29, 2017, Revised Selected Papers (2017), pp 95–216
9. ECMAScript Language Specification. Edition 5.1. http://www.ecma-international.org/publications/standards/Ecma-262.htm
10. E. Evans, *Domain-driven Design* (Addison-Wesley, Boston, 2004)
11. H. Garcia-Molina, K. Salem, *Sagas. SIGMOD '87 Proceedings of the 1987 ACM SIGMOD International Conference on Management of Data* (1987)
12. A.M. Glen, Microservices priorities and trends, in dzone.com. (2018), https://dzone.com/articles/dzone-research-microservices-priorities-and-trends
13. J. Gosling, B. Joy, G. Steele, G. Brache, *The Java Language Specification*, 2nd edn. (Addison-Wesley, Boston, 2000)
14. J. Gray, Notes on database systems. IBM Hesearch Report RJ2188 (1978)
15. C. Guidi, I. Lanese, M. Mazzara, F. Montesi, Microservices: a language-based approach, in *Present and Ulterior Software Engineering* (2017), pp. 217–225
16. M. Herlihy, J. Wing, Linerizability: a correctness condition for concurrent objects. ACM Trans. Program. Lang. Syst. **12**(3), 463–491 (1990)
17. A.M. Kermarrec, A. Rowstron, M. Shapiro, P. Druschel, The IceCube approach to the reconciliation of divergent replicas, in *Symposium On Principles of Distributed Computing (PODC)* (2001)
18. L. Lamport, R.E. Shostak, M.C. Pease, The Byzantine generals problem. ACM Trans. Program. Lang. Syst. **4**(3), 382–401 (1982)

19. B. Lampson, H. Sturgis, Crash recovery in a distributed system. Xerox PARC Research Report (1976)
20. N. Dragoni, S. Dustdar, S.T. Larsens, M. Mazzara, Microservices: migration of a mission critical system (2017). https://arxiv.org/abs/1704.04173
21. E. Meijer, B. Beckman, G. Bierman, LINQ: reconciling object, relations and XML in the .NET framework (2006)
22. D.A. Menasce, R.R. Muntz, Locking and deadlock detection in distributed data bases. IEEE Trans. Softw. Eng. **5**, 195–202 (1979)
23. C# Language Specification. Standard ECMA-334 (2001). http://www.ecma-international.org/
24. Swagger Codegen. https://swagger.io/tools/swagger-codegen/
25. TypeScript Language Specification (2016), https://github.com/Microsoft/TypeScript/blob/master/doc/spec.md

Part VI
Education

DevOps and Its Philosophy: Education Matters!

Evgeny Bobrov, Antonio Bucchiarone, Alfredo Capozucca, Nicolas Guelfi, Manuel Mazzara, Alexandr Naumchev, and Larisa Safina

Abstract DevOps processes comply with principles and offer practices with the main objective of efficiently supporting the evolution of IT systems. To be efficient, a DevOps process relies on a set of integrated tools. DevOps is among the first competencies, together with agile method, required by the industry. As a new approach it is necessary to develop and offer to the academy and to the industry training programs to prepare engineers in the best possible way. In this chapter we present the main aspects of the educational effort made in recent years to educate engineers on the concepts and values of the DevOps philosophy. This includes principles, practices, tools, and architectures, primarily the microservices architectural style, which shares many aspects of DevOps approaches, especially modularity and flexibility, which enable continuous change and delivery. Two experiments have been carried out, one at the academic level as a master program course and the other as an industrial training. Based on those two, we provide a comparative analysis and some proposals in order to develop and improve DevOps education for the future.

E. Bobrov · M. Mazzara · A. Naumchev · L. Safina (✉)
Innopolis University, Innopolis, Russian Federation
e-mail: e.bobrov@innopolis.ru; m.mazzara@innopolis.ru; a.naumchev@innopolis.ru; l.safina@innopolis.ru

A. Bucchiarone
Distributed Adaptive Systems (DAS) Research Unit, Fondazione Bruno Kessler, Trento, Italy
e-mail: bucchiarone@fbk.eu

A. Capozucca · N. Guelfi
University of Luxembourg, Luxembourg, Luxembourg
e-mail: alfredo.capozucca@uni.lu; nicolas.guelfi@uni.lu

A. Bucchiarone et al. (eds.), *Microservices*,
https://doi.org/10.1007/978-3-030-31646-4_14

1 Introduction

In a world of rapid technological development and full automation trend, *technological progress* is often identified in a new model of a digital device or a new release of a software package. In the full spectrum of technological progress, there are developments that cannot be immediately perceived or purchased by the final user, among them *process innovation*. In a competitive world, and in order to offer better prices, companies have the need to optimize their operations [1]. Innovative business models appear everywhere from the game industry to the mobile application domain, and the distinction between what is Information Technology and what is not becomes less and less obvious. Is Uber a taxi or an IT company? Is Airbnb a realtor? Software development techniques and operations need to also catch up with this trend and with the new business context.

Until now, it was clear when the next release of Windows would come out, but what about a web service (e.g., Google, Yandex search)? Agile Methods deal with this problem only from the software development point of view focusing on customer value and managing volatile requirements. However, the current effective scenario practice in industry requires much more than that, and involves the entire life cycle of a software system, including its operation. Thus, it is not surprising that today the industry is desperately looking for qualified people with competences in DevOps[2].

DevOps is a natural evolution of the agile approaches [3, 4] from the software itself to the overall infrastructure and operations. This evolution was made possible by the spread of cloud-based technologies and the everything-as-a-service approaches. Adopting DevOps is however more complex than adopting Agile [5] since changes at the organizational level are required. Furthermore, a completely new skill set has to be developed in the teams [6]. The educational process is therefore of major importance for students, developers, and managers. As long as DevOps became a widespread philosophy, the necessity of education in the field becomes more and more important, both from the technical and organizational points of view [6].

Chapter Outline and Contribution This chapter describes parallel experiences of teaching DevOps to both undergraduate and graduate students at university, and junior professional developers with their management in industry. We proceed to a comparative analysis to identify similarities, differences, and how these experiences can benefit from each other. After this introduction, Sect. 2 discusses the experience of teaching DevOps in a university context while Sect. 3 reports on the industrial sessions we have been delivering. Comparative analysis, conclusions, and future work on education are summed up in Sect. 4.

2 Teaching in Academia

The success of software development project is very often (not to say always) aligned with the skills of the development team. This means that having a skillful team is not only a prerequisite to have a chance to be successful in the software industry, but also to adopt new techniques aimed at simplifying the burden associated with the production of software in current times: i.e., remain competitive by continuously optimizing the production process. It is acknowledged that agile methods and DevOps principles and practices are nowadays among the most relevant new techniques wished to be fully mastered by team members. Therefore, we, as part of the academia are responsible of forming students with a set of skills able to cope not only with today's needs, but also those of tomorrow.

For this purpose, we have recently developed a new DevOps course offered at the master's level in our academic institution [7]. Despite the fact that the course is part of an academic program in computer sciences, it has been designed to make a pragmatic presentation of the addressed topics. This is achieved by applying the Problem-Based Learning (PBL) method as pedagogical approach. Thus, lectures are interleaved with hands-on, practical sessions and stand-up meetings where students (working in groups), along with guidance of the teaching staff, work out the solution to the assigned problem. This problem, common to every groups, consists of the implementation of a deployment pipeline. The objective then not only to engineer the deployment pipeline and demonstrate its functioning, but also justify the choices made in its design. Each group relies on a software product of its choice to demonstrate the functioning of the pipeline. Thus, it is the chosen product that makes each group's work unique.

2.1 *Experience*

Here we summarize the relevant information about the course (i.e., organization, structure, execution, and assessment), along with the lessons learnt and some reflections to be considered into its following editions.

The PBL method allows students to focus on finding one (of the many possible) solutions for the given complex problem. The problem to be solved consists of implementing a deployment pipeline, which needs to satisfy certain functional and nonfunctional requirements. As students work in groups to find out the expected solution, they will experiment in first person the problems that arise in collaborative environments. The creation of such environments is intentionally done to let students either acquire or improve (with the guidance of the teaching staff) the required soft-skills capacities needed to deal with people- and processes-related issues. Notice that it is acknowledged that DevOps culture is aimed at increasing inter- and intrateam collaboration. Therefore, soft-skills capabilities are as important as operational tools meant for automation.

The knowledge is transferred to students through lectures, project follow-up sessions (kind of stand-up meetings) aimed at having a close monitoring of the work done for each group member and helping solve any encountered impediments, and assessment talks (where each group presents the advances regarding the project's objectives). This structure favors both the cohesion of groups and the exchange of ideas among every course participant. The topics presented during the lectures are those closely related to the project's goal. They are configuration, build, test, and deployment management. Such topics are presented in the mentioned order, after a brief general introduction to the DevOps movement. It is worth mentioning that the course opens with a high frequency of lecture sessions, but soon they leave place to hands-on and stand-up meetings. Thus, a significant time of the course is spent in practices and discussions of different alternatives to achieve the targeted solution. It is during such sessions that groups soon realize the impact of the product[1] on the deployment pipeline aimed at supporting its development. It is worth remembering that one of the objectives in setting up a deployment pipeline (and of DevOps in general) is to reduce the time since a modification made by a developer is committed and pushed into the main branch of a repository until it appears in production ready to be used by the end-user, but without sacrificing quality (the development team wants to have some certainty that the modification would work as required without introducing flaws into the product). Therefore, for a product that belongs to those known as *monolithic* the deployment pipeline's throughput would be higher than for those architected according the microservices style [8, 9]. Notice that we (teaching staff) also advise in the selection of the product to be used during the execution of the course, despite not being part of the course objectives to assess the quality of such a product. The point of doing so is twofold: first, to raise the concerns related to the constraints imposed by the product over its deployment pipeline and, second, to avoid groups struggle with technical issues out of the project's scope, which could lead to frustration, and eventually dropouts (although these risks are always present). However, regardless the selected product, we drive students towards the implementation of the pipeline. This means that, eventually, they need to show us the functioning of the pipeline along with arguments that explain why the chosen pipeline is the most suitable for the product required to handle.

The experience until now has been very positive: students have provided good feedback about the course, no dropouts, and high quality project outcomes. Feedback from students was gathered through a survey filled out anonymously once the course was over: 100% agreed on the statement *the course was well organized and ran smoothly*, 75% (25%) agreed (strongly agreed) on the statement *the technologies used in the course were interesting*, and 75% agreed with the statement *I am satisfied with the quality of the course*. Therefore, based on the obtained results, we can conclude that we have a good course baseline, which can be used to derive alternative variations of the course, depending on the context

[1]This product is chosen to demonstrate the functioning of the pipeline. Each group is requested to select an open-source product for which there already exist implemented test cases.

and attained learning outcomes. More about these alternatives is explained in the following section.

2.2 *Reflections*

Definitively, the implementation of a deployment pipeline covers some of the DevOps aspects, but not all of them. However, we can argue that the backbone of DevOps is covered through the use of the pipeline as enabler to continuous product improvement. Thus, we are very happy with covering such DevOps aspects in a weekly course of 1.5 h. lasting for 14 weeks. It is also important not to forget that people-related aspects are also covered as, through the project, students need to perform in a collaborative manner developer- and maintainer-oriented tasks that have common concerns (e.g., develop provisioning scripts that need to be well structured and configurable).

If time permits, then monitoring is a worthy topic to be covered. This topic includes practices aimed at easing the detection of issues on the product once it has been released, but before they are noticed by end users. Being able to incorporate such practices will let students understand how developers and maintainers can work together to define new requirements on the product meant to solve the issues detected through product monitoring.

Yet another alternative could be to move the focus on the product rather than the deployment pipeline when the attained objective emphasize on the microservices style. In this case, both a deployment pipeline and a monolithic product are given at the beginning of the course, and then the project would be to refactor the product to adopt a microservices architecture. Working on such a project would make students aware of the important role played by the pipeline when doing refactoring. However, this idea has to be taken with caution as it addresses too many concerns at once. The most logical option would be to make this course a continuation of the one described in the previous section.

3 Teaching in Industry

We have developed extensive experience in recent years in several domains of software and service engineering, from service-related technologies and business processes [10–12] to workflows and their dynamic reconfiguration [13, 14] to formal methodologies for deriving specifications [15]. On top of this, we delivered training in corporate environments, both to a technical and a managerial audience, sometimes mixed. In particular, we had multiple interactions with Eastern and Western European companies operating in various business domains, from banking to phone service providers and others [16]. In 2018 we delivered more than 400 h of training involving more than 500 employees in 4 international companies of medium to large size, employing more than 10k people.

The delivered sessions typically last one or two full days, which can be reiterated, at the premises of the customer and cover (as general topics):

- Agile methods and their application [5]
- DevOps philosophy, approach, and tools [17]
- Microservices and applications [18–21]

The course on DevOps we offer for industry was, of course, not the first attempt ever made. DevOps, being a trend, has created a demand for proper sources of information on the topic. There are numerous courses at various levels of proficiency offered by educational platforms such as coursera, EdX, Udemy, and others [22–24], and there are also many practitioners offering their consultancy on site. DevOps courses often go along with the courses on microservices architecture style, as both were formulated to support the same quality attributes, such as deployability, scalability, etc.—in a nutshell, to work in a world of perpetual integration and deployment [25, 26].

In order for the companies to effectively absorb the DevOps theory and practice, the action has to focus not only on tools, but on people and processes as well. The target group of the sessions is generally a team (or multiple teams combined) of developers and testers, often with the presence of mid-management. Before our training we typically suggest customers to include also businesses and technical analysts, and when possible marketing and security department representatives. These participants also benefit from participating in the training and from learning the DevOps culture. The nature of the delivery depends on the target group: sessions for management focus more on effective team building and establishment of processes. When the audience is a technical team, the focus is more on tools and effective collaboration within and across teams.

For the purpose of this chapter we will summarize the experience with a particular company, an Eastern European phone service provider. Some details have to be omitted, but we describe the general structure of the training and some reflections. The detailed experience and some retrospective have been fully presented in [16].

3.1 Training Sessions

Here we describe our experience of training a team of developers of an Eastern European phone service provider which we have to keep anonymous. The training experience was structured in two sessions of 2 days, each conducted in different weeks with a gap of about 15 days. The first session was dedicated to the *Continuous Integration Delivery Pipeline* and the second on *Agile methods*.

3.1.1 Session I: DevOps

The first session was conducted over two full days at the office of our customer. Due to circumstances related to company organization, previous direct communication with the audience was not possible, and we could rely only on the information shared by the remote line manager. Our target group was expected to be a team of developers (around 30) reporting to a line manager located in a different city (reachable only by flight). There was no precise information on the team's prior level of knowledge or the usual tool chain. Therefore, the original agenda, communicated in advance to the team, had to be fine-tuned on site. However, we were given an opportunity to interview the audience through the survey.

While developing the survey, we were interested in general information about the team and the project, like

- Team size
- Roles (e.g., developer, tester, configuration manager)
- Responsibility (e.g., backend/frontend, mobile)
- Development methodology used (e.g., agile, waterfall)
- Architecture of the project (e.g., monolithic, SOA, microservices)

As in how well DevOps-related activities are spread:

- Which processes are automated (e.g., deployment, change management, migration, testing, etc.)
- How much time does it typically take to deploy changes? How often the team deploys?
- Is the team using containerization?

Also, there are question on any critical problems with quality of the project:

- How often does the deployment process lead to service disruption?
- How long does service recovery take place?
- How often are critical issues found by people (not by tools)?

We decided to divide the training into 2 days, planning to cover the theoretical aspects of the topics and *soft technologies* on the first day and practical aspects on the second day. The learning objectives for the first day included the following topics, each representing subsessions:

- Trends in IT and impact on software architectures and development
- Requirements volatility and agile development
- Challenges of distributed development
- Microservices

The second day was dedicated to the tool chains used in DevOps. Based on the survey results, we expected low prior knowledge on the topic and the original agenda was built with the idea to be more introductory rather than going into specific corners. The learning objectives were:

- Tools for supporting specific phases (emerged before DevOps)
  - Coding (e.g., Eclipse, Git)
  - Building (e.g., Maven, Apache Ant)
  - Testing (e.g., JUnit, xUnit, TestNG)
- Tools for connecting adjacent phases (make difference to DevOps)
  - From code to build to test (e.g., Bamboo, Jenkins)
  - From test to delivery to deploy (e.g., Bitbucket Pipelines)

Another huge part of the agenda, which we found to be extremely productive, was discussing the survey results. During this discussion we updated our previous knowledge on the teams and projects and were able to tune our agenda for the second day. Since the teams appeared to be more heterogeneous and some were more advanced in DevOps practices than we expected, we added the part on blue-green deployment and Kubernetes.

Having the right questions on quality and processes helped people to fire the discussion and reveal the potential problems in the project, as a result we were also asked to give a lecture on quality assurance. We have included to this lecture the general material on quality activities and artifacts as well as more specific topics like code coverage and mutation testing [27] in particular.

In general, this particular training was emphasizing the difference between *hard technologies* and *soft technologies*. Hard technologies is the large-scale industrial production of commercial items of technological nature, while soft technologies is the continuous improvement and *agilization* of development process. Agile methods were discussed in terms of requirements volatility. The final part covered distributed team development and *microservices*, which, as we mentioned earlier, are considered to be the privileged architecture for DevOps with their scalability features [19]. The key difference between monolithic service updates and microservice deployment was presented in order to motivate the need for migration to microservices. The audience therefore understood the vicinity between DevOps and microservices.

3.1.2 Session II: Agile

The second session was held for two full days at the same office. The objectives of the session according to plan were to cover *agile software development*, in particular Scrum. On site the customer required to move the focus to Kanban, which appeared to be something that could be useful in the future. At some point it become obvious that the team itself did not have a clear idea on the actual process they intended to follow, therefore we started working on identifying a methodology that could work for their development teams. The framework described in "Choose your weapon wisely" [28] turned out to be useful. This document provides information on different popular development processes:

- Rational Unified Process (RUP) [29]
- Microsoft's Sync-and-Stabilize Process (MSS) [30]
- Team Software Process (TSP) [31]
- Extreme Programming (XP) [32]
- Scrum [33]

Following this approach the information about processes was delivered according to four blocks:

1. *Overview*: short description of the process
2. *Roles*: information about positions for the process
3. *Artifacts*: to be produced, including documentation
4. *Tool support*: tools available on the market for using the process

3.2 Lessons Learnt: Who Should Attend the Sessions

Here we will summarize some reflections that we derived from our professional experience. In retrospect, the most effective training sessions were those in which the audience consisted of a mix of management and developers. The biggest challenges our customers encountered typically were not on how to automatize the existing processes, but in fact how to set up from scratch the DevOps approach itself. Generally, technical people understand how to set up the automation, but they may have only a partial understanding of the importance and the benefits for the whole company, for other departments, for the customer, and ultimately for themselves. During training sessions it is therefore important to show the bigger picture and help them understand how their work affects other groups, and how this in turn affects themselves in a feedback loop. The presence of management is very useful in such cases, while the technical perspective can be often left for self-study or additional future sessions.

4 Comparative Analysis, Conclusions, and Future Work

The last few years of experience on the field of DevOps education helped us in understanding the key aspects, and what the differences between an academic and an industrial context are. In this section we summarize our understanding of these two realities in order to help offer a better pedagogical program in the future. Each of the two domains can indeed be cross-fertilized by the ideas taken by the other. The lessons that we have learnt in the DevOps education can certainly be extended to other fields; however, we do not cover any generalization within the boundaries of this chapter.

The shared aspects between the two domains can be synthesized as follows:

- **Relevance**: The DevOps topics raises interests both in academia and industry. It is very actual and relevant.
- **Practice**: Theory is always welcome; however, students and developers mostly appreciate hands-on sessions, which should not be forgotten in the educational process.
- **Dev vs. Ops**: Classic academic education and developers training typically dedicates more time and puts more emphasis on development than operations. Sessions which present both can strengthen the understanding of the whole matter and increase efficacy of the delivery.

Given the described common aspects, certain features of the education process can and should be kept on the same line (e.g., pragmatism and synergy of Dev with ops). However, the difference between the two domains and their objectives requires some attention. The major differences we identified can be categorized as follows:

- **Entry Knowledge**: Details on the academic curriculum and specific syllabus allow a university teacher to make assumptions on the entry knowledge of the students. In a corporate environment, it is very difficult to have this complete information in advance. In these cases, the audience can be composed of people with different profiles and backgrounds about which you know very little.
- **Incentives**: For students, the major incentive is grade, which could be linked to a scholarship. This is a very short-term handle. Developers have different incentives and can look more at the mid-run in order to improve their working conditions, not only financially. Managers typically have incentives in terms of cost savings, and should be able to see things in the longer run.
- **Delivery mode**: An academic course can last 15 weeks with projects and assignments. In a corporate environment, everything has to be compressed into a few days, and there is hardly time to do anything in between. This requires and adaptation of the delivery.
- **Assessment**: At the university there is a classic exam-based system. In a corporate environment the audience is not required to be assessed at the end of the sessions, instead the success of the delivery can only be observed in the long period when it is clear whether the adopted practices bring benefit to the company or not.
- **Expectation:** Generally, a corporate audience is more demanding. This is due to the level of experience on one side and direct costs on the other. While students see the teacher as an authority, the corporate audience does not. This has to be taken into account before and during the delivery.

In terms of pedagogical innovation, the authors of this chapter have experimented for long with novel approaches under different forms [34]. However, DevOps represents a newer and significant challenge. Despite the fact that current educational approaches in academia and industry show some similarities, they are indeed significantly different in terms of attitude of the learners, their expectation, delivery pace, and measure of success. Similarities lay more on the perceived hype of the topic, its typical pragmatic and applicative nature, and the minor relevance that education classically reserves to "Operations." While similarities can help in defining a common content for the courses, the differences clearly suggest a completely different nature of the modalities of delivery.

Our current experience suggests some changes to the approach. For what concerns **university teaching**, the idea is to reduce the emphasis on final grade and to insist on the cultural aspect. Probably the relevance of practical assignments should be increased and that of final exam decreased. The understood importance of hands-on sessions should also suggest changes in the delivery. The ultimate plan is to build a Software Engineering curricula fully based on the DevOps philosophy. In future, **corporate training** is important to avoid basing everything on a university-like frontal session. As seen in our experience, customer's request can change even during the session itself, and the agenda should be kept open and flexible.

References

1. A. Bucchiarone, N. Dragoni, S. Dustdar, S.T. Larsen, M. Mazzara, From monolithic to microservices: an experience report from the banking domain. IEEE Softw. **35**(3), 50–55 (2018)
2. Preventing the AI crisis: the AISE Academy proposal for Luxembourg. http://www.itone.lu/pdf/AISE-academy.pdf. Accessed 03 Apr 2019
3. L. Bass, I. Weber, L. Zhu, *DevOps: A Software Architect's Perspective*, 1st edn. (Addison-Wesley Professional, Boston, 2015)
4. G. Kim, P. Debois, J. Willis, J. Humble, *The DevOps Handbook: How to Create World-Class Agility, Reliability, and Security in Technology Organizations* (IT Revolution Press, Portland, 2016)
5. Agile and DevOps: friends or foes? https://www.atlassian.com/agile/devops. Accessed 01 July 2018
6. I. Bucena, M. Kirikova, Simplifying the DevOps adoption process, in *Joint Proceedings of the BIR 2017 Pre-BIR Forum, Workshops and Doctoral Consortium Co-located with 16th International Conference on Perspectives in Business Informatics Research (BIR 2017), Copenhagen, Denmark, August 28–30* (2017)
7. A. Capozucca, N. Guelfi, B. Ries, Design of a (yet another?) DevOps course, in *Software Engineering Aspects of Continuous Development and New Paradigms of Software Production and Deployment – First International Workshop, DEVOPS 2018, Chateau de Villebrumier, France, March 5–6, 2018, Revised Selected Papers* (2018), pp. 1–18
8. H. Kang, M. Le, S. Tao, Container and microservice driven design for cloud infrastructure DevOps, in *2016 IEEE International Conference on Cloud Engineering (IC2E)* (April 2016), pp. 202–211
9. J. Sorgalla, F. Rademacher, S. Sachweh, A. Zündorf, On collaborative model-driven development of microservices (2018). CoRR, abs/1805.01176
10. M. Mazzara, Towards abstractions for web services composition, PhD thesis, University of Bologna, 2006
11. Z. Yan, E. Cimpian, M. Zaremba, M. Mazzara, BPMO: semantic business process modeling and WSMO extension, in *2007 IEEE International Conference on Web Services (ICWS 2007), July 9–13, 2007, Salt Lake City, Utah, USA* (2007), pp. 1185–1186

12. Z. Yan, M. Mazzara, E. Cimpian, A. Urbanec, Business process modeling: classifications and perspectives, in *Business Process and Services Computing: 1st International Working Conference on Business Process and Services Computing, BPSC 2007, September 25–26, 2007, Leipzig, Germany* (2007), p. 222
13. D. Nicola, Z. Mu, M. Manuel, Dependable workflow reconfiguration in WS-BPEL, in *Proceedings of the 5th Nordic Workshop on Dependability and Security* (2011)
14. M. Mazzara, F. Abouzaid, N. Dragoni, A. Bhattacharyya, Toward design, modelling and analysis of dynamic workflow reconfigurations – a process algebra perspective, in *Web Services and Formal Methods – 8th International Workshop, WS-FM* (2011), pp. 64–78
15. M. Mazzara, Deriving specifications of dependable systems: toward a method (2010). CoRR, abs/1009.3911
16. M. Mazzara, A. Naumchev, L. Safina, A. Sillitti, K. Urysov, Teaching DevOps in corporate environments – an experience report, in *Software Engineering Aspects of Continuous Development and New Paradigms of Software Production and Deployment – First International Workshop, DEVOPS 2018, Chateau de Villebrumier, France, March 5–6, 2018, Revised Selected Papers* (2018), pp. 100–111
17. R. Jabbari, N. bin Ali, K. Petersen, B. Tanveer, What is DevOps?: a systematic mapping study on definitions and practices, in *Proceedings of the Scientific Workshop Proceedings of XP2016, XP '16 Workshops* (ACM, New York, 2016), pp. 12:1–12:11
18. N. Dragoni, S. Giallorenzo, A. Lluch-Lafuente, M. Mazzara, F. Montesi, R. Mustafin, L. Safina, Microservices: yesterday, today, and tomorrow, in *Present and Ulterior Software Engineering* (Springer, Cham, 2017)
19. N. Dragoni, I. Lanese, S.T. Larsen, M. Mazzara, R. Mustafin, L. Safina, Microservices: how to make your application scale, in *Perspectives of System Informatics – 11th International Andrei P. Ershov Informatics Conference, PSI 2017, Moscow, Russia, June 27–29, 2017, Revised Selected Papers* (2017), pp. 95–104
20. K. Khanda, D. Salikhov, K. Gusmanov, M. Mazzara, N. Mavridis. Microservice-based IoT for smart buildings, in *2017 31st International Conference on Advanced Information Networking and Applications Workshops (WAINA)* (March 2017), pp. 302–308
21. D. Salikhov, K. Khanda, K. Gusmanov, M. Mazzara, N. Mavridis, Jolie good buildings: Internet of Things for smart building infrastructure supporting concurrent apps utilizing distributed microservices, in *Proceedings of the 1st International conference on Convergent Cognitive Information Technologies* (2016), pp. 48–53
22. J. Willis, Introduction to DevOps: transforming and improving operations (2019). https://www.edx.org/course/introduction-to-devops-transforming-and-improving
23. S. Lindsey-Ahmed, E. Kelly. DevOps practices and principles (2019). https://skillsonline.arrow.com/courses/course-v1:Microsoft+DEVOPS200.1x+2019_T1/about
24. A. Cowan, Continuous delivery & DevOps (2019). https://www.coursera.org/learn/uva-darden-continous-delivery-devops
25. MuleSoft, Microservices and DevOps: better together (2019). https://www.mulesoft.com/resources/api/microservices-devops-better-together
26. A. Balalaie, A. Heydarnoori, P. Jamshidi, Microservices architecture enables DevOps: migration to a cloud-native architecture. IEEE Softw. **33**(3), 42–52 (2016)
27. P.R. Mateo, M. Polo, J. Fernández-Alemán, A. Toval, M. Piattini, Mutation testing. IEEE Softw. **31**, 30–35 (2014)
28. J. Rockwood, Choose your weapon wisely (2014). http://gsl-archive.mit.edu/media/programs/mexico-summer-2014/materials/j._rockwood_choose_your_weapon_wisely.pdf
29. Rational unified process: overview. http://sce.uhcl.edu/helm/rationalunifiedprocess/. Accessed 01 July 2018
30. M.A. Cusumano, R.W. Selby, How microsoft builds software. Commun. ACM **40**(6), 53–61 (1997)
31. W. Humphrey, J. Over, *Introduction to the Team Software Process(Sm)*, 1st edn. (Addison-Wesley Professional, Boston, 1999)

32. Extreme programming: A gentle introduction. http://www.extremeprogramming.org/. Accessed 01 July 2018
33. K. Schwaber, J. Sutherland, The Scrum guide (2017). https://www.scrumguides.org/docs/scrumguide/v2017/2017-Scrum-Guide-US.pdf
34. D. de Carvalho, R. Hussain, A. Khan, M. Khazeev, J. Lee, S. Masiagin, M. Mazzara, R. Mustafin, A. Naumchev, V. Rivera, Teaching programming and design-by-contract, in *21th International Conference on Interactive Collaborative Learning – ICL 2018, Kos, Greece* (2018)

Author Index

A. Bucchiarone et al. (eds.), *Microservices*,
https://doi.org/10.1007/978-3-030-31646-4

Printed in the United States
by Baker & Taylor Publisher Services